Tragedy At Évian

How The World Allowed Hitler To Proceed With The Holocaust

Tony Matthews

16pt

Copyright Page from the Original Book

Copyright © Tony Matthews

First published 2020

This book is copyright. Apart from any fair dealing for the purposes of private study, research, criticism or review, as permitted under the Copyright Act, no part may be reproduced, stored in a retrieval system or transmitted in any form or by any means, electronic, mechanical, photocopying, recording or otherwise, without written permission.

All enquiries should be made to the publishers.

Big Sky Publishing Pty Ltd
PO Box 303, Newport, NSW 2106, Australia
Phone: 1300 364 611
Fax: (61 2) 9918 2396
Email: info@bigskypublishing.com.au
Web: www.bigskypublishing.com.au

Cover design: Big Sky Publishing.
Typesetting & indexing: Lensie Matthews
Printed in China

The views or opinions expressed in this book, and the context in which the images are used, do not necessarily reflect the views or policy of, nor imply approval or endorsement by, the United States Holocaust Memorial Museum.

 A catalogue record for this book is available from the National Library of Australia

TABLE OF CONTENTS

Dedication	i
Introduction	ii
Part One	1
Chapter 1: The Need for Évian	1
Chapter 2: Responses and Reactions	47
Chapter 3: Pressures Increase	104
Chapter 4: The Problems of South America	144
Part Two	172
Chapter 5: A Progression of Disappointments	172
Chapter 6: The Conference and World Disillusion	198
Chapter 7: Press Reports in South America	291
Chapter 8: Faltering Progress	297
Chapter 9: The Palestinian Question	319
Part Three	325
Chapter 10: The Aftermath of Évian	325
Chapter 11: The Ongoing Struggle	408
Chapter 12: The Courageous	442
Chapter 13: Escape and Rescue	548
Appendix A: Myron C Taylor's report to (President Roosevelt)	611
Appendix B: List of delegates at Évian	636
Appendix C: Text of resolution adopted at Évian	648
Notes and Sources	654
Bibliography	707
About the Author	713
Back Cover Material	715
Index	717

TABLE OF CONTENTS

Dedication
Introduction   ii
Part One
Chapter 1: The Need for Cuba   1
Chapter 2: Responses and Reactions   47
Chapter 3: Pressures Increase   104
Chapter 4: The Problems of Spain-America   134
Part Two   172
Chapter 5: A Progression of Desperation   173
Chapter 6: The Clutches of World Opinion   198
Chapter 7: Press Reports in Latin America   241
Chapter 8: Faltering Progress   267
Chapter 9: The Ultimatum Question   318
Part Three   325
Chapter 10: The Aftermath of Maine   348
Chapter 11: The Ongoing Struggle   408
Chapter 12: The Conference   446
Chapter 13: Hague and Radow   549
Appendix A: Byron C. Taylor's report to President Roosevelt 611
Appendix B: List of delegates to Cuba   636
Appendix C: Text of resolution adopted at Ivan   648
Notes and Sources   674
Bibliography   707
About the Author   713
Back Cover Material   715
Index   717

Dedication

This book is dedicated with love and admiration to my wife, Lensie.

As with all my books, radio programmes and television documentaries, special mention must be made of Lensie, to whom this book is dedicated. She has worked tirelessly in assisting with the many facets of the production of this book, including photographic restoration, typesetting and indexing. For her untiring efforts and encouragement I shall ever be grateful.

Introduction

The war was over. The twentieth century had brought to power one of the most malevolent forces ever known to humankind. It had given birth and infamy to a man who has been described as the most evil in creation, a mesmeric antichrist who would lead the world to war and leave over fifty million people dead.

The war had come to a bitter close and now the cost could be counted, following the trail of death and destruction from the heart of Nazi Germany through the battlefields and graves and desolation of Europe, Africa, the Middle East and Pacific.

But here, in Europe, close to the centre of the storm, lay the tattered remnants of an entire race of people who had been driven brutally into the gas chambers and crematoria of Adolf Hitler. The forces of Nazi Germany had crumbled and six million Jews lay dead, their pathetically undernourished corpses turned to ash or interred in hastily dug mass graves.

How could we have prevented this mass slaughter? How could we have allowed Adolf Hitler to murder six million men, women and children?

In the end, after all the agonising and politics, it was quite simple. We just ignored the problem.

This is a difficult and tragic history, a history of neglect, persecution and brutality, but primarily it is a history of indifference and apathy in the face of mounting tragedy and genocide. In this book are detailed the brutally indifferent dialogues of men and women who were representing their countries at an international conference concerning one of the most important human issues of the twentieth century. Those representatives of dozens of governments were filled with public moral indignation over the atrocities then being carried out in Nazi controlled areas, but still their speeches were liberally sprinkled with such phrases as: 'Charity begins at home—let's look after our own nationals as a primary concern,' or: 'We are already at saturation point, we cannot take more immigrants—and, in any case, who would pay the costs?'

These grim and indifferent words were reflected in numerous news publications of many countries. Argentina, for example, with its huge areas of undeveloped lands, was considered in 1938 to be an ideal country of refuge for those Jewish people fleeing from mounting persecution in Germany and Austria. Yet the pages of the Argentinean press continued to attack the Jews claiming that any government moves made to aid their plight would be treated by the Argentinean people with, '...deep distrust' and that they did not want an outbreak of, 'Semitic typhoid'. One newspaper cried: 'Let no one offend any of the Jews who live in the country, but let not one more enter it'.[1]

There is no doubt that during the twelve years of Nazi control, from 1933 to 1945, the Germans were responsible for the most hideous criminal act ever committed in the history of man. The persecution and attempted annihilation of the entire race of European Jews. But we should remember that this annihilation did not come about overnight. It grew in momentum, slowly at first, collecting evil as it gathered energy, direction and force. We should also recall that this evil was allowed to grow not only from a simple and illogical hatred, or a deeply entrenched policy of anti-Semitism, but through the apathy of the rest of the world. The Holocaust proved for all time that man is capable of any atrocity and is willing, even eager, to take that atrocity to unimaginable depths. It also proved that these atrocities—however hideous—can be condoned, ignored and even pardoned if the will and circumstances exist.

Even as early as 1933, shortly after Hitler came to power as the chancellor of Germany, the League of Nations, based in Geneva, was considering what it should do to help alleviate the problem of Jewish refugees. In the League Assembly the Dutch foreign minister, Andries Cornelis Dirk de Graeff, a former Dutch ambassador to Japan, submitted a resolution to the League requesting that a special sum be granted to enable an examination of the, '...economic, financial and judicial position of refugees from Germany, the influx of whom is likely to disturb the economic life of the countries in which they [take] refuge'.

However, there was reportedly a general belief that the matter would have to be referred to one of the large League commissions. Financing the investigation seemed to be the key problem. The actual cost of settling distressed refugees would have had to be raised by international voluntary contribution, in the same way as had previously been done for Russian refugees following the Russian Revolution and First World War. Administration costs would fall to the League members and would have been considerable. Many League delegates believed that the League budget committee would not accept any new burdens. Consequently this was an unlikely method of solving the problem. It was also felt that the proposition would lead to undesirable friction calculated to prejudice the disarmament negotiations which were then still proceeding—especially so in relation to Germany's claims to be allowed certain 'defensive' armaments.[2]

In July 1938 the United States, Great Britain and thirty other countries participated in a vital conference at Évian-les-Bains, France, to discuss the persecution and possible emigration of the European Jews, specifically those caught under the anvil of Nazi atrocities in Germany and Austria. However, most of those nations finally rejected the pleas then being made by the Jewish communities, thus condemning them to the Nazi Holocaust.

There is no doubt that the Évian conference was a critical turning point in world history. The outcome of the conference set the stage for the attempted complete annihilation of the Jewish race in Europe. No other international conference in modern history has played such a profoundly significant role in world events and affected the fates of so many individuals. In retrospect it is a simple matter to lay the blame for the Holocaust with Hitler; after all, it was he who sanctioned and ordered the 'Final Solution', but the question remains, could the Holocaust have been prevented, could six million lives have been saved if the delegates to that vital conference at Évian had shown more human compassion, some dignity and mercy? However, few did. America, the country that had organised the conference, and the thirty-one other participating countries, almost unanimously agreed that in light of their own immigration laws, which they would not alter to facilitate the need of the refugees, the Jewish problem was just too difficult to solve.

Yet the facts remain that at the time of the annexation of Austria in 1938 the German and Austrian Jewish population amounted to only about 570,000 people—not the six or seven million who were later embroiled in the Holocaust. These numbers could easily have been assimilated into the thirty-two countries whose representatives at Évian called themselves the 'Nations of Asylum'. In later years the United States allowed more than half a million Cuban and Vietnamese refugees to enter the country with little appreciable impact on the country's economy, politics or society. If each of the thirty-two nations represented at Évian had allowed just eighteen thousand Jewish refugees into their countries, Hitler would have been forced to reconsider his plans for the 'Final Solution'.

As Hitler rose to power during the 1930s and as anti-Semitism grew throughout Germany and its allied nations, there was mounting concern in the free world about the future of European

Jews. Hitler had made no secret of the fact that he wanted to be rid of every Jew in Germany. Indeed, the official German policy as war loomed closer during the closing years of the 1930s was to make the Third Reich *Judenrein,* purified totally of Jews. As we shall see later in this history, Hitler admitted that he was willing to place the Jews: '...even on luxury ships', in order to get them out of the country, and his hatred extended beyond the Jews to Christians of Jewish ancestry. One of Hitler's schemes to solve *die Judenfrage,* the Jewish Question, was called the Madagascar Plan. Madagascar was to be placed under the jurisdiction of *Reichsführer* Heinrich Himmler and turned into a reservation for millions of deported European Jews. However, the plan was finally aborted.

Under mounting world concern the Évian conference was organised by American President Franklin D. Roosevelt who appointed the highly successful businessman Myron Charles Taylor as his special ambassador.

As one would expect, many of the conference delegates were important men, mainly diplomats of middle to high rank in their respective countries, while others were simply low rank diplomats who would be in no position to make key decisions or significant representation regarding their countries' immigration policies. At Évian all the delegates were given the very best accommodation: luxurious suites at the Hotel Royale, and soon after their arrival they began to enjoy the fabulous amenities of the resort. The complex boasted some of the best stables in France; there were sports such as skiing, golf and tennis—it seemed that the suffering, anxiety and persecution of European Jews existed in another world, far away.

Labelled: the 'Nations of Asylum', the countries represented at the Évian conference included the U.S., Argentina, Brazil, Colombia, Denmark, Great Britain and her Commonwealth countries, Belgium, Sweden, France, Switzerland, Norway, the Netherlands, and several countries of Africa and Latin America. South Africa sent only an observer and refused to participate in the conference, Italy, allied so closely to Germany, blankly refused to attend but a small group of well-dressed Nazis, (possibly Gestapo agents, who had not been invited) were present at every conference session and took extensive notes of the proceedings.

Thirty-nine refugee organisations including twenty Jewish groups had come to give factual, firsthand evidence of the treatment then being meted out to the Jews under German control. Theirs was a simple cry in the darkness: 'Help us to get out,' they told the delegations, 'or we shall not survive.'

Unfortunately, with only a few exceptions, European Jews were not welcome anywhere in the world. Two thousand years of anti-Semitism could not simply disappear. Many countries were taking limited numbers of refugees but the only country where Jews could find a true welcome was in Palestine, and there, only by the Jewish community.

At the time Palestine was controlled by the British under a League of Nations mandate and Britain was desperately trying to control a difficult political and religious situation, the conflict between the Jews and the Arabs that was about to erupt in the Middle East.

This book is primarily based upon previously secret and highly confidential documents from the U.S. Department of State, all of which detail the entire course of events concerning the Évian conference and its ramifications to the Jewish problem. Throughout the publication quotations have been taken directly from many of these secret and confidential documents, and also from relevant press reports. These excerpts have been used to demonstrate precisely how governments, the fourth estate and the public were then regarding the issue. *Tragedy at Évian* is largely based upon the chronological sequence of events as issues unfolded at the U.S. Department of State. In order that the reader might gain an understanding of these developments, this book, generally speaking, follows that chronology. It should be pointed out, however, with some emphasis, that this is not an academic text. It has been written with the general reader in mind and utilises a simple and, hopefully, more readable style than one would expect in a thesis or more academic work. The book is divided into three parts. Part One investigates the lead up to the conference, the political and social difficulties encountered by President Roosevelt and the U.S. Department of State as they attempted to bring more than thirty countries together in what was, quite clearly, the most significant social and political problem of the century. In this section will be found the determination of Roosevelt and his staff to bring about a solution, despite the plethora of letters they received from many anti-Semites who were equally as determined to keep all Jews out of the United States and Great Britain.

Part Two gives details of what actually occurred at the conference, why the world generally found that the Jewish refugee problem in the face of Nazi persecution was just too difficult to solve, and Part Three considers the aftermath of the conference, how the decisions made at Évian were to affect the Jewish communities in Nazi controlled territories, and why, finally and irrevocably, Hitler was allowed to proceed with the Holocaust.

At the end of the text, one is, perhaps, left gasping in frustration at the inactivity and lethargy that epitomised and seemed to engulf all the events of the conference and its delegates. One almost has a mental impression of the delegates reaching for their briefcases, donning their fashionable homburg hats and walking away shrugging. They had done what they could; they could do no more.

Yet if the governments of the democratic world were to remain obstinately lethargic, then it would be up to individuals and humanitarian organisations to do what they could to rescue the Jews of Europe. Government lethargy made the task of these individuals and organisations vastly more difficult, but difficulties were there to be overcome. Within the two final chapters of this publication readers will find a wealth of information about at least a few of the many heroic efforts of people and organisations who, despite the decisions made at Évian, worked under extremely dangerous conditions, often giving their own lives, to assist in the rescue of the Jews. Their efforts, which sometimes failed and sometimes succeeded, lay bare the myth that the world, generally, did not care. It was simply the inactivity of the democratic governments, steeped in stifling bureaucracy, ineptitude and racism, which proved the major barrier in preventing the greatest massacre in world history.

The very first essential for success is a perpetually constant and regular employment of violence.

–Adolf Hitler

Part One

Chapter 1

The Need for Évian

After the rise to power of Adolf Hitler in 1933, anti-Semitism arrived at a period in time that was quite unprecedented in the history of the world. As Hitler's power grew, so did anti-Semitism on a massive scale, not only in Germany and later Austria after the *Anschluss*, but also in almost all European countries, especially in France and Poland.

The *Anschluss*, the union of Germany and Austria, was brought about under the government of Nazi extremist, Arthur von Seyss-Inquart[1] who invited Hitler to occupy Austria on 12 March, 1938, and proclaimed a union with Germany the following day. On 10 April a Nazi-controlled plebiscite recorded a vote of 99.75 per cent in favour of the *Anschluss*.

Beyond the frontiers of the countries immediately affected there was a noticeable spread of anti-Semitism. This was primarily the result of economic difficulties following the tragic years of the Great Depression, long-term industrial and business monopolisation by Jewish people and also through the malicious use of propaganda spread by the anti-Semitic states, primarily Germany and Austria. This propaganda easily and quickly found its way into the newspapers and other forms of communication in neighbouring countries, especially those of eastern Europe. President of the New Zionist Organisation, Doctor Benjamin Akzin, who was then based in London, wrote a highly confidential memorandum on the issue in April 1938, a copy of which was sent that month to the U.S. Department of State in Washington DC. Akzin and his New Zionist Organisation represented the extremely controversial revisionists who had withdrawn from the Zionist Organisation in 1935. The group advocated unlimited Jewish immigration into both Palestine and Trans-Jordan and the setting up as quickly as possible of a Jewish State following the guidelines of the famous Balfour Declaration.

The concept of Palestine as a Jewish homeland is, of course, steeped in the history of the Jewish religion but it was not until 1896 when the Viennese Jew Theodor Herzl published *The Jewish State*, that the concept began to crystallise as a real possibility. Herzl called for an international conference of Jews which took place at Basel in Switzerland in 1897 and was attended by approximately two hundred important Jewish leaders. They formulated a resolution calling for the establishment of a Jewish state in Palestine which was to be, '...secured by public law'. However, the Turkish government, which then controlled Palestine, refused to have such a state established in their territory and Herzl reluctantly accepted an offer made by the British government to have a Jewish homeland set up in Uganda. The plan was strongly opposed by other Jewish leaders, especially so since land in Palestine was being purchased on a large scale through a fund set up and backed heavily by the wealthy Rothschild family.

In 1917, Arthur James Balfour, former British prime minister and, at the time, British foreign secretary, communicated with Lord Rothschild, a leader of Zionism, advising him that the British government would support the establishment of a Jewish national home in Palestine under the provision that safeguards could be set in place to ensure the rights of the existing non-Jewish peoples of Palestine. The Balfour Declaration was quickly ratified by the Allied governments and formed a basis for the League of Nations mandate for Palestine in 1920.

Despite this, Akzin's revisionists' policies were regarded by the U.S. Department of State in confidential memoranda as being, 'intransigent and extreme'.[2]

Akzin's memorandum claimed that in some countries in Europe anti-Semitic propaganda was being carried to its extreme lengths. He said that the world was witnessing anti-Semitic activities that would deprive Jewish populations of their means of subsistence and result in '...their reduction to complete destitution'. He added that oppressive legislation was being sponsored with a view to degrading the Jewish people to, '...the position of pariahs, to denying them the most elementary protection of political status, of civil rights and of human dignity'. He ended his plea by claiming that simultaneously propaganda was being promoted that would force the Jewish people into a position where they would become, '...trapped animals with no hope locally, and with all avenues of escape closed to them'.[3]

Akzin went on to explore the concept of anti-Semitism in relation to modern political ideologies of the 1930s. He said that the roots of the circumstances lay not only in the deliberate attitudes of governments but went deeper, to the core of a rising tide of nationalism and the prevailing difficult economic circumstances. These elements combined to facilitate a powerful movement against Jewish involvement in economic affairs and appealed strongly to large parts of the population.[4]

International liberalisation of immigration laws under such difficult circumstances was an extremely unlikely proposition. Unrestricted movement of nationals from one country to another had ceased at around the time of the First World War and the possibility of nations liberalising their immigration laws to allow for large-scale migration of Jewish nationals—in the light of heightening antagonism—was less than infinitesimal. Quite the contrary, the economic and political difficulties being experienced by most countries during the 1930s only stimulated national antagonism and made the process of any kind of liberalism somewhat improbable.

But this was not always the case. Prior to the outbreak of war in 1914 there had been widespread Jewish migration, especially to such countries as the United States, Canada, Latin America, South Africa and certain countries of western Europe. Conditions then, and acceptance of Jewish people, were far more promising and governments were actually moving towards more liberal immigration policies. However, following the war—for which the Jews were partially blamed—fewer countries were willing to accept any significant numbers of Jewish people with the exception of Palestine which accepted some

300,000 in the twenty years between 1918 and 1938.[5] The primary reasons for this were the specific provisions made following the war to allow international immigration into the country. However, during the years 1933 to 1938 even this liberal immigration policy had been tightened by the British mandate holders and immigration had been severely restricted.[6]

During the post-war (1914-18) years the pressure upon areas of Jewish congestion was heightened as governments firmly and irrevocably closed their doors to Jewish migrants. This was especially so in such countries as England, France, Holland, Belgium and even Italy. Yet even so, Jewish migration continued, often clandestinely, and the numbers of Jewish immigrants in these countries grew to such an extent that they caused serious antipathies, especially over economic and environmental arguments. Ordinary diplomatic measures, and even the intervention of the League of Nations, proved ineffectual, and as Hitler rose to power through the 1930s it seemed that the monstrous problem of the Jewish population, under increasing pressure and receiving unending brutalities from the Nazi regime, was an issue for which no solution could be found.

One of the principal agencies operating to aid Jewish refugees, an agency that had been functioning since August 1914, was the American Jewish Joint Distribution Committee for German Emergency Relief. During its years of existence the committee proved to be an extraordinarily beneficial one to intending German/Jewish migrants. A 1938 report on the committee's workings included:

> The activities of the American Joint Distribution Committee begin with the most elementary help for children and orphans and general emergency relief, schooling, trade school training, and includes besides strengthening of the economic life through the establishment of credit societies, some of which extend free loans and others with interest—establishment of hospitals and medical institutions of all kinds, establishment of institutions for the prevention of disease—establishment of bath houses and sanatoria,—creation of new modes of existence—land settlements [particularly in Russia], creating new possibilities for industries and strengthening those already in existence—building of houses on a large scale in those countries devastated by the war, emigration and funding of emigration possibilities, etc. From its inception in 1914 to the middle of 1938, the American Joint Distribution Committee has spent a total

of over $90,000,000 for all activities in a great number of countries in Europe, Palestine [nearly $9,000,000], Russia and a number of overseas countries.[7]

Until 1933 the offices of the Joint Distribution Committee (J.D.C.) were located in Berlin. Because of this, immediately after the National Socialist Party came into power, the J.D.C. was able to engage in the reconstruction work and in the preparation for an orderly emigration in close contact with the Jewish organisations within Germany. The J.D.C. extended its efforts to transform the aimless emigration, which began in 1933, into a systematic well-planned one with the help of the organisations that were at first coordinated into the *Zentral-Ausschuss der Juden in Deutschland* and later into the enlarged organisation of the *Reichsvertretung der Juden in Deutschland*. (As soon as the English organisation for helping German refugees, the Council for German Jewry, was created, the J.D.C. immediately worked in close contact with that organisation in such areas as economic aid, migration, welfare, education, training and retraining).

The J.D.C. made a contribution towards the entire budget of the *Reichsvertretung*, but emphasized that its main interest was to contribute towards constructive work, namely the preparation and carrying out of emigration.[8]

Pressure Mounts

By 1938 the horror of Jewish persecution under the Germans was becoming universally known. Five years had passed since Hitler had come to power and during that time anti-Semitism had grown dramatically. In March 1933 the Nazis opened Dachau concentration camp. The following month they staged a boycott of Jewish shops and businesses. That same month they issued a decree which defined a non-Aryan as 'anyone descended from non-Aryan, especially Jewish parents or grandparents'. That month too the Gestapo was born and by July 1933 the Nazi Party was declared as the only legal party in Germany. A law was passed to strip all Jewish immigrants from Poland of their German citizenship. In September the Reich Chamber of Culture was established but excluded Jews from the Arts. That same month Jews were forbidden from owning land. In October Jews were prohibited from being newspaper editors. Month after month, year after year, the persecution continued, further tightening restrictions on every aspect of Jewish life. In 1934 Jews were banned from the German Labour Front; they were not allowed national health insurance and were prevented from obtaining legal qualifications. In 1935 Jews were banned from serving in the military and in September that year the Nuremberg Race Laws against Jews were decreed.

    Thirteen weeks prior to the conference at Évian, Hitler's troops had marched into Austria and within days of occupying Vienna the capital was in the grip of Nazi terror. Gangs of storm-troopers roamed through the streets searching for Jews to beat up, humiliate and murder. Women were forced to scrub the streets using water to which acid had been added. Jews were stripped of their citizenship, marriage between Jews and Gentiles was forbidden, sexual intercourse between Jews and Gentiles could result in the death sentence. Property was confiscated and huge punitive fines were imposed. These fines were designed to rob the Jews of the majority of their wealth. Jewish shops were smashed, Rabbis beaten up, synagogues burnt, cemeteries desecrated. Jews were banned from universities, the arts and all professions. All human rights for Jews were withdrawn. Jewish teachers were dismissed, Jewish doctors were allowed to treat only Jews. Jews were banned from working in the areas of entertainment, journalism, law, or on the stock exchange. Jewish civil servants were immediately dismissed. Shortly after the Germans walked into Austria more than half the Jewish population was unemployed. Shops carried signs in their windows stating: 'No Jews allowed inside.' Jewish families found it difficult to purchase even the simplest necessities of life, meat, bread, and vegetables.

After the *Anschluss* a further half million Jews were added to the already tragic lists of those under Nazi persecution. Finding relief for these people was of mounting concern worldwide. Even pro-German newspapers in some countries were keen to find a solution to an issue which seemed almost impossible to resolve. One newspaper in South Africa, for example, stated that it was essential, not only for political and commercial stability but also for the sake of humanity, charity and sympathy for the Jewish people that the world should work together to discover methods that might be implemented to bring all those persecuted people to safe areas and countries. The publication pointed out that if this task was not achieved then the results would be widespread social and cultural unrest and that the Jews deserved better treatment as they were an intelligent and enduring race of people who were vitally important to the economic and social wellbeing of the rest of the world.

Jewish populations had been persecuted for centuries but, as the South African press pointed out, the massive and unrelenting wave of persecution under which the Jews of Europe were then suffering might mean that they could now contract into some kind of 'secret order' for their own defence and wellbeing and that if they did coalesce defensively then their many talents and resources, especially their expertise in trade and commerce, might be lost to the rest of the world. The press article could not have stressed it more strongly: the world needed the Jews now more than ever.[9]

Yet, as Hitler had grown in his power, a solution was far more difficult to find than had ever been anticipated. During this time there were hundreds of thousands of political, racial, social and religious minorities, including the unemployed, all of whom needed somewhere to live and to work. None of the schemes for their settlement had hitherto succeeded—to any large extent—in catering for their needs, and the ability of most countries to absorb foreign immigrants was economically, socially and, (especially) politically, extremely limited.

As the South African press continued to stress, the principal reason why schemes to resettle Jewish refugees might fail lay in the commercial backgrounds of the Jews themselves. Some of these people were prominent and important businessmen, and it was a major physical and psychological undertaking for them to agree to become farm labourers in a foreign land, although some were obviously capable of that.[10]

Yet in reality a life of such primary production was far from attractive to most of the Jewish emigrants, both socially and economically. Widespread modernisation and industrialisation within rural industries, even during the late 1930s, had resulted in extensive agricultural overproduction. Farmers were often required to sell their produce below the cost of production, or to export their product at the domestic buyer's expense.

Overproduction in many agricultural industries was often at calamitous proportions. In some rural areas of South Africa, for example, coffee was being destroyed and maize was being used to fuel boilers. The press was asking the very important question: in the face of such overproduction was it viable to force Jewish people to work on the land as farmers, and, of course, would city dwellers with no experience of agriculture actually be any good at farming?[11]

The problem was as cataclysmic as it was multinational, and there were no short-term answers, nor were the answers inexpensive or politically easy to make.

Prominent American writer, journalist and social commentator, Dorothy Thompson, who would be instrumental in suggesting many concepts to the U.S. Department of State over the issue of Jewish migration, wrote a comprehensive article in *Foreign Affairs* magazine in April 1938. She stated that the world was in turmoil because, with Hitler in Vienna, every small state of the Danubian Basin was feeling increasing pressure. She said that Great Britain and France did not know how to control the situation and that the Soviet Union was, '...in a state of disintegration'. She added that with the civil war in Spain continuing, the chaos could only add to the problem of dispossessed minorities such as the Jews.[12]

Up until that time the problems of the Jews living in Germany and Austria had been considered one in which charitable institutions could give the best aid, but with rapidly mounting tensions the emphasis of the problems changed quickly from charitable to political. There was no single body set up to arrange for the emigration of Jews and other refugees from the anti-Semitic regions of Europe, although there were three temporary organisations working to aid such emigration. The first of these was the International Labour Office in the U.S.; the second—and possibly the most important—was the Nansen Office, an agency of the League of Nations; and the third was the Office of the High Commissioner for Refugees Coming from Germany, an autonomous office that was attached to the League but in only a loose fashion. These offices had carried out important work in relocating thousands of Jews from the anti-Semitic regions, primarily into Palestine. However, the limited mandates for both the Nansen Office and the High Commissioner for Refugees Office were almost over, and they were due to be closed at the end of 1938.[13]

The Office of the High Commissioner for Refugees Coming from Germany (under the direction of Sir Neill Malcolm), had been set up as an organisation attached to the League of Nations. The office was commissioned to attempt to safeguard those refugees who had already managed to flee from Germany but had not been able to gain residency permits from any other country.[14]

Sir Neill Malcolm had been appointed to the position of high commissioner in February 1936.[15] His appointment came as a direct result of the persecution then being experienced under Hitler's growing power. Sir Neill Malcolm was instructed by the League of Nations to carry out several specific tasks, the most significant of these being, '...to undertake consultations by the most suitable method with the different governments regarding the possibilities and conditions of placing refugees and finding employment for them'.[16] However, as Sir Neill Malcolm was later to state at the Évian conference:

> After very little investigation it became evident to me, and I think the private organisations were in agreement, that there was very little chance of our being able to carry through any large-scale settlement in any of the countries overseas. I think that view has been more or less borne out by the speeches we have heard in the last two days. Consequently I had to report to the Assembly that in my opinion there was no opening at that time, with or without the help of the High Commissioner, for the private organisations to do anything effective in that direction. I came to this conclusion with considerable regret, after consultation with the High Commissioners of the British Dominions and the representatives of the more promising foreign countries.
> I think I may say that I was met with universal courtesy and encouragement, but in practically every case the same real answer was given. That was to the effect that in the present conditions of labour markets in the countries of the world, any

large-scale scheme of migration could only arouse hostility, and that secondly, there was in no one of those countries any anti-Jewish feeling, but that such hostility might easily be aroused if the Government were to introduce solid blocks of foreign immigrants who would, almost necessarily, build up an alien element inside the State concerned.[17]

The Nansen Office

The Nansen Office was the most prominent of all the refugee relief organisations at that time. Its founder, Dr Fridtjof Nansen, had been responsible for the repatriation of some half million prisoners-of-war after the 1914-18 conflict, and out of this work had grown the Nansen Office which was soon involved in a wide scope of relief for refugees from many countries: Russians, Assyrians, Chaldeans and Armenians.[18]

Fridtjof Nansen was one of Norway's national heroes. Tough and profoundly resilient, he was an explorer and an internationalist. Born at Frøen near Christiania in 1861, he was the leader of the first expedition to cross the Greenland ice-cap from the east in 1888. Five years later, in 1893, he and several other men attempted to drift across the polar basin in a ship named the

Fram (translated as *'Forward'*, later preserved and set on permanent display near Oslo), which was locked in ice. They spent eighteen months on the vessel and when Nansen was convinced that the ship would continue its drift successfully, he and another man named Hjalmar Johansen travelled by skis and sledge across the ice to the position of 86 degrees 14 minutes, a point farther north than any previous explorers had reached. Riding the tide of public adulation, Nansen later entered politics and was instrumental in obtaining Norway's independence from Sweden in 1905. He became Norway's first minister to Great Britain and towards the end of the Great War was a strong advocate for the formation of a League of Nations. After the Treaty of Versailles and the formation of the League, Nansen, in 1920, was instructed by the League to arrange for the repatriation of some half million prisoners-of-war. However, the Russians did not recognise the League and would only deal with a private organisation headed by Nansen. Thus the Nansen Relief Organisation had been created. His task of repatriating approximately 500,000 former prisoners was successful. Using funds he raised himself after having his plea for funding to the League turned down, he later headed the organisation that was instrumental in bringing relief to famine-stricken Russia. He subsequently carried on similar work bringing relief to Greece and Armenia, and in 1922 was awarded the Nobel Peace Prize. He died at his home in Oslo on 13 May, 1930.

The *Office International Nansen pour les Refugies,* under the auspices of the League of Nations, was subsequently opened and did valuable work with approximately seven thousand refugees from the Saar following the 1935 plebiscite that transferred the rich coalfields region from a League of Nations administration to German control. Fridtjof Nansen's primary objective had always been to bring relief and to make that relief self-supporting. However, the Great Depression brought an end to such ideals. Governments generally were unable to fund employment opportunities or relief grants and the depression itself considerably reduced funding from private charitable institutions. Yet the relief work continued for some time. In 1938, as the problem of Jewish refugees from Germany and Austria was reaching its height, the Nansen Office itself was also awarded the Nobel Peace Prize. The office closed in December 1938, its director at the time, Michael Hansson, reporting that there were approximately 600,000 refugees still unsettled and in dire need of aid.[19]

It was generally believed at that time that the extension of the Nansen Office into a worldwide refugee organisation would have been an ideal move, especially so because of its already high profile and good reputation. It would also have been a way of increasing the somewhat tarnished prestige of the League of Nations. If the League could be associated with a nonsectarian refugee organisation it would be strengthened by public and political acceptance.

To enlarge the jurisdiction of the Nansen Office into a worldwide organisation would have required a unanimous vote from the League Council. However, this was unlikely as the Soviets were already opposing the Nansen Office because of its role in helping White Russians to emigrate from the Soviet states. The Romanian and Polish delegates would also have voted against the resolution because they did not wish to have the League of Nations interfering in their domestic affairs, and both countries were broadly—some would argue violently—anti-Semitic.[20]

In view of this it was generally believed that the Nansen Office could not win the required approval for expansion. Additionally, it seemed likely that Germany, which was not a part of the League, would fail to listen to any advances, advice or recommendations from an office of the League. The only solution seemed to be the formation of an entirely different office with sweeping powers to offer succour to refugees from a wide number of countries, specifically from Germany and Austria, but also taking into consideration, for example, the number of refugees who would want to leave Spain at the end of the Spanish Civil War.[21]

There was also considerable concern expressed that the concept of some kind of international organisation set up as a result of the proposed conference would be at odds with the organisations already in existence. As U.S. delegate to the League of Nations, Arthur Sweetser, stated to the U.S. Department of State in May 1938:

> What I very much wish is that there were some full and free cooperation between the work here and the new movement set underway by the United States. At the present moment the League agencies have no information whatsoever officially before them regarding the American initiative [of setting up the Évian conference] and are consequently in an awkward position as to referring to it in any official way. They have, of course, picked up a certain amount of material from the press or from documents handed privately to this, that, or the other official, but they cannot use this formally and they have no idea whether it is complete....

If ever a problem seemed not only to justify but to necessitate the co-ordination of all possible agencies, it would appear to be this problem of refugees. It is a terribly ungrateful task at best, with an immense amount of human suffering running through it, and certainly requires every resource that can be opened to it.... One of the first problems would seem to me, therefore, to work out a method of cooperation and coordination between the old but specialised agencies of the League and the new and universal proposal of the United States. To have these two great humanitarian efforts going along without even a speaking acquaintance seems to me unthinkable.[22]

On 27 May, 1938, James Grover McDonald, the chairman of President Roosevelt's advisory committee in New York, forwarded a confidential document to the U.S. secretary of state. The document had been written by one of McDonald's colleagues, Professor Norman Bentwich, at the League of Nations, and dealt primarily with the problems associated with Roosevelt's proposed plan to facilitate refugee emigration.

Bentwich wrote:

As regards the American President's proposal, the League and the governments are mystified. There has been as yet no communication at all about the [Évian] conference to the League, although the principal American member of the Secretariat who saw the President after the announcement was made, obtained an assurance that the League would be informed of the steps. Nor have the European governments or the American ministers in the capitals any knowledge of the proposal to be made....

It is also urged that the Organisation should submit as specific a plan as possible of the emigration and settlement which should be envisaged, and suggest a financial scheme for carrying it out. I was told by the American member of the Secretariat who saw Mr Roosevelt that in his view the liberal countries should deal with the problem of the refugees on large lines, and be prepared to receive substantial numbers.[23]

Plans, Designs and Problems

Another problem facing the democratic nations was the very strong possibility that many countries would be unwilling to open their doors to the Jews, fearing that if they did so the anti-Semitic governments would quickly unload their Jewish populations entirely onto the recipient countries. Clearly there had to be a careful dialogue between the recipient countries and the anti-Semitic countries designed to alleviate the suffering of the refugees as quickly as possible, to arrange for transport and settlement and to design methods whereby the immigrants could become useful and industrious citizens in their lands of adoption. Quite obviously the concept of moving hundreds of thousands, perhaps millions, of Jews from Europe to settle in distant countries was going to require a vast amount of money. And money was available, large amounts of cash and other valuables were owned by the very Jews who wished to emigrate, but these funds were subject to harsh exportation laws with extremely high punitive percentages being deducted prior to the financial transfers.

One plan publicly suggested at this time was that some of the massive funds then held by individual Jews in Germany and Austria be turned over to an international body committed to aid Jewish emigration, and that these funds be used to the good of all Jews wishing to flee from Nazi persecution. It was perceived that if this were done the donors of the money would receive at least the amount they would have received from the Nazis had they paid the punitive export fees, but they would be assured of emigration rights and would also be helping to assist others who were not so financially advantaged.[24] Such a plan depended entirely upon the willingness of the Nazis to release Jewish funds. However, the restrictions remained in force.

Many of the Jews hoping to emigrate from the Nazi-occupied territories wished to travel to Palestine, and during the years immediately following the introduction of Hitler's anti-Semitic laws, between 1933 and 1937, some 40,000 Jews actually managed to emigrate there.[25]) But the increase in Jewish numbers into Palestine coincided with mounting Arab hostility. In 1937 a British government royal commission decided that the concept of a Jewish homeland in Palestine and an Arab claim to self-government was impossible, and stated that the only workable solution could be the partition of Palestine. With this in mind the British government announced that the rate of Jewish immigration into Palestine was not to exceed 12,000 persons per annum. Clearly, in light of the mounting anti-Semitism in Nazi Germany where hundreds of thousands of Jews were desperately wanting to emigrate, this figure was cruelly low. Diplomatically and politically, however, the immigration restriction was seen by many countries as being a wise move.

Yet, as Arab tensions in the region were heightening into conflict and bloodshed, it was generally thought that Jews living in Palestine were faced with as much danger and open anti-Semitism as those still living in Germany.

The Palestine correspondent of the *Daily Mail* reported in October 1933 that twenty people had been killed during anti-Jewish disturbances, barbed wire had been placed around public buildings and strategic points, and the police had confiscated the weapons of all people entering the city.

They had stopped and searched all vehicles and heavy detachments of troops were barring the approaches to the central square. A large group of anti-Jewish demonstrators had surged through the gates into the square and mounted police had charged them. When the police had fired volleys the massed Palestinians had fled. Many were crushed and trampled. An unexploded bomb was found after the retreat. At Haifa the police fired in the air to disperse the demonstrators. A crowd attacking the police station at Jerusalem was confronted by a baton charge, but when this proved substantially ineffective the police fired their weapons killing two people and wounding several others. One policeman was stabbed. There was similar rioting at Nablus where a crowd attacked the railway station. One person was shot.[26]

The *Despatcher's* special Jerusalem correspondent described a chaotic scene with aircraft patrolling the skies while armoured cars patrolled the streets and Arab leaders flocked to Haifa. The military authorities were then making preparations for very serious riots and disturbances. In various towns rioting was spreading and the Jewish people were attempting to remain at home. Mobs were taking over the streets, shutters were being put up and large numbers of people were shouting, 'Down with the government'.[27]

In Jerusalem, Palestinians began a general strike and stoned a police dispatch rider. Police were forced to fire in order to rescue him. Demonstrators attacked the railway and police stations at Haifa in an effort to release Palestinian prisoners. The police fired, killing one person and wounding twenty-five others. Several British nationals were injured, two of them were stabbed in the back.[28]

Even as the Évian conference was getting underway in July 1938, Jews and Arabs were shedding blood. On 9 July, 1938, *The Times* of London reported that fifty-three people had been killed during the previous two days—twenty-five of whom were Arabs—and one hundred and fifty people had been injured. There were two British Army divisions in Palestine at the time and two more battalions were en-route to help them keep the peace. Because of this intense friction, Great Britain was actively discouraging Jewish migration to Palestine.

The press reporting the fighting at that time claimed that this wave of outrages was simply a continuation of many months of lawlessness. In just a week ten Jewish people and twelve Arabs had been killed and fifty Jews and eighty Arabs wounded.

The reports outlined that most of the violence had been committed against isolated Jewish communities in the rugged country surrounding the Tiberias area, although most of the violence had been perpetrated by Arab 'terrorists'; rather than by the general Arab population.

However, it now appeared clear that the Jews were beginning to arm themselves in whatever way they could and that some Jewish youths were forming, 'wild gangs' in order to retaliate or take 'counter-terrorism' action as it was termed. As a precautionary action the authorities were making a significant number of arrests, sometimes on a large scale, and these included the arrest of a Dr Wasthitz, the local

Zionist revisionist leader. The police had also searched the offices of the Jewish Labour Federation. British police had now largely replaced Arab and Jewish constables who, it was said, could no longer be relied upon. The British warship, *Emerald*, was preparing to land Royal Marines while local Jewish leaders were considering ways in which to restore order while the Jewish National Council had been summoned to meet.

The press was pointing out that these riots were pitting two important communities against each other when they should be learning to live together in some kind of harmony. Violence by fanatical elements, it was claimed, was not the answer, but government force might be the only way to stop the ongoing murders.[29]

In her *Foreign Affairs* article published in April 1938, Dorothy Thompson castigated those who procrastinated and who made only token gestures towards mitigating the plight of the Jewish refugees. She stated that it was time responsible political parties stopped believing that the emigration of Jewish refugees into the various countries of asylum would create massive anti-Semitic unrest, and that as the problem was a political one it could only be solved politically. She called for an international organisation headed by 'outstanding personalities' with the help of all sympathetic governments to form and place pressure on the Germans to cease the persecution, and on other countries where the refugees might find asylum.[30]

Thompson's suggestions in this article were not wasted on the U.S. Department of State. Thompson soon afterwards called a meeting of interested persons and organisations at her New York home and advised the State Department that she was anxious for a State Department representative to attend. The secretary of state, Cordell Hull, quickly agreed with her, and while pointing out that the State Department could not commit itself to adopting the many suggestions made by Thompson, he advised her that he was willing to send Mrs Ruth Shipley, chief of the Passport Division, from Washington to New York with instructions to attend the meeting.[31] At a meeting with the assistant secretary of state on 18 March, Ruth Shipley was instructed that she was, '...not to take a negative attitude with respect to consideration which was being given ... to problems arising through the increasing number of refugees from Austria and elsewhere. We should, on the contrary, endeavour to explore what positive attitude or action we might be able to take'.[32]

Shipley was seen as being the ideal person to attend the meeting because of her wide background and knowledge of passport and visa practices and also because of her knowledge of the government's general policies regarding immigration.[33]

Immigration into the United States of America was regulated by the Immigration Act of 1 July, 1924, which established quotas of immigration amounting to two per cent of the total number of foreigners who were to be found in the country according to the census of 1890.

In 1927 the quota law was modified so as to limit the number of admissible immigrants to the maximum figure of 150,000 per annum. Instructions were issued to the American consuls abroad to refuse visas to any foreigners who would appear to them likely to become a public charge in the United States. This discretionary power could be exercised even if the foreigner in question formally answered all the requirements of the immigration laws and if his country's quota had not been filled.[34] These instructions were still in force in 1938. All prospective immigrants were required to furnish affidavits of their relatives in the United States. The relatives had to furnish documentary evidence as to their capacities to support the immigrant if that ever became necessary. It rested entirely with the local American consuls to decide whether such evidence was sufficient. The applicants themselves were also expected to furnish evidence of their financial solvency; the amount of the sums varied according to each individual case, for example, the size of the applicant's family and of that of his relatives in the United States, the degree of their relationship and their respective occupations.

Between 1926 and 1930, 61,998 Jewish people were allowed to enter the United States, in other words, an average of 12,400 per annum. Between 1931 and 1935 only 19,847 Jews entered the country which amounted to an average of less than 4000 per annum. Even during the years of depression the number of Jews having left the United States was never superior to sixteen per cent of all the Jewish immigrants admitted into the country.[35]

After 1936, however, as the tyranny of Hitler's autocratic regime began to affect the Jewish communities in Europe, Jewish immigration into the United States continued to grow rapidly. Approximately nine thousand immigrants landed in 1936 and 15,288 in 1937.[36]

As a 1938 U.S. survey found:

> The influence of the depression on the immigration in general manifests itself not only in the decrease of those who are admitted to ten per cent of the annual quota, but also by a strongly marked

movement of massive repatriations. Thus during the years 1931/1935, for instance, the departures from the country have exceeded the number of entries for the first time in American history, amounting to 103,654 or to a yearly average of 20,731, while during the period 1926-1931 the surplus of immigration was of 1,120,617 or of 224,123 [sic] persons per annum. [*the average for the years 1926-1931 inclusive, with the surplus of 1,120,617 would actually be 186,770—author's note*].[37]

Meanwhile, the U.S. Department of State was certainly aware of the difficulties then being experienced by Jewish people under Nazi domination in Vienna, a fact intimated by a highly confidential telegram from the U.S. Embassy in Vienna to the secretary of state, Cordell Hull. The sender, who stipulated that the telegram was of a sensitive nature and should be closely paraphrased before being communicated to anyone, wrote:

> Private citizens may not cash dollar checks in excess of $400. Moreover, [it is] difficult for Jews to make financial transactions…. In view of desperate situation of Jews who are being fed by three soup kitchens which are allowed to operate, I suggest I be permitted to receive charitable

funds from American sources and discretely hand over mark [currency] proceeds. So far as I know this does not contravene any existing regulations.[38]

However, the next day a small note signed by a State Department officer read:

> While we would wish to be helpful in this way as far as possible, it should not be lost sight of that the authorities in Vienna would know about the financial transactions and the use to which the proceeds were being put. Knowledge that this was taking place could conceivably arouse resentment in official quarters which might prejudice the protection work for American citizens and direct American interests which the Consulate General is called upon to perform.[39]

The following day Cordell Hull sent a confidential message in secret diplomatic code stating that he had no objection to relief funds being secretly given to Jews in need. Yet he warned that the operation could only take place providing that the existing protection work and operations of the embassy could proceed without being jeopardised.[40]

***

Under mounting world concern the Évian conference was organised by American President Franklin D. Roosevelt who ordered his embassies abroad to place the proposal before their host countries' foreign offices and state departments. Initial enquiries were directed to the governments of France, Great Britain, Belgium, the Netherlands, Denmark, Sweden, Norway, Switzerland, Italy, and all the governments of the South American republics.[41]

The first indication received in Great Britain regarding Roosevelt's plan arrived via an urgent telegram, dated 23 March, 1938, from the U.S. Department of State to the U.S. Embassy in London which stated:

> Please call on the Minister of Foreign Affairs and inquire whether the British Government on its own behalf or on the behalf of the self-governing Dominions would be willing to cooperate with the Government of the United States in setting up a special committee composed of representatives of a number of governments for the purpose of facilitating the emigration from Austria and presumably from Germany of political refugees.

U.S. President F.D. Roosevelt

–U.S. National Archives

Our idea is that whereas such representatives would be designated by the governments concerned, any financing of the emergency emigration referred to would be undertaken by private organisations within the respective countries. [*Furthermore, it should be understood that no country would be expected or asked to receive a greater number of emigrants than is permitted by its existing legislation.—author's italics*].

As soon as enough replies have been received to warrant going ahead, the President contemplates appointing a representative who would proceed abroad without delay to meet with the rest of the committee. It is suggested, purely as a matter of convenience, that the first meeting be held in some Swiss city as being centrally located.

Please make it perfectly clear that in making this proposal the Government of the United States in no sense intends to discourage or interfere with such work as is already being done on the refugee problem by the Migration Bureau of the International Labour Office, or by any other existing agencies. It has been prompted to make the present proposal because of the urgency of the problem with which the world is faced, and the necessity of speedy, cooperative effort under governmental supervision, if widespread human suffering is to be averted.[42]

The first reply to these solicitations was received by telegram from Stockholm the following day, in which the secretary general of the Swedish Foreign Office advised the U.S. Department of State that the Swedish foreign minister would have to take the matter up with the Swedish cabinet.[43]

The first positive confirmation seems to have come from the Dominican Republic on the same day. The U.S. Embassy at Santo Domingo advised the U.S. Department of State that the Dominican government's representative at the conference would be its minister in London.[44]

France and Belgium also quickly replied that although no definite decisions had been made it seemed likely that those decisions would soon be forthcoming and that they would be favourable to the concept of a conference. However, the Italians were diplomatically cautious over committing themselves to any actions that might have been construed as being anti-German. On 24 March, 1938, the U.S. ambassador in Rome, William Phillips, sent the following message to the U.S. Department of State:

> In compliance with the department's circular instruction of March 23, 1p.m., I called today upon Count [Galeazzo] Ciano [*Italian foreign minister and son-in-law of Mussolini, later (11 January, 1944), executed by the fascists—author's note*] to ascertain the attitude of the Italian Government towards the proposed establishment of a committee to facilitate emigration of political refugees from Austria and Germany. While

promising to take the matter up with Mussolini, Ciano nevertheless expressed the opinion very definitely that Italy could not be represented on any such body, and pointed out that in view of the similarity of the two regimes, political refugees from Germany would be hostile to the Fascist state as well.

Although he recognised the humanitarian character of the proposal he said that it represented political considerations to Italy, that Italy could not participate in any move to care for the enemies of Fascism or Nazism, and that Italy must therefore refuse both on account of its close association with Germany and in view of its own position and form of government.[45]

Benito Mussolini

Italian *Duce*, refused to participate in the Évian conference.

–U.S. National Archives

Yet despite this somewhat frosty reply the Italians were themselves at least partially sympathetic to the plight of the Jews. Indeed, Mussolini seemed reluctant at first to persecute the Jewish people, even under pressure from

Germany to do so. It was not until Italy had capitulated and the Germans had taken control of northern Italy that widespread persecution of the Jewish people really began, and some nine thousand were killed. However, in April 1938 the Rome correspondent of the *Jewish Telegraphic Agency* informed the U.S. Embassy that there had existed for some time in Milan a private committee that worked to render assistance to political refugees from Germany. The Rome ambassador, William Phillips, asked for further details from the U.S. consul general in Milan who later replied that the *Comitato Assistenza Ebrei Profughi*, which was based in Milan, had been founded in 1933 by Jewish communities in Italy for the express purpose of assisting political refugees from Germany. Relief funds were gathered from Italian Jews and in 1937 approximately four hundred German Jews were given aid and about two hundred thousand lire had been spent. The principal work of the refugee committee lay in aiding the refugees to find work and to assist the refugees to emigrate to other countries and to join relatives abroad. They also helped with the acquisition of documents and visas. The committee worked closely with H.I.C.E.M., (HIAS-JCA-emigration association) a Jewish emigration institute in Paris that also assisted Jewish emigrants.[46]

The Rome ambassador, William Phillips, also advised the U.S. Department of State that the Italians had allowed a Jewish news reporter employed in Austria by the United Press to obtain a transit visa for Italy on '...somewhat irregular travel documents'. The ambassador advised that the Italians, '...showed considerable sympathy and cooperation and asserted that such a visa would be granted upon application to the appropriate authorities in Vienna'.[47]

However, in August 1938 the press was generally reporting that fascist unions in Italy were stating that law-abiding Jews would be permitted to live freely in Italy, adding that they would not be treated as enemies but would be prevented from participating in state affairs. Yet Jewish professors, medical men, lawyers, financiers and any Jews who were members of the Fascist Party would be, 'cut down greatly'. Jews would also be barred from the armed services.[48]

Whatever sympathetic attitudes may have existed beforehand, they were not to last. In 1938, Mussolini's cabinet passed a decree which stated that all Jews who had arrived in Italy after 1919 would be expelled.[49] The press reported:

> Jews are panic-stricken. It is estimated that 10,000 are affected including children, many of whom have resided in Italy for twenty years. Many have married Italian

Jewesses and Gentiles, many of whom had migrated from Austria and Germany during the period 1931-38. Several hundred Polish-Jews who have studied at universities and remained to practise are also affected. Indians generally welcome the decree, especially doctors, dentists and lawyers. They are relieved to find that some of their most successful rivals will disappear within six months. Where they go will not preoccupy those who will gain the advantage of reduced competition. Tradesmen also expect a revival of business, especially those engaged in the manufacture of women's clothing in which trade the competition of Austrian Jewesses was marked. Signore [Virginio] Gayda, writing in the *Giornale d'Italia* characterises foreign Jews as 'racial and political exiles unworthy as economic rivals'. He adds: 'The expulsion restores Italy's racial purity and freedom from foreign influence.'...

Lord Strabolgi said: 'This is a miserable attempt by Signore Mussolini to curry favour with Herr Hitler, of whom he is mortally afraid.'[50]

South Africa

Soon afterwards the U.S. Department of State instructed its embassy at Cape Town to ascertain the feelings of the South African government towards the proposed conference.[51] Yet it was never very hopeful that the Union would be particularly generous when it came to accepting Jewish refugees.

Immigration to the Union of South Africa was strictly regulated by the Immigrants Selection Board set up by the Aliens Act of 1937. The Board was allowed to authorise the issue of permits to enter the Union for the purpose of permanent residence to any alien who was, in its opinion, a desirable immigrant. The granting or withholding of such authority was entirely at the discretion of the board, provided that the applicants were carefully screened for good character and also for the likelihood of assimilation with the European inhabitants of the Union.[52]

Openings for Jewish immigrants to South Africa were severely restricted, although there had been an increase during the years 1933 to 1938. The U.S. State Department's confidential report on the Union in 1938 claimed that from 1 February to 31 December, 1937, 2282 applications had been received on behalf of intending Jewish immigrants. Of these, 1654 had been refused and 628 admitted. Of the latter, 167 were wives with 225 children who were joining their husbands, 94 were aged parents. In effect, the number of Jewish people being admitted into the Union was negligible.[53]

Lord Marley, (Dudley Leigh Aman, D.S.C.) deputy speaker of the House of Lords in London, later visited South Africa to appeal to the public for practical help regarding the Jewish refugee problem. He planned to deliver a comprehensive speech on the national radio broadcasting system controlled by the South African Broadcasting Corporation. However, the corporation banned his broadcast claiming that it was not allowed to broadcast appeals for financial assistance and that it would be a violation of a clause in the corporation's licence which read: 'The corporation shall not broadcast, or permit to be broadcast, any news matter or information ... likely to create public unrest or civil commotion'. This did not, however, prevent the newspaper *Cape Argus* from printing a comprehensive report of Lord Marley's speech.[54]

Marley served as deputy speaker in the House of Lords from 1930 to 1941. He was chairman of the Parliamentary Advisory Committee for the aid of the Jews in eastern Siberia and wrote a book: *The Brown Book of the*

Hitler Terror and the Burning of the Reichstag, a publication that described the conditions under which the Jews were living which did great work to raise public awareness in the U.S. about the plight of German Jews.[55]

Soon afterwards an anti-Semitic immigration bill was laid before the South African parliament by Nationalist Party member Eric Louw. The bill demanded the expulsion of all Jews who had entered the Union within the previous nine years. This was a clear indication of the degree of anti-Semitism that had been incorporated into the Nationalist Party.[56]

Louw's proposed bill called for the deletion of Yiddish from the list of European languages—and this at a time when knowledge of a European language was a prerequisite for permanent residency in the Union. He also called for a decree stating that no person of Jewish parentage would be 'assimilable' in South Africa, and, as 'assimilability' was also a prerequisite of admission, this would have precluded all Jewish immigration.[57]

Chapter 2

Responses and Reactions

Publication of Intention and Public Response

On 24 March, 1938, the U.S. Department of State released a press statement outlining its actions with regard to the proposed conference:

> This Government has become so impressed with the urgency of the problem of political refugees that it has inquired of a number of Governments in Europe and in this hemisphere whether they would be willing to cooperate in setting up a special committee for the purpose of facilitating the emigration from Austria, and presumably from Germany, of political refugees.[1]

The press release went on to explain the terms of the proposed meeting, as detailed to the invited countries, specifically pointing out that no country would be expected to change its existing immigration laws.

Yet, following widespread publicity in the world press, Roosevelt's scheme was attracting its share of critics, one of whom was the candidate for the democratic nomination for United States senator from Illinois, who, on 25 March, 1938, sent a scathing letter to the secretary of state, Cordell Hull. The nominee believed that the segregation of Jews and other 'undesirables' was justified, and that the U.S. should follow Hitler's example. He wrote:

> I want to protest vigorously against your action as reported in the press which is calculated to flood our country with racial refugees from Austria and elsewhere. We already have far too many of these racial elements, and those already here have gained far more than their just share of power over American finance, industry, radio, the press, and the government itself. They have far too much power in the State Department. What we need is to take our nation away from these elements which have seized it and give it back to the American people. That is what Hitler did in Germany. If you, as a representative of the American people, were to do your duty by the people and the nation, you would emulate the example of the German Chancellor in this respect, and restore your country to the American people. This question is fast becoming a burning issue in our country.[2]

Cordell Hull

U.S. secretary of state at the time of the Évian conference.

–U.S. National Archives

The U.S. assistant secretary, George Messersmith, was somewhat more diplomatic when he replied to this letter on 4 April, pointing out that it had been clearly stated in the press releases that no country would be expected to receive a greater number of immigrants than was permitted under its existing legislation.[3]

Shortly afterwards Albert Einstein and a number of other influential people wrote to the secretary of state, Cordell Hull, '...expressing their gratitude ... for your general initiative on behalf of the victims of the Nazi oppression in Austria and Germany.[4]

Hull responded by writing to Einstein, stating that he hoped the action of the U.S. would aid in ameliorating the plight of the, 'unfortunate people.[5]

Senator Martin Dies (who was later to head congressional inquiries into communism and espionage in the United States), pointed out to the State Department on 26 March, 1938, that in his opinion the countries that eventually did agree to take in numbers of Jews from Austria and Germany would not change their existing laws so that the immigrants could obtain work before natives of those countries. Dies added:

> ...in view of the strong feeling that exists in their respective countries that it is the duty of a nation to look after its own citizens first, and that charity should begin at home ... no matter how deeply we

sympathise with the plight of persecuted peoples, we cannot and we must not forget that our first duty is to our own people and that we have in our midst 12 or 15 million unemployed who are being supported by the overburdened tax payers of America. The admission of immigrants must result in one or two things: Either they will take jobs that Americans are now holding or the tax payers of America will be compelled to support them.[6]

Dies went on to point out that under the immigration laws of the United States the consuls did not have the right to permit any alien to enter the United States who was likely to become a public charge. He said that there were already millions of aliens in the U.S. who were being supported by the taxpayers and that others were taking work which Americans could have been doing. He added: 'If it had not been for the millions of aliens that we have admitted during the past few decades it is extremely doubtful if we would have any serious unemployment.'

Dies stated that several years previously he had formulated a method of relieving the plight of the persecuted peoples of Europe. He had outlined his concept in a bill which was to provide for the colonisation of unemployed and persecuted aliens in Paraguay. He had assembled considerable information to show that Paraguay had vast tracts of unoccupied lands and that the country was, '...anxious to welcome colonists to settle on this land'. Dies had been in touch with representatives of 'Paraguayan interests' who had, apparently, advised him that millions of acres of land were available to colonists. He called for the formation of an organisation to investigate the proposal and to consult with the Paraguayan government, although he admitted that it had been several years since he had consulted with the Paraguayan authorities and that the situation may have changed.[7]

In fact the interior situation in Paraguay was then so uncertain and changes of the government so frequent that it was difficult to judge whether migrants would or would not be accepted. However, from time to time the Paraguayan government declared itself willing to authorise the immigration into the country of 'elements useful to its economy,' but the Committee of *Asuncion*—a committee that aided immigrants—warned the U.S. Department of State in 1938 that despite all the declarations of the government in their attempts at appeasement it was not advisable to send emigrants into Paraguay.[8]

A highly classified U.S. government report stated:

> Paraguay offers but very limited possibilities for Jewish immigration. Its city population does not exceed 100,000 people and the total population of the country is under one million. It should be noted, however, that regions with tolerably good climate and fertile arable land do exist. The Government seems to be disposed to welcome Jewish colonisation but only if it has powerful financial backing of the Jewish organisations.[9]

Meanwhile, in the United States, there were supporters of the proposed immigration, even if only in a modest way. For example, on 28 March a director of the Calvert Publicity Company in Baltimore sent a telegram to Cordell Hull stating that the idea of Jewish immigration was 'splendid' and that the company would guarantee employment for one Jewish girl.[10]

But international tensions over the continued events in Austria and Germany were causing considerable public comment, especially in the U.S. press, and while the tone of these reports was sometimes anti-Semitic, most were genuinely concerned with both the plight of the Jewish people and also with the moral obligation to care as a matter of priority firstly for the citizens of the U.S. In March 1938 the *Toronto Globe and Mail*, an independent publication, accurately reported, '...it is a problem that goes far beyond what any nation might do out of decency.... Admittance is one thing, assimilation is another.... The United States has asked for a conference among European nations to deal with the forced emigration from Austria. The suspicion arises that the intention of Uncle Sam is to turn the tide anywhere else but toward his own shores'.[11]

During this time the German press was remaining remarkably silent over the issue, although this was later discovered to be because the Reich government had delayed in dictating the editorial tone to be adopted. However, on 27 March, *Angrieff*, the publication controlled by the German minister for propaganda, Josef Goebbels, issued its first editorial, an editorial which reads, in translation, suspiciously like a German government press release:

> The mixture to which America opens its gates is interesting. What is now, however, to be administered to America's blood circulation by way of foreign forces all bears a common poison, the Moscow poison. In America therefore there will be severe internal disturbances until the sound strength of the Anglo-Saxon people has

destroyed or absorbed the migrant injection.[12]

Apart from these few vituperative words in the *Angrieff*, there seems to have been little or no other press comments regarding the U.S. refugee plan, although on 25 March, 1938, Hitler himself had stated during a speech at Koenigsberg:

> We will deal with those incorrigible opponents [the Jews] through the normal methods of our state.... I can only hope and expect that the other world which has felt such deep sympathy for these criminals will be generous enough to transform this pity into practical aid. As far as I am concerned we are ready to place our luxury ships at the disposal of these countries for the transportation of these criminals.[13]

International Response

For some countries, such as the U.S.S.R., there was evidently no need even to consider sending an invitation to the conference. It was well established that the U.S.S.R. like Germany, was a profoundly anti-Semitic state. A later communication to the U.S. Department of State reported that, '...the Soviet government refuses participation in [the] solution of the refugee problem and avoids all reference to the admission of Jewish refugees to the Soviet Union'.[14]

Another country which did not receive an invitation to Évian was Trinidad, although Trinidad was, to begin with, one of the very few countries in the world to have a reasonably liberal attitude towards the refugee problem. According to confidential State Department documents it was widely known in central Europe that Trinidad was actually accepting refugees—providing they could meet modest immigration requirements, although the highly respected *Trinidad Guardian*, the country's leading newspaper, later stated that because Trinidad did not suffer from under-population, '...clearly it is impossible for us to offer aid'.[15]

The Trinidadian government's liberal policies did not remain in effect for very long. As pressures mounted an order was issued prohibiting the immigration of refugees who had emigrated during the previous two years, 'from certain European countries'. The order was to become effective on 15 January, 1939, and no exceptions were to be made other than those immigrants who had been issued with visas and were already at sea on their way to Trinidad.[16] A Trinidad government Order-in-Council dated 10 January, 1939, tightened these restrictions even more and completely banned all further entry with no exceptions.[17]

***

Three days after Hitler's speech, on 28 March, 1938, the French agreed to the formation of what would become known as the intergovernmental committee, adding in their note of agreement to the U.S. Department of State that the French government was entirely in accord with the fundamental concern expressed by the U.S. government over the refugee problem.[18]

Almost simultaneously the Uruguayan government forwarded a message to the U.S. Embassy in Montevideo also stating its willingness to respond to the U.S. call, but adding, with some considerable caution, that while refugees were welcome in Uruguay, none would be admitted if they suffered from, '...physical, mental or moral defects which might be harmful to society'.[19]

Uruguay was one of the many countries that enacted additional legislation prior to the Évian conference. The new legislation of 23 November, 1937, reduced the immigration quota to its minimum. *Llamadas* (landing permits) were admitted in only exceptional cases and then only when the case involved parents bringing their minor children, or offspring bringing their parents, or of husbands bringing their wives. However, the appellants had to be established in the country for a minimum of three years. Intending immigrants who had no relatives in Uruguay had to conform to three stipulations. Firstly they had to be bearers of political clearance certificates which declared that they were not political subversives. Secondly they had to own at least 600 pesos (£65), and they had to arrive in the country aboard a ship as first class passengers.[20]

A highly confidential U.S. Department of State report of June 1938 stated:

> As regards the emigrants who have no relatives in Uruguay it is already clear that all the ... regulations have been solely conceived in order to prevent their admittance into the country, as it was supposed that no emigrant could fulfil the three conditions required: travelling 1st class, giving a guaranty deposit of 600 pesos and obtaining a political certificate. When it transpired that there were cases when all the required conditions were fulfilled and that the authorities of the countries where their refugees resided granted them the political certificates stating that the interested parties, 'did not participate in any

conspiracy aiming at the violent destruction of the very foundation of society,' then the Uruguayan authorities addressed their European consuls an advice not to visa the passports of such emigrants. We know a case when a consul was revoked although he acted in all good faith according to the legislative regulations.[21]

In spite of the severe restrictions Jewish immigration into Uruguay maintained the same level (between 500 and 2000 per annum) during the six years prior to the Évian conference, its curve closely following that of the economic development of the country. The figures for 1938 showed a vertical slump considering the measures taken by the Uruguayan authorities against immigration, and the increasing numbers of immigrants requiring sanctuary.[22] These statistics bellied the statements later made by Uruguay's representative to the Évian conference, Senor Dr Alfredo Carbonell-Debali, who claimed that anyone was free to enter or leave his country and that Uruguay was in, '...urgent necessity of populating rural areas'.[23] Carbonell-Debali, however, qualified the statement by adding, '...I feel therefore that we will be unable to go beyond the official action ... it is our idea that immigration must be financed by private organizations in their respective countries'.[24]

U.S. Internal Reaction

U.S. public response to Roosevelt's proposal was immediate, with many people writing to the State Department offering their services in the formation of a committee. Some of these offers were made on the grounds that they not be paid for their services.

On 29 March, 1938, Dorothy Thompson wrote an informative letter to the secretary of state, Cordell Hull, in which she set out several suggestions which Hull found so helpful that he adopted many of them when the committee was later formed. Among the items suggested by Thompson was the recommendation that an official international organisation of government representatives be formed and that this organisation be backed by a private advisory body with private financial support. She pointed out that this organisation would have difficulties in preventing jealousies and intrigues and also over the question of prestige. These would be emotive issues that could well endanger the project, especially so since many of the organisations then existing had conflicting views over the methods of handling the Jewish refugee problem.[25]

Much of what Dorothy Thompson had written to the secretary of state was included in a comprehensive article she had then just completed for the publication *Foreign Affairs*. The article in this publication brought Thompson several complimentary letters, one from Charles H. Lee, the associate director of the National League for American Citizenship and another from Erwin Schattmann who advised Thompson that he was a German who had been involved in the emigration of German Jews to Palestine. He stated that prior to leaving Germany he had worked as an assistant to the president of *Palastina Treuhundstelle*, a corporation set up to handle the transfer of German-Jewish money to Palestine by means of financing the export of German goods with the money of would-be emigrants. Schattmann advised that the system then operating to get Jewish money out of the country and into Palestine meant that the emigrants received, after their emigration, the counter-value of their money in foreign currency, less a discount needed for the compensation of the difference between German prices and those of the international market.[26)]Thompson also advised the State Department concerning what organisations in the U.S. would be likely to aid the formation of a committee. These included the American Jewish Committee, the Joint Distribution Committee and six others. She also advised that the Catholic Church would be unlikely to offer aid as they were, '...completely divided,' adding that they would certainly give no aid or comfort to refugees from the war in Spain.[27]

By the end of March 1938 the U.S. Department of State still did not know whether or not the proposed committee would be formed. The replies received up to that time had been reasonably positive, but a large number of nations had not replied at all to the suggestion. As the assistant secretary of state, George Messersmith, wrote on 28 March: '...We are getting some replies from other Governments, but some of them are of a preliminary character and we cannot expect to get the definite replies before the end of this week. I think that by the end of the week we ought to know just where we stand and I feel that we will get enough encouragement to go ahead'.[28]

The American Civil Liberties Union in New York City also quickly praised the U.S. government's initiative concerning the plight of the Jews, but stressed that changes were needed to existing U.S. immigration procedures to enable a greater number of refugees to be admitted. In a letter of 28 March to Cordell Hull the director of the union, Roger N. Baldwin, stated that it was time to instruct the U.S. consuls abroad, who then required proof of, 'unreasonably large sums of money,' to change the requirement so that this stipulation was waived. It was an amendment that could be changed simply by administrative order.[29]

The American Jewish Joint Committee in New York also received the news of the proposed committee with enthusiasm, stating that they had worked to help refugees for many years and that it was heartening to have affirmation of the traditional American attitude towards those in need. The committee's chairman, Paul Baerwald, offered full aid and collaboration with other agencies in their efforts to get the Jews out of Germany and Austria.[30]

However, despite the praise, the criticism and the rhetoric, the real problems facing countries in which refugees were seeking asylum from Nazi rule were all too pervasive. Many of these countries were still reeling from the impact of the Great Depression, and unemployment was high—such forces had been contributing factors in the rise to power of Adolf Hitler in the destitute and impoverished Germany of the early 1930s. The result of this unemployment and poor business growth was the construction of strong barriers against immigration.

South American Reaction

On 30 March, 1938, the Venezuelan government officially acknowledged that it would send representatives to the proposed conference, but added, however, an intricately worded codicil to the acceptance:

> ...the capacity of absorption of immigrants is limited in Venezuela, as well as by legal provisions as by the necessity to choose immigrant elements from among agricultural workers, by the ... [problems] of demographic equilibrium which require racial diversification, and by the social security which imposes methods of rigorous selection.[31]

In other words the government at Caracas would not in any way change its existing immigration quota laws or requirements. It would only accept agricultural workers; it was particularly concerned about the intermixing of Jews within the largely Catholic population and also of having the problem of accepting immigrants who would be a burden on the social security system. In short, few Jews would be allowed into the country.

The administration practices with regard to the admission into the country did not seem to be founded on any legislation regulating the immigration. The U.S. Department of State was aware in 1938 of cases when people, having obtained visas at the Venezuelan consulates, were refused the right to land.[32] Señor Carlos Aristimuno-Coll, Venezuela's delegate to the Évian conference, was later to state, '...It must, however, be pointed out that there are certain restrictions on the welcome which Venezuela can extend to political refugees from Germany including Austria. Our capacity for absorption is limited'.[33]

Argentina also acceded to U.S. requests for the formation of an intergovernmental committee but added a codicil similar to that of Venezuela.[34] On the same date, (30 March) Panama added its weight to the committee adding that the Panamanian government had always appreciated the role Jewish immigrants had played in the reorganisation of the Panamanian public education system. However, they too were careful to point out that they would not change any existing immigration laws to provide for more immigrants.[35] The following day, 31 March, the Chilean government, through its foreign ministry, advised the U.S. Department of State that it was unable to consider taking any refugees from Nazi occupied zones. The strictly confidential message stated:

Chile has been compelled to establish severe requirements to control immigration resulting from European political events, moreover until certain studies now being made here concerning colonisation and immigration are completed, the Chilean government will be unable to sign vague and general commitments.[36]

In a note appended to this telegram the U.S. ambassador to Chile had added: 'Strictly confidential! In view of the [Chilean] Foreign Minister's anti-Semitic views, [which probably reflect (the) opinion of the government] ... the qualified nature of the foregoing reply comes as no surprise, despite [the] fact that leading papers have unreservedly supported [the] proposed plan'.[37]

The government of Chile was most concerned to restrict the numbers of Jewish migrants allowed into the country, despite an inquiry held at the end of 1937 which had investigated the results of Jewish immigration for the preceding three years. This inquiry had found that a very large percentage had been gainfully employed.[38] In spite of this evidence only extremely low numbers of Jews succeeded in penetrating into Chile in the few years immediately before the war.[39]

The country, of course, is not large, its city population in 1938 was still relatively small and industry was in its embryonic state of development. Yet the Chilean government was fully aware of the advantages of allowing Jewish immigration into the country, their statistics proved beyond doubt that industry and wages increased as a result of liberal immigration policies. The U.S. Department of State reported in June 1938:

> Nevertheless, the Chilean Government does not seem disposed to admit these elements into the country; but they do not refuse admittance to agriculturists; they even intend to reserve for them the territory south of parallel 42 degrees. Unfortunately, the country thus offered to future colonists consists of vast spaces, covered with virgin woods, the climate of which is very unfavourable,—to such extent that the Government themselves declare that only Scandinavians are likely to colonize them.[40]

Josephus Daniels, at the U.S. Embassy in Mexico, also reported at this time that he had placed the proposal of the U.S. government before General Hay of the Mexican Foreign Office. In a telegram of 25 March, Daniels reported:

He [Hay] said the humane purpose had his cordial sympathy and approval and ... he would present the suggestion to President Gardenas [sic (Lázaro)—Cárdenas] immediately upon his return to the city, and would give me an answer on Monday or Tuesday. 'You know,' Hay said, 'that Mexico has jingoists who, in Congress and out, have of late been vocal in advocacy of sending Jews, who are here on tourist visas and have remained in Mexico, out of the country.'[41]

Like many other countries Mexican immigration laws were also somewhat restrictive. They would become even more so through 1938/39 with immigration quotas being set for nearly every emigrating country. There were no restrictions for the citizens of the United States of America, for the South-American countries and for Spain, but there was a maximum yearly quota figure of five thousand for the citizens of Germany, Great Britain, Austria, Belgium, Denmark, France, Holland, Hungary, Japan, Norway, Portugal, Sweden, Switzerland and Czechoslovakia.[42] Considering that most of the refugees were attempting to flee from either Austria or Germany, this figure was brutally low. For Poland, Russia, Romania, Lithuania, Yugoslavia, where Jews were also experiencing wide-scale persecution, China, Syria and other Arabic countries—the quota number had been limited to an incredibly low 100 persons per year.[43] It should also be noted that these were figures for the entire migratory quota and included all nationalities and religions, thus the percentage of Jews allowed into the country was exceedingly small. Preference was given to agriculturists owning a sum of 20,000 Mexican pesos (about U.S.$6000).[44]

It seems clear from this that Mexican immigration for Jewish refugees would be limited in the extreme. The Mexican delegate to the Évian conference, Primo Villa Michel, was later to state that his country had been going through a great social and economic reform as a result of a programme that had taken its roots in the Mexican revolution. This reform prescribed the distribution of land to a large part of the rural population which formerly had existed in a state of serfdom. Villa Michel was to state:

Primo Villa Michel

Mexican delegate to Évian.

–*Direction General de Acervo Histórico Diplomático. Directión de Documentatión.*

In accordance with that programme my government is endeavouring, with the limited framework of our industrialization—which is now only starting—to raise to a level that is worthy of being called civilized ... the carrying out of this reform has made it necessary for my government for several years past to limit the entry of immigrants.[45]

On 29 March, 1938, the U.S. Department of State issued a press release with details of the replies then received from the various countries over the Évian proposal. At that time a total of nine countries, Belgium, Brazil, the Dominican Republic, El Salvador, France, Haiti, Mexico, Peru and Uruguay had stated they would be willing to attend the conference.[46] Although the El Salvadorian government later declined to attend.[47]

Problems of U.S. Settlement

At that time too, Senator Josh Lee of Oklahoma received several anonymous letters from American businessmen protesting at the proposal to allow Jewish refugees into the country. The letters broadly stated that an influx of such immigrants would be harmful to local business. These letters were passed onto Cordell Hull who acknowledged them, but such correspondence had little, if any, impact on State Department policy.[48]

On 1 April, Ellen C. Potter, M.D., chairperson of the Committee on Care of Transient and Homeless, based at the RKO Building in New York, pointed out to Cordell

Hull several points of importance concerning the problems of people who were transient. These included social, educational, legal, health and employment. The committee had expended countless hours on investigating these problems and forwarded a report to Hull detailing their findings and recommendations. The findings of the committee resulted in an important document, not only for immigrants into the U.S.A., but also for people who emigrated to any other country. These findings were instructional for the U.S. Department of State and may well have influenced, even in some small way, the department's outlook on immigration, but if this is so, it would only have been a marginal influence.[49]

Outlook for the Conference and Critical Attack

In an interdepartmental memorandum from George Messersmith to Sumner Welles, the U.S. undersecretary of state, on 31 March, 1938, Messersmith pointed out that the responses from the various governments to date had been so favourable that it seemed very likely the conference would proceed. Messersmith advised the undersecretary that he had been visited by a number of luminaries including Paul Baerwald of the Jewish Joint Distribution Committee and a Miss Razovsky, reportedly an expert on refugees and immigrants. Surprisingly all of these experts had, apparently, advised that no changes should be made to existing U.S. immigration laws to provide for more immigrants. They reportedly claimed that to do so would hinder, rather than aid, Jewish immigration. Messersmith also advised that according to information forwarded to him, some members of Congress were receiving hundreds of letters indicating that while the government's moves to establish such a refugee committee were applauded, '...there is a definite sentiment that *under no circumstances* must our immigration laws and practice be changed in any major respect'. (Author's italics)[50]

No U.S. member had yet been selected for appointment to the committee. At the end of March President Roosevelt was taking a brief holiday at Warm Springs but Messersmith believed that as soon as he returned he would do something about appointing a person to the position. Additionally, a venue for the conference had yet to be decided upon. Geneva had been widely accepted as the most popular location but Messersmith also believed that Lausanne or Zurich—and preferably Lausanne—would also be acceptable venues. Messersmith also advised that while there were many organisations that had offered assistance the only organisation that could be of any real help was the Jewish-run Joint Distribution Committee. This committee evidently had the power to raise significant funding to aid refugees from Austria and Germany. Messersmith reiterated his earlier views that the funding for relocating the refugees should come from private sources, adding:

> It is important also as it is through such organisations that the money will have to be raised, which will be needed in considerable sums for the transportation and settlement of refugees. This part of the problem will have to be left, I believe, to private initiative, and it is probably advisable that this should be clearly understood from the outset.[51]

A number of bills concerning proposed changes to the immigration laws had recently been introduced into both Houses, but Messersmith advised Sumner Welles that he had discreetly brought to the attention of the members the, '...desirability of hearings not being held on such bills at present'.[52]

Yet despite the good publicity, the criticisms continued. On 2 April, 1938, a Star member of the American Legion—who had obviously suffered attacks because of his outspoken attitudes towards the Jewish refugee problem—wrote a scathing letter to Cordell Hull in which he stated:

> Because of Catholic and Jewish attacks made against me and political action taken against me by Wisconsin politicians, supported by the United States government throughout the United States, I am unable to secure employment. Therefore it is respectfully requested that negotiations be made with the German government or Mr Adolf Hitler for a mutual exchange of me for a prosecuted [sic] Catholic or Jew.... My background is good. I was born and raised in the State of Georgia. My forefathers were pioneers and helped make this country. My people are honorable and well thought of. I gave to my country nineteen years of honorable service. I was with the American forces in Germany and believe I would make Mr Hitler a good citizen.
>
> It is respectfully requested that this matter be given early and serious consideration and that I be advised at an early date.[53]

Hull's reply to this letter is not known, the reply, if any, is missing from the file.

There is little doubt that most Jewish organisations in the U.S. at that time were concentrating their efforts on pressing the U.S.

government to liberalise its existing regulations to allow for greater Jewish immigration. On 5 April, 1938, William Weiner, president of the Jewish People's Committee for United Action Against Fascism and Anti-Semitism, based in New York, contacted Cordell Hull by letter, asking Hull to consider five important points:

1. That the [immigration] quota of Austria and Germany be merged and refugees be admitted from these two countries regardless of their place of origin.

2. That the quota be made retroactive and those places not filled in 1937/8 be allocated to 1938/9.

3. That the U.S. government apply to the refugees from Austria and Germany the unused quotas which had originally been intended for other countries.

4. That passport requirements for refugees be waived.

5. That the U.S. immigration laws which prevented the entry of persons who had suffered arrest, were former prisoners or who had been convicted by Nazi courts, be changed so that such people could gain entry.[54]

The possibilities of having changes made to the existing U.S. immigration laws were a source of concern to a large number of organisations.

Ten organisations such as the American Jewish Committee, (established by Rabbi Stephen Wise); the Hebrew Sheltering and Immigration Society; the National Council of Jewish Women and others, all indicated their support with a letter written by the director of the Foreign Language Information Service at Fourth Avenue New York, to Samual Dickstering, the chairman of the Committee on Immigration and Naturalization at the House of Representatives.

The letter urged Dickstein to postpone indefinitely the hearings scheduled for 21/22 April in the House of Representatives, and to discuss the possibilities of changes to the immigration laws which might allow more Jewish refugees into the country. The director wrote that Roosevelt's proposal had been met with general approval because of its humanitarian objectives and because it specified that existing immigration laws would not need to be modified. The director added that if there were to be any serious attempt in Congress to liberalise the existing immigration laws, then there would likely to be a strong reversal of feeling. He said that any public discussion of bills to change the existing quota restrictions would be bound to, '...let loose a flood of bitter anti-alien and anti-Jewish agitation'. The director also said that this would then react unfavourably on the attitudes of other countries, jeopardising the success of the proposed conference. He added the point that any proposal to amend the existing immigration laws should come afterwards, as a result of the conference, rather than preceding it.[55]

By early April the possibility that the government might be faced with very real and tangible protest against the importation of Jewish refugees was growing daily stronger. The powerful State Council of Pennsylvania's Order of Independent Americans—with some 25,000 members nation-wide—was energetically opposed to any such importation, claiming that members would resist the policy primarily on an economic basis. The State Council claimed on 7 April, 1938, that the importation of Jewish immigrants would increase dramatically the relief rolls thus substantially adding to the nation's taxation burden. Their communication to the U.S. Department of State contained various comments including the point that as refugees were not being allowed to leave the country with any of their assets then they would have to be supported financially. This, the council said, was highlighted by the arrival at New York of a number of refugees who owned just six dollars each after their passages had been paid. The State Council went on to point out that, '...one of two courses is left for these refugees—either becoming a charge [of the state] or being given employment which rightfully should be given to a citizen? Is this not placing the American citizen and American workman in the position of being a secondary citizen?'[56]

This communication went on to state that according to members of the organisation the U.S. was no place for people who were politically or morally unsuited to realise and appreciate the true privileges and opportunities accorded them by the United States, adding that rather than liberalising the immigration laws they should be tightened considerably. The letter claimed that if policy changes were to be made then it would be better for the U.S. government to concentrate on making those changes to help ameliorate the lot of impoverished Americans who could not find work and that this should be done before turning to the problems of the rest of the world. Society members also professed the belief that a more liberal immigration policy would open up an avenue for other countries to rid themselves of 'undesirables' on the pretext of oppression.[57]

How far letters such as this influenced subsequent U.S. immigration policy—especially in relation to the Jewish refugee problem—is difficult to ascertain. Certainly the organisation's misgivings were being felt by a large number of U.S. citizens and also of citizens in the almost three dozen other countries then considering taking extra numbers of immigrants. The State Council also sent a copy of this letter to President Roosevelt, and it is certain that the organisation's statement that any increase would lead to further unrest would not have been overlooked by the president and his advisers.

One man who later commented controversially on the concept of an international committee to seek a solution to the refugee problem was newspaper editor, C. Leon de Aryan, owner of a small newspaper called *The Broom*, based in San Diego, California. According to a letter written by Aryan to President Roosevelt at the end of March 1938, a subscription of *The Broom* had been sent to the White House for the previous three months, and in the latest edition, that of Volume VIII, Number 25, dated 21 March, 1938, Aryan had written an article that claimed the only solution to the Jewish refugees problem was, in fact, the creation of an international body. Aryan claimed to be 'diametrically opposed' to everything the president stood for. He said that he had written the article on 17 March. The newspaper had been sent to the White House soon afterwards, arriving there no later than 23/24 March, and that the White House had responded by sending out the invitations to the meetings almost immediately.[58] This is clearly illogical, as the invitations had been sent prior to this date, but Aryan's comments in the newspaper are nonetheless interesting. He stated that the Jews were incapable of running the committee themselves and that Gentiles should be appointed to the senior positions within the committee, with Jews being allowed only minor or secondary positions.[59]

Clearly, views such as these, even when published in relatively small circulation newspapers, could do irreparable harm to the cause of Jewish refugees. Having eulogised on the want and righteousness of allowing Jews into the United States, Aryan later wrote a scathing letter to the president claiming that Roosevelt had not thought the problem through to its natural conclusion. Aryan claimed that America no longer belonged to the horse and buggy days of the pioneers who had arrived on American shores and had done such a wonderful job of building up the nation. Now, Aryan, stated, the lands were taken up, the pioneering work was over, was there, he questioned, any real need for the Jews?[60]

***

On 28 March a resident of Owendale Alberta wrote to President Roosevelt with a warning, pointing out that opening up the country to refugees could, '...prove a grave menace', and that the entire refugee issue could have been: '...one of Hitler's crafty schemes to land an army of Nazis right in our midst without hindrance, under the guise of refugees. How are we to know that this is not a cleverly concocted scheme of Germany, Austria, England, and even your own Senate, to land an army of Nazis in the U.S. to overthrow the government?'[61]

The German-American Settlement League with thousands of members countrywide, was, of course, rabidly anti-Semitic. During the subsequent Évian conference six officers of the League were convicted of violating the state civil rights laws after conducting a violent anti-Semitic campaign. Among other things they declared that all bankers were Jews. They each received a one year suspended sentence.[62]

***

By 6 April, twenty-three countries had advised the U.S. Department of State that they would be willing to attend a conference, the only country to abstain at this time being Italy. Germany, of course, and Austria, had not been invited. The undersecretary of state, Sumner

Welles, sent a brief memorandum to the president at the White House on that date suggesting that a meeting be convened at the White House. He also suggested that the meeting should be attended by a number of prominent people who had an interest in the refugee problem so that details of the proposed conference could be examined and decided upon. Some of the people recommended for the meeting included Raymond B. Fosdick of the Rockefeller Foundation; Professor Joseph P. Chamberlain of Columbia University; James Grover McDonald of the *New York Times*; Reverend Samuel McCrae Calvert of the Federal Council of Churches of Christ in America, and several others. Strangely, although Dorothy Thompson's name was on the original list of State Department recommendations, her entry had, with no explanation, been crossed out. On 8 April President Roosevelt approved the proposal. Items to be discussed at the meeting included the proposal to amalgamate the German and Austrian quotas, thus allowing for added numbers of immigrants, the naming of a U.S. representative to the international committee, to set a date and venue for the conference, and the liaison to be established with private institutions to aid with financing the emigration from Germany and Austria.[63]

The State Department advised the White House that when the international committee was finally formed there were four points the committee should immediately address.

1. Every country would make a clear statement of its immigration laws and practice and a general statement of the number of immigrants it is prepared to receive.

2. A considerable number of immigrants will not be able to provide the documents such as passports, birth certificates, etc now required under the immigration law and practice of many states. The committee could, therefore, usefully consider the setting up of an office to issue documents to prospective immigrants, which documents would be recognised as valid for travel and other purposes by the states participating on the committee. This is one of the immediate problems.

3. The participating states would consider existing laws on the subject of economic and legal status of immigrants. In a good many receiving states newly arriving immigrants suffer from restricted treatment under the law which makes it difficult for them to make a new existence.

4. The international committee would study the various projects which may be submitted to it for settlement of refugees in participating states or in parts of their territory which may be adapted to their reception. This is the crux of the problem and it is in this field that the international committee can probably do its most constructive work. It is the long range problem.[64]

The meeting with the president was held at the White House on the morning of 13 April, 1938. During this meeting Roosevelt stated that he was about to announce the appointment of one, or possibly two, representatives to the international committee. Switzerland had previously indicated that it did not wish to host the conference, almost certainly because of its close ties with German business and because it was supplying vast amounts of military equipment to Germany, and suggested that the U.S. look for an alternative to the proposed venue of Geneva.[65] During the White House meeting Roosevelt instructed the State Department to conduct investigations to find the most suitable venue. Roosevelt also asked that those present at the meeting form themselves into a permanent U.S. based committee with the intention of assisting and advising both the president and the international committee.[66]

Three other names were added to the U.S. committee at this stage, Paul Baerwald of the Jewish Joint Distribution Committee; James M. Speers of the American Committee for Christian German Refugees, and Basil Harris a prominent Roman Catholic with significant shipping interests.[67] Raymond B. Fosdick of the Rockefeller Foundation was forced to decline the offer of a place on the U.S. committee, stating that the foundation's regulations prevented him from serving on any fund-raising committees.[68]

At the same time John Borough Dunne, the field representative for the American Red Cross, submitted some carefully conceived suggestions to the U.S. Department of State with regard to the organisation and running of the refugee effort. Dunne, who clearly had a thorough grasp of the enormity of the situation, made detailed recommendations concerning financing, budgets, methods of fund-raising, composition of committee members, pre-entry investigations of immigrants, suitability for various types of work in various areas, relocation with relatives already in the countries to which the refugee was allowed entry, post entry necessities such as checking to ensure satisfactory settlement and close contact with immigration officers, education and citizenship.[69] His suggestions were duly noted by the State Department and on 21 April, George Messersmith thanked him for his assistance, stating that the committee's organisation was in its infancy and that his suggestions would be noted.[70]

At that time too the U.S. Embassy in London advised the U.S. Department of State that the Portuguese Foreign Office had not received an invitation to the proposed international committee. Ambassador Joseph P. Kennedy (father of future President John F. Kennedy) stated in his communication: 'The Portuguese are apparently touchy on this score.'[71]

Joseph Kennedy

U.S. ambassador to London at the time of the Évian conference.

—U.S. National Archives

Despite the upsurge of public opinion in favour of the plan there was clearly a significant number of Americans who continued to oppose it. For example, a councillor of the Queens Council, Junior Order of United American Mechanics, on 9 April, 1938, wrote to the U.S. Department of State stating that, '...refugees from European countries can only prove detrimental to the best interests of the American people'. He added that he and the society were, '...diametrically opposed to this program'.[72]

The German-controlled Austrian press was remarkably tolerant over the whole issue, although the *Neue Freie Presse* in Vienna (which ceased publication in January the following year) could not avoid being somewhat cynical when it reported on 29 March, 1938:

> In case the political character of this action is not immediately obvious, this aspect of the plan is emphasized in the English press, in the *Times* as well as in the *News Chronicle*. When in Austria thousands were thrown out of employment and tens of thousands were forced to emigrate, no

finger was moved. When after the termination of the World War, German-minded Alsatians were driven across the frontier by so very democratic a country as France, and when these people were allowed to take with them only as much as they could carry on their backs, the conscience, which is now so active, was silent. The American immigration stipulations in force up to now are not of a nature to establish a moral past for the government of the United States which might entitle it to such a demonstrative step. Only immigrants fully provided with money are admitted under certain conditions. A profitable business has been made of immigration, and this continues up to today. That Italy too is mentioned among the countries which are called as guardians of such charitable actions to the side of Mr Roosevelt—who moreover has himself to provide for twelve million unemployed—reveals the political intention, whose services as corset-support for a higher morality are certainly of a very doubtful nature. To seek a moral ally for this purpose in Rome is an amusing undertaking because it shows that a moral encirclement of Germany is once more aimed at and that the existence of such a marked peace-element as the Berlin-Rome axis is considered an obstacle in this regard. One of the governments [the Netherlands] has already sent a reply according to which Austrian émigrés must be in possession of a passport of two months' validity ... they must prove moreover when they file their request for temporary residence in Holland that they are in possession of at least 500 Austrian schillings, but if they wish to take up permanent residence they must prove that they have a capital of at least 10,000 Dutch florins. In establishing these conditions, moreover, the Netherlands Government made explicit reference to its experiences with earlier émigrés from Germany. Since not only the Netherlands had these experiences, one can quietly await how this rather expensive help of Mr Roosevelt's for the émigrés will look in the end.[73]

Anti-Semitism and cynicism were not confined solely to the Germans. For example, once the decision to establish an international committee had been made, Romania's anti-Semitic government quickly made representations to the U.S. government in an effort to be rid of a large portion of their Jews. In a telegram from the

U.S. ambassador in Bucharest to Cordell Hull, the ambassador stated:

> Minister for [Romanian] Foreign Affairs today expressed his wholehearted admiration for the [U.S.] President's initiative in making a general appeal for the admission into other countries of political refugees from Germany and Austria, and expressed the hope that this might be extended to Romania. The Minister suggested as the next step the establishment somewhere in Switzerland of bureaux for Romania, Czechoslovakia, Hungary, Poland and Germany to deal with Jewish or political refugee problems in those countries.
>
> Due to the conclusion of [largely anti-Semitic] citizenship tests in this country this month, the problem of what to do with those who emerge therefrom without nationality will become active. The Minister intimated that Romania would like to dispose annually of a number corresponding to the Jewish birth rate. He seemed to think that in any case there would be no pressure to send away the old and the young under 20 or over 40 years of age.[74]

The message was evidently ignored in the State Department for several days—possibly because of its enormous ramifications. The delay prompted the U.S. ambassador in Bucharest to send another telegram on 16 April, after having again met with the Romanian foreign minister. The ambassador urged the State Department to send an answer on the Romanian proposal, adding that the Romanian Foreign Office had made a similar representation to the British Embassy in Bucharest.[75]

This telegram certainly prompted an almost immediate response and one not designed to appease the Romanian Foreign Office. In fact this kind of response was exactly what the U.S. government had feared. In a strictly confidential telegram of 21 April—which seems to have been signed by Sumner Welles—the State Department advised:

> The recent initiative of the President with regard to refugees was prompted by an emergency situation in Germany and Austria. The committee will be set up primarily to endeavor to meet the problems growing out of this situation. Whether later on the committee itself might decide to extend its work is something that cannot be foreseen at the present time, but it would be unfortunate if its mere existence should anywhere be construed as an encouragement of legislation or acts that

would create a new refugee problem as this might well result in a diminished willingness in this and presumably in other countries to consider ways and means of receiving and settling the victims of such legislation and acts.[76]

The situation in Romania at that time was clearly demonstrated to the U.S. Department of State in a report supplied by Doctor Zolly C. von Schwartz, an American citizen who had travelled through the country sometime in late 1937. Schwartz had been treated appallingly by the Romanian authorities. His suitcases and other luggage had been confiscated; he had witnessed several murders of Jewish people and was made to pay exorbitant fees to petty officials for minor services such as passport stamping. Schwartz later wrote that he had seen a soldier bayoneting an old Jew at the immigration depot; that Jews were forbidden to sell their real estate and could only offer it to the state. He reported that in business and industry, ninety-eight per cent of Romanian labour had to be used. All firms had to have an honorary president who was, 'a Romanian potentate of politics'. These men received large 'salaries' for their names to be used on the stationery. A man was not allowed to employ his own son but had to 'buy' Romanian help.[77]

***

One Jewish refugee who believed that President Roosevelt and Secretary of State Cordell Hull should have received a Nobel Peace Prize for their humanitarian efforts was Rudolph Seiden. Commenting in the *Kansas City Journal Post* in April, 1938, Seiden stated that the U.S. could offer unlimited refugee possibilities by opening the doors of Alaska to European migrants. He claimed that in the wilderness of Alaska there was sufficient room and adequate possibilities for agricultural, financial and industrial expansion, and that the state could easily absorb every single European refugee.

Seiden believed that the immigration laws of the U.S. should have been altered to allow Americans of satisfactory financial standing to become guarantors of refugees, whether such aliens be personally known to them or not. He emphasized that Alaska, Australia, New Zealand, Canada, certain South American countries and other scantily populated areas should have been opened immediately to immigration. Commenting in April 1938 he stated that agreements should be reached with the German government to ensure that what money the refugees owned might be placed into funds in Germany or Austria and corresponding credit be given to them in their adopted country, the balancing of the two funds coming about through international trade agreements.[78]

Seiden stated that the United States, South America, Australia, Canada, New Zealand and the few democratic countries still remaining in Europe should have looked at their immigration quotas. Rudolph Seiden had foreseen the Holocaust and in 1935 had escaped from Austria with his wife, Juliette, to settle in Kansas City. The couple later assisted with the provision of visas to Jewish refugees and their home became a meeting place for them. Seiden stated that up to 200,000 persons should be able to emigrate a year if democratic countries would just accept them.[79]

Seiden also pointed out that Alaska had an area of approximately 600,000 square miles and a population of approximately 60,000, about 30,000 of whom were indigenous. He stated that the climate of Alaska, particularly along the coast, is similar to that of central and northern Europe. He added that it might prove too cold for Spaniards but it would mean no hardship to Austrians, Germans or Poles.

Rudolph and Juliette Seiden became unsung heroes of Jewish migration and although Rudolph's letter to the State Department was largely ignored, this unique couple worked long and hard to find ways of assisting the plight of the Jewish people.

Rudolph Seiden pointed out that there should be space for millions of people in Alaska and, in fact, theoretically there was enough room for the entire population of Europe. He said that Alaska would be a paradise for Europeans where they would be able to live comfortably, prosper and bring up their children. He realised that working as a farmer, hunter or fisherman would not suit many of the types of people who would be fleeing Nazi persecution, but at least those people would survive and form the nucleus of new communities in their adopted homeland.[80]

However, Hull and his advisers evidently believed that Seiden's suggestions were unrealistic. In a letter of reply, Pierrepont Moffat, chief of the Division of European Affairs at the State Department, simply and somewhat coldly stated that: 'This expression of yours has been duly noted.'[81]

The President's Advisory Committee

On 18 April, 1938, President Roosevelt finally appointed the U.S. committee—formally titled the President's Advisory Committee on Political Refugees—which was to act as an intermediary between the international committee (yet to be formed) and the many organisations within the U.S. that were then working on the problem of helping political refugees. Initially this U.S. committee was to be comprised of James M. Speers, chairman of James McCutcheon and Company; Henry Lewis Stimson; Basil Harris of the United States Lines Company; Hamilton Fish Armstrong, director of the Council for Foreign Relations and also the editor of *Foreign Affairs* magazine; Professor Joseph P. Chamberlain of Columbia University; James G. McDonald of the *New York Times*; Reverend Samuel Calvert of the Federal Council of Churches of Christ; Reverend Joseph F. Rummel, the archbishop of New Orleans; Louis Kenedy, president of the National Council of Catholic Men; Henry Morgenthau Jnr., secretary of the Treasury; Rabbi Stephen Wise; Doctor Samuel McCrae Calvert; Bernard Baruch and Paul Baerwald.[82] Of these, several finally refused to serve on the U.S. committee. Henry Stimson declined, not for any political or racial reasons but because he felt that he would be unable to carry the task through before he was due to retire and that his other business commitments would otherwise keep him fully occupied until that time.[83] Henry Morgenthau also declined, stating that, '...the task is too exacting for me,'[84] (Committee member

Bernard Baruch was a highly regarded statesman. He later advised both Dwight Eisenhower and Winston Churchill concerning world problems during the Korean War).[85]

On 27 April, 1938, the publisher of the *Washington Post*, Eugene Meyer, wrote to Sumner Welles in an effort to have his brother-in-law, Charles W. Liebman, vice-president of the Refugee Economic Corporation, appointed to the U.S. committee. Evidently with little success.[86]

The U.S. committee members, while not, of course, appointed to the international committee, would do valuable work in helping to assimilate those refugees who were eventually allowed into the country.

On 29 April the president decided to appoint steel tycoon Myron C. Taylor to head U.S. representation on the yet to be formed international committee. Taylor would carry the rank of ambassador extraordinary and plenipotentiary. In a letter to Taylor, the president wrote:

> My dear Mr. Taylor:
> As you know, I have requested certain other governments to cooperate with this government in the constitution of an international committee for the purpose of facilitating the emigration of political refugees from Germany and Austria. I have hoped

that prompt and effective action by this committee might relieve the distressing situation which has arisen as a result of the persecution of so many thousands of individuals in those two countries. I am glad to say that all of the American republics and Great Britain, France, Norway, Sweden, Denmark, the Netherlands, Holland, and Switzerland have cordially agreed to cooperate in this endeavor.

As I see the problem, the task of the international committee would be primarily to meet the emergency which has arisen, through the co-ordination of efforts on the part of the several governments involved in this humanitarian endeavor, and through the expenditure of funds received from private sources within the respective nations represented on the committee to expedite and facilitate the emigration of refugees to those countries willing to receive them within the provisions of their existing legislation. The further objective of the international committee would be to undertake the formulation of long-range plans for the solution in years to come of the problem presented in those European countries where there exist excess populations.

I have designated an American committee to cooperate with the international committee, and this American committee, I hope, will act as the intermediary between the international committee and the many private organizations and individuals within the United States who are willing to extend effective assistance to these political refugees. I presume that many of the other countries represented on the international committee will take similar action.

It has seemed to me that you could represent this Government admirably as the American member of the international committee, and I hope very much that you will be willing to serve as the official representative of the United States on that body.

The representative of this government will have the honorary rank of ambassador extraordinary and plenipotentiary and, in view of the fact that this government has taken the initiative in suggesting the creation of the international committee, it is probable that the other members of the committee will select the United States representative as the chairman of that body. I can further assure you that the government will give you the technical assistants that you may find necessary.

I feel that your acceptance of this position would do much to ensure the successful achievement of the objectives which I had in mind when I suggested the creation of the international committee and in the furtherances of which I believe public opinion in this country is deeply interested.[87]

On 30 April Myron C. Taylor replied to the president's offer, stating that he was, '...pleased to accept the appointment and trust I may acquit myself to your satisfaction.[88]

Myron Charles Taylor was one of America's leading businessmen at that time and would go on to have an important and influential diplomatic career, firstly under Roosevelt and later under Harry S. Truman.

Taylor had been born at Lyons, New York State, on 18 January, 1874, the son of William Delling Taylor and his wife, Mary, (née Underhill). William Taylor was a businessman who owned and ran a tannery.

In 1894 Myron C. Taylor graduated from the Cornell Law School of Cornell University after which he returned home to Lyons. There he established a small law practice and ran twice, unsuccessfully, for the New York State Assembly.

In 1900 Taylor left New York State and travelled to New York City to join his brother, William Underhill Taylor, on Wall Street where he specialised in corporate law. Yet Myron Taylor had other strings he wished to attach to his bow. He subsequently won the U.S. government contract for the provision of mail pouches and associated equipment. An astute businessman, he bought out competitors and introduced a number of mail innovations including the now widely used transparent window in envelopes. He expanded his operations into cotton and opened a textile company which became the leading business in the supply of textile to the tyre manufacturing market. During the First World War his business became one of the principal suppliers to the U.S. military.

After the war Taylor foresaw coming economic problems and sold his textile milling interests, establishing for himself a sizeable fortune. Taylor was subsequently approached by two leading businessmen, J.P. Morgan and George F. Baker, and recruited to help turn around the failing fortunes of the massive company U.S. Steel. He was elected a director in 1925 and became the finance committee's chairman in 1929. The previous year Taylor had donated $1.5 million (a massive fortune at that time) to Cornell University for the construction of a new building at its Cornell Law School and Law Library. The library would become the repository for more than 200,000 volumes. In 1929 U.S. Steel named one of its new freighters the *Myron C. Taylor*. The ship sailed under this name until being sold in 2000. From March 1932 until April 1938 Taylor served as U.S. Steel's chairman and C.E.O. During his time with U.S. Steel he made huge structural reorganisations, upgrading and modernising the company and turning it into a major success. Taylor appeared on the cover of *Time Magazine* and in articles in *Fortune, Business Week, The New Yorker, The Saturday Evening Post* and other major publications.[89]

The President's Advisory Committee held its first meeting at the State Department at 10a.m. on 16 May, 1938. James Grover McDonald was elected as chairman and Doctor Samuel McCrae Calvert as secretary.[90]

Chapter 3

Pressures Increase

Documents in the U.S. State Department confidential files now indicate that in 1938 proposals were made by the visa division to have trust-funds set up for all refugees from Germany, Austria, Poland, Spain and certain other countries, who wished to settle in the U.S. These mandatory funds, (supplied of course by the immigrants themselves), would be used to cover their expenses for a period of five years after arriving in the United States. Amounts would be determined by the cost of living in that part of the country where the immigrant proposed to settle.[1] These stipulations, almost impossible to implement for émigrés from Germany and Austria due to the Nazi regime's policies of not allowing those émigrés to convert their funds into foreign capital, were being considered despite the plethora of information that was being made available to the State Department regarding ongoing persecutions and strict currency control. For example, on 25 April, 1938, Cordell Hull received an impassioned plea:

> Sir, I recently witnessed the change in Austria to the Nazi regime and sincerely

feel for the great number of Jewish people whom I saw humiliated. My bride ... was so distressed that she hardly slept during the five days we spent in Vienna.

I desire to participate in any way on some committee in line with your recent proposal to facilitate the emigration of the unfortunate political refugees. I shall personally bear my own expenses.[2]

As the days passed, pressure began to mount, not only on the U.S. government but also on the British government in view of the Palestinian question. *Hadassah*, the 2000 strong Women's Zionist Organisation of America, passed a resolution in April that:

> ...our government and its representative at the International Conference on refugees ... bring to the attention of Great Britain the mandatory Power for Palestine, the importance of Palestine as affording the outstanding opportunity for Jewish settlement and to plead for British co-operation in making it possible for the Jewish people through their own efforts to rehabilitate as many of the victims of persecution as Palestine can properly absorb.[3]

In Palestine itself there were mixed feelings towards Roosevelt's proposal. On 2 April, 1938,

George Wadsworth, the U.S. consul general at Jerusalem, advised the U.S. Department of State that Roosevelt's pronouncement regarding the setting up of an international committee had been received with 'generous acclaim'.[4] Wadsworth reported that he had received intelligence that the news of the proposed committee had been received with, '...gratitude and admiration in every Jewish home, in every Jewish gathering of the ensuing weekend'.[5] Wadsworth added that a leading Jewish banker who had recently returned to Jerusalem from a trip to Haifa, Tel Aviv and a number of Jewish colonies, was most enthusiastic over the reception. Wadsworth quoted the banker as saying: 'It is the biggest thing in the minds of dozens of people with whom I have talked since President [Woodrow] Wilson's plea for Peace Without Victory,' (WWI). Wadsworth stated that the U.S. Consulate's Jewish interpreter had described the state of general enthusiasm which was prevalent amongst the Jewish community, and quoted him as saying, 'My friends tell me I am the most fortunate man to be working for such a government.'[6]

Wadworth's report continued:

> The local Jewish press is equally enthusiastic. No difficulty, it is felt, will be encountered in the financing, by private organizations, of the emergency emigration;

the German Government will be forced by world opinion to permit rather than hinder it, as would be the case but for the American proposal. Its early acceptance by other Western democracies was assumed without question. As read locally, it is taken to mean at least a combining of our German and Austrian immigration quotas with the result that some 15,000 Austrian Jewish refugees will be admitted for permanent residence in the United States before July first and an equal or larger number next fiscal year.

I hear, too, the hope expressed that to South America and to Western Europe even larger emigrations will be authorized. And, in press and public discussion, a further liberalization of Palestine's immigration laws is urged.[7]

Newspapers and other periodicals in Palestine were supportive and cautiously optimistic about the American proposal and two highly regarded publications, the *Palestine Illustrated News* and the *Palestine Post*, published articles praising the United States. The *Palestine Illustrated News* was a weekly publication that had come into existence with considerable fanfare only a few years earlier in 1933 and by 1938 it had become widely respected. In their article of 28 March, 1938, the newspaper stated that in a world which was then torn by fear and 'cowed' by sharp words; it was encouraging to know that a voice was now coming from the other side of the Atlantic in support of those people most in need. The newspaper heaped praise on the American endeavours, stating that the country was then one of only a few in the world which was moving, 'unflinchingly into the future' without any fears and without backsliding or retreating from its ethical position. Similarly, the *Palestine Post*, in a comprehensive article dated 1 April, 1938, echoed those same sentiments, adding that ordinarily it was the voice of Great Britain that could usually be heard on important international matters but now there was a new and powerful voice taking the lead. These comments appear to have been generally typical of Jewish editorials at that time.[8]

Yet in the United States opposition to the proposed conference came in many forms. The Great Council of Red Men, for example, based in West Girard Avenue Pennsylvania, was vociferous in its condemnation to the concept of allowing Jewish migrants to settle on American soil and expressed opposition claiming that the U.S. was never intended to be a haven for those who 'could not appreciate' the privileges accorded to them by the nation.[9]

***

How much of a 'burden' these refugees would have been is difficult to gauge. Not all Jewish refugees were travelling in a destitute position; some had certainly managed to get their money out of Germany and Austria. For example, a Jewish refugee who arrived in Australia aboard the steamer *Morella* in 1939 had almost £4000 in solid gold among his baggage. In long thin gold bars he held 409 ounces of gold and also some paper money. There were forty-five Jewish refugees on board the vessel and together they carried more than £18,000 most of this amount was represented by bank drafts.[10] Refugees to most other countries were also arriving with substantial amounts of gold and cash.

***

By 30 April, 1938, events surrounding the organisation of the conference were beginning to crystallise. The Division of Current Information of the Department of Defense issued a memorandum after Sumner Welles had held a press conference that morning. The memorandum reported that the president had appointed Myron C. Taylor as the American representative to the international committee for refugees, and stated that Taylor was sailing for Europe on that day where he would first visit his home in Italy before travelling to France for the conference. The report advised that Roosevelt had also designated members of his advisory committee; these included James Grover McDonald who would be acting chairman until the committee could be organised formally; the Reverend Samuel Calvert; Hamilton Fish Armstrong; Professor Joseph P. Chamberlain; James M. Speers; Reverend Joseph F. Rummel, archbishop of New Orleans; Basil Harris; Louis Kenedy; Rabbi Stephen Wise; Bernard Baruch and Paul Baerwald.[11]

Cuba

Cuban restrictions on immigration were particularly harsh at this time. In order to be admitted into the country intending immigrants were required to produce—beside a passport and certificate of good character (two items so often unavailable to Jewish refugees)—a deposit of U.S.$500 payable in cash. Immigrants who were going to join their relatives already established in the country and who could display letters summoning them, were also subject to this regulation, except when they were exempt from it by special decree of the secretary of the Department of the Cuban Treasury. This law was applied very strictly and admission into the country depended upon the final whims of the Immigration Department.

The number of Jewish residents in Cuba at that time was between ten thousand and twelve thousand, representing 10.2 per cent of the total population of the island. They had all arrived in the country when immigration regulations had been far more liberal and when such immigrants were openly welcomed. In the course of 1937 three hundred immigrants, mostly from Poland, had landed on the island. The majority of the immigrants established themselves in Cuba as tailors, cobblers, peddlers or in other small businesses. A very strict law regulating the employment of foreign labour prevented the immigrants from being employed as salaried workers. Hence there were certain numbers repatriated who had not succeeded in establishing themselves in the country. The capacity of absorption of Cuba with regard to the Jewish immigrants was, as the Évian conference approached, considered to be extremely limited.[12]

Plans and Policies Progress

By early May 1938 it had been decided in the White House to hold the conference at the spa resort of Évian-les-Bains in France, a pretty holiday resort on the Swiss border at Lake Geneva. The conference was to begin on Wednesday 6 July, 1938. By 9 May the French authorities had agreed to the venue and it only remained to finalise delegates.[13]

One of the proposals the U.S. Department of State was considering at this time came from a private individual named W. Hecker, a partner in the company of Hecker and Yellen, civil engineers based in Jerusalem. Hecker had lived in Palestine for twenty-five years and claimed to have an intimate knowledge of the resources of the country and of its Jewish population. His proposition seemed logical, but politically it would have had many opponents. In brief, Hecker believed that the only way to solve the problem of the Jewish refugees was to accommodate *all* of them, some permanently, and some on a transitory basis, in Palestine. He stated, quite accurately, that refugees from European countries moving to a new land would be in need of preparation for life in another country; they would need to be able to speak the language and work at occupations which they had never before attempted; they would need to be trained, mentally and physically for the exacting tasks that lay ahead. Hecker claimed that it was necessary to strengthen the structure of the Jewish national home in Palestine and that meant mass migration into the country. However, he was realist enough to know that such a plan was politically impossible and that transients, rather than permanent residents, could be seen as something of a workable compromise. The advantages of having this training period in Palestine, according to Hecker, would have been considerable. The refugees going to places such as South America could be acclimatised to the heat. The countries willing to accept them would know that they were taking migrants who had been trained in the language of the host country and also in some kind of trade. The refugees would have time to recover their health after living in the difficult and crowded conditions forced upon them under Nazi control.[14]

Hecker also advanced the theory that, as Palestine was a country still in its embryonic stages of development, it would serve as a perfect training ground for immigrants who were travelling to undeveloped countries.[15] However, his report was received somewhat coldly at the State Department. In a confidential memorandum from Cordell Hull to the American consular officer in charge at the Jerusalem Consulate, Hull instructed that the report be, '...acknowledged with appreciation but without comment'.[16] The Americans understood very clearly that the

British would never have agreed to such a grand design.

The United Palestine Appeal organisation based in Fifth Avenue New York was also anxious to promote additional immigration into Palestine. With a fund-raising goal of U.S.$4.5 million for 1938, the organisers, led by Rabbi Solomon Goldman, placed pressure on the U.S. Department of State to have them suggest to the intergovernmental committee that they should ask the British government to increase the limited quotas set for immigration into Palestine. They also strongly suggested that the intergovernmental committee could be useful to the British government in arranging for responsible and carefully controlled immigration practices.[17]

There is little doubt that the British were, in fact, going to be intransigent over the Palestinian issue and British policies were reflected in their reservations over allowing Jewish refugees into Great Britain. None would be allowed entry without visas being issued by representatives of the British government abroad, and such visas were difficult to obtain for people without passports or money. In answer to a written question which stated, 'What new conditions have been made or are in early contemplation as to the admission into this country of refugees from Germany and the former Austria?' the British home secretary in the House of Commons on 3 May, 1938, replied:

It has been decided that in future, holders of Austrian passports who wish to enter the United Kingdom must first obtain a British visa and that a similar requirement is to apply to holders of German passports from 21st May. This step is being taken in order to carry out effectively the policy which I announced on 22 March, of offering asylum as far as practicable, to persons, who, for political, racial or religious reasons, have had to leave their own country. As I pointed out, it is impossible to admit indiscriminately all persons claiming to be refugees, and if would-be immigrants were to arrive in large numbers, without any preliminary examination, great difficulty would be created at the ports and unnecessary hardship might be inflicted on applicants whom it might be found necessary to reject. The requirement that a visa must first be obtained from a British representative abroad has been recommended by some of the organisations in this country which deal with refugees.[18]

No mention was made of those persons who had been forcibly ejected from Germany without passports, or of those people who could not leave the country because they were unable to obtain passports.

***

By 12 May, 1938, Myron C. Taylor had arrived with his wife, Anabele (also reported as Anabel) (née Mack), in Italy where he contacted the U.S. ambassador in Rome with a request for further instructions. The U.S. Department of State informed the ambassador that Taylor was to await the outcome of the first meeting of the U.S. committee which was scheduled to convene the following week. Taylor was also advised at this time that Robert Thompson Pell, a divisional assistant at the State Department, had been appointed to act as one of his assistants at the Évian conference. Pell was an expert in international conferences and a linguistics specialist. Another assistant was George L. Brandt, a foreign service officer, class III, who was well versed in U.S. immigration laws and procedures.[19]

The U.S. budget allowed for the conference was U.S.$75,000. This figure included the salaries of Myron Taylor and his assistants, stenographic reporting, translating, rent, travelling expenses, the purchase of necessary books, documents, newspapers and periodicals, stationery, equipment, official cards, printing and binding and entertainment.[20] It was estimated by the State Department that the duration of the conference and the subsequent organisation that would be set up as a result of the conference would be approximately fourteen months. Two clerks were assigned from the State Department and two more were to be employed locally in order to save travelling expenses. Taylor's salary for this period was placed at U.S.$20,416.67, and wages for all four clerks for the same period was pegged at U.S.$9,333.33.[21]

Publication of the budget for the conference and subsequent work quickly aroused the ire of at least one organisation, the Protestant War Veterans of New York City. The society's national commander, Lieutenant-Colonel Pearson B. Brown, was moved to write an indignant letter over the issue in which he demanded to know where this money was being spent, how much had been given to Jewish agencies and if any of this money had been used for Christians.[22]

George Messersmith replied on the same day, (24 May), stating that the budget was allocated solely for the expenses of the intergovernmental committee and that none was allocated for welfare work.[23]

German Intelligence Infiltration

Soon afterwards a somewhat more sinister element entered the issue. On 11 May the U.S. ambassador to Vienna advised the State Department that two, 'self appointed saviours' of the Jewish situation had suddenly appeared on the scene. These were a Dutchman named Van Gheel Gildemeester, and Arthur Kuffler, a baptised Austrian Jew who, twenty years previously, had allegedly been a prominent cotton spinner but since that time had been, 'in total eclipse'. In a strictly confidential coded telegram the ambassador advised:

> They have been officially sanctioned by the Nazi authorities, given a party member as secretary and are embarking on large-scale and apparently visionary projects to be financed by 'voluntary' contributions from wealthy emigrants. It is suspected that [the] Nazis plan to use these two men as a nucleus in order to set up [a] dummy committee which would eliminate local Jewish leaders and responsible welfare workers and forestall [any] activity of [the] international committee. It is, of course, impossible for me to intervene in anything which does not concern protection of American interests. I think, however, that

someone in the confidence of Mr Myron Taylor's committee should immediately and unobtrusively [come] to Vienna.[24]

Nothing worth noting was heard of either Gildemeester or Kuffler until 13 June, when John Cooper Wiley, the U.S. consul general in Vienna, advised the U.S. Department of State that he had received a letter from Gildemeester who claimed that his work was being jeopardised because the U.S. Department of State had allegedly advised the Gestapo that Gildemeester was working with false papers. What truth there was in this statement is difficult to prove. Wiley immediately wrote to Gildemeester stating that he had checked with the archives of the U.S. Legation in Vienna and had found no reference to any such correspondence. When Gildemeester had formerly called at the U.S. Consulate General he had presented a card to Wiley on which had been printed: 'Delegate for American Relief Action for Central Europe,' with an address in Washington DC. However, Gildemeester had no address in Washington and was unaffiliated with any U.S. relief organisations.[25] In his later correspondence to Gildemeester, Wiley coldly stated, 'May I suggest that such a calling card is apt to portray a false impression.'[26]

Organisation of the Conference

On 15 May, 1938, Taylor sent a message to Cordell Hull requesting that another assistant be added to his staff. He suggested the services of George Rublee, a lawyer and friend of President Roosevelt. However, Hull soon afterwards advised Taylor that he should attempt to arrange his organisation with the staff he had available to him, adding, however, that should he insist on increasing his staff the State Department would accede to his request. On the same day, 17 May, a meeting of the U.S. committee was held in Washington; this meeting was attended by Robert Pell who also attended a further series of meetings held in New York over the following days before he sailed for Florence where he was expected to meet with Myron C. Taylor.

Pell was originally instructed to sail from New York to Le Havre aboard the steamer *President Harding* on 8 June, 1938. This sailing would have allowed him ample time to get to Florence by 18 June for a meeting with Taylor. Pell's information was vital to Taylor. Having attended all the meetings of the U.S. committee, by the time he sailed he was fully conversant with everything the U.S. committee planned in relation to their liaison with the large number of refugee organisations in the U.S. and the fundraising activities they were carrying out.[27] The second assistant, George L. Brandt, consul at Mexico City, was also instructed to attend the meetings of the U.S. committee and was ordered to sail with Pell aboard the ship *President Harding* on 8 June.[28]

However, because of the necessity of further consultations with the president's advisory committee, both men were delayed and could not sail on the 8th.

Pell advised George Messersmith in a memorandum that the work of the U.S. committee was far from complete; there was much work to be done on such items as places of settlement for refugees, regional organisations in the U.S., and financing. All the deliberations of the many meetings had then to be co-ordinated for presentation to Taylor. As Pell stated:

> According to my understanding, the recommendations of the Advisory Committee will form an essential part of the guiding lines which will be laid down for Mr Taylor's use at Évian. It will be seen that there is virtually no prospect that these recommendations will be in anything approaching a final form before the middle of next month.... I feel strongly that in order that we may do a thorough preparation

here, in order that this problem may be thoroughly thought through in advance of our meeting with Mr Taylor at Florence, that it would be advisable to sail not before June 15.[29]

The meetings of the U.S. advisory committee were far from satisfactory. For example, at its third meeting held at the City Club on West Forty-Forth Street New York at 3.30p.m. on 2 June, 1938, there were serious problems over a number of important issues. According to the minutes of that meeting, there was, 'diffuse and pointless' discussion of various aspects until Pell, somewhat exasperated, demanded the recommendations of the meeting so that they could be formed into a letter of guidance for Myron Taylor. A confidential State Department memorandum claimed:

> The committee did not seem to have a very clear idea as to precisely what was expected of it.... In the course of an informal discussion of the points raised by Mr Pell, a sharp difference of views arose with regard to the scope of the Intergovernmental Committee's work and the injection of political issues. Some members of the committee insisted that the scope should be as broad as possible and should include refugees from all countries.

Other members of the committee insisted that the scope should be restricted to Germany alone.[30]

Present at the meeting was a Professor Stolper who outlined a somewhat overambitious plan to form a company with some 100 million to 200 million shares. These shares would, he said, be used to set up businesses in underdeveloped countries which the refugees might either part own or work in. However, during the general discussion that followed Stolper's outline, it was agreed by the committee members that the plan would be impractical for a number of reasons, among them the growing nationalism of South American countries, vested interests, untimely publicity and stiff competition from the local labour market.[31] The meeting ended with no real progress having been made.

In light of these problems Pell and Brandt were instructed to delay their departure and to leave New York aboard the steamer *Manhattan* on 15 June, arriving at Le Havre on 22 June. They were then to proceed immediately by rail to Florence.[32]

On 3 June, Myron Taylor contacted the U.S. Department of State with the suggestion that in order to save time he was quite willing to meet Pell and Brandt in Paris. He also suggested that it would be expedient if arrangements could be made to meet in Paris the U.S. ambassador to Berlin and the U.S. minister to Switzerland, so that they could, '...give us full information of [the] present situation [on] refugees as [an] aid to our efforts'.[33]

The following day Sumner Welles advised Taylor by telegram that his suggestion was, 'heartily approved,' and stated that if, after having discussions with Pell and Brandt he still felt that he wanted to meet with the Berlin and Swiss U.S. diplomats, it would be arranged.[34]

Taylor soon afterwards suggested that it would be expedient to place an 'experienced official observer' in Vienna, '...to report on refugees' conditions and developments'.[35] However, the State Department was immediately cold to the idea. Sumner Welles replied on the same day, 4 June:

> The Consul General at Vienna brought this same suggestion to our attention early in May. In reply we informed him that neither this government nor the Advisory Committee contemplated sending anyone to Europe beyond the representatives at Évian, and that it was our opinion that whatever information might be needed regarding the refugee situation in Austria might be obtained more definitely and more accurately

from the Consulate General at Vienna than from an unofficial observer.[36]

Taylor sent a telegram soon afterwards indicating that he would meet Pell and Brandt at the Ritz Hotel in Paris, and asked the advisability of inviting the German government to send an observer to the conference.[37]

Cordell Hull quickly replied: 'It is our feeling that it would be inadvisable at this time to approach the German government or to invite Germany to send a representative or observer to the meeting.'[38]

On 31 May the Belgian authorities sent a diplomatic note to the U.S. representative in Brussels, confirming that they would be sending two representatives to the conference; these were to be Monsieur R. de Foy, the administrator of the *Surete Publique*, and Monsieur J. Schneider, a director of the Administrative Section of the Belgian Foreign Office. However, the communication contained a darker element that was revealed in a 'strictly confidential' coded message from the Brussels Embassy to Washington. The message claimed:

> In connection with the appointment of Mr de Foy to serve on this committee, the Department's attention is invited to the fact that in his capacity of Director of the *Surete Publique*, his work is approximately that of

the head of the department of criminal investigation. It is part of his duty to see that undesirable foreigners are prevented from entering Belgium, or, in the case of those who are found within the country, to see that they are expelled. The fact that the Belgian government has chosen Mr de Foy to represent it on the intergovernmental committee is therefore significant in that the work of his bureau is usually just the opposite of facilitating the entry of foreigners into Belgium.[39]

As the conference loomed closer, the U.S. Department of State began to implement its planning procedure for the event. The U.S. consul in Geneva was instructed by Cordell Hull that his office was to bear a large percentage of the clerical assistance required for the conference. Hull instructed the consul that the Évian conference should take preference over the normal requirements of the consulate; the consul was to transfer three staff members to Évian, one to act as secretary and two as stenographers. Hull also made it clear that all communications regarding the events at Évian were to be coded, (Gray Code and C-1 Code) and sent by the consulate.[40] The consul was soon afterwards also instructed to reserve six single rooms and four double rooms at the Hotel

Royale, Évian. He was additionally to make arrangements to rent and install at the hotel five typewriters with desks, one safe, 'of sufficient quality to safeguard the high security diplomatic codes,' and two filing cabinets.[41] Myron Taylor and his wife had been offered the opportunity of staying in a private apartment while at Évian. However, on 28 May Taylor communicated to Cordell Hull thanking him for the generous offer but adding that he had already booked rooms at the Hotel Royale and said that he would consider it a privilege to pay his hotel costs himself.[42]

Hotel Royale at Évian

Venue for the Évian conference.

–U.S. National Archives

The venue for the conference was also at the Hotel Royale, hotel management had advised the U.S. Embassy in Paris that providing a large number of delegates stayed at the hotel, the management would be willing to provide—free of charge—a conference room with a capacity of one hundred and fifty people and an adjoining space for the secretariat.[43]

Myron C. Taylor (left) with Robert T. Pell arriving in France for the Évian conference.

–U.S. National Archives

On 6 June the State Department received a heartrending letter, addressed to President Roosevelt, written by a Jewish refugee, which was forwarded through the U.S. Legation in Prague. The letter dealt specifically with the plight of fifty-one Jewish refugees, former Austrian citizens, who were then stranded on a small French boat on the international waters of the Danube. The letter stated:

> Sir, In your high station as President of a great, mighty and democratic nation, you have often found truly human and just words for those oppressed and persecuted by racial and unreasonableness. It is this that encourages us to apply to you. We have just had to witness the heartrending fate of fifty-one human beings driven from one frontier to the other. We have gained personal knowledge of the unspeakable misery that has innocently befallen 100,000 inhabitants of Austria. We who are residing in the immediate neighbourhood of Vienna venture to entreat you with a hopeful heart to contribute by your word and deed to the immediate and truly human solution of the Austro-German fugitive problem. We citizens of Czechoslovakia cannot help alone, it is the world that must help. In the names of all that suffer we implore you, Sir, to

use your great influence to ease the fate of the unfortunate at once.[44]

It seems doubtful that the president ever saw this letter. Wilbur J. Carr of the U.S. Embassy in Prague, who had forwarded the translation of the original letter to the State Department, simply added that he had not acknowledged the communication and that unless instructions were received to the contrary, he would only make a 'purely formal reply'.[45]

German Response and Intelligence

At around the same time the U.S. Consulate General in Vienna forwarded to the U.S. Department of State a translation of a news report that made it perfectly clear to U.S. authorities what the Austrian newspapers were reporting concerning the attempted mass emigration of the Jewish people from the country. On 13 May, the *Voelkischer Beobachter* reported:

> Three months ago nobody would have dreamed in his wildest dreams that in this wonderful month of May, whose sky appears to us more blue than that of the famous Cairo, that now already, or better said, at last, the Jews stand in a queue, not to acquire the citizenship right of the City of

Vienna, but to return to us our citizenship right and to disappear themselves.

Gildemeester, whoever you may be, you are the greatest philanthropist which the Netherlands has produced up to now ... now a Dutchman, or at least a Dutch citizen, has the noble intention of freeing us from the Jews, for which project he may be sure of our far-reaching support.

Thus they leave us. We are not sorry if they leave; it is hoped that they feel the same. Our best wishes accompany them. Above all: they should at last learn to make themselves more popular in the new country which grants them hospitality than with us. For otherwise Gildemeester must establish an office in Vera Cruz, Haifa or New York—or wherever they may land—and again, as a humanitarian, initiate emigration to other lands.

We cannot refrain from giving one piece of advice ... [Jews] do not start any Bolshevist agitation in the countries which grant you hospitality. Otherwise they might think that the war of microbes with which you frequently scared the people had begun and that we had sent them the plague. Quite the contrary was our intention. We wished to be fair and to comply with the wish, so frequently expressed by the world, to have the dear Jews as their guests.

Work is for you [Jews] not only a question of livelihood, but likewise a beauty cure. Plant bananas and oranges, cactaceae and deadly night-shades in the sweat of your brow. How handsome you will become then.... But be grateful then. Do not speak badly of us, we nice accommodating Viennese, but erect over your farms, ranchos and haciendas, which it is hoped will be without bugs, a large sign: 'We owe it to the Nazis that we are working here.'[46]

Norway

On 31 May, Jefferson Patterson, the U.S. *chargé d'affaires* at the Norwegian Embassy in Oslo, advised the U.S. Department of State that he had received confirmation that the Norwegian delegate to the conference would be Michael Hansson. This should have been an extremely important decision, both for Norway and for the conference generally. Hansson, as we have seen, was the president of the Nansen Office and during the Évian conference was appointed chairman of the technical subcommittee. It seems certain that no man alive knew more about the difficulties of political refugees than did Hansson, and his advice at the conference should have proved invaluable. Hansson had previously been appointed as the president of the Egyptian Court of Mixed Appeals, a diplomatic rank equivalent to that of ambassador. However, there seems to have been some confusion as to the rank he would be awarded for the conference, (rank was important in the status of the delegate, especially with regard to his involvement and input to the conference). The Norwegians had listed him only as *rettspresident*—(presiding officer of a tribunal), but his status on the Egyptian Court of Mixed Appeals had qualified him to hold ambassadorial rank. Upon enquiry from the *chargé d'affaires*, Jefferson Patterson, in Oslo, the Norwegian government gave him the rank of minister plenipotentiary.[47]

Yet despite this promising appointment of Hansson as Norway's representative to Évian, the prospects for any large-scale immigration into the country were bleak indeed. The Norwegian official document prepared specifically for the Évian conference stated:

> Norway has never been a country of immigration. On the contrary, until after the end of the world war, emigration from Norway was very considerable; it amounted to tens of thousands of persons annually

out of a population which at the time barely exceeded two millions. It may be boldly asserted that in no country was emigration as high as in Norway in comparison with the figure of the population. When emigration stopped, chiefly because of the new immigration regulations in the United States, Norway found herself faced with the problem of finding work for this surplus population. Partly as a result of this change in the situation, it has been found necessary to bring under control the movement of immigration into Norway, and this was done by enacting the law of April 27th 1927 on the admission of foreigners. The prospects of employment are ... very slight; consequently it will be impossible to find jobs for a considerable number of refugees.... The only immigrants whom, in the strict sense of the term, Norway needs, are industrial specialists, but the need for these only arises infrequently, and solely for a few isolated individuals at a time.[48]

Additionally, by the end of the conference, Myron Taylor was less than impressed with Hansson's performance stating in his final report that Hansson had been: '...ineffective as Chairman of the Technical Subcommittee'. (See Appendix A).

The Philippines

Although the Philippines did not send a representative to the Évian conference the archipelago was considered as being a possible nation of asylum to Jewish refugees because it was an American colony and largely came under U.S. control.

Admission of immigrants into the Philippines was regulated by the United States immigration law of 1917, and, as we have seen, these laws were reasonably liberal.

People who already resided in the country, if they wished to introduce a relative or a friend, were expected to sign an undertaking to support the friend or relative during a certain period of time and in case that person later decided to leave the country, to assume his or her travelling expenses.[49]

Cases were known when passengers were not allowed to land, although their passports had received the necessary visas from an American consul. Immigrants without any country and having no national passport were only allowed to land if they had special return visas.

The Jewish population of the country comprised of only about a thousand people residing mostly in Manila. Jews—especially those of American origin—played a vital role in the industrial and commercial life of the Philippines Islands. They were at the heads of various export and import firms, motor car companies, the leather industry, sugarcane industry, and also controlled much of the mining enterprises. U.S. Department of State confidential files revealed that since 1933 about a hundred Jewish refugee families had immigrated to the Philippines and of these approximately thirty families had obtained assistance from the local Jewish community in order to get settled in the country. State Department informants claimed that another hundred families could be imported at the rate of fifty or sixty each year provided that the immigrants arrived in small groups so as not to attract publicity which might induce the government to turn its attention to the immigration problem. There was a need for workmen skilled in various branches; engineers and mining experts were very much in demand, as were businessmen and artisans, but salesmen, tailors, furriers, and needle-workers were not welcome at all. Prospective immigrants had to be, 'young, active and capable'; they had to be able to speak English and, if possible, also Spanish. They also had to have sufficient means to keep them during the first six months.[50]

Philippines President Manuel Quezon later indicated a willingness to allow, '...a rather considerable number of political refugees' to land at Mindanao, but due to powerful Muslim representation on the island this concept had to be handled carefully.[51]

Between 1935 and 1941 President Quezon would be responsible for the successful settlement of a considerable number of Jewish people at Mindanao.[52]

After the Japanese occupation of the Philippines in 1941 things would, naturally, change. Despite the terrible atrocities against both military personnel and civilians which would be carried out by the Japanese before and during the war, those Jewish people who would manage to escape to the Philippines (mainly as a steppingstone to the U.S.), would be treated by the Japanese occupation forces of the archipelago as 'stateless persons' rather than enemy aliens. The Japanese would not perceive a difference between German nationals and German Jews. Therefore the majority of Jewish people at Manila were not interned at Santo Tomas University which, during the occupation, would be transformed into an internment camp. It was not until 1943 that the Japanese, influenced by Nazi propaganda, would begin to target the non-interned Jews.[53]

Documentation

On 8 June, 1938, the U.S. Department of State finally sent circular telegrams to all the participating countries with details of the proposed agenda for the conference. This agenda included the consideration of what steps could be taken to facilitate the settlement in other countries of political refugees: both those who wished to leave the country and those who had already been allowed to leave; to consider what immediate steps could be taken within the existing immigration laws and regulations of the receiving countries and to assist the most urgent cases. It was perceived that each of the participating countries would supply confidential statements of their immigration laws, and also a statement outlining how many immigrants each country was prepared to receive. Other considerations on the agenda included the types of documentation required by refugees, especially those refugees who were unable to provide passports, and also to consider the possibility of setting up a long-range programme looking towards the solution or alleviation of the refugee problem.[54]

One of the principal purposes of the convention was the issuance and recognition of certificates of identity for refugees unable to obtain passports from their own countries, and the extension of certain legal rights equivalent to those of other aliens in receiving countries.[55]

Documentation would be, of course, one of the primary concerns discussed during the Évian conference and a special subcommittee would be formed to investigate this particularly thorny problem. Large numbers of Jewish people who were being evicted from Germany and Austria had no documentation at all, and without documentation it was virtually impossible to obtain visas into countries of refuge. The United States, for example, required substantial documentation before a refugee could obtain a visa. These included a passport or some other form of travel document such as the international Nansen passport, a birth certificate, a penal certificate to ensure that the applicant had no criminal record, a military certificate, and any other personal certificates that may have been available from the emigrant's government. U.S. authorities were in the process of liberalising these strict requirements in order to facilitate the needs of refugees with little or no documentation, however, other countries were substantially more intransigent. Chile, for example, categorically stated to the technical subcommittee formed at Évian to look at the documentation problem: '...As regards identity documents, in view of the legislation in force, my government is unable to accept passports other than those regularly issued by the respective countries'.[56] In other words, for those refugees fleeing from Germany and Austria who could not obtain a passport from the Nazi government, entry into Chile would be impossible.

Japan

Japan was never invited to Évian, however, it is worth noting that as the Nazis increased their persecution of the Jews through the late 1930s it became evident among certain government and military circles in Japan that the Japanese could actually benefit by accepting large numbers of Jewish refugees who would bring their wealth, influence and knowledge to the country. In this the Japanese were learning from their own history. During the Russo-Japanese War of 1904/05, the Japanese, suffering from a drastic lack of funds, had managed to obtain vast loans from Jewish financiers that had enabled them not only to continue with the war but to pursue it to a successful conclusion.

The Japanese now planned to settle a large number of Jewish immigrants within their newly acquired territories in Manchuria, creating a 'little

Israel', and a number of Jews would actually land in Japan in February 1941. The code-name for the top secret plan was Fugu. However, following the attack on Pearl Harbor the general usefulness of the Jews was considered to have been over.

One of the leading personalities involved in the rescue of Jews from Europe was Consul Senpo Sugihara (also given as Chiune Sugihara). In 1940 Consul Sugihara was based in Lithuania where he was actually working as a spy. He had been sent there to keep an eye on German troop movements along the border. While there he felt deep concern and empathy for the men and women who lined up each day outside the Japanese consulate. He asked for permission to provide them with transit visas but his superiors refused. However, Sugihara took it upon himself to hand out many thousands to Jews who were fleeing from Nazi persecution in Poland. His consulate in Lithuania was later closed down by the Soviet authorities. He was the last diplomat to leave Kaunas and continued to stamp visas from the open window of his departing train. After the war Sugihara was arrested by the Soviet military and incarcerated until being repatriated to Japan in 1947. There he was dismissed from foreign service but awarded a minor pension. He never spoke about those he had rescued from almost certain death and in

1985 the Yad Vashem Holocaust Memorial recognised him as being one of the 'Righteous Among the Nations', an honour reserved for nonJews who had made significant rescue efforts during the Holocaust. Sugihara died the following year. In 1996 the Polish Embassy in Tokyo stated that Consul Sugihara was to be posthumously awarded the Order of Merit for his humanitarian actions.[57]

Chapter 4
The Problems of South America

Argentina

Political, economic and social problems affecting the immigration laws of various nations were now becoming more obvious. Countries to which invitations had been sent were already scrambling to consolidate (and usually tighten) their own laws and entry requirements. An unfortunate action, especially in South America that had the potential to allow very large numbers of refugees to enter the various countries. In Argentina—where it was widely believed that many refugees could find a home—there were enormous problems facing intending immigrants. In April 1938 a U.S. diplomatic clerk named Winifred A. Hunter compiled a comprehensive report on the situation which she transmitted to the State Department on 19 April that year. Hunter's findings were dramatic. She claimed that the question of whether immigration into Argentina should be restricted or unrestricted had been an important issue for many years. It had then become a vital issue to the Argentinean administration and was being widely discussed in educational institutions and commented upon in trade magazines, cultural publications and even in the *Economia Argentina*, the most prestigious economic publication in the country. The debate was largely centered around the history of immigration in Argentina and the country's apparent need for settlers to colonise and work some 160 million hectares of fertile land then not under cultivation through the lack of manpower. Prior to the First World War the country's immigration practice had been an open one, the administration welcoming virtually anyone and in any numbers. Those men and women had produced the offspring which, in 1938, were largely seen as being the nucleus of the modern Argentinean population upon whom the backbreaking work of settling new regions was attributed. Argentinean liberalists argued that these immigrants had not taken work from the indigenous people, but rather had added to the demand for labour by opening businesses and beginning farms, breaking new ground which required additional services such as railways, roads and communications. Established businesses had prospered because of the influx of immigrants. Farmers needed tools, seeds, fertilisers, mechanical equipment, housing, fuel, animal stock, fencing, water and food, the supply of which all enriched the Argentinean economy. However, more conservative forces, opponents to unrestricted immigration—especially those who opposed immigration from European countries—were vociferous in their condemnation of allowing such unrestricted access into the country. As Hunter reported in 1938:

> The protagonists of selective and restricted immigration argue that, since Argentina lacks experience in diversified farming and therefore has few native experts to teach immigrants, it is necessary that the immigrants be selected with consideration of their skill in the various pursuits to which the soil of the different sections of the country is adaptable. They point out that today Argentina is composed of many states within a state; that is, colonies composed of the nationals of other countries, who having immigrated into Argentina and found themselves uninterested in the life of the country or unable to fit into it because of different social customs and standards of living, have gradually drawn together and formed what amounts to small foreign states. It is urged by the partisans of selective immigration that, since the colonies are all of European origin and have not

been assimilated, they are influenced by European politics and thus may eventually plant in Argentina the seeds of European unrest and political disturbances.[1]

In 1938 the partisans of selective immigration seemed to have outnumbered those of unrestricted immigration. However, as Hunter pointed out, Argentina could feed some 100 million inhabitants if one made a comparison with the European land mass which for generations had supported European populations, yet the Argentinean population at this time was only some 11.2 million.

Yet it seemed that unrestricted immigration, despite the ongoing Nazi atrocities in Europe, was to remain firmly off the Argentinean agenda. The reasons for this were complex, but largely were the result of European politics. During the previous few years Argentineans had seen the rise of Nazism and its spread to Austria; the Italian/Ethiopian conflict and the Spanish Civil War, all of which had resulted in mixed emotions and sometimes strong demonstrations in Argentina, either for or against these issues and events. The Argentinean government had therefore decided that rather than have the nucleus of political ferment in the country, it would be wise to restrain from allowing anyone into the country who might fan the flames of political unrest. In 1936 the government had tightened its immigration regulations in an effort to prevent what it perceived as 'unruly elements' entering the country.[2]

The Jews, however, were faced with a further difficulty. According to the Argentinean constitution all creeds were welcome in the country providing they could meet the entry requirements. However, the fundamental requirement was the need for people who could develop the mass of the country's agriculturally undeveloped lands. The Jewish people were largely from city areas or had held positions in towns as clerks, storekeepers and businessmen. They were not suited to agrarian pursuits and so one of the primary requirements to qualify for visa issue was generally missing—experience of work on the land.

Jewish immigrants from Germany and Austria entered the country through two methods. The first was through a colonisation programme and the second was by means of affidavits of relatives and friends in Argentina who guaranteed support. The immigration work was handled by two organisations: the Jewish Colonisation Association and the *Hilfsverein Deutschsprechender Juden*. [3]

The Jewish Colonisation Association had approximately 1.1 million hectares of land at its disposal, of which some half million hectares were already under cultivation by Jewish colonists. Throughout the republic there were twenty Jewish colonies, most of them comprised of large percentages of German Jews. According to Argentine immigration laws each family unit had to comprise of at least five people, i.e., a father, mother and three children, or husband, wife and brothers or sisters etc. One member of the family had to be a skilled agriculturist and three members had to be capable of being *trabajadores* or labourers. However, this entry requirement had always been one of the main problems with regard to Jewish immigration. As Hunter reported to the State Department in April 1938:

> The selection of colonists has been one of the association's chief problems. Many of those who want to come have been refugees for a long time in cities like Prague. Their money has been withheld from them and they have suffered so much through malnutrition that they are unable to 'labor' within the meaning of the Argentine immigration laws and to meet the requirements that each family shall include at least three adult 'laborers'. The fact also that the money which these people possess in Germany often cannot be obtained delays the work until other financial arrangements can be made.

Many of the families which the association desires to bring here for colonization purposes have no knowledge whatsoever of agricultural pursuits; so customarily no family is permitted to come until one male member has first been brought here and trained for six months in agricultural schools maintained by the association. This insures that at least one member of the family will be able to instruct the others in diversified farming and in addition have some slight knowledge of Spanish. This program gives the promise that the family, under normal conditions, will be able to look after itself and in time become a successful part of the colonization project....

A colonist's family is never permitted 'just to get along'. It must be a success. The refugees realize this and in the majority of cases devote their best efforts to making the most of the opportunities given them. The few malcontents are soon brought into line by the simple question, 'Where else in the world can you go and be welcome and permitted to earn a living?'[4]

The *Hilfsverein Deutschsprechender Juden*, on the other hand was the poor cousin of the Jewish Colonisation Association. Refugees who arrived in Argentina under the auspices of this society were usually almost penniless and relied to a large degree upon the charity of their friends and relatives. The society was run by Adolfo Hirsch who was reported as having spent his entire fortune on relief work and worked himself for no payment. He received little financial aid from the Jewish community at large because their organisations were not unified and were widely dispersed throughout the country. The society was funded largely from money that was supplied by the various Jewish charitable organisations abroad. One of these was the Refugee Economic Corporation which remitted funds into Argentina via the First National Bank of Boston. This bank was, according to Hunter, '...very careful not to let it be known that it handles this fund for the Refugee Economic Corporation because it has both German and Jewish accounts, many of which are not in sympathy with the work'.[5]

Immigrants were brought to the country aboard ship and placed in the care of the *Sociedad Protectors de Immigrantes Israelitas* (the Association for the Protection of Jewish Immigrants) who arranged to put them through the rigorous customs formalities. If relatives or friends were waiting, then the refugees were delivered to them. However, if not they were taken to one of several Jewish boarding houses where their rent was paid by the society until they could find work and their own accommodation. Finding work for the women was reported to have been a simple procedure. There was a large market for nursemaids, servants, governesses, companions, housekeepers, teachers of languages and office clerks. Yet the men found it far more difficult, especially so when it was necessary not to upset the local labour market. Within two months it was usual for approximately twenty per cent of the men to have found some kind of employment.[6] Some were provided with small loans to help them set up modest businesses. Others were sent to agricultural schools where they would undertake a nine-months' course before again seeking employment. With such experience behind them it was then generally a simple matter to find work.

At the headquarters of the *Hilfsverein Deutschsprechender Juden* there were workshops where immigrants were taught carpentry. The timber was donated by Jewish companies and the items made, breadboards, dog-kennels, miniature houses etc, were sold by the students to produce a small income. There were also other forms of training, mechanical drawing and technical instruction. Learning Spanish was obligatory, each child and adult being made to attend classes at least once a day. Young women were sent to hospitals to train as nurses.

Since the rise to power of Hitler on 30 January, 1933, the two societies combined had brought between sixteen thousand and seventeen thousand Jews to Argentina from Germany. Of these only about six thousand were capable of supporting themselves financially. Of the remainder the task of seeking work, in the face of rising nationalism within the country, had always been a difficult one. Young nationalists had already carried out persecutions against the Jewish community for allegedly taking work away from Argentine citizens.[7]

Anti-Semitism within Argentina was not on a large scale, although it certainly existed, and the government was profoundly concerned over the problems that might arise from a massive influx of Jews into the country.

As Hunter reported to the State Department in 1938:

> Both the American bank handling the Refugee Economic Corporation Fund in Buenos Aires and the *Hilfsverein* stated that there is, however, a considerable amount of 'petty' persecution of the refugees. Both organizations cited instances of small businesses having come under the eye of

the Nationalist Party from time to time and as a result, with the 'cooperation' of the police, the store had been closed up for a week or ten days on the charge of not having complied in some minor detail with respect to the law. At the end of that time the owner was usually fined from ten to twenty pesos and permitted to reopen his business.

Mr Hirsch of the *Hilfsverein*, upon being asked whether or not any open official feeling or persecution against the refugees had been noticed, replied in the negative, but added that there was 'considerable semiofficial persecution' by such government entities as the Customs House and the Post Office. He did not go into detail as to the manner of this and expressed no resentment.

It has been remarked by disinterested persons that any feeling against the Jews which might exist was pretty much counterbalanced by recent activities of the German Nazis in Argentina in connection with the Plebiscite held on April 12 which provided occasion for a number of anti-German demonstrations by students and youth organizations.[8]

Hunter went on to detail another case of discrimination against Jewish people in Argentina, a case affecting the firm of Guillermo Kraft & Cia Ltd., a large publishing house that was 'compelled' to dismiss almost thirty per cent of its personnel because they were of the Jewish race.[9]

Additionally, German companies trading in Argentina would not employ Jews, simply because they were Jews, and most Argentinean companies refused to employ them because few of them could speak Spanish. The American Chamber of Commerce had offices in Buenos Aires where many of the Jewish migrants registered for work. These were sent primarily to American and British business concerns where vacancies had been reported. However, the manager of the chamber stated in April that several members of the chamber had asked the manager not to send any more Jews, as their companies were, '...already entirely too Jewish'.[10]

In Poland where, as we have seen, there were some 3.2 million Jews, many of whom wanted to emigrate before the persecutions being experienced in Germany and Austria visited them, the Argentine Embassy had, on 16 March, 1938, suspended the issue of all visas on Polish passports. No reason was given for this sudden change in the immigration policy, but it was intimated by the *Havas* Agency, the agency that arranged much of the immigration from Poland, that the changes to government policy were primarily due to the Argentinean need for agriculturists and artisans, and that the Jewish people applying for visas were not able to meet that requirement.[11]

One of the major problems facing the various agencies working to ameliorate the plight of the refugees who wished to emigrate to Argentina was that of the lack of unity among the Jewish people already within the country. These were comprised of Spanish Jews, Italian Jews, Polish Jews and many other nationalities, and they regarded themselves still as Polish, Italian or Spanish, rather than distinctly as Jews or Argentineans. They lived in different districts and by different customs and could not be brought together as Jews in a common cause. Funding was desperately needed and such a common cause could have supplied that funding to a large extent.

Quoting an Argentine immigration official in 1939, Hunter wrote: '...if they had money no obstacles would be put in their way, if they did not, reasons would be found for refusing their entrance.[12]

Guatemala

Most of the South American countries were adopting similar practices to that of Argentina. Strict immigration procedures were designed to keep out such Jewish refugees as intellectuals, doctors, lawyers, university lecturers and businessmen. For example, early in 1938 the Jewish community in Guatemala requested from the Guatemalan Ministry of Foreign Affairs, the precise conditions under which Jewish migrants would be allowed into the country and what lands they might take up in the largely underpopulated interior. The ministry responded with an unpopular document titled, *Bases for the Establishment of a Jewish Colony in Los Andes*. The document outlined the government's preparedness to provide grants of land in Los Andes under naturalisation and work restrictions. They promised religious freedom but pointed out that the cost of the project would have to be entirely borne by the immigrants themselves.[13]

According to Fay Allen DesPortes of the U.S. Legation in Guatemala, who was quoting a Jewish informant, the terms of the regulations were not acceptable to the Jewish community in general. DesPortes later stated in a communication to the U.S. Department of State that the land which was being allocated by the

Guatemalan government was unsuitable for farming and that the government would adhere strictly to the terms of the U.S. government's proposal that no added immigration quotas be undertaken because of the refugee problem. DesPortes stated that from conversations carried out with the Guatemalan foreign minister it seemed clear that Jewish refugees would not be allowed into the country if they were members of the learned professions.

DesPortes added:

> ...the attitude of this government ... responds to Nazi influence exercised on President [Jorge] Ubico from his personal conviction that the commerce and industry of the country must be preserved for the Guatemalans themselves.... Newspaper comment during recent months has increasingly stressed the necessity for greater enterprise on the part of the Guatemalans in developing the resources of the country. This nationalism, while mildly advocated at present, may assume more militant form at any time.[14]

On 2 May, 1938, Jewish migrant Werner Holzbock wrote to Cordell Hull advising him of the difficulties many of the Jewish refugees could expect to face if they were admitted into the country. He said that skilled workers such as bakers, locksmiths, joiners, bricklayers and others all had extreme difficulty in competing with local workers, as the local man was prepared to work for very little wages, wages an immigrant would find it difficult to live on. He added that the only hope for such immigrants was to have sufficient capital behind them to purchase machinery, which the local man rarely could, and thus open a factory of some kind, however small, so that he could manufacture goods at a very cheap rate. Some Jews had succeeded in getting into the export business and, ironically, were engaged in exporting goods which were largely produced by German manufacturers. Holzbock informed the U.S. secretary of state that doctors, lawyers and other academics had virtually no prospects at all in South American countries. Lawyers and other academic professions had been forced to change commercial professions; farmers without farms and without capital had no prospects. Holzbock reported one instance of two young people who had been trained as 'husbandmen' by an organisation of the Jewish parish. One of these became a bread-baker near Santiago de Chile and lived under 'extremely bad conditions,' the other had attempted to work at a number of occupations but finally ended up, '...selling lady's clothes as a hawker and was just about to marry a disorderly woman expecting a child'.[15]

Holzbock's comments were passed from Hull to the president's advisory committee in New York.

Chile

According to confidential sources provided to the U.S. Department of State in late May 1938, the situation in Chile was similar. The U.S. consul general, Edward A. Dow, based in Santiago, advised the secretary of state that a massive Jewish congress named the Congress of Jewish Youth, had been convened at Santiago with the express purpose of discussing various topics, including the general situation of Judaism, the organisation of Jewish youth in Chile, Jewish unification, and anti-Semitism. The delegates to the congress numbered sixty, many of whom were university students. One of the topics covered was Jewish immigration into Chile. As Dow later wrote:

> Notwithstanding the pressure upon Chile to absorb Jewish refugees, particularly those from Germany within the past few years, the Chilean government has refrained from officially announcing imposition of immigration quotas but follows a policy consistent with a definite opinion among the higher Gentile intellectual groups in the form of a gentlemen's agreement. Chile is

unofficially restricting to 50 Jewish families per year. It is emphasized by the press that groups of this character which depend after arrival in Chile on success in the professional, mercantile and other non-productive fields, should not expect the encouragement which the government has offered.... Sources of information confidential.[16]

Peru

Peru quickly acknowledged its willingness to join the Évian conference, even going so far as to state that the country was definitely willing to accept refugees from Austria and Germany, but stipulated that they would only be accepted when the Peruvian government was, '...satisfied in each case that the individual bears no Communist taint'.[17]

Subsequent investigations carried out by the U.S. Department of State into Peruvian immigration procedures revealed serious discrepancies in the country's immigration practices. For example, intending immigrants were required to make a substantial deposit of two thousand soles, (U.S.$100), although this did not guarantee entry.[18] The confidential State Department document recorded:

The right to enter the country on the grounds of a labour contract is equally, generally speaking, nothing more than a theoretical privilege, as the Ministry of Labour proves extremely unaccommodating when the confirmation of such a contract is in question. In any case, this possibility can only be used in exceptional cases ... a secret circular letter recommends to consuls not to visa the passports of persons coming from the following countries: Poland, Romania, Russia, Lithuania, Turkey, Palestine. The repercussion which this circular letter must have on Jewish immigration is obvious.

It is unfortunately impossible to give the official statistics of immigration into Peru. It is only certain that Jewish immigration is insignificant and that the number of resident Jews remains to all intents and purposes stationary.[19]

According to the data of the Committee of Protection of Lima, the number of Jews who arrived in the country from 1933, when Hitler came to power, did not exceed two hundred and thirty people or about fifty persons per annum.[20]

Colombia

Colombian immigration procedures in light of the refugees situation were equally as intransigent. Colombian consuls were authorised to grant visas to all those who could furnish a deposit of two hundred and fifty Colombian pesos. This possibility, however, was only reserved for the bearers of national passports, so people without passports and bearers of refugee passports issued by the Nansen Office were excluded. Even among the bearers of national passports the authorities also made a clear distinction. Owners of German and Austrian passports were made to furnish a deposit of two hundred and fifty pesos, while nationals of Poland, Romania, Lithuania, and, in general, all other eastern European countries were forced to deposit one thousand pesos.

Immigrants who were able to procure a labour contract were exempt from the deposit but it was becoming increasingly more difficult to obtain such a contract.[21] The U.S. Department of State reported in 1938:

> The consuls, obviously, have lately received new instructions which must make the access to the country much more difficult than before. Indeed, the consuls require now certificates of good character

for the last 10 years instead of 5 years as it was before. They also require documentary evidence that the emigrant has done his military service [*livret militaire*]; and finally all the various documents submitted to them must be legalized by the consul of the country of origin of the prospective immigrant which is practically always impossible as the refugees in question come from Germany.[22]

Ecuadorian Reticence

On 6 June, 1938, Boaz Long, the U.S. diplomatic representative at Quito, Ecuador, advised the U.S. Department of State that the Ecuadorian government had at last replied to President Roosevelt's invitation stating that a representative would be attending the Évian conference and that the representative would be Senor Alejandro Gastelu Concha who would carry the diplomatic rank of *chargé d'affaires*. Concha was an Ecuadorian who had lived in France for many years. He had held various honorary and career consular positions and was then the Ecuadorian consul general at Geneva. However, Boaz Long held strong reservations concerning the sincerity of the Ecuadorian acceptance. In a confidential message to the U.S. Department of State of 6 June he wrote:

> While the Ecuadorian Government has agreed to participate in the intergovernmental committee, it is my opinion that it is doing so with little enthusiasm. Its delays in answering the Legation's first representations on this matter and my inquiry of May 25th, and the recent efforts to exclude Jewish immigrants, and the somewhat guarded wording of the Ecuadorian Government's acceptance, seem to indicate its support of intergovernmental action may prove luke-warm.[23]

Indeed, the final sentence of the Ecuadorian government's note of reply clearly stipulated that the government would give its support to the aims of the intergovernmental committee provided that, '...they do not conflict with the domestic provisions of law which govern immigration, with international conventions, and with the requirements of the national economy'.[24]

Immigration into Ecuador had been regulated by laws in no way different from those of other South-American countries except that the deposit required was comparatively modest, (U.S.$50), and that the consuls were forbidden to visa the passports of emigrants with no country.

In spite of the infinitesimal number of the Jews living in the country, a well orchestrated press campaign started during the late 1930s by a prominent Ecuadorian propaganda service had almost provoked not only the complete closure of the frontiers to Jewish immigration, but, with the exception of those engaged in agricultural work and industry, even expulsion of those Jews who had lived in the country for many years. Confidential U.S. Department of State documents revealed:

> Ecuador cannot be considered as an opening for Jewish immigration. It is true that in 1935 a Committee of Immigration and Colonization was created to which the government conceded not unconditionally, 1,000,000 acres of land, but the interest this created proved a long series of investigations. The results were all more or less identical: the country is very little developed; and in the areas surrounding the only two important cities of Ecuador—Guayaquil and Quito—malaria flourishes with extraordinary virulence. The ways of communication are insufficient, and the possibilities of establishment practically inexistent, native artisans work at extremely low salaries.[25]

Ecuador had previously opened its doors to three Jewish professors, (in 1935), and its government claimed that there were no social barriers or quota systems incorporated in their immigration laws. However, the situation in Europe had certainly caused the government to look carefully at its immigration laws and to impose several changes that sought to limit numbers significantly, primarily those of intending immigrant intellectuals. As the Évian representative for Ecuador was later to state:

> As ... Ecuador is an essentially agricultural country, we must take actual facts and national necessities into consideration and these would not admit of too great an influx of intellectual workers. My government could not remain indifferent to the results of immigration conducted under unfavourable conditions.[26]

Bolivia

Bolivia too was a country steeped in anti-Semitism and its immigration laws were tightened during the Nazi rage of persecution which then was flourishing in Europe.

Bolivia would be represented at the conference by the hugely wealthy mining magnate Simón Iturri Patino, who had made his fortune in tin. Patiño owned tin smelters in both England and Germany and by the 1940s would be one of the wealthiest people in the world. He was known as the 'Tin King' *(Rey del Estaño)*. [27]

In Bolivia immigrant admission could only be delivered by the central power but no deposit was required when this permit was granted. (Legislation of 27 December, 1926).[28]

As Hitler came to power and as anti-Semitism grew, not only in Europe but worldwide, the Bolivian government issued instructions to its consuls abroad—instructions that were repeated in the Bolivian newspapers—forbidding access into the country to, 'Negroes, Chinese, Jews, Gypsies and other undesirable elements.'[29] Confidential U.S. State Departments documents revealed:

> It is difficult to regard Bolivia as a country specially indicated for Jewish immigration…. The country draws the main bulk of its resources out from the mines and it is doubtful whether the Jewish immigration could be employed in this branch of industry. The number of Jews living in the country does not exceed a few hundred.[30]

Brazil

Throughout the preparations for, and during the Évian conference, many South American countries were openly hostile to the concept of aiding immigration to Jewish refugees. Brazil was one of these countries. Yet, as we shall see, this huge country with vast tracts of undeveloped lands desperately needed skilled migrants and should have worked actively towards aiding those who wished to migrate there.

Just prior to the Évian conference the Brazilian government introduced a series of new changes to its immigration laws. These included the right of the government to limit or to suspend the immigration of the individuals of certain races. Consuls abroad could declare an emigrant undesirable, even when the migrant could fulfil all the requirements of Brazilian immigration law.[31]

A quota system played a large part in Brazilian immigration procedures. Eighty per cent of each quota was intended for agriculturists or technical experts of rural industries, so that only twenty per cent of each quota would be left for their relatives. This provision severely affected the Jewish refugees who wished to flee from Austria and Germany. Additionally, the law forbade under the menace of expulsion any change of profession during the first four years of residence in Brazil.[32]

A confidential report prepared by the U.S. Department of State in June 1938 contained clear evidence that in light of the heightening refugee problem in Europe, Brazilian authorities, for no apparent reason, were actually reducing immigration numbers. The report demonstrated that the Brazilian government had everything to gain by increasing dramatically its immigration quotas, and that those immigrants who had arrived in the country were contributing greatly to the economy. The report stated that the new law left little for the admission of immigrants, and that the new restrictions would further reduce the number of immigrants to, '...an absolute minimum'. The government was acutely aware that the immigrants were particularly beneficial to the Brazilian economy, especially those who knew languages, accountancy and typing. According to the U.S. Department of State report these people were, '...in no way a burden to their new country, but very often answer the needs of Brazilian economy'.[33]

El Salvador

By 7 June, 1938, all the South American republics, with the exception of El Salvador, had agreed to send representatives to the conference at Évian. El Salvador had refused, allegedly because of the expense involved, but also because of the relatively small number of immigrants it could accept.[34]

The Salvadorian diplomatic communiqué from the acting minister of foreign affairs, stated, 'I beg to inform you that my government regrets not being able to appoint a representative to serve on the said committee, as it believes this action unnecessary in view of the limited number of German and Austrian political refugees to whom hospitality could be given by this country.... Furthermore the appointment of a such a representative would involve expenses which it would be difficult for my government to meet'.[35]

Part Two

Chapter 5

A Progression of Disappointments

On 20 June, 1938, Frank L. Mainz, a private citizen then living in Amsterdam, wrote to President Roosevelt with a new concept. He claimed that it would be feasible to exchange German immigrants living in the U.S.—and who wished to return to Germany—for Jewish refugees. Mainz claimed that during his recent travels to many regions in the U.S. he had come into contact with large numbers of German citizens who supported Hitler's causes. He claimed that as many of them would willingly return to Germany and support Hitler, these people should be allowed to do so in exchange for a like number of Jewish refugees.[1]

Having received only a cursory reply from the U.S. consular office in Amsterdam, Mainz was moved to write again on 13 August and was determined to make his point that the Jewish people trapped in Nazi controlled areas were desperate for assistance and that something—anything—should be done to assist them. Mainz insisted that if there was any chance at all of helping, 'these unhappy victims', then that chance should be taken. He pointed out that every day lost in bringing aid to the Jewish people meant despair and even more danger of death. He said that the persecution was growing continuously and that immediate aid was necessary, describing the events in Europe as, '...the greatest injustice in history'.[2]

On 21 June, 1938, the U.S. Department of State advised Myron C. Taylor that U.S. authorities were willing for him to hold meetings with several of the other countries' delegates prior to the main meeting at Évian, adding that it would be advisable for him to determine the views of the French, British, Argentine and Brazilian delegates, and to establish whether or not they would support in general the U.S. proposals.[3]

Nicaragua

On 24 June, 1938, the U.S. diplomat based at Managua in Nicaragua advised the U.S. Department of State that the Nicaraguan government had accepted the Évian agenda without any objections. However, the government had also advised that there were certain stipulations attached to the immigration of any Jewish refugees. These included:

> Nicaragua cannot finance [the] journey of any immigrant or finance his establishment here. Nicaragua cannot accept any but agriculturists, industrial workers and professional technical men. Nicaragua will not accept any immigrants with extremist views such as Nazis, Fascists, Communists etc. all immigrants without a country [that is, whose citizenship has been cancelled] must adopt Nicaraguan citizenship within a period set up by the Congress.[4]

These instructions were immediately conveyed to Myron Taylor in France.[5]

Luxembourg

On 27 June, 1938, the U.S. diplomat based at Luxembourg advised the U.S. Department of State that the Luxembourg government had expressed its disappointment that it had not been asked to send a representative to the Évian meeting.[6] The following day Cordell Hull replied in code, stating that invitations to attend the Évian meeting had been extended only to countries which offered any reasonable possibility of accepting a substantial number of Jewish refugees. He stated that as Luxembourg could not be considered a country of asylum, he thought it impracticable to extend an invitation to that country.[7] Hull reported the correspondence to Myron C. Taylor in France, advising Taylor that according to the U.S. *chargé d'affaires* at Luxembourg, Luxembourg itself had its own refugees problem and that it would be inadvisable to invite a representative of the country to the Évian conference.[8] In this Hull was substantially correct. The Grand Duchy of Luxembourg had realised for a considerable period that Luxembourg would be one of the first countries to bear the brunt of any mass Jewish exodus from Germany. Hull was later informed that as the pogroms increased so too did the problem of illegal Jewish immigrants in Luxembourg. Many Jewish families living legally in the country were harbouring friends and relatives who had slipped over the frontier, and members of the German border police were actively forcing large groups of refugees to run across the border. The Luxembourg border police officers were spread only thinly on the ground and it was almost impossible for them to patrol the entire border successfully—even with the help of every available man seconded from the police force. It was reported that even a significant number of traffic police had been transferred to the border in a desperate attempt to keep the refugees out of the country. George Platt Waller, *chargé d'affaires* in Luxembourg later wrote:

> The entire police force and *gendarmerie* of the country, reinforced by certain army units are maintaining as rigid a border patrol as is possible, but when hundreds of fear-crazed and desperate men are seeking in forest and mountain regions a chance to slip over an undefended frontier, [on the German side] it is easy to comprehend that a good many will be successful. If the situation were reversed, it is safe to say that very few Luxembourgers could get into Germany, but in this case the German authorities are not only eager to allow Jews to get out, but in many cases ... [have] bundled hapless groups over the frontier in unwatched places and threatened them with dire punishment if they attempted to return or confessed that they had been forcibly put into Luxembourg.[9]

Guatemalan Representation

We have seen in the previous chapter the methods Guatemala was adopting in order to restrict Jewish immigration into the country. No immediate commitment was made by Guatemala to attend the conference but on 20 June the Guatemalan government finally advised the U.S. Department of State that its representative at Évian would be Senor Jose Gregorio Diaz, adding, '...the immigration law in effect in this republic, restrict in a definite manner the entry into the country of persons who come to work'. The Guatemalan statement ended by claiming that the representative to the conference would, however, be willing to state that his government would accept, '...a small number of agricultural immigrants'.[10]

The Guatemalan government also commented:
> ...one of the principal commissions of the international committee, whose organisation the United States has proposed, would be, naturally, the establishment of strict and real guarantees that the immigrants do not constitute a menace or danger from the point of view of social interest and of the collective well-being. And in this sense pertinent precautions will have to be taken to avoid in time the risks that might come from all that element of immigration undesirable because of the danger which its ideology might constitute for democratic institutions.[11]

Poland

One of the European countries that had, until now, been reticent in appointing representatives to the Évian conference, was Poland. As we have seen, Poland too was a particularly anti-Semitic state at the time and was only too willing to promote an active and aggressive emigration programme for Polish Jews. At a confidential meeting between the assistant secretary of state, George Messersmith, and the Polish ambassador in Washington on 24 June, 1938, the ambassador advised Messersmith that his government had appointed two representatives to attend the conference, adding that the government hoped the agenda of the conference could be widened to discuss the possibility of emigrants from countries other than only Germany and Austria.[12] In other words, Poland, even before the Nazi occupation of that country, was also keen to be rid of its Jewish population.

The question of Poland in respect to the proposed plans constituted a particularly difficult problem for the U.S. Department of State. Poland had been courting anti-Semitism since the Dark Ages and widespread publicity of the events in Germany and Austria was doing little to alleviate this attitude. Following an article published in the *Warsaw Jewish Press* on 26 April, 1938, which had called for a plan to relocate to Palestine 500,000 of the approximately 3.2 million Jews then living in Poland, Doctor Joseph Schechtman, the leader of the Zionist Revisionist Movement in Poland, contacted the U.S. Embassy in Warsaw to request an interview with President Roosevelt. The alleged purpose of the requested interview was to congratulate the president on his initiative in forming the international committee, and, ostensibly, to offer the services of the Revisionist Movement on matters regarding the emigration of Jews. However, as the U.S. ambassador to Poland, A.J. Drexel Biddle, Jnr., stated in his subsequent communication with the U.S. Department of State:

> In my opinion they would also welcome the opportunity of being received by the President as [an] occasion for focusing favourable publicity on [the] Zionist Revisionist Movement and its determined aim and arguments in respect [to] the development of Palestine.
>
> Though Zionist Revisionists comprise only about 3% or 96,000 of Poland's approximate total of 3,200,000 Jews, [the] Polish government sees eye-to-eye more with Zionist Revisionist leader Zabotynski and his representative Dr Schechtman than with other Jewish leaders in Poland, for

[the] Polish Government feels the aforementioned are the most objective and cooperative in efforts to solve the Polish-Jewish problem.

Zabotynski and Schechtman are distinctly at odds with Weitzman [*sic, actually Dr Chaim Weizmann, president of the World Zionist Organisation and head of the Jewish Agency for Palestine—author's note*] in terms of Palestine. The former earnestly advocates the development of Palestine as the logical and practical centre for expansion as an outlet for Jewish emigration from European disturbed areas. Weitzman, they feel, would be likely to accept the shadow for the substance in terms of Palestine's possible expansion due to Weitzman's paramount desire to have a toy state which he could head.

I should appreciate the Department's placing me in a position to reply to Dr Schechtman's inquiry.[13]

The undersecretary of state, Sumner Welles' strictly confidential reply was drafted in code four days later. 'I hope that you will be able to discourage, without the issue being presented to us in more concrete terms, any trip to the United States of a committee representing the Revisionist Zionists.'[14]

Confidential State Department documents detailed some of the history of the Revisionist Movement, claiming that they constituted only seventeen per cent of the Jews in Palestine while having relatively few adherents in the U.S. and western Europe. Their strength was reportedly drawn mainly from Jews of eastern Europe, from areas in which the pressure to migrate was the greatest such as Germany and Austria, and who consequently were most concerned with ways in which unrestricted migration to Palestine could be established. The New Zionists were advocating a migration of some 1.5 million Jews to be relocated to Palestine over a period of ten years.[15]

Biddle was finally able to, 'discreetly dissuade' Schechtman from visiting Washington, as he reported on 28 May:

> Just about the time I received the Department's ... cable the local press carried a report of the President having appointed Mr Myron Taylor as Chairman of the American Delegation to the International Refugee Conference, whereupon I telephoned New York City in order to ascertain Mr Taylor's whereabouts. Upon finding he had sailed for Italy, I traced him to Florence. This placed me in a position to divert Dr Schechtman's attention from

Washington to Mr Taylor. Accordingly, I suggested that Dr Schechtman and his associates make direct contact with Mr Taylor, explaining the latter's position as chairman of the American Delegation. Dr Schechtman, as spokesman for his group, expressed his appreciation of this suggestion, and stated that he would await word from me as to when and where Mr Taylor would be willing to meet him.

I have today received Mr Taylor's reply to my letter addressed to him care of our Consul General in Florence and explaining the circumstances of Dr Schechtman's desired interview. Mr Taylor was of the opinion that the Conference should first care for the main business at hand, namely the question of refugees from Austria and Germany, before undertaking the broader aspects of the Jewish problem in general. He would communicate with me at a later date as to where and when he could receive Dr Schechtman. I thereupon accordingly apprised the latter who expressed his appreciation and understanding of the situation.[16]

Not long after this event, U.S. Ambassador A.J. Drexel Biddle, Jnr. in Warsaw advised the State Department that the Polish government was beginning to put added pressure on him regarding the large number of Jews that the Polish government would like to have deported from that country. Biddle was told that if nothing were done to alleviate the problem then this would only serve to, '...provoke acute anti-Semitism amongst the ranks of radical anti-Semitics, not only in Poland, but also in Romania, Hungary and other countries where the Jewish problem is steadily becoming a more acute social-economic-political issue'.[17]

Biddle was instructed to inform the Polish government that while the U.S. government realised a problem of Jewish concentration existed in Poland, it was more important for the intergovernmental committee to concentrate on those refugees who were then bearing the brunt of Nazi persecution in Austria and Germany.[18]

Shortly afterwards it became clear that the Poles were in no way prepared to soften their attitude and indeed, had introduced more severe legislation to ensure that all Jews who had fled from Germany to Poland were forced to leave the country, including approximately eleven thousand former Polish Jews who had moved to Germany during better times and were now forced to cross the Polish frontier near Zbaszyn where they lived in crowded and impoverished conditions. Even the Polish ambassador in the

U.S. later admitted that these people were, '...strangers in their own land and were destitute'.[19]

Traditionally, Austrian Jews in Poland were treated more sympathetically than German Jews. During the previous four or five years Austrian Jews bearing Austrian passports had been permitted to live and work in Poland. However, as anti-Semitic feelings grew within the country these people were forced to exchange their Austrian passports for German documentation and the Polish authorities assumed a much stricter attitude towards them. Ambassador Biddle reported: 'The natural assumption is that the Polish authorities desire to force these new "German citizens" to depart from Poland, possibly with the assistance of the intergovernmental committee.[20]

Soon afterwards the pressure increased dramatically. Biddle informed his superiors that a fresh wave of anti-Semitism was rapidly mounting, adding:

> Increasing sections of the press are taking up the cry for large-scale emigration, leading parliamentarians are loudly calling for an early solution of the so-called Jewish problem through mass emigration, other politicians are seeking to enact anti-Semitic legislation, and the youth organisation of the

Ozon Party is plastering the city with posters calling for what literally amounts to a boycott of the Jewish shops and pointing out with contempt the dominant position of the Jews in the economic and professional structures of the nation. This surge of anti-Semitism presages not only an added hardship for the unfortunate Jews in Poland, but also an augmentation of a rapidly rising state of political confusion.[21]

These were interesting comments and clearly demonstrate that anti-Semitism was then deeply entrenched in Europe, not only in countries dominated by the Nazi influence, but also elsewhere. If Poland, a relatively free and democratic country, with 3.2 million Jews within its borders, could so blatantly discriminate against Jews in such a fashion, then what possible hope could the Jews under Nazi dominance have?

The eleven thousand Jews who were then living precariously on the Polish border at Zbaszyn were originally not considered as part of the problem to be tackled by the intergovernmental committee. They had managed to escape from Germany and were therefore 'free'. However, as anti-Semitic activity in Poland rapidly increased, these people were again considered to be a part of the overall problem and provisions were later made for them to be included within the scope of the committee's work.[22]

As we now know, Poland was to be a particularly terrible killing ground for the Jews of Europe and the Germans would build several extermination camps within the country including, Treblinka, Sobibor and Belzec—no 'ordinary' concentration camps like Auschwitz which, in addition to its gas chambers had a huge population used as a workforce, but camps constructed specifically to murder on an industrial scale, camps built close to railroads so that large numbers of Jews destined for the gas chambers could be delivered to them quickly and with relative ease. In 1942 more people would be murdered at Treblinka than at any other place in the history of humankind.

The Situation Deteriorates

On 13 June, 1938, John Cooper Wiley, U.S. consul general in Vienna, advised the State Department in Washington that the situation in Austria was deteriorating rapidly. Wiley wrote:

> In respect of Jewish activities in general, there seems to be no relaxation whatsoever in the pressure which is being applied by the authorities. Wholesale arrests continue on an ever-increasing scale. There is,

moreover, a new wave of Jew-baiting in various sections of Vienna, as well as in several of the provincial cities of Austria.

There are innumerable cases where individuals are given the choice of leaving Austria within a given period, varying between two and eight weeks, or of being sent to Dachau.... The authorities are encouraging clandestine emigration. I have received what I believe to be a conservative estimate from an authoritative source that over 1000 have been obliged to cross the frontier at night into Belgium. A few days ago 350 were sent in sealed cars to Greece whence they will be shipped to Palestine without visas or permits of entry....

A section of the population that is in particular distress are the *Mischlings* or part Jews. I know one case of a distinguished composer whose property was sequestered and who is now seriously ill. He was refused admission to the Jewish hospital on the grounds that he was not a Jew. The municipal hospital refused him admission because he was. He is now at the home of a friend living on private charity. He is 59 years old; despite the fact that he is a former officer, three times wounded in the [Great] War, [for Germany] he was sent to forced labor in Styria where three days of work in the flooded areas brought on his illness. I cite this case as typical of the treatment meted out to Jews. So far there are no soup kitchens or other effective philanthropic activities for these people.[23]

In order to help alleviate the problems which might arise from a public perception that, following the Évian conference, a flood of Jewish immigrants would arrive in the U.S., the State Department issued a press release claiming that in line with its adopted policy towards the Jewish refugees there would be no changes to the current immigration laws. Using the press release for a major part of its report, the *New York Times*, the only mainstream newspaper to print anything of importance on the matter, reported (in part) in June:

> James G. McDonald, formerly League of Nations High Commissioner for Refugees from Germany, doubts that the exodus of political minorities from Germany and Austria to this country will reach such proportions as to lead to a change in American immigration laws. Before departing for Quebec, whence he sailed yesterday to participate in the International Conference of Refugees at Évian-les-Bains, France, Mr. McDonald cited statistics on comparative

immigration and emigration of Germans to support his contention. These figures, prepared from government records by the President's Advisory Committee on Political Refugees, of which Mr McDonald is chairman, show that since Hilter's rise to power the excess of German immigration over emigration [from the U.S.] has been only 7108. The annual quota for Germany was set at 25000 by the Immigration Act of 1924, which remains unchanged.[24]

Secret Conference

On 2 July, Myron C. Taylor communicated with Cordell Hull, relaying details of a secret conference he had attended with one of the British representatives to Évian, Sir Charles Michael Palairet. (Palairet was descendant from a refugee Huguenot family named Palayret whose members had fled to England when Louis XIV had revoked the Edict of Nantes in 1689).[25] Precise details of that meeting remain obscure but in his confidential communication to Hull, Taylor stated, among other things, that there had been no specific indictment against Germany for causing the whole problem in the first place, and too much indictment against several other countries such as Poland and

Romania which, while being antiSemitic, had not actually caused the major problems. Another subject under discussion at the meeting was the highly controversial character Dr Chaim Weizmann, the head of the Jewish Agency for Palestine. Weizmann was possibly the most important Jewish person to attend the Évian conference. Born near Pinsk in Russian Poland, he had been subjected to anti-Semitism from an early age. He later emigrated to Britain where, as a biochemist, he held a 'responsible position' with the British Admiralty from 1916 to 1919. The British government, even at that time, recognised him as being the powerful leader of British Zionism and he had been consulted prior to the vital Balfour Declaration in 1917. By 1920 he was head of the World Zionist Organisation and in 1929 became the head of the Jewish Agency for Palestine. Ten years after the conference at Évian he was to become the first president of Israel. Communicating through Rabbi Stephen Wise of Roosevelt's U.S. committee, Weizmann requested that Taylor grant him the privilege of a private interview prior to the Évian conference so that he could explain in clear detail the plight of the Jewish people and the need to establish a homeland in Israel. This man was in a position to give Taylor a large volume of important information regarding the requirements of Jewish refugees, information that would clearly have been of enormous and vital assistance to Taylor during the talks at Évian. However, Taylor refused to meet with Weizmann prior to the conference.[26]

Chaim Weizmann

Head of the World Zionist Movement, and the Jewish Agency for Palestine. First president of Israel in 1948. His advice was ignored at Évian.

–U.S. National Archives

Iceland's Stance

At this time too, the government of Iceland refused to participate in the conference. The reasons for this are not clear although the general feeling as the run-up to the conference began was one of extreme caution on the part of almost all the countries involved. Iceland was, in any case, not generally considered to be a country that would have the resources or climate for any significant number of refugees. Its wild interior with large snow-fields and deep fjords constitutes a profoundly hostile environment, and four/fifths of the country is virtually uninhabitable. For the refugees from Nazi domination it would have been, at least, a free country, but they would have been severely restricted to a number of small industries such as sheep farming or fishing or associated manufacturing projects. Clearly this would have been impractical for people who were used to warmer climates and metropolitan industries.[27]

The Proposed Permanent Committee

During his secret talks with Sir Charles Michael Palairet, Taylor had been informed of the British government's reservations regarding the possibility of a permanent committee being established somewhere in Europe to aid Jewish refugees.[28] The government of Canada was also quick to point out that it had strong reservations over the setting up of a permanent committee, stating that neither the Canadian prime minister nor the Canadian undersecretary of state for external affairs had, '...given their consent to participate in this [long term] meeting'.[29] The Canadian diplomatic note, written by the Canadian secretary of state for external affairs and passed through John Farr Simmons, U.S. *chargé d'affaires* at Ottawa, also stated: '...I should be less than frank, however, if I did not intimate to you at this stage that ... [there are] real difficulties from the point of view of the Canadian Immigration Service. Under Canadian law and regulations, there is no provision for immigrant quotas and no commitments could therefore be made to receive any quota or specified number of refugees. Existing legislation does not permit immigration from the continent of Europe except for very restricted groups'.[30]

In spite of these difficulties and the reservations concerning the setting up of a permanent intergovernmental committee to aid the refugees, and despite the fact that no multinational decision had been made concerning the issue, Myron C. Taylor, in line with his instructions from Roosevelt, was pushing ahead with plans to have such a committee established—probably in Paris. Taylor's friend, lawyer George Rublee, was prominent among a small number of candidates to head the permanent committee, but another name had also been presented—possibly by the president's U.S. committee in New York. The name was that of committee member, Hamilton Fish Armstrong. However, Taylor held deep reservations over the appointment of Armstrong and in a telegram to Cordell Hull on 2 July, he presented his case:

> The name mentioned to me in connection with this activity by the President was Hamilton Fish Armstrong although the particular office we now have in mind was not then indicated.... It seems to me that the office of Secretary General should be filled by a man of real distinction in our business or public life who will have the

ability and energy to make the best practical use of the impetus which will be given to the solution of the refugee problem by the Évian meeting. I am considering several names and will welcome any suggestion which you might wish to make.[31]

Two days later, on the night of 4 July, 1938, Myron C. Taylor left Paris for Évian.[32]

On 5 July, 1938, after the departure of Taylor for Évian, the U.S. ambassador to Paris, William C. Bullitt, sent a highly confidential telegram in diplomatic code to Cordell Hull which stated:

> It has been a great pleasure to me to work with Myron Taylor who has made a most excellent impression in Paris. The best solution of the question of our representation on the committee which is to be set up to deal with Jewish refugees would be ... [to ask] him to remain in Paris as our representative. Since there seems to be no chance of persuading him to do this it will be necessary to find some other man of comparable ability, energy, and standing to represent us after Taylor's departure. The job will require the full time and energy of a man of the first order and at least one assistant from the Department of State supported by an efficient secretariat. The

present demands on my own time are such that I should not be able to give more than fragmentary attention to the work of the committee and none of the officers or clerks now on duty at this mission can be spared.

I am cabling you with regard to this matter in order to make certain that no one in the Department should remain under the misapprehension that this problem can be handled by the addition of an officer irrespective of the clerks to this mission. If it is the intention of our Government to deal with this question seriously, a man of Taylor's calibre who is willing to devote several years to the task is needed.[33]

The task of setting up a permanent committee to aid the refugees was considerable. The U.S. Department of State was aware that the setting up of such a committee would be an incursion upon the traditional ground of the League of Nations, although there was little alternative. The League was virtually powerless with regard to the question of German and Austrian refugees because Germany was not a signatory to the League. The Nansen Office was due to close at the end of 1938, its charter ended. With the closure of this office there would have been only small organisations working, sometimes diametrically, to assist the Jewish refugees. Yet the setting up of such an international committee was seen by some politicians and diplomats as being a form of usurpation of the League of Nations' mandate. The possibility of having the committee based permanently in Paris was thwarted when the French objected early in July. However, the British stated that they would have no objection to having the permanent committee based in London.[34]

Chapter 6

The Conference and World Disillusion

The Évian conference began on 6 July, 1938, with the French delegate welcoming almost two hundred representatives, journalists and observers. Conference delegates arrived in somewhat belligerent, pessimistic and cautious moods. They were mostly concerned that they were not to be bullied by the major powers into allowing unacceptable numbers of refugees into their countries. There also seems to have been an underlying concern over the choice of the U.S. delegation. Members of other delegations believed that if the U.S. had really meant to do something forcefully to ameliorate the plight of the Jews of Europe they would have sent more powerful representatives to the conference. Myron C. Taylor who was, after all, only a part-time diplomatic appointee, was assisted by a small group of relatively low level diplomats and staff.

Évian-les-Bains, France.

–U.S. National Archives

The conference opened with heated debates concerning which country, the United States or Great Britain, should chair the proceedings. The U.S. was finally chosen and after this decision had been made the thirty-nine representatives of the various refugee organisations were called upon to make their presentations. One would normally assume that such detailed presentations on such a vital subject concerning the fate of millions of people would have been scheduled to be heard over at least a week, possibly two weeks. However, each representative was given just ten minutes in which to make his or her claims. Many of the delegates found these representations tiresome and left the conference to enjoy the more relaxing pursuits on the golf course or in the casino. As that long afternoon wore on the time allowed to the refugee organisations was cut by half. The World Jewish Congress, representing about seven million Jews, was given just five minutes, and the delegation *specifically* representing German Jews was given no time at all. They were told simply to provide a written submission which would be, '...considered in due course'.

U.S. Opinion

First to speak at the conference was Monsieur Henri Berenger, the French delegate, whose traditional role—as delegate of the host nation—was to welcome the other delegates and to open the conference officially. Soon afterwards the U.S. ambassador, Myron C. Taylor, rose for his first address. The auditorium was hushed, there was an expectant silence as the delegates, the press and the world waited to learn what the U.S. would offer. Speculation was rife that the U.S. would set a high quota of Jewish immigrants from Germany. Many, in fact, believed that the U.S. would announce they were prepared to take up to 600,000 refugees. Taylor's speech began with details of the need for rapid action on behalf of the Jewish refugees and later continued:

> I shall not at this point dwell at length upon the technical aspects of the problem

with which we shall have to deal. May I merely suggest that it will be advisable for us to exchange, for the strictly confidential information of the Committee, details regarding the number and the type of immigrants whom each Government is prepared to receive under its existing laws and practices, details regarding these laws and practices and indications regarding those parts of the territory of each participating Government which may be adapted to the settlement of immigrants. Then, there will be the problem, which must be carefully considered, of documenting political emigrants who have been obliged to leave the country of their original residence in circumstances which render impossible the production of customary documents. It will also be incumbent upon us to consider the various studies which have been made in the respective countries of the problems of aiding the emigration and the settling and the financing of political refugees....

Évian delegates: Henri Berenger (France), Myron C. Taylor (US), and Lord Winterton (UK).

—U.S. National Archives

You will have noted that my Government's invitation to this meeting stated specifically that whatever action was recommended here should take place within the framework of the existing laws and practices of the participating Governments.... The American Government has taken steps to consolidate both the German and the former Austrian quota so that now a total of 27,370 immigrants may enter the United States on the German quota in one year.

From the inception of this present effort on behalf of political refugees it has been the view of the American Government that the meeting at Évian would serve primarily to initiate the collaboration of the receiving Governments in their assistance to political refugees and that the work would have to be carried forward subsequently in a more permanent form. It is the belief of the American Government that this permanent collaboration might be most effectively maintained by the regular meeting of the diplomatic representatives of the participating Governments—or such other representative as a participating Government may wish to designate—in a European capital.... The problem is no longer one of purely private concern. It is a problem for intergovernmental action. If the present currents of migration are permitted to continue to push anarchically upon the receiving States and if some Governments are to continue to toss large sections of their populations lightly upon a distressed and unprepared world, then there is catastrophic human suffering ahead which can only result in general unrest and in general international strain which will not be conducive to the permanent appeasement to which all peoples earnestly aspire.[1]

In effect Taylor was stating that America's quota system could not be changed to any great degree in order to accommodate the Jewish problem. He acknowledged that there was widespread anti-Semitism among many of the U.S. consuls throughout the world, consuls who often made hasty racial judgements concerning the migration of Jews to the U.S. He added that these prejudices were going to cease and that a full quota of German and Austrian immigrants—amounting to slightly more than 27,000 people—would be accepted for the following year. However, he failed to point out that a large percentage of these immigrants would be comprised of Christians.

The Jewish representatives at Évian were stunned into silence at the U.S. ambassador's words. The country that had promised so much (albeit obliquely) was now offering virtually nothing beyond those measures already in place, and Taylor's proposals were to set the example for the tragic series of events that followed. Documents later tendered to the conference delegates set out full details of the U.S. immigration procedures and stipulated that the U.S. was willing to allow unrestricted immigration to certain classes of people. These included university professors, spouses of U.S. citizens and their children, ministers of religion, and students who had enrolled in accredited college or university courses.

The documents clearly stipulated that other than the limited number who would qualify for unrestricted immigration: 'No preferential treatment may be accorded to so-called political refugees, as such, as distinguished from other immigrants.'[2]

Nahum Goldmann

—Wikimedia Commons

It seems almost incredible that the U.S. administration, having called the conference, was now blocking any further immigration quotas to the country. Evidently Roosevelt *wanted* to do something; it was as much part of his conscience as his duty to protect innocent people from oppression, no matter what their nationality or religion. However, as Nahum Goldmann, a representative of the World Jewish Congress and a delegate who attended Évian with Golda Meir later pointed out, Roosevelt personally may have wanted to increase the immigration quota but realised that in the face of stiffening public opinion against Jewish immigration he would have met with considerable resistance from Congress. As Goldmann stated, on this occasion Roosevelt was just not courageous enough to fight Congress over the issue. Goldmann, who had been stripped by the Nazis of his German citizenship in 1935, would move to America from Geneva in 1940 to settle with his family in New York. He also stated that when he was working with the State Department in efforts to implement policies to save the Jews, he became aware that most of the State Department staff were bureaucrats who were firmly against increasing the immigration quota. He did not realise at the time that it was official State Department policy to do so.[3]

Great Britain

Lord Winterton (Edward Turnour) the British delegate, was eloquent but equally as intransigent. Speaking after Taylor, he stated that it was a traditional policy for the British to offer refugees asylum and that immigrants who had come to the country had never failed to enrich it. However, Winterton stated that: '...the United

Kingdom is not a country of immigration. It is highly industrialised, fully populated and is still faced with the problem of unemployment. For economic and social reasons the traditional policy of granting asylum can only be applied within narrow limits'.[4]

Unemployment was certainly a problem in Great Britain at that time. According to figures released by the International Labour Office in Geneva the unemployed in Britain totalled 1,778,805.[5]

Winterton stated that his country was willing to allow certain numbers of refugees into the United Kingdom for the purposes of training or retraining, but the specific reason for this was to enable them to be accepted and to assimilate more readily in another country and not to settle permanently in Britain. Winterton added that his government was primarily concerned with assimilating those Jews who were already in the country before consideration could be given to allowing any more to enter. He claimed that serious consideration was being given to the introduction of refugees into the country's dominions, but stated that many of these dominions were already overcrowded or were unsuitable for European settlement because of political considerations or climates. He stated: 'These factors impose strict limitations on the opportunities for offering asylum to European refugees, but H.M. Government are not unhopeful that some of their colonial territories may in their turn be able to take a part, if only a relatively minor part, in assisting to solve the problem.'

Winterton said that his government was examining the possibility for settlement in East African territories but claimed that even these could take only limited numbers of refugees. He also said, '...my colleagues will appreciate that at the present stage it would be premature for me to make any positive statement on the subject'.[6]

Winterton called upon Germany to allow immigrants to leave both Germany and Austria with sufficient funds to provide for themselves in their countries of adoption. He said that no thickly populated country such as Great Britain could be expected to accept people who had been deprived of their means of sustenance. Clearly, humanitarian ideals for desperate, poverty-stricken people were not on Winterton's agenda. Sometime later Winterton explained further details of Britain's policies. He said that people with capital, students for educational and technical courses, people with academic qualifications who could find work before their entry into the country, and a limited number of doctors would be admitted. Yet he refused to speculate on what number of people would be allowed to enter the country.[7]

There is little doubt that before the Second World War England too was tendentiously anti-Semitic. Jews were barred from many organisations and, as A.J.P. Taylor points out in his *English History,* many public schools exercised a *numerous clausus* ('closed number') against them.[8]

Jew baiting in London, although not commonplace, certainly occurred. For example, in August 1938 on a delicatessen and snack-bar in North London the words, 'Jew shop' were painted. Following this an advertisement appeared in the personal columns of a North London newspaper which stated: 'Miss Frances Fleming, proprietress of a cooked meats business at 83 Bower Road, begs to state she was born at Edmonton, North London. Her father and mother still living are of Irish and Welsh parents. She demands the right as an English citizen to carry on her lawful business without cowardly and unwarranted attacks similar to those of last Saturday.'[9] Soon afterwards a swastika and the words, 'Jews keep out' were burned onto the fourth green at Potter's Bar golf course, Middlesex. Caustic soda had been used to burn the grass; the swastika was about twelve feet high and the words were spread over an area of around one hundred feet.[10]

Instances of Jewish persecution in London by fascist groups had been presented to the House of Commons in 1936. These instances included that of a fascist, a professional boxer, who had regularly struck Jews. Fascists threatened a Jewish woman, telling her that her millinery shop would be burnt down and calling her a 'dirty Jewish cow'. Labels had been pasted onto houses and shop windows with the inscription: 'Get back to the Ghetto,' and, 'Perish Judah'. A spokesperson for the British Imperial Fascist League stated that the Jews in Britain exceeded the unemployment figures. This was a statement similar to that upon which the Nazis had based their uprising in 1933.[11]

A dramatic police move to prevent frequent attacks on Jews in the East End was made after an appeal from leaders of the Socialist Party conference in Edinburgh to: 'Restore the confidence of the East End.' Special foot-patrols of police were allocated to Stepney Green and the mayoress of Stepney, Mrs H. Roberts, stated that residents were in daily need of protection against roaming gangs of fascists. She said that people were afraid of going out at night and that those who lived in the streets where there had been disturbances kept to the back rooms of their houses. She added: 'I have at the Town Hall a collection of weapons found after recent street meetings including a poleaxe, a bent poker, lumps of lead and pieces of railings.'[12]

At a meeting held in the East End of London in 1936, a 'Council of Citizens' had been formed to: 'End grave disorders'. Citizens at the meeting had urged the boycott of demonstrations of a combatant and provocative nature and the *Herald* in an editorial claimed that Jew baiting in the East End had gone beyond a joke. The editorial was unambiguous in pointing out that re-enforcing the police would bring hope to the people and relief from ongoing persecution. The press stated that the cause of all the trouble was a deliberate fascist campaign designed both to insult and harass the Jewish people in the area. The newspaper went on to state that a Mr Herbert Morrison, a member of parliament, had spoken at an anti-Nazi demonstration claiming that he was totally opposed to these kinds of developments and it appeared that the East End was being prepared as a kind of battleground for organised fascism and communism.[13]

Racial violence was becoming endemic to the region and people went in fear for their safety. The East End suffered from such notoriety but this was something more. Yet despite acts of vandalism such as these it should be pointed out that Nazi vilification of the Jewish people did more than anything to heighten British feelings against Nazism. Later in the year, as anti-Semitic hatred increased, the British press was stating very forcefully that the pogrom against the Jewish people would clearly affect British foreign policy. Neville Chamberlain's candidates in four by-elections which were then soon to be held in the country were attempting to persuade their electors to back Chamberlain's appeasement policy. Of course we now know how ineffective that policy was to be but at that time all the people and press could do was to speculate at its possible efficacy. The press was very strongly posing the question of how could anyone become supportive for a proposed friendship with a regime which was bent principally on war, destruction and cruelty. There were enormous risks facing the world, the press stated, risks that did not arise from any kind of bellicose spirit in Britain, but from those who were outraging the collective conscience of humankind.[14]

In the British House of Commons it was revealed that certain German firms in London, allegedly under instructions from the Nazi government, were terminating the employment of Jewish employees, some of whom had worked for the companies for up to twenty years. The

British home secretary, Sir Samuel Hoare, promised to, '...look into the matter'.[15]

***

Lord Winterton later stated at Évian that the possibilities for emigration to Kenya for small scale Jewish settlement had been under consideration by the British government for some time. He added that investigations were underway and that after preliminary discussions with the private organisation concerned, a representative had been sent to Kenya to investigate the question. The subsequent report proved favourable and claimed that a scheme would be implemented by which small numbers of Jewish migrants would be allowed to settle in Kenya.[16]

In any event, the concept was hopelessly optimistic. Confidential documents later revealed that applications for entry were numbering approximately forty or fifty per week, but of these many were rejected on economic grounds. From October 1937 to 24 November, 1938 only 178 refugees were admitted into the country, and while no new Kenyan laws had by then been passed, the Kenyan Legislative Council in Nairobi was working actively towards passing laws to make immigration even more difficult.[17]

Proposals were later discussed to send a large number of German Jews to Tanganyika (later Tanzania) and British Guiana, (later Guyana). However, the major restricting element to these proposals was, as we have seen in so many other proposals, the lack of financing. The governors of Tanganyika and British Guiana had been asked if land could be made available for leasing on generous terms for the purpose of large-scale settlements—and this was certainly approved providing the refugee organisations undertook the costs of preparing the land and settling the refugees.

The press reported:

> In a long statement on refugees from Germany, Mr Chamberlain dealt with the consideration which his Majesty's Government had been giving this problem, and reviewed the results of its inquiry into the possibilities of the settlement of refugees in the colonial Empire and British mandated territory.
>
> Mr Chamberlain said: 'In conformity with the recommendations of the Évian meeting ... his Majesty's Government has had under examination the contribution it can make in respect of the United Kingdom and colonial Empire to international efforts to facilitate the admission and settlement of involuntary immigrants from Germany. It also had in mind the view expressed by the

Évian meeting that the countries of origin of refugees should make their contribution to this problem of migration by enabling intending migrants to take with them their property and possessions. The extent to which countries can be expected to receive immigrants must depend very largely upon the conditions under which they are able to leave the country of origin'.

'His Majesty's Government had been greatly impressed by the urgency of the problem created by the anxiety to migrate overseas of sections of the population in Germany and of individuals who, in consequence of recent events in that country had found temporary asylum in countries of first refuge,' added Mr Chamberlain, 'and in the light of these circumstances and of the Évian recommendations the Government had again reviewed the situation.' Referring first to the position in the United Kingdom itself, he observed that the number of refugees Great Britain could admit, either for temporary stay or permanent settlement, was limited by the capacity of voluntary organisations to undertake the responsibility of selecting, receiving and maintaining them....

The Prime Minister introduced the subject of openings in the colonial Empire with the reminder that, despite the great extent of territory, it was not necessarily capable of absorbing refugees in large numbers, and it and the mandated territories contained native populations of many millions, whose interests must not be prejudiced. This already had been made clear at Évian, but the Governors of Tanganyika and British Guiana had been asked whether land could be made available for leasing it on generous terms, for the purpose of large-scale settlement, to voluntary refugee organisations, provided the latter undertook the responsibility for the cost of preparing the land and settling refugees of a suitable type.[18]

The U.S. consul at Johannesburg later visited Tanganyika and reported that the local government and white residents were very much in favour of allowing Jewish refugees into the country. The consul claimed that the government was thinking in terms of approximately fifty thousand immigrants, but local opinion placed the figure much lower, somewhere in the region of twenty thousand. The Tanganyikan government knew full well that most of the Jewish migrants would not be agriculturists and that the influx of so many refugees would cause considerable business competition with the Indian community which virtually controlled business activities within the country. But this was seen as a healthy change. Indians were known to export their profits back to India where they would not help Tanganyikan economic growth, whereas it was perceived that Jewish businessmen would make their homes in Tanganyika and keep their money within the country.[19]

Another country then under British rule to be considered for agricultural settlements was Rhodesia, (now Zimbabwe). However, the proposal depended upon Hitler allowing the Jews to leave Germany and Austria with sufficient funds to cover the costs of such a venture. In light of Hitler's attitude to the export of Jewish money, the project never materialised.[20]

Britain's intransigence with regard to opening the doors for further Jewish immigration remained in force even after the conference. There seemed to be a special reason for not allowing professional people into the country. Apart from small numbers, refugees with medical qualifications were particularly singled out. In the House of Commons on 11 July, 1938, the prime minister was asked how many refugees' applications for visas had been made since the incorporation of Austria into the Greater German

Reich, and how many of these applications had been granted. The undersecretary of foreign affairs replied: 'During the period in question the number of visas for the United Kingdom granted in Austria was 2,740, while 420 were refused.'[21] Three days later there was a discussion regarding the immigration of doctors to the country. On being asked for details of such immigration, the home secretary replied:

> It has always been recognised that a policy of unrestricted admission would be out of the question. Only a small number of foreign practitioners can be absorbed into the medical and dental professions, and it will be necessary to select this number with care.... I have had discussions with representatives of the principal medical organisations and we both agree that discrimination must be exercised.[22]

France

Henri Berenger, the French ambassador, was next to speak at the Évian conference. He told the delegates that since the end of the First World War, France had become the home of some two hundred thousand refugees and exiles. He said that in a total population of approximately forty million, France then had about three million aliens, adding that such numbers were, '...already the source of many difficulties.[23] Berenger said that many millions of francs had already been expended on hundreds of thousands of refugees and that the country had, '...already reached the extreme point of saturation as regards admission of refugees'.[24]

In a later written confidential statement to the technical subcommittee formed at Évian to examine ways in which refugees might be introduced into the various countries, Berenger commented that France could not accept any quota placed upon her by decisions which might be made at Évian and added that during the previous three months some three thousand refugees had crossed the border into France and that more were arriving daily.[25]

Shortly afterwards the first meeting at Évian ended with a warning to the journalists present to take care in framing their reports and not to publish anything inflammatory that might prejudice the work of the committee or further deepen the plight of those refugees who were still attempting to flee from Germany and Austria. It seems clear, however, that writing anything positive about the events at Évian would have been an almost impossible task. Interestingly, one of these reporters was Hans Habe who later became an internationally acclaimed novelist. His novel, *The Mission,* was based upon his experiences and observations at Évian.

Brazil

The following day, 7 July, the conference resumed with an opening statement by Senor Helio Lobo of Brazil. Despite his country's strict immigration laws, this man was to be of enormous help to the U.S., French and British delegates in tempering the often racially discriminate reactions of many of the delegates of other South American countries.

Lobo stated that Brazil had depended for more than one hundred years on immigration to build the wealth of the country. He said that between 1820 and 1930 more than 4.5 million immigrants, almost all Europeans, had entered the country.[26] In fact, in 1920 some seventeen thousand Jews had been living in Brazil. By 1930 that figure had risen to forty thousand and in 1937 some fifty-five thousand Jews were resident within Brazil.[27]

Lobo pointed out that his country was prepared to increase its immigration quota somewhat, but stipulated that eighty per cent of these immigrants had to be agricultural migrants or technical experts in agriculture.[28]

Indeed, much hope was being placed on Brazil. The country badly needed a large intelligent workforce, it needed an influx of money and business acumen. However, when the U.S. had first proposed the Évian conference the U.S. Department of State had made it quite clear to the participating countries that they would not be expected to change their existing immigration laws. Just prior to the opening of the conference, Brazil did change its immigrations laws, enacting a new law which clearly stipulated that every visa application would have to be accompanied by a certificate of baptism. This new law effectively prevented any Jewish immigration into the country.[29]

Yet perhaps the policies of Brazil (and also of Argentina) in relation to the Évian conference have been somewhat harshly dealt with in this history. Both countries subsequently altered their polices sufficiently to allow reasonable numbers of Jewish refugees to migrate. Brazil had previously allowed some 30,000 Jewish migrants into the country, that number arriving between 1920 and 1930. A growing xenophobia led to severe restrictions by 1934 and before the coup that established the *Estado Novo* of 1937 a top secret communication was released which forbade the granting of visas to Jewish people. At Évian, as we have seen, Brazil joined with almost all other countries in preventing Jewish immigration, but restrictions were subsequently loosened, somewhat. When Oswaldo Aranha, a pro-Jewish foreign minister, was appointed, new rules governing Jewish immigration were issued which reopened Brazilian boarders to Jewish refugees.

During the war, despite specific orders from his government not to do so, the Brazilian diplomat in France, Luis Martins de Souza Dantas would illegally issue diplomatic visas to hundreds of Jewish refugees in Vichy France, literally saving them from the gas chambers.[30]

Belgium

The next to speak at Évian was Monsieur R. de Foy, the Belgian delegate. De Foy claimed that his government had already accepted large numbers of immigrants including 8800 Russian refugees, 2000 German refugees, 800 Austrian refugees and eighty stateless people. He was careful not to point out that many of these refugees were Christians. He then went on to state that he had noted the U.S. government had no intention of extending its current immigration quota of 27,370 people. He also said: 'In view of the large number of refugees already established on her territory, Belgium, to her great regret, is nevertheless under the urgent necessity of reconsidering the problem of refugees before she accepts fresh international obligations.[31]

In a confidential document tabled at the Évian conference, De Foy had written:

> The outlook in the social and economic spheres and the statistics of the country's population have convinced the Belgian authorities of the need for seriously restricting immigration. It is important in the first place that the social organism should absorb the foreign elements which have been allowed to enter and that a remedy should be found for the serious scourge of unemployment which, notwithstanding rises and falls, affects annually about 250,000 Belgian workers....
>
> As regards Jewish immigration, more particularly, Belgium has at present 80,000 Jews, many of them recent arrivals, and the Belgian authorities feel that to avoid provoking social disturbances and perhaps even a wave of anti-Semitism, it is advisable to refrain from settling further numbers of Jews in the country. Belgium is of course prepared to grant transit facilities to German and Austrian émigrés who are, or will in future be holders of permits to settle in the neighbouring countries or in overseas lands, but she cannot agree to her territory

being a waiting room for emigrants who leave their country with the fallacious and purely subjective hope of being allowed to settle in another country.[32]

Australia and New Zealand

Even as late as 27 June, 1938, just ten days before the Évian meeting was due to commence, the Australian and New Zealand governments had still not indicated that they would be attending the conference. This in itself, may be taken as an indication of the reluctance of those governments to allow further migration of Jewish refugees to their shores. In a telegram to the U.S. ambassador in London (the U.S. invitation to Australia and New Zealand had gone through the British government), Sumner Welles had asked, '...have you had any indication whether Australia and New Zealand will be represented at the Évian meeting?'[33] In fact Australia was finally represented by Lieutenant-Colonel Thomas Walter White, Australian minister for trade and customs. New Zealand's delegate was C.B. Burdekin.

Australia's delegate, Lieutenant-Colonel White, had served as a pilot during the Great War. From an early age he had taken a keen interest in military affairs and at the age of thirteen years had joined the citizen forces as a trumpeter in Monash's battery. He was the founder of the aero club at Point Cooke, Victoria, inaugurated in 1914, and qualified as a pilot at Point Cooke, leaving as a captain with the first Australian flying unit in April 1915.

Thomas Walter White

Australia's delegate to Évian.

—*Australian Parliamentary Handbook* – Eleventh edition, 1945 to 1953.

He served for some months in Mesopotamia and, with Captain Yeats-Brown, his observer, was captured by the Turks near Baghdad on 13 November, 1915. He escaped from Turkey into Russia in August 1918, was twice mentioned in dispatches and awarded the Distinguished Flying Cross in recognition of gallantry in landing by aeroplane behind enemy lines in Mesopotamia to destroy telegraph wires. White served in the army continuously until his retirement on the unattached list in 1932. He later wrote a book, *Guests of the Unspeakable,* which includes chapters on his imprisonment. He served again during the Second World War until retiring, medically unfit, in December 1944. He was appointed Australia's high commissioner to London in 1952.[34]

There is little doubt that Australia, being a democratic country, a country with enormous expanses of land, a sound economy and rich in mineral wealth, should have been one of the major asylums for intending Jewish refugees. However, this was not to be the case. According to the immigration regulations in force at the time, every foreigner wishing to settle permanently in Australia had to obtain a landing permit from the government. Australia certainly had liberal immigration laws and it should not have been difficult for intending migrants of good character to enter the country. Close relatives of people already established in the country were welcomed, as were more distant relatives. People who could guarantee that they could incorporate themselves into economic life without prejudice to Australian workers and who would not become public charges were also welcomed. Entry requirements stipulated that each immigrant had to own at least £50 at the time of his or her arrival. Strictly confidential U.S. Department of State files reveal details of a report written in 1938 concerning Australia's ability to accept large numbers of Jewish refugees. The report claimed:

> Australia is at present one of the countries with regard to which greatest hopes can be entertained for future [Jewish refugee] immigration. This country in fact requires labour not only for its agricultural but also for its industry.... The number of Jews who have immigrated into Australia between 1920 and 1929 amounts to 5000—6000. After 1930 Jewish immigration also underwent, for several years, a period of an almost total inactivity ... [although] quite recently it seems to have resumed its steady flow....
>
> Although little important in itself, this increase certainly is a consequence of the change for the better.... Considering that real possibilities present themselves in Australian industry as well as in agriculture,

there is every ground to believe that the movement will go on increasing.[35]

Refugees were welcomed to the country by three organisations, the Australian Jewish Welfare Society, the German Jewish Relief Fund and the Polish Jewish Relief Fund. The type of people the Australian government was willing to allow into the country included, '...tailors, mechanics of all descriptions, industrial workmen such as founders, turners, moulders, adjusters, draughtsmen, diesel-motor experts, toolmakers, electrical engineers, wireless experts and designers, plumbers, upholsterers, clockmakers, watchmakers, engravers, English stenographers and typists, milliners, domestic servants'.[36]

When the time came for Australia's representative, T.W. White, to speak at the Évian conference, it was widely believed that at last here would be a country that would offer generous and positive action in an effort to alleviate the sufferings of hundreds of thousands of people. Australia was a country with vast potential for large numbers of immigrants, and even the British tended to believe that an antipodean liberality over immigration would ease the pressure then being placed on the British over the Palestine issue. However, there is little doubt that the Australian government had no reason to be proud of its performance at the Évian conference.

Lord Winterton had already stated the case of Britain and her colonies, although Australia, as a dominion rather than a colony, was a free partner in the Commonwealth and, as White stated, '...arbiters of their own economy and national destiny'.[37] White claimed that Australia had its own particular difficulties with regards to economy and unemployment. He added: '...[The] United States and Australia owe their development to migration from the old world. This is so, and in Australia's case such migration has naturally been predominantly British, nor is it desired that this be largely departed from while British settlers are forthcoming'.[38]

White said that the Australian government would include a small number of Jewish migrants on a pro-rata basis, but qualified the statement with:

> Under the circumstances Australia cannot do more, for it will be appreciated that in a young country, manpower from the source from which most of its citizens have sprung is preferred, while undue privileges cannot be given to one particular class of non-British subjects without injustice to others. It will no doubt be appreciated also that as we have no real racial problem

we are not desirous of importing one by encouraging any scheme of large-scale foreign migration.

Moreover, it will, I hope, be also realised that in the particular circumstances of our development we are confining migration principally to those who will engage in trades and occupations in which there is opportunity for work without detriment to the employment of our own people.[39]

In fact Australian immigration laws had been somewhat liberalised during the preceding few years. At the time of the Great Depression alien immigration into the country had been confined almost entirely to close relatives of people already living in the country or to people who could prove that they owned at least £500—a not inconsiderable figure in the days when a reasonable house could be purchased for half that amount. However, in March 1936 the Australian government decided to liberalise the immigration laws providing for people who could be nominated by friends already in the country and dropping the financial requirement to £50 for people with guarantors or £200 for people without guarantors.[40]

At this time no encouragement at all was being given to the immigration of Jews and it was official Australian government policy to allow only five hundred Jews per annum to enter the country, a policy designed to prevent the setting up of Jewish colonies. In fact, White grossly overstated his government's intentions concerning Jewish immigrants. In the decade 1933 to 1943, only nine thousand Jews were allowed to emigrate to Australia.

In Manchester, Lord Summers, a former governor of Victoria, publicly described Australia as, '...a hoop with nothing in the centre and people living on the rim in which there are enormous gaps'. Yet despite this, Summers went on to say that Australia was unable to absorb a large number of migrants.[41]

Of course Australia was simply following the British and U.S. examples concerning Jewish immigration. Great Britain stated at the conference that an influx of Jews from Germany would, '...arouse anti-Semitic feelings in Great Britain,' adding that none of the British dominions were suitable for large-scale resettlement. No mention was made of Palestine.

A graphic example of Australia's attitude to the Jewish problem may be seen in an event that occurred shortly after the Évian conference. As anti-Semitic activity increased dramatically throughout Germany and Austria many Jews, of course, managed to escape. Some travelled to

Australia as 'tourists', admitting as they arrived without immigration permits that they were desperate. In October 1938, three months after the Évian conference, the steamship *Nieww Holland* arrived at Brisbane from Holland loaded with hopeful Jewish migrants. On board were also twenty-two Austrian Jews, three German Jews and two Czechoslovakian Jews, all of whom were not permitted to land. Although they had purchased return tickets beforehand, these 'tourists' all admitted to Australian immigration officials that they wanted to find employment in Australia and to make Australia their permanent home. Their occupations varied from medicine, engineering and law, to textile manufacturing. They all had letters of credit assuring the immigration officials that they could be self-supporting, and all had at least £200, the minimum then required under existing Australian immigration laws. This money had been smuggled quietly out of Austria and Germany and sent to friends in Belgium and Holland. For a while it seemed that the intransigence of Australian immigration laws would mean that the refugees would have to be returned to their countries of origin, in effect a virtual death sentence. Shortly afterwards the *Nieww Holland* left Brisbane for Sydney and immigration officials referred the case to Canberra. Finally, the minister for the interior,

John McEwen, (later prime minister), stated that the Jews could land. In light of the news of Nazi atrocities, a blank refusal on behalf of the Joseph Lyons' United Australia Party government would have meant political suicide.[42]

Some time previously, Lyons had received a letter from a Jewish lady in London which had stated:

> A great number of Australia's puny population, I believe, are foreigners. Why not encourage Jewish refugees to come to your country.... This plea is made on behalf of exiled German and Austrian Jews.[43]

However, Lyons later publicly confirmed the government's policy that no encouragement would be given to the migration of Jewish refugees.[44]

In London, Liberal politician Sir Percy Harris, speaking in the House of Commons, stated that it was distressing that more encouragement had not been given to using the vast territories of Australia as an answer to the Jewish question at Évian. He said that many countries were casting hungry eyes on some of the Empire's undeveloped lands and that it was a pity Australia was not more sympathetic.[45]

Shortly after Évian the Australian minister for the interior, John McEwen announced new and stringent laws to prevent the growth of alien communities in Australia. The local press reporting:

> The Federal cabinet has decided to check the growth of alien communities in Australia. This is one of the series of important migration decisions announced by the Minister for the Interior. The decision applies specifically to the [sugar] cane-field areas of Queensland and the Murrumbidgee and Shepparton irrigation areas.
>
> No special facilities are to be granted for the admission of European Jews, and there is to be a general tightening up of the examination system which precedes the issue of landing permits.
>
> 'We will not approve or facilitate the group migration of aliens, and propose to prevent the continued aggregation of foreign nationals in certain areas.' said Mr McEwen, in announcing the Government's future policy.
>
> 'I have refused hundreds of applications from foreigners who wished to go to the sugar-growing areas of Queensland. There already is ample labour in those areas, and further extension is not practicable. All aliens now seeking admission must satisfy me that they will not seek employment in the sugarcane industry.... Since Germany's

occupation of Austria ... many inquiries have been made regarding the position of Jews who desire to settle in Australia. Each case is dealt with on its merits, but no special facilities can be granted for the admission of groups of Jewish migrants'.[46]

Australia's representative at Évian, T.W. White, was almost certainly aware of these impending changes to the Australian immigration laws when he made his disappointing speech in July 1938.

In November 1938 the Australian Jewish Welfare Society formed a company, Mutual Farmers Pty. Ltd., with the intention of settling Jewish migrants on farms in the Murrumbidgee area of New South Wales. However, the society stated that it was definitely against group settlement, adding that it was the fixed policy of the society to assist only such Jewish refugees who would not come into competition with Australian workers. Preference would be given to agricultural workers, skilled technicians and children. The society also insisted upon all Jewish migrants applying for naturalisation at the earliest opportunity. An organisation that preferred to remain anonymous sent £10,000 to Sydney to be expended on the purchase of equipment for farms on which experienced and locally trained migrants could be placed. The money was given on terms of call for neither interest nor guarantee of payment. The sole requisite being that the security of the capital was guaranteed.[47]

The Australian press was also cautious over the refugee issue. For example the *Maryborough Chronicle,* in Queensland, reported:

> It would be absurd, however, to take up the attitude that there is no room in Australia for a controlled flow of migration. If there is no inclination by British people to migrate to the Commonwealth, it is reasonable that the Commonwealth should open its doors to the foreigner; but it is entitled to say what type of foreigner shall make his home in this country. To open wide the doors to an unrestricted flow of foreign migrants, irrespective of type or their financial position, would be to create unnecessary difficulties in Australia itself, social and industrial....
>
> It is hardly necessary to add that Australia is not under obligation to admit thousands of foreign migrants who might become a charge on the nation, or who might, if the flow were uncontrolled, undermine the high economic standards which Australia is endeavouring to build up. There is, however, a welcome in this

country, or there ought to be, for the foreigner who is not afraid of work, who is guaranteed financially by his friends already settled here, or has sufficient funds of his own to make him independent of governmental assistance.[48]

In January 1939 a steamer named the *Oronsay* carrying approximately one hundred and twenty Jewish refugees arrived at Fremantle. They brought with them tales of hardship and suffering, the loss of their funds and of careers cut short. Most were bound for Melbourne and others for Sydney. About half the men had been in prison since the *Anschluss* and all had lost most of their property. The party included a doctor, a scientist, a lawyer, musicians, photographers and manufacturers. The press reported:

> Only a few would discuss their experiences in Austria and they kept an eye opened for men onboard whom they suspected of being Nazi spies. One refugee was telling a story and stopped suddenly until a man who passed was out of hearing distance. 'That man is a German, we are not sure of him.'[49]

***

New Zealand—allied to Australia in so many ways—also had fairly liberal immigration laws.

The conditions of immigrant admission being very similar to those of Australia, although as the country is far smaller than Australia the number of immigrants allowed entry was somewhat restricted.

Applications were made through two major societies, the Jewish Philanthropic Society in Wellington and the Council for German Jewry in the same city.[50] Those most likely to be allowed entry included, '...qualified artisans, skilled workmen such as tailors, joiners, carpenters, turners, adjusters, motorcar mechanics, masons, founders, metallurgical workmen, plumbers, and engineers'. The New Zealand government also welcomed people who owned sufficient capital and were capable of establishing new industries that would contribute to the economic development of the country.[51] Documents tendered at the Évian conference pointed out that persons of non British origin came under the regulations of the Immigration Restriction Act of 1919 which stipulated that permits had to be obtained by anyone not of British heritage before they could enter the country. However, there was no quota system nor was there a requirement for a minimum amount of capital. Yet the New Zealand delegate to the Évian conference, C.B. Burdekin, made no specific promises of how many European refugees would be allowed into the country.[52]

Burdekin later stated publicly that, '...it would only be raising false hopes to suggest that the acceptance by New Zealand of any large number of refugees could be anticipated'.[53]

Canada

Following the Australian delegate at Évian the representative of Canada, Humphrey Hume Wrong, rose to deliver his message. H.H. Wrong was a professor, diplomat and historian who would serve as the Canadian ambassador to Washington from 1946 to 1953. His brother, Harold Verschoyle Wrong, had been killed fighting the Germans on the Somme during the First World War.[54]

Wrong said that in the past his government had not been ungenerous in allowing large numbers of migrants to stay in the country and added that after the First World War no fewer than ten thousand political refugees had found a permanent home in Canada. However, Wrong also stated that because of the Great Depression the country had experienced severe economic hardship, and, as a result of these circumstances, the Canadian government had been forced to alter its immigration laws. He said that it was impossible to absorb immigrants in any significant numbers and added that these stringent immigration laws were still in force and it was not foreseen that any liberalisation of the laws could be made in the immediate future. Using Roosevelt's own original stipulation that no country would be required to alter its current immigration laws to facilitate greater immigration, Wrong pointed out that under the present circumstances and within these laws it would be impossible to take more than a token number of refugees. He added, 'Unfortunately the continuance of serious unemployment and of economic uncertainty and disturbance still limits severely Canadian power to absorb any considerable number of immigrants.'[55]

According to Canadian immigration laws only close relatives of Canadian residents, farmers provided with the sum of £1000 or other refugees with a minimum capital of £5000 (an extraordinary amount of money at that time) were entitled to enter the country.[56] In order to enter Canada it was necessary to obtain a permit from the central government in Ottawa. The granting of this permit, even to close relatives of Canadian residents, was subject to the deposit of varying sums of money.

Applications for Jewish residency in Canada were usually presented by the Jewish Immigrant

Aid Society of Montreal. This was affiliated with the HIAS-JCA organisation which submitted the applications to the Department of Immigration and Colonization in Ottawa. Since 1931 the strict application of the immigration law had been somewhat severe, and, according to a confidential U.S. Department of State report of 30 June, 1938, instructions had been given to the Canadian Railway and Navigation companies, who were charged with recruiting foreign agricultural labour, that they were not to accept any demands emanating from Jewish agriculturists, even in cases where such candidates satisfied all of the regular conditions of the law. However, as the U.S. report stated:

Humphrey Hume Wrong Canadian delegate to Évian.

—National Archives of Canada

This deplorable state of affairs has been recently modified and the Director of the Department of Colonization and Agriculture has just informed the President of the Jewish Immigrant Aid Society that from now on the applications of 'bona fide' Jewish agriculturists will be examined under the same conditions as those emanating from the prospective immigrants of other nationalities.[57]

The person responsible for Canadian immigration was Frederick Charles Blair, the director of the immigration branch of the Department of Mines and Resources. Blair believed that the doors of Canada should be closed entirely to all Jews, no matter what their predicament. It was a direct result of Blair's stringently enforced immigration regulations that Canada, one of the 'Nations of Asylum' with enormous potential for the induction of immigrants, actually allowed less than five thousand Jewish refugees into the country during the twelve years of Nazi domination in Europe.

Such stringency had not always been the case. In 1923 the Canadian government authorised the JCA to admit into the country five thousand Russian Jews stranded in Romania. The authorisation was granted on the express condition that the association would assume the responsibility with regard to their reception and later with regard to their establishment in Canada. A confidential U.S. Department of State report claimed that in 1924 over three thousand refugees had been established in the country and were distributed to various centres according to a 'preconceived plan'. If the Canadians could do this for Russian refugees then why could they not offer the same service to the desperate Jewish refugees from Germany and Austria?[58]

Argentina

Doctor Tomas A. Le Breton of Argentina told the Évian conference that his country had already accepted large numbers of immigrants. He stated that for every forty-eight refugees who had been allowed to enter the U.S., thirty-eight had entered Argentina. Le Breton pointed out that this was proportionately a far higher quota by land mass than the U.S. and that the country would continue to accept immigrants under its existing immigration laws. He warned, however, that intending migrants had to be primarily agriculturists. He said that any migrant group could enter Argentina but only if they adopted Argentinean ways and left their old lives and privileges behind. Le Breton stated, 'Our extreme liberality will never go so far as to lead us to grant to new immigrants a situation of advantage or privilege as compared with nationals of the Argentine or other immigrants who have already established themselves in our country.[59]

After the war, of course, Argentina was only too willing to allow fleeing Nazis into the country. According to an Argentinean government inquiry conducted in the late 1990s, senior officials had met at the *Casa Rosada* palace in Buenos Aires in order to discuss the possibilities of allowing Nazis into the country, particularly those who could bring scientific or technical skills.[60]

Netherlands

Netherlands representative, W.C. Beucker-Andreae, head of the legal section at the Ministry of Foreign Affairs, was next to speak at Évian. His message was even more resolute, stating that no more refugees would be allowed into his country. Yet the refusal was eloquent. Beucker-Andreae stated that his country desired to play a part in contributing to finding a solution to the refugee problem by, '...encouraging the organisation of the migration of refugees'. He said that as his country was a neighbour to Germany his government had become one of the countries of first refuge. He added: 'My country has followed an age-old tradition in granting generous hospitality to such refugees. When the inflow continued, however, it became increasingly aware of the fact that it was impossible for it to continue to absorb such great numbers.' He said that his government had established a number of agricultural training establishments for the training for various industrial occupations so that the refugees could be trained prior to emigrating to countries of permanent residence. He concluded:

> The density of our population, which had already led the Netherlands Government to encourage the emigration of its own nationals, the very serious unemployment in the country—an average of 400,000—were facts that prevented the Netherlands government to its great regret from admitting any continuation of the inflow of refugees. For the moment, the Government is not in a position to admit any refugees.[61]

Sweden

Sweden was represented at Évian by the highly respected Gosta Engzell, head of the legal department of the Ministry for Foreign Affairs, and later the Swedish ambassador to Finland.[62] He was assisted by C.A.M. de Hallenborg, chief of bureau at the Ministry for Foreign Affairs. Secretary of the Swedish delegation at Évian was Eric Drougge—the secretary of the 'Administration of Labour and Social Affairs'.

Gosta Engzell

Head of the legal department of the Ministry for Foreign Affairs.

–Gosta Engzell

Their official immigration manifesto as presented to the conference was ambiguous. The document claimed that since the end of the First World War Sweden had experienced an influx of refugees from countries east of the Baltic Sea, and during the years following Hitler's rise to power the country had accepted large numbers of refugees from Germany and Austria. Yet the Swedish delegation claimed that Sweden was not a country with great resources or the availability to absorb tens of thousands of Jewish refugees. The immigration laws did not adhere to any quota system but rather relied on each case being examined individually. The confidential Swedish document ended:

> The unemployment that, to a certain degree still persists in Sweden is, however, being particularly felt in ... branches of economic life. This evidently means a serious obstacle in the matter of finding work for the refugees. It has further been found that the economic structure of the country, the absence of big cities and generally the conditions of work and life in Sweden, considerably different as they are from those of the continent, involve difficulties as to the assimilation of refugees coming from central Europe.[63]

To its credit, however, the Swedish *Riksdag*, later appropriated the sum of half a million crowns for the relief of political refugees, although members of the *Riksdag* were split over the issue. Some members of the Peasant Unionist Party confessed to strong anti-Semitic reservations, stating that if the government eased its restrictions the country would soon have a Jewish problem of its own. Other political parties took a different view. The Social Democrats protested 'very vigorously' over statements made by the Peasant Unionists and professed that they were pro-Semitic. The outcome of the debate proved that the majority of the government, while restrictive, was indeed pro-Semitic. Swedish press reports often differed in this view. These differences were highlighted when a plan was announced to allow a certain number of Jewish doctors, dentists and chemists into the country. The press roundly condemned the plan and 1500 students of the University of Uppsala demonstrated against it—the largest such university demonstration in the history of the country up until that time. The students strongly resented such an immigration allowance, claiming that the government should not allow any intellectuals into the country to assume the duties that might be filled by Swedish men or women. They sent a resolution to the king protesting against the immigration and a similar resolution was later signed by students of the Caroline Medical Institute at Stockholm. These demonstrations caught the Swedish press off balance. Journalists and editors, despite their own often strongly anti-Semitic stance, had been expecting a somewhat more liberal attitude from the country's blossoming intelligentsia.[64]

Finland

Finland too was finding trouble in establishing a sound policy regarding the Jewish refugees. When fifty-five Jewish refugees later arrived from Austria aboard the steamer *Ariadne*, they were detained aboard the vessel for a day before being allowed to land. Later the Finnish cabinet decided at a special meeting to permit them to remain in Finland as long as the local Jewish communities would provide food and lodgings for them until they could obtain a permit to enter some other country. Those who were not able to leave Finland were informed that they would be returned to Germany. Yet when these people had reluctantly been issued visas to enter Finland by the Finnish vice-consul in Vienna, they had been forced to sign an agreement never to return to Greater Germany.

Up until that time very few Jews from Austria or Germany were reported to have sought refuge in Finland. However, the increasing number of refugees, according to a statement made to the press by the Finnish minister of justice, forced the Finnish authorities to take new and forceful measures to control refugee immigration.

Finnish newspapers and other forms of periodical publications largely followed the rest of the world in their attitude towards Jewish migration. Many pointed out that the country did not then have a 'Jewish problem' and that Finland would struggle to find the resources to allow for any kind of mass migration. There were the typical concerns that Jewish refugees would not be able to support themselves and that without financial means they would present a burden on the Finnish economy. These were all fairly standard arguments being used to prevent any kind of mass migration into the country. Some publications were wholly sympathetic towards the plight of the refugees, but hearts were being steeled against too much compassion, and newspapers in particular played an important role in hardening public attitude towards creating a strongly conservative approach to the issue.[65]

This attitude was not confined only to regional publications with agrarian readerships. Much larger publications were also of the same opinion and they mainly stuck to the accepted argument of economic unviability. How could a small country like Finland with its limited resources support such mass migration? The publications quite clearly stated that one country like Germany making the lives of so many innocent people intolerable was terrible, but the difficulties that such persecution would cause to other nations would be economically impossible to resolve.[66]

However, despite these rather hard-edged policies the government of Finland would, during the war, refuse to deport almost all of the Finnish and refugee Jews to Germany. Finland was a co-belligerent with Germany, fighting with them against the Soviet Union and its allies, and did not consider itself as having any real 'Jewish problem'. However, the Finnish secret police did arrange for the deportation of more than fifty Austrian and German Jews, although after considerable protest these deportations were cancelled.[67]

Jesus Maria Yepes

One of the Colombian delegates to Évian.

Professor Yepes was a legal counsellor to the permanent delegation accredited to the League of Nations.

Doctor Luis Cano

Permanent delegate to the League of Nations, with the rank of envoy extraordinary and minister plenipotentiary. Cano was one of Colombia's representatives to Évian.

—Government of Colombia, supplied by Fernardo Navas de Bridgard. Australian Ambassador of Colombia.

Colombia

The representative of Colombia, Professor Jesus Maria Yepes, was next at the Évian podium. Yepes made an eloquent speech but it ended, unsurprisingly, on a negative note:

...we have already received a large number of European political refugees and sometimes the Government has officially entered into contract with them to secure their services in education or other national undertakings. Unfortunately, and despite our humanitarian feelings, we could not indefinitely maintain this policy and we found ourselves compelled to limit immigration so that it includes only agricultural workers of honourable character who are prepared to come and work on the land. Such immigrants will always be welcome in Colombia, but we cannot accept—nor would we tolerate—the entry of undesirable persons on the pretext that they were going to engage in agricultural work, thereby entering our country illegally. As regards intellectuals or traders, middlemen of all kinds, we cannot encourage their immigration into our country; for, as we are above all an agricultural country, we do not desire to bring about an organised foreign competition with our own workmen, who are not very numerous in our cities, nor do we wish to upset national trade or the liberal professions, which are already overcrowded with our own nationals.[68]

Yepes went on to berate France, Great Britain and the Netherlands for their tardiness in not opening up their various colonies to large-scale immigration. He ended by stating quite emphatically, '*Messieurs les Francais, Messieurs les Anglai, Messieurs les Hollandais,* it is for you to act first, it is to you that this appeal is addressed.'[69]

Yet these were empty words, designed perhaps to bring about policy changes in those countries whose intransigence was assiduous. Yepes possibly hoped that by attacking those larger countries, forcing them to reconsider their strict policies, it would effectively take the pressure from smaller, less developed nations such as Colombia. Yepes later went into great detail of Colombia's immigration restrictions, pointing out to the Évian technical subcommittee that his government was concerned over the possibility of having large numbers of Jewish refugees who might eventually become politically destructive. He quoted statistics to show that Colombia had already allowed a significant number of refugees into the country, adding:

> The fact that most of these immigrants are of the Semitic race, and in particular the fact that more than 95% of those who recently entered Colombia are competing in a ruinous and not always honest manner

with national traders, has evoked very widespread and deeply felt opposition to this current form of immigration. The government and parliament are constantly being asked by public opinion to impose fresh restrictions on immigration. In these circumstances it would be impossible to secure the necessary ratification by the legislature of an international agreement implying an undertaking to facilitate explicitly Jewish immigration, even in small proportions.[70]

Indeed, after the Évian conference was over and the text of its resolutions had been communicated to the Colombian secretary general, Senor Alfredo Michelsen, Michelsen stated that the class of Jewish refugees who had already been allowed into the country was, 'very low,' and that they had caused constant trouble. He claimed that they had caused considerable political agitation and many had been expelled.[71] In Germany there were several honorary Jewish consuls representing Colombia and these, according to the Colombian government, had improperly issued a great many visas to Jewish refugees. Many of these refugees had been businessmen and merchants and the influx of so many Jewish people of the business class was,

'...seriously disturbing the Colombian merchants' trade'.[72]

To his credit, Yepes was later to state that the conference was becoming a farce and called upon the other delegates to act according to their principles, rather than merely on facts.

The Dominican Republic

The Dominican Republic was one of the very few countries at Évian to offer any concrete proposals, although, in retrospect, even those were limited. Virgilio Trujillo Molina, the Dominican representative to Évian, made a moving statement which lead the small number of real humanitarian gestures made at Évian. Molina said:

> Men, women and innocent children, without a country and without a home, lacking food and lacking employment, deprived not only of a livelihood but also of their rights as individuals, would perish from hunger if we here did not make it our urgent task to alleviate their grievous hardships. If we place our sense of public duty at the service of this noble humiliation and hardship, the whole world will be grateful to us and President Roosevelt's

name will be blessed by present and future generations.

The Dominican Government which for many years past has been encouraging and promoting the development of agriculture by appropriate measures and which gives ample immigration facilities to agriculturists who wish to settle in the country as colonists, would be prepared to make its contribution by granting specially advantageous concessions to Austrian and German exiles, agriculturists with an unimpeachable record who satisfy the conditions laid down by Dominican legislation on emigration.

For colonisation purposes my Government has at its disposal large areas of fertile, well-irrigated land, excellent roads and a police force which preserves absolute order and guarantees the peace of the country. The Department of Agriculture could give colonists, in addition to land, seed and the technical advice which they need.[73]

Virgilio Trujillo Molina, later made the only concrete offer at Évian, initially stating that his country would accept up to ten thousand immigrants. For a small Caribbean island this was indeed a remarkable offer. Yet even more remarkably, the offer was later increased to, '...between fifty and one hundred thousand refugees'. However, classified U.S. Department of State intelligence soon afterwards ascertained that this could only be a gesture and that the country was not in a position, either financially, socially, or from an aspect of policy, to accept such numbers. R. Henry Norweb, the U.S. ambassador to Santo Domingo, stated that the Dominican government's real intentions were to import, 'neo-white' agricultural workers from Puerto Rico, '...where they would be sent to the frontier provinces to form a bulwark against Haitian infiltration'. Norweb added that the Dominican offer was merely a gesture and that it should not be taken at face value.[74] Because of this and through subsequent events inside Germany, the rising tide of antiSemitism that swept over intending refugees, only a few hundred Jews eventually found refuge in the Dominican Republic. Two thousand applied soon after the Dominican announcement, but of these only twenty were found to have the necessary capital and entry requirements. The U.S. Department of State was later advised that most of those who were finally allowed into the country considered the island merely a stepping stone for future immigration into the U.S.[75]

According to U.S. intelligence, internally the Dominicans were largely against any significant Jewish immigration, and a later report stated that there was no real capacity in the republic to set up Jewish colonies unless the refugees themselves were able to bring substantial sums of money with them.[76] Strict Dominican immigration laws stipulated that an entry fee of $500 was required for intending immigrants.[77]

A fact-finding mission to the Dominican Republic later found that there were large areas of land that could be made available to Jewish refugees. Some of this land was owned by the Dominican government and substantial holdings were owned by President Rafael Leónidas Trujillo who anticipated making an enormous profit by selling his holdings to the refugees. Clearly there were cynical aspects to the country's immigration policies—the flooding of a border region with a population that might help prevent enemy infiltration, and a profit-making venture of the most repugnant nature.[78]

Despite these reservations and problems the Dominican efforts of assimilating Jewish refugees into the country have, historically speaking, been well regarded. The Dominican Republic Settlement Association (DORSA) was formed with the objective of settling Jewish people on the northern coast, and five thousand visas were issued. Of these only eight hundred people actually reached the settlement. There the town of Sosua was founded. $5000 in gold was reportedly paid to President Trujillo for every Jewish refugee taken in by the Dominican Republic, the money coming from the organisation called Jewish International in New York.[79]

In 1998, on the sixtieth anniversary of the Évian conference, at a special Israel Council meeting on foreign relations, the Canadian Jewish Congress joined with other world leaders in paying tribute to the Dominican Republic for its efforts during and after the conference.

Nicaragua, Costa Rica, Honduras, Panama and Haiti

Representatives of the governments of Nicaragua, Costa Rica, Honduras and Panama evidently believed their own immigration problems were so similar that they decided to offer a joint declaration to the delegates of the Évian conference. This statement provided for an agreement in principle of setting up a permanent intergovernmental committee to seek resolutions to the refugee problem, but also added:

> Though new countries like our own are saturated with foreign elements, we cannot deny that the arrival of the latter had

contributed to raising the level of our wealth and civilization. We are, however, limited by the scantiness of our resources and our small powers of assimilation, and, while we cannot refuse, we can equally not exceed the quota which, territorially speaking, would be in proportion to that of other nations here represented.

We must also declare that our own governments cannot undertake to bring in or settle at their own expense any refugee. Consequently, any immigrant who wishes to settle must do so at his own expense and risk. Further, we declare that no traders or intellectuals can be accepted as immigrants by our countries which may already have a glut of these elements.[80]

These sentiments were also later echoed by the representative of the Haitian government, lawyer Leon Robert Thébaud.[81]

Paraguay

Paraguay representative, Gustavo A. Wiengreen, issued a similar statement. Wiengreen admitted that Paraguay, '...possesses an immense territory of extraordinary fertility,' which was much too thinly populated. He added that Paraguay took a highly favourable view of immigration of industrious individuals capable of developing the nation's wealth, but ended, as so many other delegates had already done, by saying that any immigration into the country would have to be subject to strict selective procedures and that only trained agriculturists would find a ready welcome.[82]

Cuba

Cuba's representative, Juan Antiga Escobar, pointed out at Évian that his country had been wracked by internal political turmoil for years and as a result many people had been forced to flee from Cuba and had received asylum in a wide diversity of countries. Therefore the Cuban people, he claimed, realised the importance of finding refuge for people who were forced to flee from persecution. However, Escobar pointed out that Cuba was dependent almost entirely on the production of sugar, and the low world prices of sugar were barely covering the costs of production. There were, he said, fifty thousand unemployed workers and intellectuals in Cuba, and in such a depressed situation, '...in spite of our great desire to help in the solution of this question, the government of Cuba is in a very difficult situation for receiving fresh immigrants'.[83]

Indeed, as Charles Patterson details in his history, *Anti-Semitism—the Road to the Holocaust and Beyond* (p 78) one of the more tragic events concerning Jewish immigration to Cuba was that of the case of the steamship *St. Louis* which left Hamburg on 13 May, 1939, (about ten months after Évian) with 937 Jewish refugees on board. These refugees all possessed landing permits for Cuba. However, upon their arrival at Havana the Cuban government authorities decided not to permit them to land. The ship left port and cruised somewhat aimlessly for a while as various nations, including the United States, refused them entry. Some were eventually allowed to land in England others in France, Belgium and Holland. Many of those who were returned to Europe were, of course, later engulfed in the spreading evil of Hitler's regime.

Among the passengers of the ship was Rudolf Cohen (later Dr Rudolph Jacobson), the son of Margarete Jacobsohn. Rudolf had been born on 11 May, 1933, at Insterburg, East Prussia, although his parents were divorced the following year. In October Rudolf's mother married Erich Jacobsohn and the family moved to Bamberg. During the terrible events which became known as *Kristallnacht,* (9 November, 1938) Rudolf's stepfather was arrested and subsequently incarcerated at Dachau. However, Margarete was able to secure his release by obtaining landing permits for Cuba and purchasing tickets for the family aboard the *St. Louis*. The ship left on 13 May, 1939, but after it had been returned to Europe the family was able to find refuge in Holland. They went to Rotterdam and were subsequently interned in the Heijplaat region (also reported as Heijplatte). However, they were later allowed to emigrate to the United States having received sponsorship and funding from Erich's cousin, Fanny Osterdman. They arrived at New Jersey on 9 February, 1940.[84]

Rudy Jacobsohn with his aunt, Elsie Spickler shortly after arriving in the United States.

—United States Holocaust Memorial Museum, courtesy of Dr Rudolph Jacobson.

Two young members of the Hermanns family outside their home in Moenchengladbach, Germany.

—United States Holocaust Memorial Museum, courtesy of Kurt & Jill Berg Pauly.

Far sadder was the case of the Hermanns family (pictured above). Julius Hermanns was a textile merchant who lived with his wife, Grete and teenage daughter, Hilde, at Moenchengladbach, Germany. He would later be arrested, sent firstly to Dachau and then Buchenwald, but was released having promised the Nazi authorities that he would emigrate as soon as possible. He was able to purchase a ticket aboard the *St. Louis* but being unable to pay for his wife and daughter was forced to leave them behind in the hope that he would later be able to get them to safety. After the *St. Louis* had been returned to Europe Julius found refuge in France, but he was again arrested as an enemy alien and sent to an internment camp at Saint Cyprien, on the Spanish border. He was subsequently transferred to the Drancy transit camp at Paris and deported to Auschwitz, described as being 'the most heinous place on earth', where he was killed. Grete and Hilde were deported to the Riga Ghetto where they too were probably killed.[85]

Other passengers of the *St. Louis* included Kurt and Else Stein and their infant son, Werner. After the *St. Louis* had been returned to Europe the family would go to Holland, hoping that they would be safe there. However, following the German invasion of the Netherlands they were to be arrested and interned at Westerbork where a special transit camp had been set up for Dutch Jews who were to be held until trains could take them on to Auschwitz. They remained at the Westerbork camp until September 1943 when they were deported to Auschwitz where they all died. Else and Kurt were gassed immediately upon arrival.[86]

Kurt and Else Stein with their son, Werner.

—United States Holocaust Memorial Museum, courtesy of Gerd Siegel.

More fortunate among the *St. Louis* passengers were Adolf [Aron] Aberbach and his wife, Anna. Both Adolf and Anna had been born in the Ukraine but at the time of the *Anschluss* were living in Vienna. Their sons, Julian and Joachim, who were both then living in the United States, managed to secure visas and entry tickets to Cuba for their parents and Adolf and Anna sailed aboard the *St. Louis*. The sons, meanwhile, caught a bus to Miami and then went on to Cuba to meet their parents. However, when the *St. Louis* passengers were unable to land, the sons managed to acquire a small dinghy and went out to the ship which was then in the centre of the harbour. After the ship had been returned to Europe the parents disembarked in France, uncertain of their future. Julian then flew to France and was able eventually to succeed in bringing both his parents safely to the United States.

German passport issued to Viennese Jews, Adolf (Aron) Aberbach and his wife, Anna.

–United States Holocaust Memorial Museum, courtesy of Julian Aberbach.

Venezuela

Venezuela's representative at Évian, Carlos Aristimuno-Coll, admitted that his country would be excellent for immigration purposes, stating that it was a vast country which was thinly populated. He warned, however, that it was also a difficult country with high mountains and extremes of temperatures, and that such formidable conditions were not always suitable to some people. He added, 'It is therefore essential to make very detailed and minute surveys before deciding what nationalities, what categories and what number of people we can admit to increase our population and stimulate our economic development without injuring our national interests.[87]

Ireland

Francis Thomas Cremins was Ireland's delegate to Évian, a highly experienced diplomat, he was Ireland's permanent delegate to the League of Nations. When the original invitations had been sent to the various countries requesting their participation at Évian, the U.S. Department of State had deliberately omitted several countries, including Ireland, because it was perceived that those countries could have offered little in the way of immigration possibilities for the hundreds of thousands now wishing to flee from Nazi Germany. Ireland almost immediately protested, claiming that diplomatically they should have been invited to the conference. When the U.S. Department of State received the diplomatic protest they soon afterwards apologised and forwarded an invitation. However, diplomatic niceties having been observed, Ireland, in reality, could do nothing at all to help alleviate the problem, and Cremins openly admitted this at Évian. When one reads his statement, it is difficult to understand why the Irish had insisted on attending the meeting at all. Cremins said:

Ireland is a small country with jurisdiction over a population of something less than three million people. Notwithstanding the steady progress which has been made in recent years in regard to the creation of new industries, by far the greater part of our people still derive, and will continue to derive, their living from the land. I need not attempt to explain the land problems which have arisen in Ireland; it is sufficient to say that there is not enough land available to satisfy the needs of our own people.

Although every effort is being made by the Government to expedite industrialisation in a country which had been greatly under-industrialised, the new industries are not yet capable of absorbing the regular increase in our population, so that each year numbers of young people are forced by circumstances to emigrate. While such emigration remains imposed upon our national economy, it is obvious that we can make no real contribution to the resettlement of refugees....

It has, I think, emerged from the speeches already made that there is little likelihood that the fully-settled countries will be able to provide homes for more than a fraction of the unhappy persons with whom we are now concerned. The only alternative solution which has been suggested is the opening up of new or underdeveloped territory. The Irish Government have no such territory under their control, and they are accordingly reluctant to urge the taking by other Governments of measures in which they themselves could not participate.[88]

Cremins later added that Ireland would only accept aliens whose training and experience may have been of some value, for example, for the setting up of new industries, but he qualified the codicil that even these people could not be guaranteed permanent residency.[89]

Switzerland

Over the following days each of the Évian delegates rose to explain why their respective countries could take no more Jewish refugees. The Swiss representative Dr Heinrich Rothmund, director of the police division at the Federal

Department of Justice and Police, stated that because of the large numbers of refugees who had flooded into Switzerland after the Great War, in 1919 the Swiss government had been forced to introduce stringent controls over the entry of foreigners. The census of 1930 demonstrated that the population was comprised of nine per cent foreigners, or, in a total population of four million, 355,000 were immigrants. Unemployment, it seems, was at high levels and Rothmund was moved to state, 'Switzerland finds that it is essential to exercise severe control over the admission of any further foreigners into the country.[90] After the *Anschluss,* around four thousand Jews had fled east across the narrow border between Italy and Germany into Switzerland. (Many of these had received backdated papers from Swiss commander of police Paul Grüninger, who issued the documents to more than three thousand refugees. After the war he would be arrested for fraud and sentenced to a prison term and a stiff fine. As a convicted criminal he would later find difficulty in obtaining employment and would die in poverty in 1972 without his humanitarian efforts being recognised).[91]

Rothmund stated at Évian that his country had already been liberal enough in accepting such refugees. However, he did not state publicly that he had recently been in secret discussions with the Nazi authorities and had advised them that his government intended to stop all immigration of Jews into Switzerland. Rothmund was alleged to have confided confidentially to colleagues at Évian: 'Switzerland, which has as little use for these Jews as has Germany, will herself take measures to protect Switzerland from being swamped by Jews with the connivance of the Viennese police.' Shortly after the conference had ended Rothmund insisted to the German authorities that all German passports issued to Jews should be clearly stamped with a red J—thus jeopardising the attempts of any holders of such passports in finding asylum—not only in Switzerland—but anywhere else in the Western world.[92] The British later sent a representative, Lord Duncannon, to Switzerland with instructions to investigate the refugee situation in that country. Duncannon reported that the Swiss were placing all refugees into 'establishments' but that they would all later be deported to another country. The Swiss claimed that all refugees were first interrogated by the police and through these interrogations it had been discovered that a gang of smugglers was responsible for getting many of the refugees across the Swiss borders. These smugglers allegedly offered their services for a specified cash payment; two were later arrested and prosecuted for violation of the federal laws governing the residence of foreigners in Switzerland.[93]

Among the most prominent of those who were to assist Jewish refugees to get into Switzerland was Mrs Recha Sternbuch, a powerful opponent of Rothmund. Mrs Sternbuch was responsible for smuggling forged visas to Jews in Austria and Germany, thereby allowing those Jews to escape, initially into Switzerland and then on to other countries. She even made it possible for some inmates from Dachau to be released through the use of these visas, playing upon the German's desire to rid themselves of as many Jews as possible. She spent time both in Italy and France where she was able to obtain further visas. Arrested by the Swiss authorities and charged with bribery, her trial and imprisonment dragged on for three years before finally being thrown out of court for lack of evidence. During the war her struggle to save the Jews of Europe would intensify as she and her husband worked to smuggle refugees across the Swiss border and to send food parcels and medical supplies to those who were held captive within the ghettos of Lodz, Krakow and Warsaw.[94]

Switzerland was never to alter its policy concerning Jewish refugees and it was not until 1997 that any official apology was made concerning the World War Two refugee problem. In March that year the Swiss foreign minister, Flavio Cotti, while attending a formal dinner in New York, apologised for Switzerland's lack of courage towards the refugees stating that his country's policy had been, 'inexcusably wrong'. He added that there had been some, '...very dark moments,' in Switzerland's history during the 1930s and 1940s.[95]

Today there exists a list a Jewish arrivals in Switzerland from 1938 until 1945 which provides details of 21,730 Jewish refugees who managed, in one way of another, to gain entry into Switzerland (an average of just 4346 per year). Extensive police files were maintained on their residences and activities in the country.[96]

Peru

On 11 July, 1938, the U.S. *chargé d'affaires* in Lima, Peru, sent a translation of a news report written in a Lima publication on 8 July, 1938, in which the editorial claimed that Peru was in no position to accept thousands of Jewish refugees and that charity for the needy should begin at home.[97] The press in Lima questioned what representatives of South American countries were even doing at Évian, claiming that if resolutions of mass migration were to be adopted for large scale immigration into Latin America then the continent would end up carrying what was described as being a 'killing load'. The press pointed out that countries such as France, Great Britain and Belgium had already quite clearly stated that they had reached saturation point so how were South American countries to cope?

European countries were vastly more economically stable than the countries of South America and therefore better able to manage these waves of enforced migration from Germany and Austria. South American economies were far more fragile and therefore those countries should be 'on guard', as the press stated, and should not accept thousands of European migrants.

The press also claimed that European problems should be settled by Europeans alone and that South Americans should not interfere with issues arising in what was described as, 'the Old World'.

It was also pointed out that many South American countries had political and economical issues of their own which it would be necessary to resolve before attempting to assist in alleviating the problems of other countries. Generosity was always to be respected and offered, but it would be of primary importance to settle all the issues at home before offering aid to others.[98]

In spite of these comments Peru's minister to Évian, Francisco Garcia Calderon, stated at Évian that his country would be glad to assist a limited number of colonists, agricultural labourers with some experience and technical experts, adding, however, a stringent codicil: '...if traders or workmen came it might disturb her [Peru's] economic system or create problems similar to those which other countries have to tackle ... to prevent the growth of an intellectual proletariat, restrictions would be laid on the settlement of a large number of lawyers or doctors'.[99]

Chile

Chile too was experiencing enormous social difficulties during this time, and while there were large tracts of undeveloped and fertile lands still available for settlement within the country, its government was extremely reluctant to liberalise its immigration policy in order to allow an influx of Jewish immigrants. As Fernando Garcia Oldini pointed out during the Évian conference, there were enormous problems associated with the refugees question. There were territorial, shipping, financial and social issues to be overcome, and only when these problems had been solved could a humanitarian solution be found to the refugee conundrum. Oldini stated—as many of the other

Évian delegates had also claimed—that the impact of the Great Depression was still being felt in his country and, as a consequence, the Chilean government had been forced to act with extreme caution before allowing any kind of wide-scale immigration into the country. He added that one of the major problems would be to find outlets for the oversupply of production which would be the immediate result if a large number of refugees was allowed into the country. Oldini said that within this difficult framework he and his government would listen to any proposals the committee at Évian were prepared to make. Yet the prospect of the Chilean government accepting large numbers of Jewish refugees was slight.[100]

There is no doubt that Chile was experiencing social and political problems caused, primarily, through the events unfolding during the Évian conference, as Wesley Frost, counsellor of the U.S. Embassy in Santiago, advised the U.S. secretary of state in July 1938. Frost reported that Chile's immigration policy in relation to the Évian conference had recently been discussed during a session of the Chilean senate. He stated that Senator Maximiliano Errazuriz, a Catholic conservative, had declared that while he was not unsympathetic to the humanitarian considerations of the refugee problem, he thought that special attention should be focused on the large numbers of Jews who were then arriving in Chile. Many of them, he claimed, were entering illegally and were doing so by bribing immigration officials.[101]

Press reports in the country did much to persuade public opinion against any kind of mass migration, pointing out that a quota system for migrants already existed and, in fact had been surpassed at that time.

Chile was not a wealthy nation and its resources were finite. Like so many other countries there were very serious concerns over the issue of migrants being unable to work as agriculturalists, and therefore taking work and employment in cities or towns that should have been going to local people. It was feared that large scale migration would lead to mass unemployment and that the people of Chile would be far worse off.[102]

One local newspaper accurately pointed out that during the few days that Évian had been in session no real progress had been made. Almost all the nations represented had made it perfectly clear that their immigration laws prevented them from taking a large number of migrants and that they were permitted only to investigate the need for additional migration on an individual basis. The article pointed out that with such structural rigidity towards migration laws it would be almost impossible to achieve anything beneficial at Évian. The article predicted that the conference would end up being a gesture of 'noble human significance', but that was all. Évian would become simply a gesture.[103]

Holland and Denmark

There were, however, several positive moves being made at Évian. Three more countries stated that they were willing to give aid. Holland was one of the most densely populated countries represented at the Évian conference. Its Jewish population of approximately 140,000 had enjoyed full civic rights for about 150 years.[104] The government had already accepted about 25,000 Jewish refugees and now offered temporary refuge to many thousands more.

Denmark, also badly overcrowded, stated it would continue to accept refugees. Denmark's representative at Évian, Gustav Rasmussen, said that his country was one of emigration rather than immigration. He quoted statistics which demonstrated that some eight thousand persons had emigrated from Denmark each year up until the First World War, after which time emigration had fallen to around six thousand per annum. By the time of Hitler's rise to power, emigration had virtually ceased.[105] Rasmussen said that his country did not have a quota system but that Denmark would be prepared to accept a number of refugees. He could not stipulate what these numbers would be.[106]

Gustav Rasmussen

Denmark's representative to Évian.

—Ministry of Foreign Affairs, Denmark.

As we now know, Denmark was to be occupied by Nazi forces as from 9 April, 1940, and it will here be of value to move forward a little in time as the events that occurred in Denmark during the war, in relation to its Jewish population and refugees was unique.

In 1940, realising that resistance would be futile, and in order to preserve civilian casualties, the Danish government almost immediately surrendered to the Germans. However, the Germans claimed that it was not their intention to disturb the political independence of Denmark and allowed the Danish government to remain in place with King Christian X retaining his throne.

This was an important and lifesaving factor in the survival of Danish Jews and those Jewish refugees who had sought refuge there. The Danish Cabinet steadfastly rejected any notion that a 'Jewish question' existed in Denmark. No anti-Semitic legislation was passed, nor was the much-loathed yellow badge introduced. The Jews of Denmark breathed a collective sigh of relief, at least temporarily. Here, at last, was a government willing to stand up to Nazi domination and terror and to reject any ideological concept that the Jews were an inferior race and should be exterminated. Germany was handling its relationship with Denmark with kid-gloves. Danish agriculture was important to German food supplies and millions of Germans relied upon continuing supplies of meat, butter and other essential foodstuffs.

However, by 1943 all that was about to change. Following a series of strikes and protests, illegal under German law, the Nazis issued an ultimatum to the Danish government demanding a ban on strikes, a curfew, and the death penalty for those found guilty of sabotage. The Danish government believed that these terms were unacceptable and declared a state of emergency. The Germans then took about one hundred prominent Danes hostage, including the chief rabbi, Dr Max Friediger and many other Jews, and placed them into a camp near Copenhagen. The Danish government resigned and the Germans took complete control of the country's administration. This meant that all the Jews of Denmark were now at risk of imminent deportation to the concentration camps.

On 1 October, 1943, Adolf Hitler ordered the arrest and deportation of all Danish Jews. However, German diplomat Georg Ferdinand Duckwitz, was able to tip off Danish politician Hans Hedtoft, the chairman of the Danish Social Democratic Party. Hedtoft moved quickly to alert not only the Danish resistance but also Jewish leaders C.B. Henriques and the acting rabbi, Dr Marcus Melchior, who immediately urged the

Jewish community to go into hiding. Thousands were hidden in private homes.

Events that followed were to form one of the most remarkable chapters in the history of the war and demonstrate the astonishing courage of the Danish people.

Georg Ferdinand Duckwitz (centre).

—Photograph courtesy German Federal Archives, Bundesarchiv, B145 Bild-F008672-0027, Wikimedia Commons.

Plans were then made to move the Jewish community out of the country and over the following few months, (August to October 1943) more than 7500 of Denmark's 8000 strong Jewish community were ferried in fishing boats, rowboats and even kayaks over the choppy Oresund Strait from Zealand to neutral Sweden.

Jewish refugees are ferried out of Denmark aboard Danish fishing boats bound for Sweden.

—United States Holocaust Memorial Museum, courtesy of Frihedsmuseet.

Some of the refugees, mainly the younger generation, were sent to Sweden in sealed railcars. The underground movement had been able to break into the cars after they had been inspected and sealed by the Germans. Once the refugees were installed inside the railcars the cars were resealed with forged or stolen German seals. Unfortunately some of the Jewish refugees committed suicide before they could be deported or were captured by the German military and most of these were sent to the Theresienstadt

Ghetto/concentration camp in Czechoslovakia. On 2 October, 1943, the Germans, assuming that all Jews would be in their homes, carried out a sweep to arrest them. They were surprised to discover that almost all the Jews of Copenhagen had vanished. Only about 450 Jews were subsequently arrested and deported including the 200 who had been held hostage. These too were sent to Theresienstadt, but Danish officials were able to ensure that those prisoners were not shipped into the death camps. Additionally, the Danish Red Cross was able to provide these Jewish prisoners with food parcels and made regular inspections to ensure that they were being held under at least survivable conditions. About fifty Jews died of disease at Theresienstadt, many of them being elderly.

Swedish diplomat Count Folke Bernadotte was able to ensure the release and transport to Denmark of the surviving imprisoned Jews during the latter stages of the war.[107]

Another person who would do much to save the Jews of Denmark was Frederick Jacques 'Frits' Philips, an industrialist and chairman of the Dutch electronics company Philips which had been founded by his father and uncle. During the German occupation of his country Frits Philips would save 382 Jewish people from deportation by telling the Nazi authorities that they were indispensable to his business operations.[108]

***

As the Évian conference ground to its predictable close it became patently obvious to the representative countries—and particularly obvious to Hitler—that the world generally had little time for the Jews. The official resolution of the conference—which was passed unanimously—stated that the delegates of the 'Nations of Asylum' were not willing to undertake any obligations towards financing involuntary immigration.

In effect this meant that apart from the existing strict immigration quotas those Jews who were accepted would have to finance their own immigration costs and have sufficient money for support in the adopted country. On the surface this seems a fair and reasonable resolution, but it had clearly been explained to the delegates beforehand that Hitler had passed a law preventing Jews from leaving Germany with any of their wealth. They were permitted to take only ten Reichmarks, or about seven dollars.[109]

Chapter 7

Press Reports in South America

The diatribe emanating from Évian was not essentially a fair representation of public feeling. Some newspapers in South America seemed to be swinging on the issue. On one hand the editors were considerably concerned over the problems of allowing mass migration into their respective countries, while others remained fairly liberal in their attitudes. Various articles in most of the major South American newspapers remained undecided concerning the refugee problem. Editorials often seemed to reflect the popular prejudices of the day and the Jews were regularly portrayed as the *eminences grise* behind the countries' difficult economic problems. However accurate or inaccurate this may have been, Chile's Senator Errazuriz's decidedly anti-Semitic remarks of July 1938 struck an unusually discordant note with the country's newspapers. Both the leading conservative morning newspapers *El Mercurio*, and *La Nación*, were prompt to disagree with the senator, and Socialist deputy, Ricardo Latcham, soon afterwards gave a strongly worded reply to Errazuriz during a session of the Chamber on 13 July, 1938. Latcham delivered a resounding rebuke to Errazuriz over his profound anti-Semitism. He also took the Ministry of Foreign Affairs to task for attempting to restrict Jewish immigration through an allegedly illegal quota arrangement which provided for only fifty Jewish families to be allowed to enter the country each year. The rebuke was particularly effective in light of the fact that two officials of the Chilean Foreign Affairs Ministry, Benjamin Cohen and Enrique Bernstein, were both Jews, and that many of the Chilean upper classes were, '...heavily tinged with Jewish blood'.[1]

An editorial in the influential news publication *La Nación* concluded an extensive report by stating that in Chile racial problems had never been an issue and that where the country had experienced anti-Semitism those rare examples of discrimination had been isolated which did not reflect the opinions of the masses. The press article went on to claim, however, that Chile would not be able to accept people who might form political affiliations which might undermine the sovereignty of the country, adding, however, that a warm welcome, tolerance for religious beliefs and liberty for work and business undertakings would be offered to those who arrived in the country as refugees.[2]

The other major newspaper, *El Mercurio*, also treated the subject in similar fashion. The editorial reviewed Chile's traditionally fairly liberal policy and advocated that no changes were necessary to the immigration laws providing that immigrants obeyed the Chilean laws and established roots in the country, leaving behind, '...the memory and activities which may have caused their exodus'.[3]

In a message to the U.S. Department of State of 16 July, 1938, Wesley Frost of the U.S. Embassy in Santiago stated that Senator Errazuriz's public remarks would have the affect of bringing about a more liberal attitude in the conservative elements of the country. He said that this could well serve to reverse the trend which, in his opinion, had been profoundly '...unfriendly to Jewish immigration, and tending to become more so all the time'. He added that an undertone in the press comment was the impression that Chile was unsympathetic to the refugee problem and that the people in general were, 'not disposed to allow such a situation to develop here.[4]

***

Uruguayan public comment over the Évian conference was also fairly predictable. During the conference and for several days afterwards most of the newspapers in Montevideo devoted one or more articles to the refugee problem. William Dawson, U.S. diplomat in Uruguay, stated that these articles were, however, of little significance.[5]

In general, Uruguayan press comment reported that while the country needed immigrants, those immigrants should be agricultural workers rather than city dwellers. Several articles expressed sympathy with the plight of the Jewish refugees and paid tribute to the humanitarian motives which had induced President Roosevelt to call the conference. But the same editorials clearly pointed out that while the U.S. had been responsible for calling the conference, U.S. immigration laws remained intransigently closed to other than standard quotas. Several newspapers implied accurately that the conference had been a cynical attempt to shift the U.S. immigration problem onto third world countries, that the U.S. government was attempting to find refuge for millions of people whom the U.S. was unwilling to receive. One of the publications was the *La Tribuna Popular*, an independent sensational pro-fascist and anti-American publication, which, as U.S. diplomat

William Dawson reported on 12 July, '...has no sympathy whatever with the unfortunate Jewish refugees and notes with satisfaction that the discussions at Évian prove that the whole world has had enough of its "parasites" and has decided to repudiate them'.[6]

William Dawson claimed that, in general, Uruguayan opinion would strongly oppose the immigration of any considerable number of Jews unless those immigrants could be settled quietly into rural districts. Montevideo, he claimed, already had a substantial and commercially active Jewish community which was, '...viewed with dislike in some quarters and with concern in many others'. He added that the Jewish people were experiencing a real lack of sympathy and this was due less to race prejudice than to economic causes. Dawson claimed: 'As ... competition becomes more effective and makes itself increasingly felt, the sentiment against ... [the Jews] is likely to grow in intensity; and it is not improbable that the Nazi Germans will take advantage of any opportunity to foster and exploit this sentiment'.[7]

Despite this, there would be a significant act of humanitarian kindness from Florencio Rivas the Uruguan consul-general in Germany. Rivas, would not only hide one hundred and fifty Jews during *Kristallnacht,* but would also provide them with passports.[8]

Chapter 8

Faltering Progress

On 9 July, 1938, the U.S. Department of State advised Taylor, 'for his strictly confidential information', that George Rublee had been appointed by President Roosevelt to head the permanent committee.[1] George Rublee has been described in classified State Department documents as, '...one of the outstanding lawyers in the United States, with wide experience in international law'.

Left to right: Myron C. Taylor, Henri Berenger, Lord Winterton and Robert Thompson Pell.

–U.S. National Archives

George Rublee

–Wikimedia Commons

This was certainly true. Rublee had been born in 1868, just three years after the end of the American Civil War. He had graduated from Harvard in 1890 and from the Harvard Law School in 1895. During his career he served as a member of the Federal Trade Commission in 1915-16, having been appointed by President Woodrow Wilson. He later served as a member of the Commercial Economy Board appointed by the Council of National Defence in 1917. Other appointments included Special Council of the Treasury Department in 1917, delegate to the Allied Maritime Transport Council in London, 1918-19, and as adviser to the American delegation of the London Naval Conference in 1930. He worked as a legal adviser to the U.S. Embassy in Mexico City and played an important role in the negotiations with the Mexican government between the years 1925-30. From 1921 he was a partner in the law firm of Covington, Burling and Rublee in Washington. At the time of the Évian conference he was also an overseer of Harvard University.[2]

Shortly after Rublee's appointment he asked Robert Pell if he would accept the position as his assistant on the London-based permanent committee. The U.S. Department of State advised that he could take leave of absence without pay and Pell accepted the position.[3]

Technical Subcommittee's Report

Finally, on 13 July, 1938, the technical subcommittee at Évian brought out its written findings. Chairman of the subcommittee, Judge Michael Hansson, seemed pleased with the results of the committee's reports and stated that many of the countries had indicated a willingness to accept further numbers of refugees. However, he qualified the statement by reporting that, '...all governments are prepared to cooperate to the extent permitted by their laws and individual situation'.[4] What Hansson failed to point out in his carefully worded report was that most of these countries had laws and other social, political or economic requirements that would preclude any further Jewish immigration into their territories. He did, however, speak briefly of restricted entries, claiming: 'Certain countries have expressed a willingness to receive experienced agriculturists. Others have indicated their willingness to accept selected classes of workers for whom suitable employment is available.'[5] Hansson added that many countries were facing serious economic difficulties with large numbers of unemployed, a situation that would preclude significant numbers of immigrants being allowed within those borders. He also pointed out that most of the refugees were impoverished, a point that formed a major obstacle to their reception into any other country.[6]

The Pogrom Continues

Meanwhile, the pogrom in Europe continued unabated and the newspapers were reporting:

Berlin, Saturday,—Thousands of Jews have been plunged into a state of terror as the result of anti-Semitism. The Gestapo is hourly rounding up dozens, and it is estimated that nearly 16,000 were arrested during the week, their relatives not being informed of the reason or their fate.

Jewish shops throughout the city are being closed for fear of violence. Insulting notices are being posted on residences and shops with warnings of reprisals against those who dare to remove them. In many instances there is manhandling, but the Government insists that the arrests are purely directed against criminals.

Despite every effort to whip up public resentment the crowds watching the persecutions appear sympathetic towards the Jews. The campaign is obviously offending public opinion.

The official explanation of the arrests is:

'The attitude of 1000 Jews from Vienna was so insulting and provocative that many Germans were increasingly indignant. The Jews were put into custody to prevent worse happenings.... The Gestapo is aiming utterly to demoralise Austrian Jews, and persecution is very bitter in Vienna. Not a day elapses without arrests. Thousands wait all night outside the British and American consulates for the purpose of registering for migration which usually is impossible owing to liability to finance their departure.

'There can be no Jewish families throughout the country without one or two members under arrest. Austria is experiencing an orgy of Jew-baiting such as Europe has not known since the Middle Ages.'

...Children are being told in lectures in schools throughout Germany that they are not allowed to play with Jewish children and are also forbidden to enter Jewish shops. The authorities claim that the lectures are necessary because by favours, the Jews become provocative, resulting in the growing indignation of the population.[7]

On 6 July, 1938, world newspapers were reporting that some twelve thousand Jews had succeeded in escaping from Nazi Austria. One newspaper in London stated: 'Jews who, after having been released from prison, have been told to quit Austria by a certain date in July or be re-arrested, have sought visas in vain. They have asked in despair, 'Where can we go?' and were told, 'Well, the road to the Danube is open.'[8]

Indeed, suicide, as the notorious Danube remark suggested, was certainly an option that many of the Jews took in their desperation. On 7 July the press reported: 'The correspondent of the *Telegraph* at Vienna says that evidence abundantly confirms the reports that eight hundred Jews and Jewesses have attempted to commit suicide in the past few days. The majority of the eight hundred succeeded, and as a result rabbis have been so busy at funerals that they were occupied after sunset.'[9]

A semiofficial German statement later denied that the Jews were killing themselves in large numbers. However, there was no doubt that the deaths were occurring and foreign correspondents were reporting the events accurately.[10]

On 21 July, 1938, John C. Wiley who held the unenviable position of U.S. *chargé d'affaires* at Vienna, instructed the U.S. Department of State that there was a plan—evidently organised through the German secret agent Gildemeester—to smuggle a large number of Jewish refugees into Palestine. As Wiley explained in his highly confidential and coded telegram, the plan was devised expressly with a view to embarrassing the British government during the conference at Évian.

Wiley wrote:

Three hundred and sixty persons of the Jewish race and faith are involved. They have a community chest of some 500 schillings per head, and some 7500 pounds have been transferred abroad with the approval of the Devisen Central and the Gestapo.

I am told that when Mr Norman Bentwich, a British member of the Council for German Jewry, was in Vienna, the matter was discussed with him. He protested against the carrying out of the project, but was finally persuaded, with considerable difficulty, not to inform the British authorities.

The *Kultusgemeinde,* or Jewish community, of Vienna does not appear to have sponsored this group emigration. Indeed, it appears to regard it with misgivings. It was apparently arranged and financed through the Gildemeester-Kuffler organisation by the German authorities.

The question of Jewish emigration to Palestine is one of some delicacy. The fact that a substantial sum in foreign exchange has been allocated by the German authorities [for Austria an unprecedented generosity] to further the illegal immigration of a relatively unimportant number of

Austrian Jews suggests the possibility that there may be a political motive in the background; perhaps that of embarrassing further British relations with the Arabs. This supposition is strengthened by reliable information that the Italian authorities are collaborating with the Gestapo; that the transport will be in charge of an Italian officer after it leaves German territory.[11]

According to another classified communication written by John C. Wiley, the press in Vienna was careful to ignore the proceedings at Évian. Wiley informed his superiors in Washington that the German authorities in Vienna were following the proceedings in Évian very closely and that the Jewish community in Vienna was being represented by three Viennese Jews: Dr Joseph Lowenherz, Professor Heinrich Neumann and Herr Berthold Storfer. Wiley stated that Doctor Lowenherz was provisionally the director of the *Kultusgemeinde* (the Austrian Jewish Community), Professor Neumann was a leading throat specialist who had received wide publicity as physician to the Duke of Windsor, and Herr Storfer was in some way connected with financial matters having previously given banking advice to Professor Neumann. Wiley stated:

Professor Neumann and H.A. Goodmann during the Évian conference.

–U.S. National Archives

I do not believe that this delegation will be found to be particularly representative or helpful. Dr Lowenherz, following the *Anschluss*, was in custody at Dachau. It is suspected that his spirit is not entirely resilient and that he is somewhat under the influence of the Gestapo. Professor Neumann shines in his particular field. Otherwise his career has not been particularly successful. Moreover, his personality is not prepossessing. Herr Storfer, as a personage, is somewhat obscure.

It was not the desire of the Jewish community to be represented at Évian, indeed, I am reliably told that it was formerly decided not to send anyone to the conference. It was held that the Austrian Jews were not defendants and dared not be plaintiffs, that, therefore, there was no proper or helpful roles for them to play at Évian.

The change in plan, according to an informant, was dictated by the Gestapo, which selected the three persons mentioned above.

Mr Arthur Kuffler, who is associated with Mr Gildemeester, in the latter's somewhat obscure enterprise ... has also proceeded to Évian. I am told that he has succeeded in attaching himself to the British delegation.

It appears that the activities of Gildemeester and Kuffler in furthering illegal transport of emigrants to Palestine indicate close collaboration with the Gestapo, the Italian authorities and the ultra Zionists led by Mr Jabotinsky, the Jewish 'Hitler'.

The increasing pressure which the Gestapo and the criminal police have exerted on the Jewish population during recent weeks is generally interpreted as an effort designed to influence the conference at Évian in order to accelerate mass Jewish migration from Austria.[12]

Influence Over Germany

The question of whether a permanent committee would have any influence over the German government was vital to the mandate and structure of the committee. On 9 July, 1938, Cordell Hull sent a strictly confidential message in code to the U.S. ambassador in Berlin, asking his opinion on the matter.

> We would appreciate receiving your opinion whether the German government would be willing to deal with the head of such an organisation on such questions as the orderly migration of refugees, the export from Germany of at least a part of their capital and other questions of a similar nature.
>
> We assume it would be undesirable, at least for the present, for you to approach the German authorities in this matter.[13]

The following day the Berlin ambassador replied that he thought the German authorities would cooperate, especially as arranging the deportation of Jewish people was what they urgently wanted.[14]

A Veil of Secrecy and South American Restraint

As the conference progressed there arose a strong feeling among the delegates of the South American countries that they were not being fully apprised of the talks, and that a veil of secrecy had descended over the whole affair. They complained that the U.S., Britain and France had dominated the talks and that much of those talks had been carried out privately. Jesus Maria Yepes, the Colombian delegate, at the end of one of the morning sessions, asked Taylor whether the creation of a permanent committee would be discussed by the entire conference or only by the executive. Colombia was strongly opposed to the formation of a full time committee, allegedly on the grounds that it would infringe upon the League of Nations mandate. After reading various news reports concerning this secrecy, Hull sent a message to Taylor in which he stated the press reports were claiming that the U.S. was not acting in the spirit of its good neighbour policy.[15]

***

Adopting resolutions as a result of the conference was a difficult matter. For example, many of the Latin American countries were under pressure from the German government over commercial arrangements, and these countries were unwilling to take any action or adopt any resolutions that might damage those relations. According to Taylor, notable among these reticent countries were Colombia, Venezuela, Chile and Uruguay.[16]

Uruguayan rejection of the Jewish refugees seemed profound. At a later cabinet meeting in Montevideo the government was reported to have tested ways of tightening its immigration laws considerably. At the same meeting a proposal placed before the cabinet to allow five hundred Jewish refugees to form an agricultural colony somewhere in the country was flatly refused. The local press was also inclined to editorialise against Jewish immigration. One pro-government newspaper approved of the Cabinet's actions and called for further examples that would emulate, '...certain totalitarian countries to keep the race pure'.

Of course these were words largely echoed from those propagandist publications then being released regularly in Germany and Austria and it was not difficult to understand why so many publications around the world became ultra-conservative when it came to finding ways to deal with the issue of Jewish migration.

Various publications in Uruguay were only too willing to point out that Jewish people were not agriculturists and would be, 'completely useless' on the land, as one publication described the Jews. The press added that offering Jewish migrants agricultural work would place enormous pressures on the stability of the economy and social structure and even endanger the existence of the country's nationality which might disappear—become smothered beneath the weight of foreign elements. It was claimed that migration into the country had already reached saturation point and that it was vital to preserve national defence, patriotism, the love of the country's traditions and racial structure because it was these elements which constituted the individuality of the people.

The press was also advancing the disturbing possibility that large scale migration to the country could create significant and widespread hostility which might manifest itself into a more 'disquieting' element, even violence, particularly if Uruguayans could clearly see that the presence of so many migrants was displacing local people from their employment and other important activities.

As usual, fears of an overwhelming number of migrants brought out significant anxieties for the personal control of one's life, prosperity, safety and comfort. Everyone feared the unknown.[17]

Yet some Jewish people were certainly being allowed into the country, despite government action and scathing anti-Semitic reports in the press. Steamers such as the *Cap Arcona* were arriving at Montevideo with immigrants who claimed that they were intending to remain for only a short period before attempting to gain access into the U.S. Many of these, however, were fully aware that entry into the U.S. would be very difficult and were quite prepared to remain in Uruguay. Some of these refugees had evidently managed to smuggle substantial sums of money out of Germany. Indeed, the entry requirements at this time for Uruguayan immigration called for the intending immigrant to own at least US$400. Those who had got out with considerably more than this were able to purchase residential property in Pocitos, the foreign quarter of the city where many U.S., British and other non-Uruguayans lived.[18]

The Conference Ends

The Évian conference closed on 15 July, 1938, with the participating governments deciding to establish a continuing body that was to set up a permanent organisation in London. The U.S.

Department of State instructed all its diplomatic officers to send copies in duplicate of any reports pertinent to the issue to the U.S. Embassy in London.[19]

Despite the many difficulties, on 14 July, 1938, the day before the end of the conference, the Intergovernmental Meeting on Political Refugees adopted its resolutions. (For the full resolutions, see Appendix C). In closing the session, Taylor made a comprehensive speech declaring the success of the conference and ending:

> It is vital that orderly emigration should replace disorderly exodus. It is essential that the emigrants should leave their country of origin with their property and possessions if they are to take root and sustain themselves in countries of settlement. It is imperative, in consequence, that the countries which are willing to receive emigrants in refuge or in permanent settlement should have the collaboration in these respects of the country of origin. In closing, I am anxious to emphasize that we are seeking to approach this human problem with which we must deal in an objective manner, and we seek a solution promptly that will lighten the burden of many who

are suffering and are in sorrow, in sickness and in want.[20]

The London committee was to be composed of a British member as chairman, with four vice-chairmen, initially thought to include an American, Brazilian, a Frenchman and a Norwegian. However, this concept was later to change. The work of the committee would be carried out under a director assisted by a small secretariat. By 14 July, George Rublee had agreed to be appointed as director of the permanent committee.[21]

Mexican News Reports

On 12 July, three days before the end of the conference, Josephus Daniels, the U.S. diplomat based in Mexico, wrote to Cordell Hull with reservations he held following news reports that the Mexican delegation to Évian had stated that Mexico would be prepared to receive large numbers of Jewish refugees. Daniels wrote:

> With reference to the work of the Committee to Facilitate Emigration From Austria and Germany Of Political Refugees, I have the honor to inform the Department that the statement of the Mexican delegate to this Conference, Primo Villa Michel, to the effect that Mexico offer asylum to

foreigners who fear for their lives, has been given much prominence in the Mexican press. It has been pointed out in the dispatches that Mexico and the Dominican Republic are the only countries which have offered definite assistance to the refugees and that the United States does not propose to amend its immigration laws despite the fact that the latter country was responsible for calling the Conference now in session at Évian. It will be noted, however, that Mexico has made no concrete proposal regarding the number of the refugees which she is willing to accept and it is considered doubtful that her offer will include a large number of them.[22]

This message was immediately sent to the newly forming committee in London which was due to hold its first meeting on 13 August.[23] Some time afterwards President Lazaro Cardenas del Rio of Mexico granted a press interview in which he stated that there was no cause for alarm and that the numbers of Jews arriving in the country would be few.[24]

However, one Mexican national who would later stand out for his humanitarian efforts was Gilberto Bosques Saldivar, the general-consul for Mexico based at Marseilles. Gilberto Bosques Saldivar and his consular staff would issue visas to Jews, Spaniards and political refugees. In all he would issue around forty thousand visas for entry into Mexico. He rented a castle and a summer holiday facility at Marseilles and maintained that these were officially Mexican territories under international law. Within these facilities he would house many Jews and other refugees.

Saldivar, his wife and two children, along with about forty consular staff, would be arrested by the Gestapo in 1943 and sent to Germany to be detained for about a year. However, the Mexican president, by that time, Manuel Ávila Camacho, would retaliate by ordering the arrest of a number of German citizens living in Mexico. The Mexican and German government would then reach an agreement and Saldivar, his family and staff would be released as part of a prisoner exchange.[25]

Brazilian Press Reports

On 15 July Alexander W. Weddell of the U.S. Embassy in Buenos Aires wrote a detailed report to the U.S. secretary of state, voicing this concern over publications that had appeared in Brazil following the Évian conference. His concerns were warranted. At least two major publications came out with very strong warnings of the country accepting large numbers of migrants. There was a distinct element of resentment in these warnings; some editors expressing their concerns that Évian was simply attempting to place even more pressure on nations to accept migrants that were not really necessary or wanted. Some of the ways these sentiments were expressed could also be both colourful and injurious to the whole concept that Évian was actually a badly needed and desperate attempt at some form of rescue mission.[26]

One Brazilian newspaper, a popular, fascist publication, on 9, 11 and 13 July under the respective headings of *Water from Évian Brings Typhoid; 600,000 Jews;* and, *The Evil Road of Évian*, referred in sarcastic terms to the 'generous' initiative of President Roosevelt. The newspaper claimed that the '...peaceful city of Évian, whose waters had always enjoyed great prestige,' would now bring its own brand of 'Semitic typhoid'.

The second article also bitterly attacked the Jews and the publication stated that the country had a right to defend its race with the same energy displayed by European countries in defending theirs, ending. 'Let no one offend any of the Jews who live in the country. But let not one more Jew enter it.'

In the third article the newspaper also claimed: 'Why do not England, France and the

United States—if they wish to protect the Jews driven out of Germany—give them shelter in their own colonies?'[27]

The London Committee

On 19 July, Myron C. Taylor informed the U.S. Department of State that the vice-chairmen's positions to the London committee would probably be filled by an American, a Frenchman and a Dane, although no definite decisions had then been made, the British favouring a Danish representative. The fourth position was open to a representative from a South American country, and, as the Brazilian representative to Évian had been so helpful, Cordell Hull later stated: 'In view of the cooperation which the Brazilian delegate gave you at Évian ... he would seem an appropriate choice for the position of vice-chairman, and his election would be agreeable to this government. I am sure that you will appreciate of not, repeat not, giving the impression that we are initiating or sponsoring the election of the Brazilian delegate as vice-chairman'.[28]

Chapter 9
The Palestinian Question

The problems of Jewish immigration into Palestine were immense. Here two peoples were living together in mutual hostility. As anti-Semitism grew throughout the 1930s, and as Jewish immigration into Palestine increased, so too did the animosity that finally resulted in widespread rioting and violence. In July 1937 a royal commission under the chairmanship of Lord Peel was formed to investigate the problems. This commission finally recommended a partition of Palestine into a Jewish state, an Arab state, and a British mandate for both Jerusalem and Bethlehem with an access corridor to the sea. However, the Zionists were indignant over the recommendation and in 1938 a partition commission under the auspices of Sir John Woodhead reported that the two peoples were 'inextricably tangled up' and that such partition was not possible.

British diplomatic circles in Palestine were apprehensive that the United States would, under pressure from powerful American Jewish lobby groups, advocate a mass refugee immigration programme into Palestine. The British stated that such a move would, '...add to [the] difficulty of solving an already distressingly complicated problem.[1]

The Jewish Agency representative to the Évian conference was Dr Arthur Ruppin, a Zionist member of the Jewish Agency executive and an authority on the complex problems of Palestinian colonisation. On the day of his departure for Évian, the *Vaad Leumi*—the National Council of Palestine Jews—issued a six articled resolution concerning Jewish immigration into Palestine. The resolution protested against the persecutions of Jews 'merely and solely because they are Jews'. It voiced an appreciation that Roosevelt had taken the initiative in calling the conference and appealed to the conference delegates to put an end to the process of extermination. It also strongly requested increased immigration to the countries represented at the conference, demanded that Palestine be opened to Jewish immigration and called upon all sections of the Jewish community in Palestine to increase opportunities for absorbing the refugees.[2]

The Arab press was carrying very little on the subject, although on 2 July, 1938, the *Palestine and Trans-Jordan* newspaper published an editorial asking why, if Great Britain, the United States and France were sincere in their attempts to assist with the plight of the Jewish people, they did not open up their own lands to significant immigration. The editorial stated that this would be preferable to forcing Jewish immigration onto Palestine with, a 'force of arms' The article claimed that Arabs generally and their governments would be perfectly willing to support the endeavours of the Évian conference but only on the understanding that every country participating should unilaterally accept a number of Jewish refugees in direct proportion to its density of population and its area of lands.[3]

On 11 July, 1938, George Wadsworth, the U.S. consul general in Jerusalem, wrote a detailed dispatch for the U.S. Department of State in which he stated that Arabic reaction to the Évian conference had been both immediate and profoundly anti-Semitic. He stated that Arab sentiment lay firmly in the belief that Roosevelt and his administration had bowed to Jewish pressure and that pressure had been brought to bear by the U.S. on Britain to allow for extra Jewish immigration into Palestine. However accurate or inaccurate this may have been, the Arab press was reporting that the decisions made at Évian would cause irreparable damage to, '...this innocent Arab land'.[4]

Wadsworth informed the U.S. Department of State that the Évian conference and Britain's handling of the Jewish immigration programme into Palestine had done much to harm both countries' reputations throughout the Middle East. Wadsworth quoted a leading Arab lawyer, the secretary of the National Defence Party, as stating: 'We Arabs, because we can see in all of this the controlling influence of Jewish pressure on Washington, have given up hope that any consideration of our rights can be expected from public or official opinion in the United States.'[5] The lawyer's wife, who was the secretary of the Arab Women's Committee, allegedly telephoned members of the Évian conference on 10 July to state that to permit further Jewish immigration into Palestine would be to, '...convert it into an inferno, by adding fuel to already smouldering fires'.[6]

Various widely read local newspapers held very strong views over the issue of Jewish immigration into Palestine and published powerful but populist editorials while the Évian conference had been in session. One of these publications pointed out that it would be pointless and futile to impose the pain of one race of people on another race. Yet another prominent press report claimed that it would be impossible to resolve the issue of Jewish persecution and migration simply by 'transplanting' individuals onto the colonies or dominions of various countries, adding that to do so would simply lead to the creation of even more tensions in countries that were, at that time, free of the 'anti-Semitic scourge'.[7]

At the close of the Évian conference, British delegate, Lord Winterton stated:

> It has been represented in some quarters that the whole question, at least of the Jewish refugees, could be solved if only the gates of Palestine were thrown open to Jewish immigrants without restriction of any kind. I would like to say, as emphatically as I can, that I regard any such proposition as wholly untenable.[8]

And thus the Évian conference ended. Nothing concrete had come from the many days spent in intense discussion, other than a general agreement that a permanent committee would be established in London. What became obviously clear to all the delegates was the fact that the represented nations were unwilling to do anything more than advance token gestures in their endeavours to solve the refugee problem.

On 20 July, 1938, Myron C. Taylor wrote a detailed report on the Évian conference, giving a full account of the events leading up to and during the conference. Without doubt this was one of the most important documents to come out of Évian. Filled with a mixture of praise and criticism, Taylor was sure that the conference had been a success and that as the work continued a solution would, almost surely, be found to the problem of Jewish refugees. He ended his report by writing: 'In conclusion, I am convinced that it is of the highest importance to maintain the continuity of this work and not to let it drop for a single instant. It has got off to a good start; it must be carried on in the spirit of the Évian meeting and with the same energy and determination.'[9] For the full text of Taylor's report see Appendix A.

Part Three

Chapter 10

The Aftermath of Évian

Following the conference at Évian the British press reported varied analyses over the issue. *The Times* in London claimed that the work had been worthwhile, as did the *Sunday Times*. However, the *Manchester Guardian,* a newspaper that had been an enthusiastic supporter of the conference, reported considerable disappointment over the outcome, with the exception that the conference had, '...perpetuated itself by means of a permanent committee'. The report pointed out that the principal disappointment of the entire conference had been the complete lack of offers from any of the participating nations to take significant numbers of refugees. The article very clearly demonstrated that Britain's offer to settle a number of refugees in Kenya was completely negated by not allowing any emigration into Palestine. Meanwhile, another influential publication, the *Sunday Times*, stated that all the discussions that had taken place at Évian had simply served to focus attention on the problem rather than offering any conclusive solution.[1]

The *Manchester Guardian* was rather more forceful when it highlighted the fact that a 'Jews Not Wanted' poster might frequently be seen at the entrances to establishments in Nazi Germany and Austria, and given the current attitude in those countries that was not surprising. However, it was both astonishing and particularly disconcerting to discover that the same sign might well have been displayed at Évian.

The article published in the newspaper stated that it was a sad reality and a terrible admission that the Nazis' taunt of Jews not being welcomed anywhere, including the 'great democratic nations', was apparently true. The newspaper stated categorically that nations everywhere were not willing to help and that Évian had been particularly disappointing.[2]

In the United States, *Debrest's Weekly News Service*, published in New York, raised a number of questions regarding the outcome of Évian and pondered on the efficacy of the continuation of the work in London. The news service claimed that Évian had been nothing more than a conference of 'Gentiles' whose conscience had needed appeasement because that would have been better than doing nothing while thousands of years of civilisation was in the process of being 'strangled' by the Nazis.

The agency claimed that the question of rescuing the Jewish people was not really a Jewish question at all: it was a Christian question with Christianity in the balance, pointing out that conscience is very much a private matter and that we all have to make our own decisions based upon our Christian beliefs.

What the London conference would achieve was anyone's guess, but its result would determine what two thousand years of Christianity meant to the individual. If we abandoned the Jews, the agency claimed, left them to their fate, then we might all simply go back to the jungle and cease our platitudes about love of God or social justice.[3]

Following the conference at Évian, Myron C. Taylor was somewhat at a loss concerning how approaches should be made to the German government and admitted so in a highly secret letter he wrote to Hugh Wilson, the U.S. ambassador to Berlin, on 24 July, 1938. Emphasising the point that the contents of the letter were secret and that they were being seen only by Taylor himself and his personal secretary, Taylor asked for Wilson's advice on the matter. Wilson's secret reply, also seen only by himself and his private secretary, pointed out the need for such secrecy and stated that, at some time in the near future, after various policies had been hammered out, there would be a need for the director and other members of the London committee to go to Berlin and have direct and formal talks with representatives of the German government.[4]

The first meeting of the London committee met in the Locarno Room of the British Foreign Office at 11a.m. on 3 August, 1938. Myron C. Taylor was standing in as chairman until the arrival of George Rublee who was due to leave the U.S. aboard the liner *Queen Mary* on 10 August.[5] The only governments present at Évian and not represented in London were Switzerland, (officials of which claimed that they could not attend, 'for obvious political reasons')[6], Paraguay and Costa Rica. The Costa Rican government stated that because it had no diplomatic representative in Great Britain it would be too costly to send a representative to London.[7] Later, as though to emphasize the point, the Costa Rican consuls abroad, and all immigration authorities within the country, were, '...instructed to refuse admission into Costa Rica to all Jews other than unquestionable tourists'.[8]

Paraguay later introduced a bill to its chamber of deputies to, 'strictly forbid' all Jewish immigration, with the exception of legitimate visitors.[9] The Paraguayan government also passed a decree (number 12277) which stipulated that ten thousand or more Czechoslovakian families would be allowed into the country. However, stipulations of the decree included the requirement that the immigrants all be agriculturists, that they possess at least fifty gold pesos, that they held the necessary entry documents and were, quite emphatically: '...*not of the Semitic race*'. (Author's italics). There was also provision for artisans and industrialists, providing that these people had, in the case of artisans, five hundred gold pesos and industrialists, one thousand five hundred gold pesos. None was to be of the Jewish race.[10]

The situation in South America was further exacerbated by the Nazi policy of cramming a large number of Jewish people onto German steamships and sending them uninvited to South American ports, as Cordell Hull stated: 'The German authorities should realize that such travel, even if it removes a substantial number of Jews from Germany immediately, will make it far more difficult for larger numbers of such persons to obtain admission into the American republics in the future.'[11] South America was not the only region to be affected by this practice. Countries bordering the Mediterranean, the Black Sea and the Caribbean were also subject to these expulsion ships. The British strongly protested to the German government but the Nazi authorities only replied that it was not their responsibility and that they cared little what happened to the Jews once they had left Germany. The Germans stated that they could not prevent Jews from buying passage aboard German ships even without the proper documentation.[12]

Meanwhile, Myron C. Taylor was on notice from the State Department not to make any inflammatory statements that might annoy the German authorities and therefore jeopardise the ongoing negotiations concerning the refugees.[13] Even approaching the Germans over the issue was an event of considerable diplomatic manoeuvring and, as Taylor informed the State Department, it was pointless to ask the Germans to release significant numbers of refugees if there were no countries of asylum prepared to take them. Taylor claimed that unless the U.S. would change its existing immigration laws to provide for a vastly increased immigration quota from Germany, none of the other countries—all of whom were closely watching the U.S. immigration policy—would change theirs. Taylor went on to state that if this were to be the case then it would be useless to approach the German government at all. He ended his lament by pointing out that the entire system was fragile in the extreme and stated: '...As you know the original idea of the British, which we scotched at Évian, was to reduce the intergovernmental committee to the role of advisory body to the League Commission. Should the negotiations with Germany not succeed, I am convinced that the British will return to their original position and we shall then have to decide whether to go along with them in this idea or to withdraw from the work altogether'.[14]

***

In an attempt to break the deadlock forged by the Germans of not allowing the Jewish refugees to take any of their wealth out of the country, Julio Metal—evidently an economist of some vision—who lived in Zurich, wrote to the State Department with a concept whereby the Jewish people could be allowed to leave and settled into other countries through the raising of gold bonds. He claimed that if most of the countries represented at Évian issued gold bonds, the cost of relocating the Jewish people and their upkeep for ten years, including the money needed for development and interest (at two per cent) would cost two milliards (two billion in modern terms or two thousand million) gold dollars. Metal claimed: 'Will not then every thinking human being prefer to accept and keep a gold certificate guaranteed by twenty-seven states which furthermore yields two per cent interest per annum than gold or fluctuating currency ... the area of settlement with its property and installations and their increasing value will provide a guarantee'.[15] Metal's plan was as detailed as it was visionary, and if it could have been instigated, even on a far smaller scale than that proposed, it would certainly have solved some portion of the refugee problem.

However, the U.S. Department of State—possibly overawed at the scope of the proposal, simply instructed its consul general in Zurich to, '...address an appropriate noncommittal acknowledgement'.[16]

***

At the first meeting in London, Taylor told the other countries' representatives:

> We are met in London now to take a second vital step. It is incumbent upon us to set in motion the machinery for negotiations which we have established, to evaluate the extent of our problem on the basis of information assembled at Évian, and to receive from the representatives of each of the governments participating here a more specific statement of what it is

prepared to do in eliminating a major factor of unrest in international politics.... Fundamentally, this problem of involuntary migration is one which challenges Western civilization. Briefly stated, Western civilization is the degree of progress of order under law in the struggle against anarchy and chaos. It is the ... march of humanity away from the rule of force to an orderly system of society where good neighborliness is the rule, where there is real security for the individual and for the nation to which he belongs.[17]

After a 24 July communication from Myron C. Taylor, the U.S. ambassador in Berlin, Hugh Wilson, contacted the German government with the request that it consider the recommendations made at Évian. At first the Nazis indicated that they were not ready to cooperate, and Wilson later communicated with the German minister of economics, Dr Walter Funk, (who, in 1946, received a sentence of life imprisonment at the war crimes trials in Nuremberg). Funk stated that the competent German authorities were, '...ready to receive and enter into exploratory discussions with [the] director of the committee.[18]

The U.S. Department of State officials were cautiously pleased with this unexpected development and Taylor was instructed to have the London committee representatives, '...explore the most suitable and constructive approach to the German government with a view to ... securing the cooperation of that government in facilitating the orderly emigration of refugees.[19]

After Rublee's arrival in London he held talks with Taylor and Pell and was not at all happy with the situation. He soon afterwards sent a telegram to the State Department, 'I find the situation here somewhat different and more discouraging than I had supposed, and I feel that I shall need all the support that the department can give me in order that I might accomplish my mission.'[20]

***

On 19 August, 1938, British courts imposed sentences of six months with hard labour on three Jewish refugees who had managed to smuggle themselves into the country. The refugees, John Bocker, Mendel Flerman and Henrietta Weiss were recommended for deportation after completion of their sentences. The magistrate responsible for their imprisonment, when passing sentence, had reportedly stated: '...The way stateless Jews from Germany were pouring in ... is becoming an outrage'.[21]

That same day (19 August) members of the U.S. delegation to London moved into their newly furnished offices at Central Hall Westminster. This is where the London committee would, from then on, hold its meetings.[22]

Further work of the committee was delayed for some days. The Brazilian government had become diplomatically cautious because of the possibility that Argentina may have had its representative appointed to a vice-chairmanship of the committee and that the Brazilian delegate may have been relegated to a mere member. The Brazilian government was anxious that it was not being placed into a minor role as compared to Argentina. This furore created a considerable amount of diplomatic correspondence. A further delay was caused by the inability of Senator Berenger or any other French representative to be present at the meeting. The French, it seemed, were becoming somewhat bellicose over the issue of what to do with the many hundreds of thousands of Jewish transient refugees then in France for whom no permanent home had yet been found.[23]

A fairly typical example of these may be seen in the later case of a group of children who would originate from Germany and Austria. During the year preceding the outbreak of the war around one thousand children between the ages of four and seventeen would find refuge in Belgium, some coming individually and others as part of an organised transport from Cologne in Germany. The rescue of these transport children would be arranged through the *Comite d'Assistance aux Enfants Juifs Refugies* (CAEJR). This organisation was founded by Madame Goldschmidt-Brodsky whose husband, Alfred, was a member of the Red Cross in Belgium.

The children, one hundred in number, would be taken originally into Belgium as it was thought that they would be fairly safe there. However, following the German invasion of Belgium in May 1940 it would quickly become necessary to evacuate the children once more and they would be taken to an old farm at Seyre, south of Toulouse. In charge of the group would be a couple named Lucienne and Gaspard de Waay, and also Elka Frank. Conditions at the farm would be fairly basic; food and clothing were in short supply; the older children cared for the younger ones and also worked on nearby farms. Meanwhile the Goldschmidts had also fled from Belgium into France and were then living at Cahors. They were able to prevail upon Maurice and Elinor Dubois of the *Secours Suiss aux Enfants* (the Swiss Children's Aid—an agency of the Swiss Red Cross) to aid the refugee children. In the autumn of 1940 the *Secours Suiss* were to take charge of the group of children at Seyre, which, by that time, would be under the charge of Alexander and Elka Frank. Some very badly needed supplies were brought to the children's group and it was decided to move the group into a more remote region, the abandoned *Chateau de La Hille,* situated closer to the border with neutral Spain. Soon after making the move Roesli Naef took over the directorship of the home. In 1941 seventeen of the younger children would be evacuated to the United States, the evacuation being arranged through the U.S. Committee for the Care of European Children with the assistance of the American Friends Service Committee (AFSC). Two more teenagers would also be evacuated to America that summer.

Unfortunately, in 1942 the French police would raid the *Château de La Hille* and arrest forty of the children. These would be sent to the *Le Vernet* internment camp to await deportation back to Germany. However, with the assistance of Maurice Dubois of the Swiss Red Cross, who was able to place pressure on the Vichy authorities by threatening to close all the Swiss camps in France, the children would later be released and returned to the colony at *La Hille.* The director of the colony, Roesli Naef, would later make arrangements to smuggle the older children over the borders into Spain or Switzerland. Some of these children would be caught while crossing but others would evade the border police. Of the original one hundred children at *La Hille*, ninety would survive the war. Twelve teenagers and one adult would be transported to the Auschwitz and Majdanek concentration camps. One teenager, Werner Epstein, miraculously survived Auschwitz. The Yad Vashem Holocaust Memorial would later recognise both Maurice Dubois and Roesli Naef as 'Righteous Among the Nations'.[24]

***

On 23 August, 1938, it seemed that there was some hope for those Jews still trapped in Austria. The *Frankfurter Zeitung* newspaper announced that a central bureau would be established in Vienna and that all Nazi Party and German government agencies had been instructed to refer all Jewish emigration applications to the bureau. Exactly what the bureau could do for the refugees and how it would function was still something of a mystery, Hugh Wilson, the U.S. ambassador in Berlin, could only state laconically: 'The Embassy has not yet ascertained the character and functions of this bureau.'[25] One of the first actions of this bureau seems to have been the imposition of a special passport tax levied against all citizens issued with departure documents. The scale of the tax varied and was calculated according to the wealth of the intending emigrant. Funds gathered through this tax, according to the *Jewish Telegraphic Agency* in New York, would allegedly be used to assist poorer emigrants.[26]

By 25 August it seemed clear that the bureau, headquartered at the confiscated Rothschild-Palais in Prinz Eugenstrasse, was a central clearing house for immigration procedures which had the full cooperation of the German secret police. Chief of the section of Jewish Affairs, Dr Lange, told U.S. diplomatic representatives that the introduction of the bureau would greatly speed up the deportation of the Jews in line with urgent government policy. He said that the secret police, who had previously handled all applications for documentation, had gladly handed over this responsibility to the bureau.

The operations of this bureau were, of course, designed to rid the Reich of its 'Jewish element' as quickly as possible and in any manner deemed necessary. It was certainly not at odds with the German practice of forcibly and clandestinely driving Jewish people over the borders of neighbouring countries. For example, shortly after the opening of the bureau the U.S.

Department of State learned that German troops had secretly evicted further Jewish people across the Luxembourg frontier. These people were described as being, '...penniless, insufficiently clothed and without passports'. All the evictions had occurred at night and at unguarded parts of the frontier. There had been similar incidences on the Swiss frontier. The Swiss were aware of the practice but were unable to make any strong protests because it could have disrupted German/Swiss diplomatic, business and military relations.[27]

A similar situation existed on the Belgian border and, according to a highly confidential memorandum in State Department files, the Belgian Ministry of Justice had issued a communiqué on 26 August, 1938, stating that arrangements had been made to, '...drive back all foreigners who shall illegally enter Belgium'.[28]

This practice of forcibly evicting the Jewish people across the borders of other countries served a duel purpose. Firstly, it was a method of obtaining the Germans' primary objective of ridding their country of Jews, but it also created strong anti-Semitic feelings in those countries that were now being flooded with Jewish refugees. Thus, the Germans theorised, with a rising tide of powerful anti-Semitism occurring throughout Europe, German anti-Semitic policies would be proved to be right. No-one wanted Jews and whatever measures were then taken to rid Europe of Jews would be justified. Even if it meant extermination.

In Aachen, close to the Belgian border, a Belgian citizen of German descent was running an underground refugee operation. He would meet with desperate refugees and for the sum of six thousand Reichsmarks smuggle his charges across the Belgian border. His *modus operandi* was to have his charges arrive at Aachen where they would be forced to wait for up to six days before the 'correct personnel' were on duty at the frontier. He would then place the refugees—up to six at a time—into the back of his motor truck and hide them beneath piles of straw. At the frontier the German guards were bribed with an undisclosed amount of Reichsmarks and the Belgian frontier official was paid eight hundred Reichsmarks. The refugees were then taken to Antwerp and hidden until they could be moved quietly to Copenhagen where they would apply for U.S. immigration visas.[29]

German and Italian ships were also 'dumping' large numbers of refugees at Shanghai and Rublee was told to bring the matter up with the German government because it was, 'creating a serious problem'.[30]

Jewish refugees from Austria disembarking at Shanghai from the Italian ship Conte Verde.

—United States Holocaust Memorial Museum, courtesy of U.S. National Archives and Records Administration.

On 29 August, the State Department was informed by the U.S. Embassy in France that the *Jewish Telegraphic Agency* in Paris had reported that because several statements made by President Roosevelt had been seen by the German government as containing, '...severe attacks against the German Reich,' the Germans were now unwilling to open negotiations with the London committee over the refugee issue.[31]

Meanwhile, in Austria and Germany it seemed that the Gestapo was continuing its efforts in aiding the illegal importation of Jewish refugees into Palestine. Exactly what role the Gestapo played in this migration is not entirely clear but it is clear that they were under instructions to increase the exodus for two reasons. Firstly to rid the Reich of as many Jews as possible, and secondly to embarrass the British government which could never hope to seal off Palestine effectively to the Jewish people. U.S. consul general to Jerusalem, George Wadsworth, wrote a detailed report for his superiors in August 1938, just as the London committee was becoming established. Wadsworth stated that the British government was indeed being placed in an embarrassing situation. Prior to the Nazi pogroms, illegal Jewish immigrants in Palestine, although not being welcomed, had been tolerated to a certain degree. They were generally allowed to remain in the country not by law, but through a policy of social acceptance. They were not, of course, allowed to sponsor the immigration of friends or families, as were legal migrants. As the Nazi pogroms increased so too did the numbers of illegal migrants and, as one British official stated: 'Humanitarian considerations aside, to what country could we deport them if we were to intensify efforts for their apprehension.'[32]

At this crucial time in the Jewish refugees debate several countries were working quickly to tighten up their immigration laws in order to prevent the immigration of Jews. Argentina, for example, which was represented at both Évian and London, altered its laws, severely restricting Jewish immigration from 1 October, 1938, and advised its consul in Berlin that the six hundred visas that had then just been issued to Jewish refugees would be invalid unless those refugees could get to Argentina before the new law came into force. As it was now 3 September this was clearly impossible as all the immigrants would be travelling by sea.[33] The U.S. Department of State was horrified at the implications of the Argentinean move and claimed that the exclusion would, '...create a most unfortunate impression in this hemisphere and in Europe'.[34] This furore resulted in a storm of diplomatic messages between the U.S. and Argentina, with Argentina claiming that the U.S. should be doubling its immigration quota to provide for desperate and homeless refugees. Patiently the U.S. Department of State once again explained that no country had been asked to make any changes to its immigration laws, neither tightening nor liberalising them. The Argentineans argued that the refugees were mainly musicians and artists, the type of people definitely not needed in Argentina. However, under considerable diplomatic pressure the Argentinean government finally relented and stated that providing those refugees who had been issued with visas left Germany before 1

October, they would be allowed into the country.[35]

***

Even under the considerable public pressure that was by this time mounting, the U.S. authorities were still not prepared to change, even temporarily, their existing immigration laws. In early September the editor of the *Chattanooga News*, George Milton, wrote to Cordell Hull's office asking what changes were being contemplated to facilitate the Jews. Harry McBride of Hull's office replied, '...we do not believe that any material change in our immigration laws and regulations based on conditions abroad rather than conditions in this country, is either necessary or desirable.'[36]

As the weeks passed there seemed to be no concrete solution to the many problems. Unable to pinpoint effectively any chance of direct discussions with the German government, the London committee languished, its members becoming increasingly discontented. In late September the committee was obliged to request that it temporarily wind up its work.[37]

Cordell Hull informed Rublee that in his opinion the work should continue, but as the salaries of both Rublee and his staff were being paid out of combined funds supplied by all the nations involved, the State Department would be forced to accede to the vote of the majority.[38]

As tensions grew between Great Britain and Germany it seemed clear that the committee's work would, in the event of hostilities, have to cease. There was also considerable consternation over the funding for the committee. The U.S. had paid a portion of its share of $5000; Peru had paid U.S.$450 but even Great Britain was procrastinating with its payment. Ambassador Kennedy in London lamented: 'The British informed us originally that they would make their payment on October first. Now they say that in view of the crisis they will be unable to pay their contribution for some time to come.'[39]

The French were being equally as uncooperative over their payment. Five governments had acknowledged that they had received a demand for payment and all other governments failed to reply to the demand. Clearly, despite the resolutions made at Évian, there was considerable silent and passive opposition to the continuation of the London committee and its goals.[40] As the annual budget of the committee was estimated to be U.S.$40,000, the funds paid to this point were obviously grossly insufficient to keep the organisation running for any considerable length of time.[41]

In late September 1938 Myron C. Taylor returned to the United States and issued a lengthy press release detailing his actions and those of the other delegates to the Évian conference. A few days later the secretary of state, Cordell Hull, received a telegram from Albert Einstein and Thomas Mann in which the two men stated:

> We turn to you in the sake of humanity to help and probably save the lives of the German refugees in Prague who are ordered to leave Czechoslovakia before next Tuesday alternative to extradition to Germany. These men and women who, in most cases are even without passports and among whom there are many important artists and scientists, are in imminent danger of life. Therefore we beg you to help us in any way.[42]

The assistant secretary of state, George Messersmith, replied that there was little to be done and that the U.S. government was watching the situation carefully.[43]

***

Meanwhile, in London, nothing further was being done to approach the German authorities over the problem. George Rublee was becoming increasingly frustrated. He badly wanted to approach the Germans but the British were stalling for time. Rublee claimed: '...They are still of the opinion that the work of the intergovernmental committee should be subordinated to high policy and they are therefore not [repeat not] really anxious that I should go to Berlin where my conversations with the German authorities ... might have some repercussion on other developments to which they attach importance'.[44]

Rublee went on to state that in his opinion the remaining nations represented at London were all firmly sticking to their intransigent policies of refugee immigration, at least until the German authorities changed their policy and allowed the refugees to take ample funds for their support into other countries. He said that the Germans were almost certainly willing to talk but that the British were unwilling for him to open negotiations. Rublee lamented, '...it is being said already that the intergovernmental committee has been in existence for several months and it has accomplished virtually nothing, that, in fact, it has provided an incentive to the governments of refugee and settlement to increase their restrictions'.[45]

In mid October Ambassador Kennedy in London telephoned the U.S. ambassador in Berlin to ask his opinion of approaching the German government over the issue. The U.S. ambassador at Berlin was not available but a guarded conversation was carried on with another member of the embassy staff: 'What's the weather like in Berlin?' The diplomats knew, of course, that their telephone conversation was almost certainly being monitored by the German secret police and the reference to the weather was actually referring to the attitude of the German government.[46]

Shortly afterwards, despite British objections, the U.S. Department of State instructed its embassy in Berlin to approach the German Foreign Office with an informal request that Rublee be received by the German government. The request was made but the response, as usual, was far from promising.

Meanwhile, in Czechoslovakia the refugee problem had become a huge one for the authorities. By early October 1938 it was estimated that some two hundred thousand Jewish refugees had fled across the border and the Czech authorities had issued a forty-eight hour expulsion order. However, the execution of this order entailed such hardship for the refugees that it was virtually impossible to implement and little more was done to deport them back to Germany. They were accommodated in temporary shelters and the government was providing a crown per day for food. Yet the government knew that it would be impossible to find work and homes for them in the short term, and with winter approaching, with food, shelter and clothing in short supply, it seemed that the situation for the refugees would quickly become very grim.[47]

***

The Gestapo was also instrumental in allowing Jewish refugees to flee into Lithuania with temporary 'summer resort' visas. On 13 October, 1938, the U.S. legation in Lithuania informed the State Department that one hundred and twenty Austrian and German Jews had been allowed to cross the border using such visas, and they had been told when receiving permission to leave Germany that despite their temporary visas, if they returned either to Germany or Austria they would be deported to concentration camps. Desperate measures were made by a number of Jewish organisations to have their Lithuanian temporary visas extended into permanent ones, but the intransigent Lithuanian authorities advised that, '...while the Lithuanian government was sympathetic to the plight of the Jewish refugees ... it was not prepared to grant these refugees a permanent haven'. The government added that Lithuanian resources were far too limited to provide food and shelter, even for such a small number of people, adding that the country did not want to establish a precedent that might attract other refugees.[48]

The Lithuanian cabinet finally agreed to issue temporary residency permits to those refugees who held the summer permits. Some received visas valid for two months, some for one month and several for only seven days. Those refugees who did not apply for these temporary visas were being hunted down by the Lithuanian police and faced immediate deportation. The Hebrew Immigrant Aid Society continued to make representations to other governments in efforts to gain access for them, and it seemed likely that most would eventually find homes in South American countries, although Paraguay continued to state categorically that it would take no more Jews.[49] This statement was backed by action. When a ship filled with Jewish refugees suddenly arrived at the river port of Asuncion soon afterwards, the intending immigrants were not allowed to land despite the fact that they all possessed visas. Under considerable pressure the government finally permitted them to land, but regulations concerning their employment as agriculturists were immediately enforced.

Jews who had arrived earlier and sent into agricultural areas to work had been subjected to considerable scrutiny; those who had ceased agricultural pursuits to become businessmen had immediately been rounded up and expelled.[50]

***

Following the Sudetenland transfer from Czechoslovakia in September 1938, the problem of Jewish refugees intensified considerably, and tens of thousand more Jews attempted to flee from Nazi persecution. Many of these were fleeing west into the Netherlands, and Netherlands authorities quickly took steps to strengthen their borders in an effort to prevent the refugees from entering. J. Webb Benton, the *chargé d'affaires* at the Hague, informed his superiors in Washington:

> The Minister for Justice, alive to the necessity of keeping out of the country undesirable aliens, has ordered a strict watch day and night along the frontiers, in addition to the regular supervision already exercised at the various frontier stations. The constabulary has not, however, sufficient men for the purpose, and it is for this reason ... that the Ministry of Justice had arranged with the Ministry of Defence for the temporary loan of men from the frontier defence battalions to assist the

constabulary in carrying out their increased frontier patrol duties.[51]

Yugoslavia responded similarly, advising that the authorities would continue to follow the same policy they had adopted after the *Anschluss*, that is, under no circumstances would they accept political refugees from the German Reich.[52]

***

Romania pressed harder for the London committee to consider not only Germany and Austria, but also to have other countries 'plagued by Jews' on an agenda for deportation.[53] At a later meeting held between a member of the Romanian government and the British minister to Bucharest, the Romanians asked if it would be possible to send fifty thousand Romanian Jews per year to Palestine. Naturally, the request was not regarded seriously by the British government.[54]

***

It appears that, at Évian, not a great deal of credibility was given to Albania as a source of possible refugee intake. Albania was not on the Évian invitation list. However, despite the dangers and difficulties involved in successive Italian, German and communist control, Albania was one of the few European countries occupied by Axis powers which ended the war with a larger Jewish population than it had contained before the war. Approximately 1200 Jewish families would be hidden by Albanian families during the war.[55]

Albania is credited with not only saving its own Jewish population during the war but also saving those Jewish refugees who had fled to the country. In 1943 when the Nazi authorities ordered Albania to hand over all its Jews they completely refused to comply. Under threat of mass deportations the Jews were taken from the cities and hidden in the country. Non Jewish Albanians would steal identity cards from police stations so they could be used by the Jews. The Albanian underground resistance warned that they would execute anyone handing Jews over to the Germans.[56]

The pro-Jewish attitude was amplified in the case of the Gerechter family. Alice and Siegbert Gerechter lived in Hamburg where Siegbert Gerechter was a merchant and manufacturer of work-gloves. Alice's forebears had lived in Hamburg since 1763. Her two sisters had now emigrated to America and the couple, with their young child, Johanna 'Jutta' wished also to emigrate to the U.S. However, Siegbert had been born at Posen and the U.S. authorities considered him to be Polish, rather than German, so he was allocated a far high quota number than his wife and child. The Gerechters decided, therefore, not to emigrate at that time but to remain together as a family unit. In March 1939, nine months after Évian, they left Hamburg for Albania. From that time until the Italian invasion and occupation of Albania (invaded 7 April, 1939) the family lived at the city of Durazzo. Even after the Italian occupation the family was treated well by the Italians, although during the Italian-Greek War of 1940-41 they were moved to an internment camp at Berat—not because they were Jews but because they were simply 'undesirable aliens'. Finally returning to Durazzo, the Gerechter family continued living at the port city until the German invasion and occupation of September 1943. After that time they were always in imminent danger of arrest, although they were aided by a couple named Njazi and Lizalotte Pilku. Lizalotte actually harboured Nazi sympathies but this did not influence her decision to help the Gerechter family. She and Njazi would introduce the Gerechters as relatives from Germany. While in hiding Alice and Siegbert were able to support themselves by taking in washing from Italian truck-drivers. The Germans mined the city of Durazzo, fearing a possible Allied landing, and all civilians were evacuated to the capital, Tirana. During the period of the German occupation the Albanians did not hand over Jews to the German authorities. Instead the Albanian government told its people to say, when asked by the Germans, that they did not know of any Jews, only Albanians. King Zog, then living in comfortable exile at the Ritz Hotel in London, wanted to give all the Jewish refugees Albanian citizenship in order to protect them from the Germans.

From left to right: unknown, Johanna Gerechter, Alice Gerechter, Luan Pilku and Lizalotte Boetge-Pilku.

—United States Holocaust Memorial Museum, courtesy of Johanna Neumann, (née Gerechter [pictured]).

However, despite every effort to protect the Gerechter family they were registered for deportation during the summer of 1944. That would mean only one thing—death at a Nazi concentration camps.

The family now went on the run, fleeing from town to town, always hiding. When communist partisans took control of Albania in late 1944 they suspected everyone of collaborating with the Germans. The communists launched a tremendous terror campaign, shooting intellectuals and arresting and torturing thousands of innocent people. In such a state of chaos it became almost impossible for Jews to obtain exit permits. However, when an epidemic broke out the communists found themselves badly in need of vaccines to fight typhoid and cholera and so agreed to exchange one hundred Jews for the required doses of vaccine. In 1945 the Gerechters were able to go to Italy where they lived in the *Tricase Porto* displaced persons' camp. It was here that they came into contact with survivors of the Nazi concentration camps and learned for the first time what had been happening in Germany and Poland to the Jews of Europe. The following year Alice Gerechter and her daughter Johanna left for the U.S. Siegbert went to Rome where he managed finally to obtain a U.S. visa and he joined his wife and daughter the following year. In 1998 Njazi and Lizalotte Pilku, who had done so much to assist and hide the Gerechters, were recognised by Yad Vashem Holocaust Memorial as being 'Righteous Among the Nations'.[57]

***

Meanwhile, returning now to 1938, the Czechoslovakian situation was becoming increasingly more difficult and news of the plight of the refugees stranded there was further emphasized over the killing of a man named Peter Forster. Forster had escaped from a Nazi concentration camp and found temporary refuge in Czechoslovakia. He had later been extradited to Germany for execution. The International Bureau for the Rights and Aid to Political Refugees, based in Paris later reported:

> Although it was a known fact that death awaited him, the government ... turned a deaf ear to the appeals and petitions which were sent from all over the world to save him from extradition. Handed over to the Gestapo on the morning of December 19th, Peter Forster was 'judged' by a special tribune and condemned to death the same day. His head fell under the axe 24 hours after his departure from Prague.[58]

There were overcrowded refugee camps scattered throughout Czechoslovakia at this time, places such as Cerveny Hradec, Kladnoer, Cornicice, Klattau and Pinsck. Rations were only issued to the inmates during weekdays and not on weekends. They received a very small monetary allowance but at Cerveny Hradec and possibly at other camps this allowance was cut from six crowns per day to 4.5 crowns and then four crowns.[59]

As the political situation deepened across Europe other countries tightened their immigration procedures. Norway, as we have seen, was particularly intransigent. Applications for admission into the country—especially after the Sudetenland transfer, rose to staggering proportions. One consulate alone was reported to have received fifty-two thousand applications within the space of a few months. Yet Norwegian authorities claimed that it did not matter how many applications they received, Norway was not, '...a land for immigrants.' Not even professional men or businessmen would be admitted.[60]

The influential and widely read Norwegian newspaper, *Aftenposten* published an editorial outlining the country's reasons for not being able to take in refugees, claiming that it would have been impossible to offer satisfactory living conditions and that therefore it was necessary to monitor the control of the flow of migrants. As a result the importation of migrants had, at that time, virtually ceased.[61]

The newspaper went on to state that there had been many terrible scenes at the borders as large numbers of Jewish people were turned away. They quoted an instance of one Jewish man refused entry who had leaned from the train window, waved his passport clearly displaying the large red J, and shouted: 'It is a catastrophe for personal freedom.' Immigration procedures had been considerably tightened. Refugees could no longer claim that they were marrying Norwegian citizens, nor were they successful in smuggling themselves ashore at the many ports. The report ended by advising that immigration into the country had now largely stopped and as this was becoming so well known intending refugees would no longer try.[62]

***

The situation, as we have seen, was much the same everywhere. In Mexico, for example, when a group of twenty-one Jewish refugees wished to land from a steamer they were denied permission to do so and President Cárdenas himself stated that although his government was willing to cooperate with the Évian and London committees, no person would be allowed to enter the country without first having undergone the rigorous admission procedures.[63]

European refugees denied entry to the United States and Mexico aboard the SS Quanza when the vessel called into Norfolk, Virginia, for refuelling, 11 September, 1940.

United States Holocaust Memorial Museum, courtesy of AP/Wide World.

The Mexican government later indicated its willingness to ease restrictions slightly, in accordance with, '...our population and our economic resources'.[64]

***

Meanwhile, efforts continued to have the German government agree to a visit by George Rublee. On 20 October, 1938, the U.S. ambassador to Berlin, Hugh Wilson, had a luncheon meeting with Reich State Secretary Brinkmann and his chief assistant, *Ministerialdirektor*

Bergmann. Brinkmann agreed that something had to be done to help alleviate the problem and promised to speak with *Reichsmarschall* Hermann Göring (also spelt: Goering) on the matter. Brinkmann stated that it might have been possible to work out a system whereby the Jews who wished to leave could purchase goods and take these goods with them. This would have to be in addition to normal trade and served the purposes of leaving Jewish capital in Germany. Wilson reported this to the U.S. Department of State, but with little enthusiasm.[65]

A later report stated that Göring and Dr Walter Funk had both indicated their willingness to meet with Rublee, although there was considerable consternation in U.S. diplomatic circles concerning Göring's influence over the issue and it was believed that the real decisions affecting Jewish emigration would be made at a higher level, possibly by *Reichsführer* Heinrich Himmler in consultation with Hitler himself.[66] Wilson soon afterwards reported that the German government seemed to be becoming even more deeply entrenched in its anti-Jewish policies and was taking the position that its members and representatives wanted to consult with no-one over the issue.[67]

Meanwhile, the Polish ambassador to the U.S. paid an unexpected visit to George Messersmith at the State Department. The ambassador conveyed the impression that his country was being especially patient in waiting for the U.S., and particularly the London committee, to reach a decision regarding the overpopulation of Jewish people in Poland. He said that he had a plan that might solve the problem. He claimed it might be possible for the Polish government to purchase a part of Portuguese-owned Angola and to ship a large percentage of the Polish Jews there where they could form a substantial Jewish colony. Messersmith was noncommittal in his reply, stating only that the concept should be thoroughly discussed with the Polish and Portuguese governments.[68]

***

After Myron Taylor's return to the United States he wrote a considerable report of his activities at Évian and London for the State Department. He also suggested that he go to Canada to hold private talks with the Canadian prime minister, MacKenzie King. Canada, like Australia at the time, was a vast underpopulated area badly in need of immigrants. However, Canada's policy regarding the Jewish refugees throughout this period was nothing less than shameful. Rublee's subsequent conversations with King proved unsatisfactory and during the period leading up to and during the Second World War, only approximately five thousand refugees found a home there. King was an expert on Canadian immigration. In 1906 he had represented Canada during negotiations with Britain regarding British immigration and was later the Canadian representative to India with special emphasis on Indian immigration. In 1938 Canadian immigration chief Frederick Blair was particularly zealous in holding back the tide of Jewish immigration, a zealousness that was directly attributable to the country's profound anti-Semitic policies. A post war poll showed that forty-nine per cent of Canadians considered Jews to be undesirable immigrants.[69]

The *Toronto Globe and Mail* reported that applications from Jewish doctors and other professions were being received but because there were a great many young people then eligible for registration into those professions applications from Jewish immigrants had to be approved by special order-in-council before they could be admitted.[70]

The press displayed mixed commitments over the issue of Canadian immigration and most of the newspapers commented with considerable revulsion upon the Jewish persecution, adding their voices of anger and bitterness over the, '...brutal policy of the authorities in Germany'.

However, as a later U.S. Department of State report claimed, '...the fact remains that little progress has been made either by the National or the Provincial Government in contributing materially to the relief of Jewish refugees'.[71]

The *Vancouver Sun* declared, on 11 November, 1938, that Germany and Italy had not conformed with their declared policy of conciliation and toleration in persecuting the Jews ruthlessly, and that any policy of 'appeasement' should include appeasement of European Jews.[72]

The *Victoria Daily Times* praised Roosevelt's options with regard to Germany's policy toward Jews and claimed that he was, '...the logical leader in foreign affairs of the Western Hemisphere'.[73]

The *Vancouver News-Herald* castigated the Canadian government for hesitating to offer refugee aid, claiming that Jewish immigrants would be, 'a definite help in building a new and more prosperous Canada, and in making more solid the broad basis of the justice and freedom of the British Commonwealth of Nations'.[74]

A report on press comments to the U.S. Department of State concluded that, '...unanimous emotional reaction of repugnance to the brutality in Germany together with the traditional prejudice against the Jew as a colonizer has produced a conflict which has nullified concrete attempts to alleviate the Jewish situation'.[75]

There is little doubt that the country was divided over the issue. The French Canadian element, both in the press and privately, was seen as having misgivings and was, in general, determined not to relax, 'in the slightest degree' the strict immigration procedures that had been in force in Canada since 1930. On the other hand English speaking Canadians seemed to have been more liberal in their attitude, and leftist groups were particularly emphatic that the immigration procedures should be relaxed to ensure a steady flow of refugees into the country. Confidential State Department documents revealed that the Catholic Church was profoundly against any such mass immigration and the *Action Catholique*, a Roman Catholic publication, stated that Canada had already taken in too many Jews and that they had caused, '...vexatious problems' in Canada.[76]

Some Catholic journalists used their editorials to point out that the Jews were seen as having 'serious faults', which would need to be pardoned by the Christian world.[77]

The U.S. Department of State was confidentially informed in February 1939 that the Canadian Corps Association had sent a strongly worded plea to Prime Minister Mackenzie King, begging him not to allow any more Jews into the country.

One newspaper pointed out that while the Canadian people were sympathetic to the many problems associated with the difficult issues of Jewish emigration, and particularly to those refugees who were attempting to flee from Germany and Austria, there were many other issues to be confronted including the thorny problem of unemployment in Canada. There was also the problem of assimilating German speaking people into a country where the residents spoke either French or English. Yet it was the problem of unemployment that was first and foremost on the agenda for Canadians, and that while their empathy went out to those in need, the Canadian authorities had decided to maintain the country's immigration restrictions.[78]

Meanwhile, as the politicians shuffled and procrastinated, the Holocaust grew in horrific momentum.

The problem was exacerbated on 7 November, 1938, with the shooting of German diplomat Ernst von Rath at the German Embassy in Paris. The assassin was a seventeen-year-old Jew named Herschel Grynszpan, the son of a deported Polish Jew. Although Von Rath lingered for a while his injuries were severe and death was virtually a certainty. He died on 9 November. This event led to what was later described as the greatest pogrom in history.

Following the shooting of Von Rath, Göring issued a decree fining German Jews one thousand million marks, the equivalent of £80 million at that time. He also decreed that all Jews were barred from retail and wholesale trade, Jewish owners of shops and residences damaged in the riots would have to pay for all damages while the Reich confiscated all the insurance claims. The fine was calculated at £136 per head.[79]

The pogrom included the suppression of cultural performances, bans on imports of all Jewish publications and the banning of meetings. Jewish children were refused admittance to German primary schools.

The Berlin correspondent of a British newspaper stated that Jews remained indoors all day for fear of riots and that Nazi leaders were about to meet to draw up plans for, 'an intensified anti-Jewish drive'. The report continued:

> The shooting of Dr von Rath will complicate the Polo-German negotiations over the Polish Jews in Germany. The entire press has broken out in hysteria reported to be inspired by Herr Hitler. Screaming red headlines demand the extermination of the Jewish menace. Herr Streicher's[80] paper says: 'It is evident that Germany will reply to Judaism in a manner opening the

eyes of the too tolerant world as to where the enemies of peace can be found.'[81]

Over the following few days, about four months after the Évian conference, the infamous *Kristallnacht*—the 'Night of Broken Glass', exploded in a violent and mindless rampage of anti-Semitic fury right throughout both Germany and Austria. The date was 9 November, 1938. This was a carefully orchestrated programme of destruction that raged through almost every city, town and village in those countries. A total of 267 synagogues and congregational buildings were burnt to the ground. Thousands of Jewish shops and other forms of Jewish businesses had their windows broken, Jews were evicted from their homes and thrown from trams and moving trains. Thirty thousand Jewish men were arrested and sent to the concentrations camps at Dachau, Buchenwald and Sachsenhausen. Women and children were harnessed to wagons and whipped through the streets like beasts of burden. There was a particularly cruel flurry of lynchings and even the Germans themselves admitted to hanging summarily thirty-three people—although according to various British and American journalists present at the time this figure was grossly understated by the Nazis and hundreds of Jews were actually murdered.

Within days the press was quoting German newspapers as reporting:

> German Jews were answerable because they worked on a worldwide scale against Germany in the hope of deteriorating her relations with other Powers. They must bear the consequences. It disgraced the spirit of German art to sit next to Jews in a cinema theatre. There would be no future occasion to damage Jewish shops because these were passing immediately into Aryan hands. The hatred of the foreign Press left Germans unworried.[82]

Foreign and national newspapers were reporting that the value of Jewish property in Germany was estimated at £660 million. It was rumoured that no Jew would be allowed to retain over £250. Only four doctors were left to attend hundreds of patients at the largest Jewish hospital and two clinics were without doctors. The arrest of Jewish lawyers left their compatriots legally defenceless. Patients suffering from tuberculosis at Soden sanitarium were turned out to fend for themselves. An orphanage at Caputh was closed on half an hour's notice. Jews dared not assemble even for private prayers.[83] The press reports continued:

> The outrages are continuing at Clogau and elsewhere, and many Jews are hiding in

the woods in the hope of crossing the frontier. Others sit dazed in their homes dreading the summons to concentration camps. All shops in Munich are displaying signs 'No Jews admitted'. The signs are exactly similar to those shown in Berlin restaurants, says the Berlin correspondent of the British United Press. A mob in a small town in North Germany destroyed all Jewish shops and cut Jews' clothes and underwear to pieces, as well as removing bedding. The mob also took Iron Crosses, won in the Great War, from the Jews.[84]

As the pogrom continued President Roosevelt was reported as stating:

> News of the past few days from Germany has deeply shocked public opinion in the United States. Such news from any part of the world would inevitably produce a similar profound reaction on American people in every part of the nation. I myself could scarcely believe that such things could occur in the 20th Century civilization.[85]

Soon afterwards the National Negro Congress in the U.S. asked Roosevelt to, '...provide in America a free haven for oppressed Jewish people,' and the *New York Sun* in a powerful editorial remarked, '...it is hard for a peace-loving democracy to deceive itself that it can ever achieve appeasement with such barbaric ferocity'.[86]

The *New York Evening Post* declared in a leader entitled, 'German Moral Leprosy' that Germany had to be isolated and quarantined until the country could, '...throw off the loathsome affliction that is Hitlerism'.[87]

The tragic events of *Kristallnacht* finally prompted the citizens of many of the so-called 'Nations of Asylum' to petition their respective governments to accept more Jewish refugees, irrespective of their social or financial status. Under considerable pressure Great Britain accepted a further nine thousand, Belgium took in several hundred, Holland another 1700, but these numbers were far too insignificant to make any real impression on the problem and none of the countries officially liberalised their immigration laws.

During the four or five months after the events at Évian, Mexico, Chile and Uruguay did change their immigration laws, adding a number of quite severe restrictions designed to preclude Jewish people from those countries.[88] Uruguayan consuls abroad were informed that no visas were to be issued unless they were referred firstly to the Uruguayan Ministry of Foreign Affairs, and the Uruguayan consul at Bern was relieved of his office for issuing too many visas to refugees.[89]

In Uruguay itself there was widespread anti-Semitic activity. Pro-fascist organs and also some of the country's principal publications conducted campaigns against Jewish immigration and stated that the Jews were responsible for a number of crimes. These allegedly included the bribery of Uruguayan officials on a very large scale, that many of the refugees were, 'dangerous agitators,' that the refugees were working for starvation wages thus displacing Uruguayan nationals, and that they were entering the country illegally to engage in 'nefarious and criminal activities'. The papers were evidently following the same lines of propaganda as the Nazi press. They claimed that the Jewish refugees were threatening the livelihood of Uruguayan doctors, dentists and businessmen and that they were buying up properties at an alarming rate. The newspapers castigated the Uruguayan government for not being strong enough with regard to the refugees and stated that immigration laws should be more strongly enforced. More moderate newspapers also expressed their concern over the issue, although with somewhat less vitriol.[90]

In November 1938, as tighter restrictions were enforced, the Western press was reporting:

The wandering Jew may not even wander the streets of Berlin in future, or camp in Grunewald forest around the city. The taxation authorities have received an order to refuse Jews certificates ... this means that no Jew may quit the country as the certificate is essential for departure.[91]

Following the *Kristallnacht* pogrom George Rublee called upon all of the thirty-two 'Nations of Asylum' to act quickly and to accept twenty-five thousand Jews each. If just half of the nations had agreed to this proposal the German and Austrian Jews could have been saved from the Holocaust.

While some nations such as Great Britain and Denmark were secretly allowing a small number of refugees into the country—keeping this from the press and public—most nations ignored Rublee's plea. Guatemala was one of the exceptions. On 29 November the Guatemalan government—in spite of its earlier intransigence, advised the U.S. Department of State that it was now willing to allow one hundred families into the country. These people would have to be agriculturists and would be carefully selected by a panel of judges formed to scrutinise their qualifications to work on the land. The Guatemalan government also advised that there would, at some time in the future, be limited openings for people trained in such industries as 'pottery, chemistry, plumbing, teaching, experimental botany and physiology'.[92]

In Denmark, the Danish minister for justice, Mr K.K. Steincke, was under considerable pressure over the issue. He was being attacked by the communist elements in the country who claimed that he and the government's policies were under the influence of Berlin. The National Socialists in the country stated that he was a 'Jew lover' and that as a result of Évian some five thousand Jews would be allowed into the country. Steincke responded to these allegations by allowing himself to be interviewed on radio, during which he stated that despite press reports it was not true that Denmark had agreed to take up to five thousand Jewish refugees. He pointed out that the conference had not, thus far, influenced his country to take any more refugees but that it would now be necessary to act as humanely as possible. However, he added the codicil that Denmark was limited in what it could realistically achieve in efforts to find a solution to this European problem.[93]

Australia was now allowing a pathetically thin trickle of Jews into the country but the government was being especially careful not to be seen by the public as opening the gates to Jewish refugees. Despite this, much of the press was alarmingly set against further immigration. The *Truth*, in Brisbane, stated that the issue needed, '...a firm check at once,' and claimed that, '...more Jews have already arrived here than this country can absorb'. This was far from the truth. Australia had the potential for very large-scale immigration, yet the newspaper continued, '...the percentage of Jews to the Gentile population in Australia must not be increased ... the only thing that will satisfy Australia is an absolute ban upon the alarming tidal inflow of these refugee aliens—hunted from lands where apparently they were a problem, coming here to provide us with a problem no less intolerable'. The *Truth* had apparently adopted the slogan, 'No More Refugee Jews'.[94]

The Australian government soon afterwards released details of its immigration proposals concerning the refugee issue. Despite Rublee's plea these included an allowance of only fifteen thousand people over three years and the government pointed out that these were not to be people of only Jewish descent, but, '...Aryans, non-Aryan Christians—that is, people wholly or partly of Jewish race, and of the Christian religion, and Jews'. These people would be allowed into the country on the condition that existing labour standards were not disturbed, the immigrants met the requirements of the infamous

White Australia Policy, each of the immigrants was of good health and good character, and each had the required amount of money. The government pointed out that these refugees would be distributed as widely as possible to ensure that no Jewish enclaves sprang up.[95]

***

Rublee was astounded at the lack of response to his pleas following *Kristallnacht* but he was determined to impress upon his own government the urgency of the situation. Four days after *Kristallnacht* he sent a cable to the U.S. secretary of state, Cordell Hull, in which he stated:

> The attack on the Jewish community on the one hand, and the indifference of the participating [Évian] governments to the fate of the victims on the other, has brought the affairs of the intergovernmental committee to a critical state where, in our opinion, immediate action is required if the President's initiative [in calling the Évian conference] is to lead to a positive result.... With the exception of the United States ... doors have been systematically closed to involuntary migrants since the meeting at Évian.[96]

In this Rublee was stating cold hard facts. As we have seen, following the Évian conference many of the representative countries had actually tightened their immigration laws. Uruguay, Argentina, Chile and Mexico, all adopted new and tougher legislation in a determined effort to keep the Jews out of their countries.

Rublee reported that in the countries surrounding Germany the illegal crossings by refugees had risen to such staggering proportions that those countries could no longer cope with the problem. He added: 'The consequence is that they have been obliged to ship refugees back to Germany indiscriminately and with a disregard of the probable consequences to the unfortunate people, many of whom have been immediately thrust into prison camps.'[97]

Rublee stated that upon his request the Belgians and Dutch had temporarily ceased shipping the Jews back to Germany but only on the understanding that he was about to go to Germany where it was hoped that arrangements would be made to allow the refugees to take a portion of their money with them when they fled from Germany and Austria. Rublee added however, '...but ... if my visit to Germany fails to materialize, they will be obliged to ... throw back into Germany many of the people whom they are now holding in special camps'.[98]

Rublee was profoundly disappointed with the responses he was receiving to his diplomatic overtures to the various so-called 'Nations of Asylum'. He reported to the State Department that he had discussed the possibilities of refugee immigration with representatives of the Latin American republics and the British dominions and in every case had met, 'with a negative response'. He said that news and decrees were being published and promulgated each week that rendered the prospects of immigrant reception more and more unlikely. He added that new places of settlement were not being opened up and the likelihood that he would be received in Berlin was becoming more remote.[99]

This was even more especially so when, on 14 November, under mounting diplomatic hostility, the U.S. Department of State under orders from President Roosevelt recalled Hugh Wilson, the U.S. ambassador to Berlin. The German ambassador to Washington, Hans Dieckhoff, reported to the German Foreign Office that a, 'hurricane is raging here' over the *Kristallnacht* pogrom, and was himself recalled to Berlin on 18 November. Neither diplomat ever returned to his post.

President Roosevelt was horrified by the events of *Kristallnacht* and publicly denounced the terror at a press conference he held on 15

November, 1938. However, when asked by American journalists if new changes were to be made to existing U.S. immigration laws; even temporary changes to allow added immigration of the persecuted Jews, Roosevelt's reply was a terse: 'No.' No changes were then being considered. This attitude was mirrored throughout the remainder of the 'Nations of Asylum'. All of these countries publicly denounced the horror of *Kristallnacht* and expressed a strong disapproval of the Nazi government but they all steadfastly refused to make any changes to their immigration laws.

Prior to his departure from Berlin, Hugh Wilson was successful in gaining an interview with Joachim von Ribbentrop, the German foreign minister (later hanged at Nuremberg). Ribbentrop stated that he thought it would be impossible for the German government to deal with Rublee or his committee because the German government did not recognise the authority of the committee. He then asked if Rublee was a Jew and Wilson, somewhat startled, told Ribbentrop that Rublee's ancestors were French Huguenots. Ribbentrop then said that although the German government could not meet officially with Rublee, and as the Germans badly wanted to find ways of ridding the Reich of the Jews, there might be scope for a clandestine meeting in a country such as Holland.[100]

Rublee was by now becoming desperate. Despite considerable diplomatic moves at various levels it seemed that the German government and the intergovernmental committee in London had reached an impasse. The problem was further compounded because Rublee did not seem to have any concrete plans to present to the Germans, even if they did agree to meet with him. No country had given any definite statements concerning how many extra refugees they were willing to take, and many countries were actually in the act of expelling them, just as the Germans were doing. At this stage Rublee was forced to question seriously the value of the intergovernmental committee and whether it would have any impact at all on the problem. Hugh Wilson, the U.S. ambassador to Berlin, left Germany later in November, travelling by sea via Southampton. Rublee met Wilson at Southampton and Wilson reiterated his belief that the Germans would not see Rublee in Berlin and that it would be best to consider a clandestine meeting in a 'neutral' country. Rublee agreed with this and informed the U.S. Department of State that efforts along these lines should not be abandoned.[101] With the situation rapidly deteriorating President Roosevelt instructed

Myron C. Taylor to return to London. Taylor sailed from New York aboard the steamer *Normandie* on 26 November, 1938, to attend a meeting which was to be held in London on 2 December that year.

***

Shortly afterwards Conrad Hoffman Jnr., the director of the International Missionary Council based at New York, wrote to Roosevelt claiming that, as Nazi atrocities had reached new heights in Germany and Austria, there was no time left for political or diplomatic manoeuvring. Hoffman had spent four years inside Germany during the First World War where he had worked for the Y.M.C.A. in serving the interests of Allied prisoners-of-war. He claimed that during the war Germany had captured some three million Allied soldiers and these men had been accommodated, with quite reasonable success, in ninety specially constructed camps. Hoffman claimed that if Germany alone had been capable, in times of war, to care for an added three million unwanted people, then surely the same could be done in a number of countries for the one million Jewish refugees who wished to flee from Nazi persecution. He said that if France, Britain and others all constructed camps where the Jews could be housed and fed until homes could be found for them then at least the immediate problem of getting them out of Germany and Austria, where many of them were being killed, persecuted, or were committing suicide, was a realistic alternative.[102]

The U.S. Department of State replied to Hoffman pointing out that in some countries such camps were already in existence, although the department failed to point out that in truth these were simply minor centres accommodating only those refugees who had been able to smuggle themselves across the borders.[103]

***

Meanwhile, in London, diplomatic moves were continued in an endeavour to offload the Jewish problem onto third-world countries. In November 1938 a discussion took place between Joseph Kennedy, the American ambassador to Great Britain, and Prime Minister Neville Chamberlain, at which the Jewish problem was discussed in some detail. The possibility of enticing the Brazilians into changing their intransigent stance was reviewed and the U.S. offered large sums of money to the United Kingdom virtually to take the Jewish problem out of the Americans' hands, although such efforts were only marginally successful.[104]

In Warsaw the leaders of Jewish communities urgently appealed to Jewish welfare workers in Great Britain, France, the United States, Argentina, South Africa and Australia to organise to hasten relief for the thousands of Jews who had been banished from Germany to Poland. Of course there was to be no escape.

When Hitler's troops marched into Poland the following year the Jews of that country and those who had been thrown out of Germany were rounded up and most were finally sent to the extermination camps.

For several days in late November it seemed for a while that a breakthrough may have been possible. The Germans agreed to hold a secret meeting with Rublee in Brussels, but would not name their negotiator. Shortly afterwards the Germans reneged on the agreement claiming only that their mysterious negotiator was ill and could not attend the meeting. The French pressed the German foreign minister on the matter but Von Ribbentrop had become decidedly intransigent. Avoiding the issue of the meeting he reportedly stated:

> ...the Jews in Germany without exception were pickpockets, murderers and thieves. The property they possessed had been acquired illegally. The [German] government had therefore decided to

assimilate them with the criminal elements of the population. The property which they had acquired illegally would be taken from them. They would be forced to live in districts frequented by the criminal classes. They would be under police observation like other criminals. They would be forced to report to the police like other criminals were obliged to do. The German government could not help it if some of these criminals escaped to other countries which seemed too anxious to have them. It was not, however, willing for them to take the property which had resulted from their illegal operations with them.[105]

These statements, coming from such a high level diplomat, were received in Washington with considerable alarm. President Roosevelt himself ordered that they be verified so that, '...if there is any truth in it, the time will come when we can bring it out for the benefit of humanity'.[106]

Within days the U.S. Department of State received intelligence that Ribbentrop's words had been prophetic. Jews were to wear yellow star badges and there would begin large-scale arrests and deportations to camps. The mass assimilation of the Jews 'with the criminal classes' was in the process of being carried out.[107]

The Western world could not, of course, have envisaged where this mass discrimination would lead, and it seems clear that most Germans at this time had no idea that they were on the verge of butchering more than six million Jews.

The plan for the destruction of the Jewish race would only be fully outlined during the infamous Wannsee conference in Berlin on 20 January, 1942. Presiding over the conference was Reinhard Heydrich, head of the Reich Security Head Office (R.S.H.A.) which embraced the SS's own intelligence service, the Gestapo and Kripo (criminal police) and who had earlier established the Reich Central Office for Jewish Emigration, based in Berlin. It was Heydrich, second only to Himmler in absolute power, who would be in charge of the mass deportations in Poland and the creation of the *Einsatzgruppen* (special action squads) which would trail behind the German Army into its conquered territories such as Poland and Russia to massacre thousands of Jews, communists, prostitutes, the mentally ill, the intelligentsia, Gypsies and political adversaries. *Obergruppenfuehrer* Heydrich would later be assassinated in the Prague suburb of Holesvice (June 1942) by Jan Kubis and Josef Gabcik, two Czech Special Operations Executive operatives working in conjunction with the Czech Resistance.

The S.O.E. had code-named the mission 'Operation Anthropoid'. In retaliation Hitler would order a savage *vergeltungstaktion* (reprisal action) and in consequence the Nazis would obliterate the small coal-mining village of Lidice, thirty-two kilometres north-west of Prague, murdering a large percentage of its occupants including all its men who would be shot and eighty-two children who would be sent to Chelmo concentration camp where they would be gassed. Most of the women would be deported to Ravensbruck concentration camp. Two weeks after Lidice the small Czech village of Lezaky would also be destroyed; all its men and women would be shot and the children deported to concentration camps.[108]

Hitler had, of course, long maintained the vision of a Europe free of Jews and had made himself perfectly clear on the issue during at least five of his celebrated speeches, one of which was made to the Reichstag on 30 January, 1939: 'If the international financiers ... should again succeed in plunging the nations into a world war the result will be ... the annihilation of the Jewish races throughout Europe'.

But in December 1938 Hermann Göring had held a meeting with a group of German *gauleiters* (district leaders) and much of the content of this meeting was later provided to the U.S.

Department of State. In a highly classified report dated 9 December, 1938, the U.S. Embassy in Berlin advised the U.S. Department of State that Göring—who, after the war, claimed that he had never heard of the 'Final Solution'—was already using such terms as, 'liquidation of the Jewish problem,' and that Germany fully intended to, '...proceed forthwith to its solution,' and the '...complete elimination from Germany of all Jews within three years'.[109]

On 29 December, 1938, the leader of the World Zionist Organisation, Dr Chaim Weizmann, visited Turkey and met with executives of the Turkish government to whom he offered a 'substantial loan' if the government would allow two hundred thousand Jews to emigrate immediately to that country. It is not clear where this loan would come from, but it was presumably to be raised through Jewish bankers in the U.S., Britain and possibly Palestine. U.S. Department of State documents now reveal that the Turkish authorities were largely in favour of the plan but it was finally rejected by the cabinet on the grounds that such a large influx of Jews into the country would have substantial anti-Semitic ramifications.[110]

Interestingly, it was the Turkish consul general at Marseilles, Necdet Kent who would be responsible for saving a large number of

Jewish people. Kent was able to grant Turkish citizenship to hundreds of Jewish refugees, thus saving them from the Holocaust. On one occasion, at great personal risk to himself, he actually boarded a deportation train bound for Auschwitz and rescued seventy Jews to whom he had granted Turkish citizenship.[111]

***

In mid December 1938 Rublee was jubilant when he discovered that Hitler's chief financier, Doctor Hjalmar Horace Greeley Schacht,[112] who was then president of the German Reichsbank, was to present a plan, in London, outlining German deliberations on the refugee problem. Could it be that here, at last, was a possible breakthrough? Schacht was not acting under plenipotentiary powers but was simply to present the plan and not to discuss it.[113]

The meeting went ahead a few days later and Schacht presented details of a 'solution' outlined by the German government. In simple terms he stated that there were six hundred thousand Jews still inside Nazi controlled territories. Of these, two hundred thousand were old and would have to remain. He added that two hundred and fifty thousand were women and children. Of the remaining one hundred and fifty thousand these were men of working age and could emigrate at a rate of fifty thousand per year for the following three years. The women and children would be permitted to follow at a later date. Schacht made no statement regarding the fate of the older people other than to state that they would be, 'assured satisfactory conditions of existence'. To finance this emigration Schacht stated that Jews outside Germany would have to raise a loan equivalent to one milliard, five hundred million marks (1.5 billion) in foreign currency, either all at one time or in three annual instalments. He said that as a condition of the plan persecution in Germany would cease, although, in reality, there could be no guarantees of this as Schacht presented his plan orally without committing anything to paper.[114]

Once again the executives in the State Department were appalled. In a memorandum to Rublee and Taylor dated 19 December, 1938, Sumner Welles wrote:

> We have been in close touch with both the [U.S.] Treasury and the President's Advisory Committee with relation to Schacht's plan. No one who has been consulted believes that it would be possible to raise the sum mentioned, or even an appreciable part of it, under the terms

outlined. The plan is generally considered as asking the world to pay a ransom for the release of hostages in Germany and to barter human misery for increased exports.... Neither Advisory Committee, Treasury nor the State Department feels that the plan holds out any hope of acceptability.[115]

The British too considered the plan to be not only unworkable but a flagrant attempt at ransom on an enormous scale, and immediately rejected it.[116]

While in London, Schacht also stated that Rublee would be welcome in Berlin at any time during the following few weeks. He said that the details of his plan could there be worked on more thoroughly. Soon afterwards it was decided that Rublee would travel to Berlin for a meeting with Schacht and other top level Nazi officials sometime early in January 1939.[117]

On 2 January Schacht met with Hitler and Hitler approved of the Rublee meeting which was then scheduled for 11 January.[118]

The meeting was held on schedule but without any concrete results. Rublee clarified a number of points regarding the mechanics of emigration and then told Schacht that such a large sum could never be raised for the operation. Schacht was not surprised and even stated that a smaller sum would suffice. The conversation continued with financial technicalities, most of which Schacht claimed would have to be cleared with Hitler. He added that some of the points raised would be, 'rejected out of hand'.[119]

A second meeting was held two days later on 13 January, 1939. The conversation centered mainly on the technicalities of large-scale emigration and Schacht promised—after being pressed by Rublee—that the first group of people allowed to emigrate would be those who were already in concentration camps.[120]

While Rublee was in Berlin a window of a private apartment occupied by a member of the German consulate staff in Amsterdam was broken by a boy's slingshot. The window of a hotel room in the Hague which served as the office of a member of the German legation, was also broken, this time by a boy with an air rifle. The incidents were immediately represented by the Nazis as '...new Jewish attacks on German representatives,' and the press soon afterwards reported:

> The German Minister to the Netherlands was ordered to protest, and he obtained an official expression of regret at The Hague. The Nazi press warned that such incidents might result in 'more severe reprisals' against the Jews in Germany. The

Jews, thrown into panic, with the memory of the pogroms following the Ernst von Rath slaying in Paris still vivid in their memories, turned frantically to foreign consulates in Berlin for information about the incidents, but the consulates knew only what they read in the German papers. The Jews' fears were not allayed by the memory of the recent warning by *Das Schwarze Korps* [*a profoundly anti-Semitic Nazi publication*—author's note] that '...the day a Jewish or Jewish-bought weapon is employed against a German there will be no more Jews in Germany'. While negotiations with Rublee were in progress the Reich went about enforcing emigration in its own way. Police launched a systematic roundup of German and stateless Jews unable to obey expulsion orders, evidently with the intention of interning them in concentration camps. Berlin's rich Jews were forced to pay illegal police levies for passports when seeking to emigrate. They have been mulcted of from four to five million marks in recent months through this method.[121]

By now the rates of immigration into various countries should have been greatly increasing, but from official figures and estimates compiled by the U.S. Department of State it seems that this was certainly not the case. The U.S. and Great Britain remained at the top of the list, allowing approximately 27,000 new immigrants from Nazi controlled areas into their countries every year, although it should be stressed that not all of these were Jewish refugees. Palestine with a little over five thousand and Australia, also with five thousand, had the next largest acceptance of immigrants. These were followed by Bolivia and France, each allowing some two thousand. In total no more than eighty thousand refugees were being absorbed by all nations at this time. At that rate it would have taken almost eight years to absorb just the refugees then in Germany and Austria, without considering the many other nations such as Romania and Poland then also doing their best to rid their countries of Jews. Clearly, with the political situation deepening towards a war that would break out within nine months, a war that would mean not 600,000 refugees but many millions, this rate of absorption was hopelessly inadequate. It should also be pointed out that these figures were only theoretical, that in each individual case the intending immigrants had to meet very stringent immigration requirements such as financial independence or to have an agricultural background. This, in many cases, was not possible. Raymond H. Geist, the American consul at Berlin, issued a desperate statement to his superiors in Washington telling them that even as people were waiting for visas promised them by countries such as the U.S. and Britain, the Germans were becoming increasingly impatient and were placing these people into concentration camps. Geist lamented: 'Increasingly cruel pressure will be put on these people so that their situation in Germany will become intolerable, even unbearable.... If restrictions continue concerning the admission of aliens into other countries as they are today, the situation will become desperate indeed'.[122]

The official figure of eighty thousand people per year was further confused because many of these people had been admitted or were about to be admitted into other countries only on the basis of temporary visas, and with the strict provision that permanent visas be issued by other countries. Highly confidential State Department documents reveal that this figure could not be sustained, and there was also considerable debate about its accuracy. Most U.S. officials involved in the issue believed that as each of the 'Nations of Asylum' tightened immigration restrictions even further, then the flow of refugees would be subjected to an effective stranglehold that would spell the end of any kind of Jewish exodus from

Germany. No one could then foresee what the result of such a stranglehold would be.[123]

Public sympathy in the U.S. was certainly increasing. This is evident not only from the many pro-Jewish editorials appearing in the press but also from the large number of private letters sent to executives at the State Department. Some offered money, others stated that they would employ or would board and feed a number of Jewish families. The sentiment was not universal, of course, and detractors of Jewish immigration remained. One of these, a resident of Oklahoma City wrote to Senator Josh Lee in Washington:

> The Democratic nations of the earth should not, at great cost and inconvenience to them, pull Hitler's chestnuts out of the fire. I am sure that attitude upon the part of the other nations, will mean great suffering by the German Jews, but ... it is a domestic problem which Hitler has created. If the German people will stand for his murdering the Jews of their country then so it will have to be.
>
> Practically every nation has a minority problem. Some people in this country would favor persecuting the Negroes if we could thus induce England or some other country to take them off our hands.

So my opinion is that we should not open our doors and permit large numbers of German Jews to enter this country. We already have a Jewish problem in the East, particularly in New York City.[124]

Yet some of the letters expressed heartfelt concern. Students of the tenth grade history class of Calvin High School in Louisiana wrote to the U.S. president in January 1939 telling him that they and their teacher, a Miss Pepper, had agreed that they were willing to adopt, '...one Jewish baby' and to bring up the child to be, '...one of the most outstanding citizens in the United States of America'. They stated that Miss Pepper had agreed to become the child's guardian but that they would all have a hand in its upbringing.[125] The president even received a letter from a Frenchman named S. Barkon who had written from Paris to state that the diplomats had failed in their efforts to alleviate the refugee problem. Barkon described himself as a manual worker and, enclosing a one hundred francs note to aid the refugees, stated that the only person who could now save the Jews was Roosevelt himself.[126]

***

On the evening of 3 January, 1939, the U.S. ambassador to Italy, William Phillips, presented a letter from President Roosevelt to the Italian dictator Benito Mussolini. The letter, in part, asked Mussolini to consider allowing a number of Jewish refugees to emigrate to the plateau region in southern Ethiopia (then under Italian control). The meeting was held at Rome's Palazzo Venezia in the presence of Count Galeazzo Ciano, the Italian foreign minister. Mussolini had just returned from a two weeks' skiing holiday and was still dressed in his skiing clothes when he received Phillips. Phillips himself later stated that contrary to widespread reports that claimed Mussolini's health was ailing, the *Duce* [leader] looked, '...the picture of health and vitality'. The *Duce* told Phillips that the idea of Jewish immigration to Ethiopia was impracticable, and that the region referred to in Roosevelt's letter was, '...inhabited by people who were wholly unsympathetic to Jews'. Mussolini produced a map and explained to Phillips that he had already suggested another region north-east of Addis Ababa but that the Jews themselves had allegedly not received his suggestion favourably. Phillips knew that he was treading on very thin diplomatic ice. His later report to the U.S. secretary of state claimed he had told the *Duce* that relations between Italy and the U.S. were strained, that this was largely the result of Italy's 'infatuation' with Germany and the fact that

German methods of dealing with the Jewish people had, '...greatly shocked public sentiment in America'. Phillips continued:

> The *Duce* interrupted me by recounting the iniquities of the German Jews and of Jews in general, their lack of loyalty to the country of their residence, their intrigues, and the fact that they never could assimilate with any other race. He admitted that this lack of assimilation was a strong point in their favor and showed their remarkable racial strength. He told me of the financial frauds which were being practised by the Jews and showed me a little book in German containing photographs of counterfeit bills for huge amounts of German marks. I was impressed by his apparently genuine antagonism to the Jews. He went on to say that, in his opinion, there would not be one Jew left in Germany, and that other European countries—and he mentioned in particular Romania and Hungary—were confronted with the same problem and were finding it necessary to rid themselves of their Jewish elements. There was no room for Jews in Europe, and eventually, he thought, they would all have to go.[127]

Phillips later added that throughout the entire interview with Mussolini, Count Ciano, dressed in his civilian 'livery' had stood at a respectful distance without uttering a word, and that he had given Phillips the impression that he was, '...a thoroughly well-disciplined footman'.[128]

***

Meanwhile, in Berlin, Dr Hjalmar Schacht had been, '...relieved of his functions,' as the intermediary concerning discussions over the refugee problem and Rublee was forced to admit that the Germans had now adopted, '...a hardening of the German position on several points'. Rublee reported to Washington that the German government seemed to have no intention of continuing discussions and that as a result he was leaving Berlin to return to London for consultations with other members of the committee.[129]

Even so the German government indicated that it was still willing to negotiate and appointed Doctor Helmuth Wohlthat, an official from the Economics Ministry, as its negotiator. Rublee also received an invitation to meet personally with Göring. The meeting took place on the afternoon of 21 January, 1939, and Göring repeatedly made the point that he and his government were anxious to find a solution to the 'Jewish problem'.

Other than this, however, the meeting proved fruitless.[130]

While in Berlin Rublee had a total of thirteen meetings, three with Schacht, nine with Wohlthat and the one with Göring. Rublee pressed for further details of the outline that had been given to him in London by Schacht. He asked how the German government proposed to organise the emigration; how those left behind would be cared for and what would become of the Jewish money held in trust. The Germans indicated that they were still not willing to recognise the London committee but they would arrange for orderly emigration and would put such an emigration programme into effect only when they were satisfied that the countries of immigration were disposed to receive large numbers of Jewish refugees. In other words they would do nothing until the 'Nations of Asylum' had opened their doors. Rublee came away from those meetings with mixed feelings. He feared the more radical elements within the German government but stated that he believed the conservative elements were, '...sincerely anxious to modify the Jewish policies because they do not approve of the methods which were previously followed and are conscious of the adverse effect on Germany and on German trade in the outside world'.[131] Further negotiations eventually resulted in what became known as the Rublee-Wohlthat plan. This plan was based upon the concept that a trust-fund would be established to aid the departure of 400,000 Jews and the creation of an international corporation to oversee the project. The plan was labelled as a Nazi blackmail plot by many Jewish organisations and the later outbreak of war ended the activities of the foundation.

In February 1939 came the first powerful indication (there had been many minor indications) that the entire concept of the Évian conference and its subsequent removal to London—as a means of determining ways of ameliorating the plight of the refugees—was falling apart, that members were losing interest in its manifesto of terms and that the internal political issues of each country were creating enormous pressure to have the entire project dropped. On 11 February that year Myron C. Taylor, then still in London, advised the U.S. Department of State that the French had decided not to be represented at any further meetings in London. This was a serious blow as the French, diplomatically and geographically, were in a prime position to help solve the problem. Under considerable diplomatic pressure the French soon afterwards changed their minds but stated that there would be no high level participation and that French representatives in London would be prohibited in taking any active part in the meetings.[132]

The Spanish Civil War was now drawing to a close and France was experiencing another refugee problem at its borders as members of the Spanish government's Republican Army fled from Nationalist atrocities. This added refugee problem was, it seems, one of the reasons why France had decided not to participate further in the intergovernmental committee meetings.[133]

Indeed, the Spanish were also being particularly intransigent regarding German Jews already in their country. According to 'reliable sources', such people, when applying for registration, were ordered to report to the German consulate where they were turned over to the Spanish police and jailed.[134]

On 11 February the U.S. Department of State was advised that British statesman Sir Herbert Emerson had agreed to take up the appointment of the director of the intergovernmental committee, replacing Rublee who had resigned several weeks previously. Temporarily, Rublee's position was taken up by his assistant, Robert Pell.[135]

It is not entirely clear how the officials at the U.S. Department of State felt about the appointment of Emerson. Emerson was then the

League of Nations' 'high commissioner for refugees from Germany,' and during all of the negotiations of the intergovernmental committee, both at Évian and at London, the U.S. had been at pains to keep the League and the objectives of the intergovernmental committee quite separate.[136]

Soon afterwards English banker Lord Rothschild, who was heavily involved in the British aspect of refugee immigration, visited the U.S. with a profoundly disturbing message. Having interviewed many of the Jewish refugees, some of whom had been incarcerated in Nazi concentration camps, Rothschild was convinced that, despite German rhetoric which claimed that the Germans only wanted to expel the Jews from Nazi-controlled areas, the Germans were, in fact, gearing themselves up for genocide. During a luncheon reception held on 22 February, 1939, he told members of Roosevelt's advisory committee that in his opinion, based upon information he had gleaned from his many interviews, all the Jews in Germany would be dead within two years. This was a staggering statement, a warning of a concept never before envisaged in the U.S. That the Germans were actively planning to kill millions of people was totally unthinkable, Rothschild had to be wrong. Highly confidential State Department documents now reveal that Rothschild's statements were considered as being, '...exceedingly pessimistic, so pessimistic that ... he is indulging in propaganda'.[137]

Rothschild's comments were substantially confirmed in a letter written by Mr S. Adler-Rudel to the National Coordinating Committee for Aid to Refugees and Emigrants Coming from Germany. Adler-Rudel, a prominent German philanthropist living in Berlin, advised the committee that since the end of Rublee's discussions in Berlin the situation had become substantially worse, despite German claims that Jewish persecution had eased and that emigration was being placed on a more organised footing. He said Adolf Eichmann, head of the Gestapo's Jewish section and architect of the 'Final Solution', had been called to Berlin and ordered to, '...apply the methods which have proven successful in Vienna to mop up the Old Reich'. As persecution increased Adler-Rudel stated that the people would be forced to lose once again all hope of any kind of organised emigration and to, '...cross the border at night [and] ... be forced to buy tickets to Shanghai and Trinidad and such horrible places'. He added the powerful warning that:

> No negotiations with reference to large-scale immigration have proved successful thus far. Delegations have been

sent to various parts of the world, but until they get back and submit reports the last Jew will probably have been buried in Germany. This is the situation as I see it. I don't think it's exaggerated.[138]

This important document was sent immediately to the U.S. Department of State by the committee's executive secretary, Cecilia Razovsky. There does not seem to have been any official reaction to this chillingly prophetic report.

***

Myron Charles Taylor, the man who had chaired the Évian conference, later went on to enjoy a hugely successful diplomatic career. In 1939 he became Roosevelt's personal envoy to Pope Pius XII. He served in this capacity throughout the remainder of Roosevelt's administration and into Harry S. Truman's. Among his many diplomatic accomplishments were persuading Spain's dictator, Francisco Franco, not to join with the Axis powers, and also lobbying successfully to allow an Allied air-base to operate from neutral Portugal. After the war Taylor established the organisation: 'American Relief for Italy' which subsequently was responsible for raising more than $37 million to purchase relief supplies for Italians suffering because of the war.

In 1950 Taylor resigned as envoy and officially retired. He returned to his country home at Locust Valley, New York State, where he lived quietly with his wife, Anabele, never seeking public recognition for his work. Anabele Taylor died on 12 December, 1958, and Taylor passed away at his home, just five months later on 5 May, 1959.[139]

Chapter 11

The Ongoing Struggle

The ultimate results of the Évian conference and its ramifications for the world Jewish community are difficult to define fully. For such a definition one must look substantially at subsequent events. During the discussions with Nazi officials held in London and Berlin in the early months of 1939 the Germans repeatedly agreed to arrange for a more orderly emigration of the refugees, to facilitate the necessary documentation and to arrange for a trust-fund to be set up so that the Jewish people could take at least some of their wealth with them. Of these promises not one was met. As the German government rushed headlong towards precipitating the world into war these promises, conveniently, were forgotten. For the Jewish people the exodus remained far from organised. As they clamoured to gain their freedom all semblance of organisation broke down, allowing only a straggling few to flee as the mounting rage of anti-Semitism swept them firstly into the ghettoes, then the concentration camps, and eventually into the gas chambers and crematoria of the 'Final Solution'.

The United States of America, the country that was supposedly leading efforts for Jewish relief, was suffering considerable public vilification over the issue, and, as we have seen, there were certainly groups strongly opposed to any further Jewish immigration.

Among these was the extreme right wing Christian Front. In January 1940, J. Edgar Hoover, chief of the United States Federal Bureau of Investigation, announced the arrest of eighteen members of the Christian Front. Members of this group had been operating for at least six months prior to their arrest and Hoover had them charged with conspiracy to create a revolution to overthrow the government and to establish a dictatorship. Hoover stated that his investigators had unearthed a small arsenal in New York City intended for revolutionary purposes. The arrested men had functioned as a sports club. The club planned, among other things, '...terrorism, the eradication of Jews, the seizure of public utilities including power and waterworks stations, railroads, communication and transport, [and] also the bombing [of] the Jewish newspaper *Daily Forward*. The seizure of the Customs House and the main post office in New York city as well as Federal Reserve Banks throughout the United States and National Guard armouries'.[1]

Hoover told the press that principals among the arrested men were John Cassidy, leader of the Christian Front who was addressed as its führer, and William Bishop, the leader of the sports club. Federal Bureau of Investigation agents confiscated bombs, rifles and thousands of rounds of ammunition. Hoover stated that it was the purpose of the group to establish a government in America similar to Hitler's. At least one member of the Christian Front was a member of the German/American Bund and many were connected with the United States reserved forces. They planned to assassinate twelve leading congressmen.[2]

***

In Berlin Hitler viewed the resolution of the Évian conference with considerable contempt. He had been hoping that the 'Nations of Asylum' would take the Jewish problem off his agenda. Now, however, he believed that he was left with little alternative. Jews were not welcome anywhere in the world, and so there was only one solution.

Extermination.

When the Évian conference and refugee question were later again raised in the British House of Commons, Chancellor of the Duchy of Lancaster, Earl Winterton, who had been leader of the British delegation at Évian, said: 'The problem of refugees required most careful and delicate treatment.'

Golda Meir, future Prime Minister of Israel was later to state, 'After the conference at Évian-les-Bains, it became chillingly clear that the Jewish people were entirely on their own.'[3]

Following the Évian conference a leading German publication the *Danziger Vorposten* clearly stated that the reaction of the delegates at the conference only served to, '...justify Germany's policy against Jewry'. A damning article also appeared in the *Das Schwarze Korps*, the official newspaper of the SS, which stated: 'Because it is necessary, because we no longer hear the world screeching, and because, after all, no power on earth can hinder us, we will now bring the Jewish question to its totalitarian solution.' There followed detailed steps that would be taken towards the internecine slaughter which was to be implemented. The article ended: 'The result will be the actual and definite end of Jewry in Germany and its complete extermination.[4]

German newspapers reported heavily on the results of Évian, claiming that anti-Semitism was right and just and that the results of Évian proved that no one wanted the Jews. The *National Zeitung* reported: '...We have reports from Australia and South Africa that those countries are closed to Jews. Poland refused to take her own nationals, Holland will not accept Jews in her colonies, [*which was untrue*—author's note] thus overpopulated Germany is forced to tolerate these parasites'.[5]

In February 1939 the Limited Refugee Bill was introduced in the U.S. Senate. The bill was introduced by Senator Robert F. Wagner and called for the introduction of 20,000 refugee German children under the age of fourteen years. The bill proposed that over the following two years the children would be allowed into the country in addition to all other immigration quotas. Charities across the country, religious organisations and prominent politicians strongly backed the bill. However, organisations such as the American League and the American Coalition of Patriotic Societies opposing the bill claimed that the introduction of so many refugee children would deprive American children of aid and pointed out that the Jewish children should not be separated from their parents or guardians. After several months of debate the bill was defeated.

***

Discussions concerning the exact time when the world generally became aware that the Holocaust was taking place have been going on since the end of the war. When the Germans launched their unexpected attack against the Russians in 1941 more than half a million Jews were annihilated by special execution squads during the first six months of the campaign. News of these mass murders was often carried home by ordinary German soldiers going on leave—yet few people—even in Germany—wanted to believe what was happening on the Eastern Front. But this was not yet the mass murder on an extensive scale that was quickly to follow. Soon the extermination camps were operating like massive killing factories constructed and operated like abattoirs, most of which had only two purposes—to provide slave labour and to exterminate the Jews like cattle.

After the war few German people would admit that they knew what was going on in the camps, even those Germans and Poles living close to the extermination centres. Yet many *must* have known. Millions of people could not simply disappear—there were enormous statistical problems. Life insurance policies had to be paid out, property had legally to change hands, wills had to be enacted. Employees had to be informed that they were now out of work because their employers had disappeared. There was the problem of explaining why food and clothing ration stamps were no longer needed—banks had to be informed that the holders of accounts were legally dead. And what of the personal items provided by these mass exterminations? Teeth filled with gold, gold spectacle frames, gold rings, and other valuables such as currencies and jewels were transported directly to the *Reichsbank,* but other less valuable items, clothes, children's dolls, shoes and suitcases, shaving brushes were distributed to the German public and military. Even human hair shorn from the female victims of the gas chambers was taken to the Alex Zink fur factory near Nuremberg for use in clothing manufacture for the war effort—the recipients of these items must have known—or at least strongly suspected—what was happening to the Jews.

People living close to the death camps and those working in the slave factories of Krupp and I.G. Farben—all complained of the hellish stench emanating from those camps, and nightly they watched the massive flames, sometimes five metres high, roaring from the crematoria chimneys.

Contrary to popular belief the mailing system was still operating in Europe at this time and letters were sent to relatives and friends overseas warning of the atrocities. Yet few believed the stories—such mass extermination simply could never happen, not even in a totalitarian state.

Many thought that such news was merely enemy propaganda. They remembered the hotly contested avalanche of propaganda that had taken place during the First World War, both British and German, most of which was later publicly disproved as being totally false—people asked themselves; was it happening again? Polish, Hungarian and even German smugglers filtered out accurate information that the exterminations were taking place and finally the press began to take notice.

One man, now considered a hero, was Witold Pilecki, the only person who actually volunteered to be incarcerated at Auschwitz. In 1940 Pilecki convinced his associates in the Secret Polish Army *(Tajna Armia Polska)* that it was necessary to find out exactly what was happening inside Auschwitz and then to convey that intelligence to the Allies. Up until that time it was believed that Auschwitz was simply an internment camp and people on the outside had no knowledge that it was, in fact, a death factory. Pilecki's resistance associates approved the plan and he was issued with false identity papers under the name of Thomasz Serafinski. On 19 September, 1940, Pilecki deliberately placed himself on the road to extreme danger by going out into the streets during a Nazi roundup. Along with about two thousand other people he was caught in the Nazi trap and imprisoned temporarily at the Light Horse Guard barracks where prisoners were beaten with rubber truncheons and suffered other forms of physical and psychological torture.

Soon afterwards Pilecki was sent with most of the other inmates to Auschwitz where he was given the identification number 4859.

Witold Pilecki

–TBór Komorowski 'Armiapodziemna' Warsaw 1990, Wikimedia Commons.

In the death camp Pilecki managed somehow to survive. He suffered starvation and pneumonia but was able to form an active resistance movement within the camp. This was known as the *Zwiazek Organizacji Wojskowej* (ZOW), the Union of Military Organisation. The movement set itself the tasks of improving the morale of the inmates, obtaining news from outside, providing additional clothing and food, setting up an intelligence network and training men to take over the camp if an attack could be made on the facility by the Polish resistance or the Polish 1st Independent Parachute Brigade which was then based in Britain.

Pilecki was able to send firsthand reports on the camp atrocities to the Polish government in exile which, in turn, passed them on to the Allied powers.[6]

These reports were received by the British as early as 1941 but the British authorities refused to believe them, considering the numbers to be gross exaggerations and mere propaganda emanating from the Polish government in exile.[7]

Following an extraordinary escape from the death camp at Auschwitz, Witold Pilecki had a varied and distinguished underground career but after the war he was arrested by the Communist Ministry of Public Security and after suffering terrible torture was executed at the Warsaw

Mokotow Prison on 25 May, 1948, having been found guilty during a 'show trial' of a variety of 'crimes'. Today he is considered a national hero and has been posthumously awarded the Order of the White Eagle, the highest Polish decoration.[8]

In June 1942, about twenty-one months after Witold Pilecki had heroically allowed himself to be incarcerated at Auschwitz, the *Daily Telegraph* in London published a cautious account of the exterminations, and by the end of that year the atrocities were known worldwide. Yet still there were no details concerning how many were being killed.

Like Pilecki, Eduard Schulte, a German industrialist, was, reportedly, one of the first to inform the Allies about the exterminations which were being carried out at the Nazi death camps. Schulte, who controlled vast business interests in Poland, often had the opportunity to travel to Switzerland where he had important contacts including Polish and French intelligence agents and Allen Welsh Dulles, U.S. diplomat and later head of the C.I.A.

Schulte had learned of the intended destruction of European Jews in 1942 and informed Gerhart M. Riegner, the secretary of the World Jewish Congress in Geneva.[9]

Riegner had firsthand experience of Nazi persecution; when the infamous 'Boycott Day' occurred in Berlin on 1 April, 1933, soon after Hitler had been sworn in as chancellor, Riegner had been working as an assistant to a judge. He immediately lost his job, as did many other members of his immediate family including his father, a lawyer.[10]

On 10 August, 1942, Riegner sent a startling telegram through various diplomatic channels to the British consul general at Geneva for forwarding to Mr S.S. Silverman, M.P. chairman of the British section of the World Jewish Congress in London.

The telegram read:

> Received alarming report stating that, in the Fuehrer's Headquarters, a plan has been discussed, and is under consideration, according to which all Jews in countries occupied or controlled by Germany numbering 3 1/2 to 4 millions should, after deportation and concentration in the East, be at one blow exterminated in order to resolve, once and for all the Jewish question in Europe. Action is reported to be planned for the autumn. Ways of execution are still being discussed including the use of prussic acid. We transmit this information with all the necessary reservation, as exactitude

cannot be confirmed by us. Our informant is reported to have close connections with the highest German authorities, and his reports are generally reliable. Please inform and consult New York. (Ends).[11]

The telegram, however, was largely ignored.

In November 1942 the *Washington Post* published a small article on page six quoting Associated Press of 24 November with the headlines: *Half of Jews Ordered Slain, Poles Report*. The report went on: 'Rabbi Stephen Wise, chairman of the World Jewish Congress, said last night that he had learned through sources confirmed by the State Department that approximately half the estimated four million Jews in Nazi-occupied Europe had been slain in an "extermination campaign."[12]

A survey carried out in the U.S. during 1943 found that most people believed only a hundred thousand Jews had been killed—and the American authorities did nothing to correct this error. Indeed, for most of the war the U.S. Department of State kept the numbers of deaths from the American people and even managed largely to stem the flow of such information which was then filtering out through Jewish agencies in Switzerland.

Jewish organisations in Palestine, Switzerland, Britain and America called upon the Allies to attempt rescue missions—anything was worth trying as millions continued to be gassed. Yet the British refused to contemplate such a move. The infamous White Paper of 1939 had abandoned any concept of establishing a Jewish Commonwealth and had completely forbidden the immigration of Jews into Palestine. The British also refused to allow Jewish people into England in any appreciable numbers, claiming it was: 'Because of the difficulties of disposing of a considerable number of Jews should they be rescued.'

The American government—in a complete fit of paranoia—voiced the opinion that many of the rescued Jews would be German espionage agents.

President Roosevelt himself broadcast a speech in which he said:

> Today's threat to our national security is not a matter of military weapons alone. We know of new methods of attack; the Trojan horse, the fifth column that betrays a nation unprepared for treachery, spies, saboteurs and traitors are the actors in this new strategy. These dividing forces are undiluted poison. They must not be allowed to spread in the new world as they have in the old.[13]

Jewish organisations called upon the Allies to stop the extermination by any means possible—the bombing of railway lines leading to the death camps could have prevented—or at least slowed the death factory process—the bombing of the factories themselves could have saved millions of lives—Yet the Allies steadfastly refused to carry out such raids claiming that most of the death camps were out of bomber and protective fighter range. However, following the Allied invasion of Italy in 1943 bombers could easily and with relative safety have reached Auschwitz. Indeed Allied bombers did attack military targets in the region, ignoring the death factories as they did so.

At the height of the Holocaust, in April 1943, another Allied conference on the refugee problem was held at Bermuda. Delegates to the conference by this time knew exactly what was happening to the Jews in Europe. They had secret and very accurate estimates of the numbers of deaths in the extermination camps. They even knew where the camps were situated. Papers from Winston Churchill's secret wartime intelligence archives clearly demonstrate that the British were fully aware of details of the camps by August 1942. From intercepted Nazi reports the British learned that more than eight thousand people had been killed at Auschwitz in just one month. Yet history repeated itself, the delegates to the Bermuda conference also decided to do nothing to help those innocents who were then being systematically killed.[14]

The Bermuda conference began on 14 April, the eve of the Jewish Passover. Many of the original countries at Évian had not been invited, including Canada, although the Liberal government of Prime Minister Mackenzie King had been warned by the British that they should expect to permit entry for at least a further two thousand Jews as a result of the conference.

The objectives of the Bermuda conference were, in any case, somewhat limited, and the British particularly had no intention of increasing Jewish immigration other than to discuss further plans for the Jewish colonisation of its dominions. Bermuda, like Évian five years previously, was a complete betrayal of the Jewish cause. The delegates to the conference knew, even before they met that the conference would achieve nothing. The U.S. wanted it to be used as a public forum to explain to the American people that added immigration quotas were not only impossible for America, but also impossible for almost every other country in the democratic world.

The Bermuda conference ended after ten days with thirteen 'secret' proposals. However, these proposals were only administrative recommendations such as the reconstruction and reorganisation of certain refugee organisations and an agreement to incorporate refugees from all Nazi-controlled areas into the so-called relief system. It is certain that the Bermuda conference did nothing to ameliorate the plight of the European Jews who were then dying in their millions.

The *New York Times* published a profound editorial claiming, 'The truth is, the dead hand of yesterday's politics is still at the throat of European Jews.'[15]

The Jewish people of the U.S. universally agreed that the object of the Bermuda conference had not been to find ways of rescuing the Jews from the gas chambers, but through secrecy and diplomatic management, to rescue the western democratic governments from a rising tide of public anger, shock and bitterness.

Since the end of the war there has been widespread criticism concerning the lack of Jewish aid in America, Great Britain and Palestine, but individually, the Jewish people in those countries could do little—apart from petition their governments and to supply funds to the many Jewish agencies. The various aid organisations that were set up in order to facilitate emigration and rescue work were also somewhat ineffective without the strong and forceful intervention of their countries' governments.

The sad fact remains that as the war ground mercilessly on the requirements of manpower and the social gearing of the nation shifted its emphasis towards fighting and surviving the war. Social rescue work made way for military strategy, and the plight of the Jews, although not forgotten, was conveniently considered to be of only secondary importance. Few military strategists, if any, believed that the extermination of the Jews was a military matter. Yet this was in fact so. If the Germans wanted to destroy the Jewish people then the U.S. military should have wanted to prevent them from doing so, irrespective of the humanitarian necessity, but simply because it was in direct opposition to German wishes. Militarily, the enslavement and final destruction of the Jews was also providing the Germans with enormous masses of materials and wealth that could be used to further the German war effort, clothing, gold, hair, fertiliser, forced labour, food, spectacles, shoes, bank accounts and confiscated housing. U.S. military authorities seemed reluctant to admit that this was the case and throughout the war would make no special effort to end the Holocaust through military action.

The War Refugee Board

Millions of European Jews had been reduced to ashes before the War Refugee Board came into existence in the United States in 1944. This was the country's first major attempt to create a body that could do something positive to ameliorate the plight of those few surviving Jews then under Nazi control.

What had become patently obvious to those organisations and individuals who were doing whatever they could to help the Jews of Europe, was the fact that official government policy was in place to block Jewish refugees. By early 1944, by presidential degree, all that was about to change but it was now far too late.

Josiah E. DuBois was a young lawyer working for the U.S. Treasury Department when he learned of a document, written in 1940 by the assistant secretary of state, Breckinridge Long, officially blocking Jewish immigration. The policy note had been sent to all those staff members who were involved in immigration.

DuBois was incensed and frustrated. He responded by writing a strongly worded report of his own. It was bluntly titled: *Report to the Secretary on the Acquiescence of this Government to the Murder of the Jews.* This damning report stated that the State Department was guilty of procrastinating and failing to act on behalf of the Jews of Europe and also guilty of actually implementing policies and actions which prevented steps to be taken to rescue the Jews. It was, in effect, a highly powerful document. DuBois sent this report to his chief, Henry Morgenthau Jnr., a close friend of the president, who resisted having it sent to Roosevelt. There has been a claim that Morgenthau only agreed to forward the report to the president after DuBois threatened to resign and to call a press conference at which he would, '...rip the lid off the entire State Department scandal'.

Finally Morgenthau agreed but insisted that the title of the document be changed to *Personal Report to the President*. The report was laid on the presidential desk in the Oval Office on 16 January, 1944.

Under pressure from a number of other organisations such as the Bergson Group (see below), Roosevelt got busy very quickly and formed the War Refugee Board with three Cabinet members. These were Cordell Hull, the secretary of state; Henry Morgenthau, the secretary of the Treasury, and Henry Stimson, the secretary of war. The executive order creating the board was signed by Roosevelt on 22 January that year.

John W. Pehle who was then the assistant to the secretary of the Treasury was appointed the board's first executive director. He was aided by a staff of about thirty people.

The board rapidly implemented a number of policies and actions. The assistance of numerous foreign governments and relief organisations were enlisted and several neutral countries such as Switzerland, Sweden and Turkey gave their cooperation. Refugee camps were established in North Africa and safe havens were prepared in Palestine, Switzerland and Sweden. The board worked with the U.S. Treasury Department to transfer funds from the U.S. to neutral countries where the money could be used by its representatives to aid in the rescue, transport and accommodation of people living under Nazi domination. The board also obtained clearances to have food parcels and other items distributed to inmates held in concentration camps. It has been calculated that during the period of its existence the board was able to rescue as many as 200,000 Jews. About 15,000 Jews and around 20,000 non-Jews had been rescued from Nazi controlled areas with a further 10,000 Jews having been protected within Nazi controlled areas. About 48,000 Jews were rescued from Transnistra and taken to Romania and around

12,000 Jews in Budapest managed to survive the war thanks to the efforts of the board.

John Pehle was later replaced as the director of the board by Brigadier General William O'Dwyer who would remain in that post until the board was dissolved in September 1945.

Yet Pehle later admitted that the board had been formed too late in the war and its achievements were relatively minor compared to the full extent of the Holocaust and the number of lives lost. The organisation should have been created right at the beginning of the war, if not before. Realising that the board's achievements had been limited, Pehle said that this was a, 'very disturbing experience' and that he had found himself sick to his stomach at the board's incapacity to be effective in any great way.[16]

Among the more successful representatives of the War Refugee Board was American businessman Ira Arthur Hirschmann who was responsible for saving the lives of tens of thousands of people.

In February 1944 the press reported that Ira Hirschmann, who previously had been investigating the difficulties associated with refugee problems in the 'Near East' had been appointed as a special attaché to the United States Embassy at Ankara. The decision to appoint Hirschmann was announced by Mr John Pehle who was then the active executive director of the War Refugee Board. From that time Hirschmann would become the board's representative in Turkey. Pehle told the press that Hirschmann had arrived in Ankara on 14 February and that he was being employed upon the development of programmes and also on the implementation of measures which might assist with the rescue and relief of the Jewish people and other persecuted minorities in Europe.

Pehle also informed the pubic that Hirschmann had not only spent considerable time in both Central and Western Europe but had also attended the Évian conference as an observer for the United States.[17]

Ira Hirschmann was actually a business executive and one of the pioneers of radio broadcasts in America. Born in 1901 to a wealthy Baltimore family, he attended Johns Hopkins University prior to commencing work at L. Bamberger and Co., in Newark where he subsequently became the advertising and sales manager.

He then took up consecutive appointments at Lord and Taylor, Saks Fifth Avenue and later Bloomingdale's where he was vice president.

In the 1930s he commenced experimenting in television and FM radio broadcasts and was responsible for the broadcast of classical music concerts during the 1940s.

He commenced his anti-Nazi activities during the mid 1930s by organising a boycott of German-manufactured goods. Following service for the War Labor Board he received his appointment to the War Refugee Board and was sent to Turkey.

It was here that his efforts to assist the persecuted Jews of Europe would come to full fruition. With the assistance of the American ambassador to Turkey, Hirschmann was able to convince the Turkish government to open its doors to Jewish refugees. Almost seven thousand Jews were able to reach Turkey and ultimately Palestine through these efforts.

Hirschmann then offered a Romanian diplomat visas for himself and his family if the diplomat could arrange for the gates to the Transnistra concentration camp to be opened so that its inmates could be returned to Romania. This was carried out and tens of thousands of Jews were able to get away, many of whom finally found their way to Turkey and Palestine.

Ira Hirschmann died of heart failure at his home in Manhattan in October 1989.[18]

The Bergson Group

Hillel Kook, who, in America, went under the pseudonym of Peter Bergson, was one of the harshest critics of the U.S. administration and of many Jewish organisations in America for their laxity in doing anything to assist, protect or rescue the Jews of Europe. During the war Kook was to the fore in attempting to awaken public opinion to the plight of the Jews and to force the U.S. administration into action. It was Kook who fought desperately, but in vain, to make the U.S. authorities understand that military action was necessary to help to save the Jews and that bombing raids should have been made against rail-lines transporting Jews to the extermination camps. He also pointed out, very forcefully, that as the Germans were using poison gas against the Jews they should be warned that chemical weapons would be used against them if they continued the practice. Kook stated that Germany had made it a war aim to destroy the Jews and therefore it should have been a war aim for the Allies to have prevented their destruction. The U.S. administration, however, remained ambivalent despite the fact that Kook and his various committees were able to do more than any other single Jewish organisation in awakening public awareness and conscience to the plight of the Jews of Europe.[19]

Hillel Kook was one of those controversial, outspoken and single-minded figures in Jewish history who found that he attracted considerable friends and even more foes. He had been born on 24 July, 1915, at Kriukai, within the Russian Empire, which is now a part of Lithuania. His father was Rabbi Dov Kook whose elder brother was the well known Abraham Isaac Hacohen Kook, the first Ashkenazi chief rabbi of the British Mandate of Palestine. About nine or ten years after his birth, Kook was taken with his family to Palestine. There his father became the first chief rabbi of Afula. Hillel Kook was educated at Afula and later attended the Hebrew University where he was a student of Jewish Studies.

Following the Arab riots of 1931 Hillel Kook helped to found the *Irgun, (Irgun Zvai Leumi* [IZL]) the military arm of the Revisionist Zionist movement. The goals of the Revisionist Zionist movement were to force Britain to grant Jewish statehood on both banks of the Jordan River, to establish a Jewish majority in Palestine and to create trained Jewish military regiments.

Kook fought with the *Irgun* in Palestine throughout the 1930s. In 1936 he was an *Irgun* post commander and finally became a member of the *Irgun* general headquarters.

In 1937, the year before Évian, as a Revisionist Zionist spokesperson for *Irgun,* Kook travelled to Poland. There he worked at fundraising, establishing *Irgun* cells in Eastern

Europe and organising the transfer of Polish Jews to Palestine. While in Europe Kook met Vladimir 'Zeev' Jabotinsky and his son, Ari Jabotinsky—founders of the Revisionist movement. At their request, in 1940, Kook travelled with Ze'ev Jabotinsky to the United States. He served as the head of the *Irgun* in America with the principal tasks of mobilising support for the *Irgun*, the creation of Jewish military units and gathering support for the creation of a Jewish State in Palestine. Kook now took the name of Peter Bergson—reportedly to prevent embarrassment to his family and especially to his famous uncle, Chief Rabbi Abraham Isaac Kook.

Kook formed the nucleus of a group of ten *Irgun* activists which became known as the Bergson Group. This group worked in close association with a number of Jewish organisations and also founded its own separate entities including the Committee for a Jewish Army of Stateless and Palestinian Jews whose goal it was to form a fighting force of Jews.

Working initially on *Irgun* fundraising and propaganda activities, the outbreak of the war brought about a transformation in the group's focus. When the true extent of the pogrom in Europe began to become known in America, particularly after the *Washington Post* report of 25 November, 1942, which claimed that half the

Jews of Europe had been murdered, Kook immediately instructed his colleagues that their entire focus would now be centered upon saving the Jews of Europe from destruction. He and his group moved quickly to begin raising awareness and to find ways of forcing the U.S. administration and Jewish organisations to act. The Bergson Group took out full page advertisements in many of America's leading newspapers, bringing the Holocaust sharply into focus for the people and government of America.

One of the group's principal publicity coups was the production of a huge pageant titled: *We Will Never Die* which was performed in Madison Square Garden on 9 March, 1943. The production had been written by Bergson Group member, Academy award winning author and screenwriter Ben Hecht who became an active Zionist shortly after the Holocaust began in Germany.

The pageant was a memorial to the two million Jews who were then known to have been murdered in Europe. The production was a huge success in gaining public attention. Reports of the event appeared in national newspapers; around forty thousand people attended on that night, and the production went on to be performed in five other cities, including Washington, where it was attended by Eleanor

Roosevelt, six Supreme Court judges and around three hundred senators and congressmen. Author Ben Hecht later stated that despite the massive reception of the pageant it had been disappointing. 'Actually, all we have done is make a lot of Jews cry, which is not a unique accomplishment,' he subsequently noted.[20]

That same year Kook was instrumental in establishing the Emergency Committee for the Rescue of European Jewry. This committee lobbied the U.S. government and Congress to take immediate action for the Jews of Europe. It also disseminated information to the general public about the Holocaust. It was largely on account of the pressure brought to bear by this group that the War Refugee Board (q.v.) came into existence.

On 6 October, 1943, about five hundred Orthodox rabbis marched on Washington. The event had been organised by Kook who had convinced the rabbis to march. It was one of the more controversial events surrounding the entire issue of U.S. response to the Holocaust and no representatives from Conservative Judaism or Reform Judaism were in attendance that day. In fact Rabbi Stephen Wise believed that the march was destructive and would stir up anti-Semitism in America. He stated that the protesters did not represent American Jewry.

The protesters, however, were able to get Vice President Henry Agard Wallace to interrupt a session of the Senate and to ask all the senators to come to the steps of Capitol Hill to receive them. Wallace made a speech (reluctantly) and was presented with a petition after which the rabbis marched on the White House to meet with Roosevelt. However, Roosevelt was careful to avoid the protesters. Shortly before the rabbis arrived at the White House, and in line with advice he had received from some of his Jewish aides, including Stephen Wise, and his speechwriter Samuel Rosenman (a member of the American Jewish Committee) he left the White House through a back door to attend a ceremony at an army base and then go on to a weekend in the country. Roosevelt could easily have met with the rabbis. His schedule was open that afternoon. Between lunch with the secretary of state and a scheduled 4p.m. departure time for the army base there was nothing in his diary. The rabbis and Hillel Kook were incensed that they had been snubbed. One Jewish newspaper thundered: 'Would a similar delegation of 500 Catholics have been thus treated?'

Following the end of the war Kook served extensively in the cause of the *Irgun* and also in the first Israeli Knesset, from 1949 to 1951 having by that time abandoned his pseudonym of

Peter Bergson. Since then his work has been largely ignored or conveniently forgotten and it has been suggested that his story is politically 'problematical' as it illustrates that the main priorities of the U.S. government and many Jewish organisations during the war were not centered around doing anything positive to stop the Holocaust or assist realistically in rescue efforts. Hillel Kook died near Tel Aviv in 2001.[21]

As a footnote it might be worth mentioning that Ben Hecht, the man who wrote the pageant *We Will Never Die*, later stated that he had become involved in activism after meeting Kook. He described the meeting saying that he had, '...accidentally bumped into history'. He then felt a burning need to do everything in his power to save the doomed Jews of Europe. He wrote the script for the Bergson's Group's production *A Flag is Born* which opened in 1946 starring Marlon Brando. The proceeds from the production were used to purchase a ship which was renamed the *S.S. Ben Hecht*; in March 1947 this was to carry nine hundred refugees to Palestine. Unfortunately the ship was captured by the Royal Navy and six hundred of its passengers were sent to detention camps in Cyprus. The ship later became the flagship of the Israeli Navy. Films written by Hecht were blacklisted in England and those few which were allowed to be shown had Hecht's writing credit removed. Hecht was immensely proud of his association with *Irgun* and its battle against the British mandate in Palestine. He later stated: 'Every time you blow up a British arsenal or wreck a British jail, or send a British railroad sky high, or rob a British bank, or let go with your guns at British betrayers and invaders of your homeland, the Jews of America make a little holiday in their hearts.'[22]

***

Today the sequence of events that led up to the Holocaust, and the Holocaust itself, are issues that are still steeped in controversy and guilt. Some revisionist style historians are proudly proclaiming that the Holocaust, in fact, never took place, but such views are obscene, grossly inaccurate and profoundly dangerous. The people of Germany have lived with the guilt of the Holocaust since the end of the war and there is a general swell of opinion that perhaps it is time to end what may be termed, '...the cult of past guilt'.[23]

Leading German intellectuals have stated that it is time to forget, to bury the past, that Germany's responsibility for the past should be abrogated, and, naturally enough, sentiments such as these have been enthusiastically embraced by far-right factions around the world. History is one of the basic elements of learning; as has often been stated, we learn from the past in order to attempt not to make the same mistakes again. If we deny the Holocaust, if we allow the memories of those six million murdered people to fade into the past; if the guilt is allowed to wither and die, then there is every chance that at some time in the future, a group of medium level diplomats will once again be gathering reluctantly at some prestigious resort to discuss another refugee problem in the face of mounting persecution and genocide. The events centered on the Kosovo crisis which prompted the 1999 NATO bombing of Belgrade and other areas under the control of Slobodan Milosevic is dramatic testimony to this argument. Milosevic's brutal treatment of ethnic Albanians closely paralleled Hitler's treatment of the Jews under Nazi control. When Milosevic revoked Kosovo's autonomy in 1989, strengthening Serb control over Kosovo, Albanians were robbed of control over their own affairs. Serbs were able to take over all the main jobs in government, the courts, schools and universities. As we now know, Serbian persecution also took the form of widespread murder and deportation of ethnic

Albanians. These events are chillingly similar to the Jewish persecution of the 1930s and 1940s.

More recently, the brutal actions of ISIS terrorists in Iraq and Syria have created a massive refugee problem, just as significant as the Jewish exodus of the 1930s and 1940s. What is interesting, and frightening, about this more modern refugee issue is that it has led to a significant increase in right-wing policies across Europe and even into the U.S. where the election of Donald Trump as president is testimony to current attitudes towards widespread xenophobia and a dangerously corrosive political agenda.

It is, of course, logical and right that the sins of the fathers and grandfathers should not be placed on the shoulders of new generations. Guilt should not be hereditary. Yet it is equally right that those monstrous crimes are never forgotten. History has judged Nazi Germany for the incredible evil that it perpetrated on the world in general and the Jews in particular, and no-one, especially the far right or individuals who propound an indecent revisionist style of history can erase the obscenity of the Holocaust from the collective memory of the peoples of the world.

Chapter 12

The Courageous

It took an astonishing amount of courage to defy the Nazi doctrine of ruthless, unmitigated, murderous intent; it took fearlessness, heroism, daring, nerve, audacity, deep human spirit, empathy and compassion. All essential elements that would be needed if at least some of the Jews of Europe were to have any chance of surviving the Holocaust. As outlined in earlier chapters of this book, almost all the governments of the world including the U.S. unashamedly shunned the Jews of Europe when it would have taken only a small alteration in policy, a little 'courage' to provide the simple changes to their immigration laws allowing the refugees to escape and survive. In light of the intransigence of almost all the foreign powers it would be up to individuals and organisations to find ways in which at least *some* of the persecuted Jews of Europe could survive. The governments had failed, their courage had never really existed, only the sham of conscience had lived in their combined and ineffectual efforts. If powerful governments had been unable, or unwilling, to do something positive to aid the persecuted Jews then what possible help could simple individuals offer? As it turned out, it would be individuals, single-minded, courageous people, who would place their careers, freedom and often their lives into extreme danger to assist people they did not even know.

In Europe, right at the 'coal-face' of persecution and death, many people defied the Nazis and most of those were murdered. Naming all of these courageous individuals and organisations would be beyond the scope of this relatively concise history but some stand out as being at the fore of rescue operations.

El Salvador

Colonel José Castellanos Contreras

El Salvador did not send a representative to the conference at Évian. However, between 1942 and 1945, Salvadorian diplomat Colonel José Castellanos Contreras, while working as El Salvador's consul general at Geneva would be responsible for saving thousands of European Jews from Nazi persecution by providing them with false documentation.

Colonel José Castellanos Contreras was born at the city of San Vincente, El Salvador, on 23 December, 1893, the son of General Adelino

Castellanos and Isabel Contreras de Castellanos. He trained for a military career and would serve as a high ranking officer of the Salvadorian Army for twenty-six years. He was later appointed as a Salvadorian consul general and served at Liverpool England, Hamburg Germany, and Geneva Switzerland (1941-45). It was during his time at Geneva that he was able to do so much to save the Jews of Europe. While there the colonel was approached by a Jewish businessman named György Mandl (also known as George Mandel or George Mantello) who explained that he needed documentation for himself and his family so that they would not be arrested and deported to the concentration camps. José Castellanos Contreras gave Mandl a position as first secretary to the consul and issued Mandl and his family with Salvadorian nationality papers (bearing the name George Mantello). These prevented the Gestapo sending Mandl and his family to Auschwitz. José Castellanos Contreras and Mandl now proceeded to issue thousands of certificates of Salvadorian citizenship to Central European Jews. The certificates, mainly issued through the Swiss consular office of Carl Lutz, stated that the bearers were entitled to receive the protection of the International Red Cross and of the Swiss consul in Budapest. Up to forty thousand desperate refugees from Czechoslovakia,

Bulgaria, Hungary, Poland and Romania quickly became newly minted 'Salvadorians' and were saved from Nazi extermination.[1]

The Netherlands

Miep Gies

In the Netherlands one person who is now well known was Miep Gies, the woman who, with her husband, Jan Gies, attempted to save Anne Frank and her family. Miep and Jan sheltered Anne Frank, her father, Otto, mother, Edith, older sister Margot and four other Dutch Jews, Hermann van Pels, his wife, Auguste, son Peter and Fritz Pfeffer for twenty-five months in Nazi-occupied Amsterdam.

Miep Gies, 1931.

–Wikimedia Commons

Miep Gies had been born Hermine Santruschitz (also given as Santrouschitz), in Vienna, Austria, on 15 February, 1909. Yet conditions in Austria, particularly after the First World War, were somewhat difficult. There were severe food shortages and many Austrian children were sent to Holland to be cared for by Dutch families. In 1920 Hermine, with 'legs like sticks' was sent to Leiden. She later recalled waiting on the Leiden railway station until a 'strong looking man' came along, inspected Hermine's name tag and took her away for a few months with the intention, at least, of 'fattening her up'. Miep later remembered her first drink of warm frothy milk and a soft warm bed.'

While living with the Nieuwenburg family she was given the nickname of Miep. She became their foster daughter and was very attached to them. Eventually Miep's birth mother agreed that she should remain in Holland and the Nieuwenburg family adopted her.

In 1922 the family moved to Amsterdam and in 1933 Miep became the secretary to Otto Frank who was an overseer for a German company Opekta which sold a pectin preparation used in jam manufacture. Frank, a Jew, had fled Nazi Germany and had later been joined by his wife and family. Miep and the Frank family became close friends. In May 1940 Germany invaded the Low Countries and the Jews of the Netherlands faced an uncertain future. By July 1942 thousands of Dutch Jews were being deported to concentration camps and the Frank family went into hiding in an annex comprising a few unused rooms above Otto Frank's office.

Otto asked Miep to help in supporting the family and Miep unhesitatingly agreed. The van Pels family plus Fritz Pfeffer, Miep's dentist, soon joined them. At their own apartment, a short distance away, Jan and Miep Gies also hid an anti-Nazi university student. For hiding these people both would have been facing a death sentence had they been caught.

The end of the endeavour came in 1944 when the *Grüne Polizie* received a tip-off from some person who has never been identified, although more recent research appears to demonstrate that a Nazi collaborator named Tonny (Anton) Ahlers was responsible for the betrayal.

The Gestapo raided the annex and arrested all the Jewish occupants but Miep was spared because the police officer who interrogated her had also been born in Vienna. Miep and her husband Jan were to live safely in Amsterdam for the remainder of the war.

Miep later collected all of Anne Frank's handwritten notebooks and loose papers and kept them together in the hope that Anne would one day return to claim them. Anne, however, died at Bergen-Belsen in northern Germany. Her parents were sent to Auschwitz where Edith Frank died. Otto Frank survived and returned to Amsterdam after the camp had been liberated.

He was the sole survivor of the family. Miep gave Anne's journals to Otto and they were published in 1947. Anne Frank's diary has since been translated and read by millions of people.

Miep Gies remained almost completely anonymous until persuaded by an American writer to tell her own story of the months she kept the Franks and others in hiding. She then wrote her memoirs *Anne Frank Remembered*, which was published in 1987. After the publication of the book Miep became recognised around the world for her humanitarian efforts. Then in her eighties she travelled the world while carrying out speaking engagements against intolerance. Her husband, who had served in the Dutch resistance, also survived the war. He died in 1993. Miep died in January 2010.[2]

Gertruida Wijsmuller-Meijer

Miep Gies was not alone in her humanitarian endeavors; she and Jan were among the best known but there were literally thousands of other people in the Netherlands who assisted with hiding and rescuing Jewish refugees, mainly ordinary families who risked deportation to the camps and death should they have been discovered.

One of the more prominent leaders in the field of humanitarian endeavour during the war, a woman known as the 'Mother of 1001 children', was Gertruida Wijsmuller-Meijer (also given as Geertruida Wijsmuller-Meijer).[3]

Gertruida Wijsmuller-Meijer

(known as Aunite Truus)

—Wikimedia Commons

Gertruida Meijer, a banker's daughter, was born at Alkmaar, in the north of Holland, on 21 April, 1896. She was educated at the School of Commerce in Alkmaar. In 1912 the family decided to move to Duivendrecht, south of Amsterdam. In 1914 Gertruida was appointed to her first job at a bank where she met her future husband, J.F. Wijsmuller. The couple married in 1923 and Gertruida subsequently resigned from her bank job as she anticipated having children and wished to spend her time in raising them. However, she was unable to conceive. As Nazi influence gained momentum across Europe and as anti-Semitism expanded dramatically, Gertruida decided to do what she could to assist in the plight of refugee children.

As outlined in earlier chapters, Holland was not an anti-Semitic state and the Jews of Holland, numbering about 140,000 at that time, had been enjoying full civic right and complete assimilation for around 150 years. When war was declared in 1939 the Dutch believed that they had little to fear from the Germans. As with the First World War it was generally thought that Holland would not be affected or drawn into the conflict. However, all that was to change with the Nazi invasion of the Low Countries in May 1940. The invasion of Holland came both as a shock and surprise to the people of the country and the Jewish population was completely unprepared for the pogrom that was to follow. The Dutch government was largely unable to do much to assist or protect the Jews and as a result of this a very large proportion of the Jewish population of Holland would find themselves in Nazi concentration camps, principally Auschwitz and Sobibor.

The Nazi plan for the Jews of Holland was extremely organised and this was made even more effectual by the efficiency of the Dutch civic records. Prior to the war the Dutch civil service had recorded extensive information on every Dutch national. These records made it a simple matter for the Germans to determine who was Jewish and who was not.

From 1941 the Jewish population of the country found themselves herded into a system designed specifically for their murder. Firstly they lost their jobs and were crowded into a ghetto at Amsterdam. This was the beginning of the end. In February 1941 the Germans deported a small number of Dutch Jews to the Mauthausen concentration camp. The deportations created a furore in Holland and a nationwide protest and strike quickly took place. The Nazis reacted in their usual manner and the leaders of the strike were executed.

The next phase in the Nazi plan for genocide was to move the Jews to a large transit camp at Westerbork, south of Assen, from where they could be deported on weekly trains to the death camps. Of the 140,000 Jews who had been living in Holland at the outbreak of war, approximately 110,000 perished in the camps. As Dutch author and journalist Daphne L. Meijer points out in her excellent essay: *Unknown Children, the Last Train from Westerbork,* by the summer of 1944 there were no longer any Jews on Dutch streets, all had either been deported and killed or were in hiding.[4]

It was during the lead-up to this dark scenario of mass murder that Gertruida Wijsmuller-Meijer began her work to save as many Jewish children as she could. She was a good friend of Mies Boissevain-van Lennep, a resistance fighter and it was with Mies' assistance and the assistance of others such as Nicholas Winton (q.v.) that she arranged children's transports from Germany and Austria via the Netherlands to the U.K.

Before the German invasion of the Netherlands in May 1940 Gertruida was able to travel regularly into Germany where she worked with the wife of a Berlin rabbi, Recha Frier. Gertruida was a strong-willed, determined woman. She would bribe railway officials and charm German officers into doing what she wanted. In 1938 she travelled to Vienna where she met with Adolf Eichmann who was then involved in arranging the transportation of Austrian Jews for the 'Final Solution'. Eichmann told Gertruida that there would be no negotiation; she could have six hundred Viennese Jewish children, these being mainly orphans. Gertruida arranged to have the children transported to the Hook of Holland where about five hundred of them were immediately sent to England. The remaining children were given refuge at The Hague. After this time Gertruida was allowed to take up to 150 children at a time. She would travel into Germany every week to collect them but the invasion of the Netherlands put to stop to the *kindertransports*.

At the time of the invasion Gertruida Wijsmuller-Meijer was in Paris. She hurried back to Amsterdam where she arranged for the removal of all the Jewish children at the Amsterdam Municipal Orphanage, about forty in number. Hiring a bus, she took them to the port of IJmuiden where they boarded a ship, the *S.S. Bodegraven,* bound for England. En route she collected a number of other children making a total of seventy-four. This was the last ship to leave Holland for England before the Germans took complete control of the country.

Once the ship arrived in England the children, however, were prevented from landing because of their German nationality. One child had died during the journey. The ship then took them on to Belfast but finally arrived at Liverpool where the young refugees were allowed to land. The children spent the remainder of the war with various English families.

However, Gertruida Wijsmuller-Meijer (known affectionately as Auntie Truus) now continued to carry out a large amount of humanitarian work. She took Red Cross parcels to refugee camps in southern France and transported Jewish children into Vichy France and Spain. In 1942, the Gestapo arrested her in Amsterdam as they suspected her (correctly) of planning to smuggle dozens of Jews into Switzerland. However, Gertruida was released as the Gestapo did not have sufficient evidence.

Gertruida continued with her endeavours. Working with a resistance group she sent thousands of packages of food to the Westerbork orphanage and the camp at Theresienstadt. In July 1944 she received a message advising her that she should discontinue sending packages to Westerbork as the orphanage was about to be closed and the children transported to Auschwitz. Gertruida went immediately to the head of the security police in Amsterdam, Otto Kempin, (later sentenced to ten years imprisonment for persecution of the Jews) telling him that the orphans there were not Jewish at all but the children of Dutch women with German fathers. It was a complete lie, of course, but the result was that Kempin was able to change the orders so that the children were sent instead to Bergen-Belsen where they might have stood a slightly better chance for life than at Auschwitz.

Despite her humanitarian work in opposition to the Nazi regime, Gertruida Wijsmuller-Meijer managed to survive the war. From 1945 to 1966 she served as a member of the Amsterdam City Council and was involved in the creation of workplaces for the disabled. Gertruida also served as a board member for Anne Frank House. A sculpture of her by Herman Janzen was unveiled at *Oosterpark,* Amsterdam, in 1965 and Yad Vashem recognised Gertruida as 'Righteous Among the Nations'. She died at Amsterdam on 30 August, 1978.[5]

Greece

The Jewish population of Greece had little reason to fear the Nazis until the German occupation suddenly arrived in 1941. Upon taking control the Nazis ordered that all Jews be handed over to the occupying power. Many resisted this order. For example, on the island of Zakynthos the people worked together to save its Jewish population of around 275 people. When the Germans issued the order to hand over all Jews, the mayor of the island, Lucas Karrer. and Bishop Chrysostomas returned to the Germans with the names of just two people on the list: their own. The bishop additionally wrote personally to Hitler stating that all the Jews of Zakynthos were under his personal care and supervision. The general population of the island did everything in their power to hide and protect the Jews. After the war, following the great earthquake of 1953 when the island was almost completely destroyed, the State of Israel was the first to send relief with a message which read: 'The Jews of Zakynthos have never forgotten their Mayor or their beloved Bishop and what they did for us.'[6]

Another example of Greek generosity was seen in the Greek community of Volos which experienced fewer losses than any other Jewish community in Greece.

Princess Alice of Battenburg and Greece, the mother of Prince Philip, Duke of Edinburgh, remained in occupied Athens during the war sheltering Jewish refugees, which later saw her being recognised as 'Righteous Among the Nations' by Yad Vashem.[7]

Archbishop Damaskinos (Dimitrios Papandreou)

In Athens Archbishop Damaskinos (Dimitrios Papandreou) is still remembered for his kindness towards the Jewish population. While serving as the archbishop of Athens during the German occupation, Damaskinos ordered that all the churches under his jurisdiction were to issue fake Baptismal certificates to Jews fleeing from Nazi persecution. Thousands of Jews in Greece were thus able to claims that they were Christians and evade the deportations. The archbishop even defied the orders of the Germans who threatened to place him in front of a firing squad.[8]

Archbishop Damaskinos

(Dimitrios Papandreou)

—Photograph courtesy Kessel archive, Wikimedia Commons.

Ukraine
Omelyan Kovch

Omelyan Kovch was a priest with the Ukrainian Greek-Catholic Church. He had been born in the Western Ukraine in 1884. Following his studies in Rome he was ordained and served as the parish priest in various areas including the Church of St. Nicholas at Peremyshliany, a small town in Western Ukraine. He was the father of six children.

During the war Omelyan Kovch handed out more than six hundred baptismal certificates to Jewish refugees.

On one occasion a group of Jewish people had been driven into the local synagogue and the Nazis were in the process of throwing bombs into the building when Father Kovch ran up and with the assistance of several brave parishioners was able to block the door to the building so that the Germans were unable to throw any more bombs inside. Father Kovch spoke fluent German and was able to convince the Nazis to stop attacking the Jewish group inside. Astonishingly, the Germans listened to Kovch and the trapped Jews were rescued from the burning building. On one occasion Father Kovch conducted a mass baptism of about one thousand

Jews so that they would be saved from deportation. Father Kovch even wrote to Hitler personally, denouncing the crimes against humanity.

However, the Gestapo finally caught up with him; on 30 December, 1942, Father Kovch was arrested and interrogated. He admitted to having baptised people of the Jewish faith and also refused to state that he would not do so again in the future. Severely beaten, Father Kovch refused to give up his humanitarian work and continued to serve as a priest to many of his fellow inmates. Having failed to extract his compliance to their wishes, the Gestapo sent Father Kovch to the Majdanek concentration camp, near Lublin in Poland. There, under terrible conditions, he continued with his religious ministrations, despite brutal treatment, until he developed medical problems and subsequently died.

The Jewish Council of Ukraine awarded Omelyan Kovch the title of 'Urkaine's Righteous' in September 1999. Father Kovch was later canonised by Pope John Paul II.[9]

France

Le Chambon-sur-Lignon

One of the most well known instances of the protection of Jewish people occurred at the village of *Le Chambon-sur-Lignon* in the *Haute Loire* department of south-central France, the residents of which sheltered several thousand Jews at a time when such protection could well have led to a death sentence for the protectors. Led by their local minister, Pastor André Trocmé, and Pastor Edouard Theis, the people of the village believed that it was their duty to assist the persecuted Jews to evade the Nazi roundup and deportation to the death camps. The Jews were hidden in village homes and public buildings and when the Vichy police came on search patrols the refugees were sent into the woods to hide. After the police had left, villagers would walk through the woods singing a particular song to let the Jewish people know that it was all clear. The church leader, Pastor André Trocmé, had been a teenager at the time of the First World War and had been greatly influenced by a German soldier who was a conscientious objector. Both André Trocmé and his assistant Edouard Theis were pacifists who had established the *Ecole Noubelle Cevenole*, an international pacifist school to educate Jewish children. In 1938 there had been just eighteen children but by 1944 that number had grown to 350. Daniel Trocmé, André's cousin, was the head of the school. When the Germans discovered the school Daniel was arrested, interrogated and sent to the Majdanek concentration camp in Poland where he was gassed in 1944.

The Germans and Vichy French knew that Jews were hiding in and around the village but not one of the village residents ever gave them any information. The refugees were provided with forged ration cards, food and accommodation and some were able to escape into Switzerland. No written records of the events at *Chambon* ever existed but it has been estimated that the villagers saved between 3000 and 5000 Jewish refugees during the war. In 1981, in recognition of its humanitarian efforts, the entire community was awarded an honorary degree by Haverford College in Pennsylvania. Additionally, in 1990 the Yad Vashem Memorial to the Holocaust awarded the community the 'Righteous Among the Nations' Award.[10]

Eduardo Propper de Callejón

Another case of wonderful humanitarian effort was displayed by Eduardo Propper de Callejon who was working as the first secretary at the Spanish Embassy in Paris when France surrendered to the Germans in June 1940.

Working from the consulate at Bordeaux and in cooperation with Portuguese diplomat Aristides de Sousa Mendes, (see below) Callejón and Sousa Mendes were responsible for issuing more than thirty thousand transit visas to Jewish refugees so they could escape through Spain to Portugal.[11]

When the Spanish foreign minister, Ramon Serrano Suner, discovered that Callejón was issuing visas without the proper authorisation he had Callejón transferred to a 'backwater' diplomatic post at Larache in the Spanish protectorate of Morocco. Suner is now known to have been actively assisting the Axis powers. Despite Spain's neutrality he was then working with the Japanese Foreign Office to assist a network of Japanese espionage agents to function in 'neutral' Spain. (For details on Suner and the Japanese 'TO' network see, *Spies for Nippon* by Tony Matthews, Robert Hale Ltd, London, 2010).

In 2008 Eduardo Propper de Callejón was posthumously recognised by Yad Vashem as 'Righteous Among the Nations'. He was the father-in-law of the Honourable Raymond Bonham Carter and the grandfather of the well known British actress Helena Bonham Carter. He died in 1972.[12]

Aristides de Sousa Mendes

Aristides de Sousa Mendes, who worked closely in cooperation with Eduardo Propper de Callejón, was a Portuguese diplomat appointed to Bordeaux in France during the early part of the Second World War. He had been born on 19 July, 1885, and later studied law with his twin brother at the University of Coimbra. In 1908, the same year he qualified in law, Sousa Mendes married his childhood sweetheart, Maria Angelina Coelho de Sousa. The couple would have fourteen children.

Aristides de Sousa Mendes

—Photograph courtesy Wikimedia Commons

Soon after marrying, Sousa Mendes began his diplomatic career, being appointed subsequently to a number of posts including Zanzibar, Kenya, Brazil, the United States and Belgium before being transferred to Bordeaux.

Following the outbreak of war, Sousa Mendes, in association with Eduardo Propper de

Callejón, defied his own government and issued over thirty thousand Portuguese visas, free of charge, to refugees fleeing Nazi persecution. On some occasions a single visa might cover an entire large family. Despite being ordered by his government to stop issuing the visas, Sousa Mendes feverishly continued with his humanitarian work; he set up a kind of factory-line with his sons and wife and was processing visa applications and issuing visas even during German bombardments of the city.

In 1939 Portuguese premier Antonio Salazar had issued orders to his consuls abroad that they were forbidden to issue visas to: '...foreigners of indefinite or contested nationality; the stateless; or Jews expelled from their countries of origin'.[13]

However, Sousa Mendes continued ceaselessly with his work although he knew it would be the end of his career.

Sadly, Aristides de Sousa Mendes, like his contemporary, Eduardo Propper de Callejón, was never recognised during his lifetime for his amazing humanitarian efforts. His career was brought to an abrupt halt in 1941 when Antonio Salazar, forced him out of his job. Disgraced by the dictatorial Portuguese government and prevented from continuing with his law work, stripped of his pension, abandoned by many of his colleagues and friends, Sousa Mendes died in poverty in 1954, his wife, Maria Angelina, having died in 1948. It took many decades for Sousa Mendes' humanitarian actions to become known to the public and to have his name cleared of any wrongdoing. However, eventually Sousa Mendes' diplomatic honours were posthumously restored; he was promoted to the rank of ambassador and awarded the Cross of Merit and Order of Liberty.[14]

Abdol-Hossein Sardari

In Paris the head of consular affairs at the Iranian consular office was Abdol-Hossein Sardari. While today it is not usual for people of the Moslem faith to have a great deal of empathy with the Jewish people, Sardari was responsible for saving many Iranian Jews then trapped in France by arguing with the German authorities that Iranian Jews were protected from German acts of aggression by previous agreements made between the German and Iranian governments. Sardari also handed hundreds of blank Iranian passports to nonIranian Jews so they could be saved from the Holocaust. He did this without the permission of the Iranian government. Unlike so many other cases where diplomatic staff have provided visas to refugees and then been vilified for their actions, the Iranian government later supported Sardari fully in his humanitarian efforts.[15]

Sardari's later life, however, was to be plagued by personal difficulties. His Chinese lover disappeared under mysterious circumstances in 1948 during the Chinese Civil War and during the postwar era of Iran Sardari was charged with embezzlement. After the violent Iranian Revolution of 1979, Sardari lost his pension rights and property. Poverty stricken, he went to live in a small bed-sitter at Croydon, London, finally moving to Nottingham where he died in 1981.[16]

Belgium

In Belgium during the war the Belgian resistance was able to stop one of the death trains to Auschwitz and free 231 people who had been destined for the gas chambers. Additionally, several local government authorities were able to slow down or prevent the registration process for Jewish people. Many private individuals assisted by hiding Jewish children in houses and boarding schools.

Henri Reynders (Dom Bruno)

Henri Reynders was born on 24 October, 1903, the fifth of eight children to a middle class Catholic family. Upon completion of his school education he was accepted as a postulant at the Benedictine Mont-César Abbey in Leuven, Belgium. In 1922 he completed his noviciate and was given the name of Dom Bruno.

For the following three years Dom Bruno studied theology and philosophy at both the Catholic University of Leuven and the Saint Anselm Athenaeum in Rome. In 1925 he took the Benedictine vows and bound himself to monastic life at Mont-César where he continued his intellectual studies focussing on the writings of Saint Irenaeus. In 1928 Dom Bruno was ordained a priest and three years later earned a Doctorate in Theology from the University of Leuven.

When war broke out in 1939 Dom Bruno was assigned to become a chaplain with the Belgian 41st Artillery Regiment. However, when the Germans overran Belgium in May 1940 he was captured, having received a serious leg injury, and for the following six months was held in prisoner-of-war camps at Wolfsburg and Doessel in Germany.

Following his release from the camps Dom Bruno returned to live at Mont-César. However, he had now become an ardent opponent of Nazism. He joined the Belgian resistance and some of his work with them included the repatriation of British pilots who had been shot down over Belgian territory. He was subsequently appointed to work at a home for the blind at Hodbomont and soon became aware that the home was being used as a place of refuge for a number of Jewish adults and children. The home was subsequently closed and the refugees moved to other relatively safe locations but Dom Bruno returned to Mont-César and thereafter dedicated himself to assisting the relief of the Jewish people of Belgium and to finding ways in which they could be hidden from the Nazis.

Dom Bruno was assisted in his endeavours by other monks at Mont-César, members of the resistance and even some members of his own family including a nephew, Michel Reynders. Dom Bruno was able to construct an underground network, establish contacts with other resistance groups and also with individuals who were helping to assist the plight of the Jews. He was instrumental in finding many families who, risking death or deportation, were willing to offer a place of refuge in their own homes.

The Gestapo finally learned of Dom Bruno's underground activities and sent men to arrest him at the Mont-César Abbey. However, Bruno was not in the abbey when they arrived and was able to go into hiding, abandoning his habit for civilian clothes and covering his tonsure with a beret.

Dom Bruno survived with the assistance of his friends in the resistance and a fellow monk who supplied him with some forged identity papers. Mounted on a bicycle he continued to ride around the countryside, visiting those Jewish people who were in hiding, bringing them food, news and other forms of comfort. While the Gestapo kept a close watch for Dom Bruno, they never succeeded in capturing him.

When Belgium was liberated in September 1944 Dom Bruno rejoined the Belgian armed forces as a chaplain. He served until the end of the war. Following the cessation of hostilities he assisted with the repatriation of Jewish refugees and in reuniting, where possible, family members and children.

In 1954 Dom Bruno was able to publish his lifetime's work, the study of Saint Irenaeus' writings. In 1964 Yad Vashem proclaimed him one of the 'Righteous Among the Nations'. In 1968 he was granted permission to join the monks at Chevetogne Abbey. During his final years he suffered from Parkinson's Disease and this forced him to enter a nursing home in 1975. In October 1981 he suffered a bone fracture and did not survive the resulting surgery. Dom Bruno was interred at the Abbey of Chevetogne.[17]

Bulgaria

Dimitar Peshev

The history of the treatment of the Jewish people under Bulgarian control remains highly controversial. Bulgaria was, of course, allied to the Nazi regime. Indeed, the Bulgarian government under Prime Minister Bogdan Filov was active in assisting the Germans with implementing the Holocaust in the areas of Yugoslavia, Macedonia and Greece which it had occupied under orders from the Nazis. King Boris of Bulgaria joined an alliance with the Nazis in 1940 which agreed to follow Germany's anti-Semitic course and on 27 September, 1942, both Romania and Bulgaria, under German auspices, signed the 'Law for protection of the nation'. Like the Nuremberg Laws passed earlier in Germany, these new laws depicted the Jews as being subhuman and enemies of the state. On 10 March, 1943, the Bulgarian government under Prime Minister Bogdan Filov signed an agreement that would see the deportation of all of Bulgaria's Jews, more than 48,000 people. The deportation was to be organised by SS officer Theodor Dannecker, a close associate of Adolf Eichmann. Many of the Jewish people slated for deportation would later owe their lives to the actions of one man, Dimitar Peshev.

Born at Kyustendil in 1894, Peshev had fought during the First World War and later completed his law studies. He was regarded as an honest and reliable man and in 1938 became deputy speaker in the Bulgarian Parliament.

In March 1943 all the Jews of Kyustendil were ordered to leave their homes as they were about to be deported.

However, Dimitar Peshev and the Bulgarian Orthodox Church rebelled completely against the deportation order. After he had been advised of the planned deportation Peshev attempted on several occasions to obtain an audience with Bogdan Filov. However, Filov refused to see him. Undaunted, Peshev went to see a close friend and colleague, the interior minister Petur Gabrovski, who had the authority to cancel the deportations. It took a great deal of persuasion but Peshev was able to convince Gabrovski that stopping the mass deportation was the right thing to do. Gabrovski finally called the governor of Kyustendil and ordered him to stop making preparations for the deportations. At 5.30p.m. on 9 March, 1943, the order was cancelled. The Jews of Bulgaria had been saved but the order to cancel the deportations had come too late for the Jewish people living in Thrace and Macedonia where the roundup had already commenced. Almost all of the Jews living in Thrace were arrested (around four thousand of them) and sent to Treblinka where most were murdered. About 1200 Thrace Jews were arrested moved to Salonika and then sent to Auschwitz for gassing. Almost all the Jews of Macedonia received similar treatment, being rounded up and send to Treblinka where only a handful survived.

After the war Peshev was charged by the Soviets with anti-Semitism and anti-communism. He was found guilty and sentenced to death. However, following an outcry from the Jewish community in Bulgaria his sentence was subsequently commuted to imprisonment for fifteen years. Of this he served just one year before being released.

After the war Peshev lived in poverty and anonymity. His work in saving the Jewish population of Bulgaria was generally unknown. However, in 1973 his actions were recognised by Yad Vashem and Peshev was awarded the title of 'Righteous Among the Nations'. He died on 25 February that year, aged seventy-eight years.[18]

Italy

Father Rufino Niccacci

In Italy the situation was difficult. Mussolini had promulgated racial laws in 1938 but generally speaking the Italian people were not particularly anti-Semitic and many Jewish people had been able to escape from places such as Germany, Austria, Poland and other countries to find at least temporary refuge in Italy, especially before the German occupation.

From the lowest parish priest, many members of the Catholic Church aided Jewish refugees. Among these was Father Rufino Niccacci who, in September, 1943, was the father guardian at the Franciscan Monastery of San Damiano at Assisi. Under the directions of Bishop Placido Nicolini and the chairman of the Committee to Aid Refugees, Aldo Brunacci, Father Niccacci issued false identity papers to the Jews and also provided about three hundred of them with sanctuary in the monastery, convents and private homes. Father Niccacci was recognised by Yad Vashem as 'Righteous Among the Nations' in 1974 and in 1983 President Ronald Reagan, while addressing the American Gathering of Jewish Holocaust Survivors remarked: 'The picturesque town of Assisi, Italy, sheltered and protected three hundred Jews. Father Rufino Niccacci organised the effort, hiding people in his monastery and in the homes of parishioners. A slip of the tongue by a single informant could have condemned the entire village to the camps, yet they did not yield.'[19]

Giovanni Palatucci

In Fiume, then an Italian territory (now Rijeka, the principal seaport and third largest city in Croatia), the chief of the Foreigners' Office, Giovanni Palatucci, began to forge documents and issue visas to large numbers of Jewish refugees. He was instrumental in destroying all the documentation concerning about five thousand Jewish refugees who were then living in Fiume. He issued them with false papers and also provided them with some funds. He then sent the refugees to an internment camp in southern Italy which was being run by his uncle, Giuseppe Maria Palatucci who was the Catholic bishop of Campagnia.

With the disintegration of Italian fascism in 1943 and the fall of Mussolini, Fiume came under German control. Giovanni Palatucci continued his clandestine operations of aiding the Jews in association with the resistance movement. However, the Gestapo eventually learned of his activities and his arrest was imminent. A close friend, the Swiss consul to Trieste, offered safe passage to Switzerland but Palatucci refused, sending his Jewish fiancée instead. Giovanni Palatucci was arrested on 13 September, 1944, and sentenced to death. His sentence was later commuted to deportation to Dachau where he died on 10 February, 1945, just weeks before the camp was liberated. The cause of his death is unknown but is variously given as starvation or gunshot wounds. He was just thirty-six years of age.[20]

Giorgio Perlasca

There were other Italian nationals who, while working outside Italy, also distinguished themselves through their actions in helping to save Jewish people. These included Giorgio Perlasca, who, under the guise of a Spanish ambassador to Bucharest, was able to protect thousands of Jews destined for the Nazi gas chambers.

Much has been written and produced about that other and far more well known humanitarian Oskar Schindler yet the deeds of Giorgio Perlasca were not only similar in scope but Perlasca was able to save far more Jewish refugees from the death camps.

Giorgio Perlasca was born at Como, Italy, on 31 January, 1910. As a young man he became interested in fascism. He fought for Mussolini during the second Italo-Abyssinian War (1935-36) and for Francisco Franco during the Spanish Civil War (1936-39) when Franco employed the services of more than 50,000 Italian 'volunteers' (actually sent to Spain by Mussolini). However, when Franco allied Spain, ideologically, to Germany and anti-Semitism, Perlasca became disillusioned with fascism. It was the overwhelming wave of Nazi anti-Semitism that influenced Perlasca to break with fascism.

During the Second World War he worked initially at the task of obtaining supplies for the Italian Army based in the Balkans and was then appointed an official delegate with diplomatic status to Eastern Europe. Having previously worked for a meat importing business in Italy, his task was the procurement of meat to feed the Italian forces then fighting alongside Hitler's army on the Russian front.

Following the Italian capitulation to U.S. forces in 1943 Giorgio Perlasca, then serving in Budapest, chose not to join with the newly formed Italian Social Republic but to remain loyal to the king. The Hungarian authorities imprisoned him but he was later able to take advantage of a medical pass to gain access to the Spanish Embassy where he requested and was granted political asylum—due largely to his previous commitment to fighting for Franco during the Spanish Civil War.

In 1944, following the Soviet crossing of the Hungarian border, the pro-Nazi Arrow Cross Party leader Frerncz Szalasi, a fanatical anti-Semite, was installed as prime minister and Hungary was even more deeply immersed in a tidal wave of brutal persecution—particularly those Jews living in Budapest. Hungarian ruler Admiral Horthy then abdicated.

In association with the Spanish *chargé d'affaires*, Angel Sanz Briz, Giorgio Perlasca and several other similarly-minded diplomats worked at smuggling Jewish refugees out of Hungary. The situation became even more dangerous as Soviet forces approached Budapest and Sanz Britz was forced to flee the country. Yet Perlasca, now masquerading as the Spanish ambassador, continued with his dangerous humanitarian work.

Due largely to his distinguished appearance and fluency in Spanish, Perlasca was able to carry through his subterfuge convincingly when dealing with Hungarian authorities. During one sensational meeting he convinced the Hungarian minister of internal affairs that the Spanish government would actually take retaliatory action against Hungarian citizens living in Spain if the Hungarians did not allow Jewish refugees to remain under Spanish protection. Over the following months literally thousands of false documents were handed out to refugees. Perlasca and Spanish Embassy staff provided refugees with 'protection cards' which placed them under the asylum of Spain. He also hid the Jews in safe houses and mansions which were under the diplomatic protection of various countries. Within a fairly short period, from 1 December, 1944, to 16 January, 1945, Perlasca was able to save more than five thousand Jews from the death camps—about four times more than Oskar Schindler. Perlasca also bought medicines and other necessities on the black market and handed them over to the refugees.

In December 1944 Perlasca encountered one of the most dangerous figures in Nazi history. Two Jewish boys were being herded onto a deportation train when Perlasca stepped in and rescued them, pushing them into the back of his car, despite the presence of a forbidding German lieutenant-colonel on the scene who challenged Perlasca's authority. Also present that day was the now famous Swedish diplomat Raoul Wallenberg who later stated that the German officer had been none other than the much loathed Adolf Eichmann—the officer in charge of organising the deportations to the concentration camps and Hitler's 'architect' of the 'Final Solution',. During the war around 600,000 Jews from Hungary or territories annexed to Hungary were deported and killed.

When the war ended Giorgio Perlasca returned to Italy but told no one about his humanitarian activities in Hungary. It was not until 1987 when a group of saved Hungarian Jews finally found him that the story became public. Since that time at least two books have been written about his wartime activities, one of which had been made into a film. Giorgio Perlasca died of a heart attack in 1992, having received a host of international awards for the work he did in saving Jewish refugees.[21]

Angelo Guiseppe Roncalli

Angelo Guiseppe Roncalli, who would later become Pope John XXIII, while working at the Apostolic Delegation at Istanbul, helped a great many Jews and non-Jews to escape Nazi persecution by issuing transit visas. His work in this regard was varied. Jewish refugees arriving in Turkey were assisted in getting to Palestine and other safe destinations. Slovakian children were able to leave the country after Roncalli's interventions on their behalf. Orphaned children were able to leave Constanta for Istanbul and later Palestine with the assistance of Roncalli and Jews held at the Sered concentration camp in Slovakia were spared from deportation to the death camps as a result of interventions made by Angelo Roncalli. Similarly, Jewish prisoners held at the Jasenovac concentration camp (in the German occupation zone of the independent state of Croatia, one of the largest camps in Europe and the only camp not actually operated by the Germans) were freed after Roncalli intervened on their behalf.[22]

Guelfo Zamboni

Another Italian hero of the Holocaust was Guelfo Zamboni, a career diplomat who was responsible for saving many hundreds of Greek and Italian Jews from the concentration camps.

Zamboni had been born at Santa Sofia, then part of Tuscany, in 1897, one of eight sons. His parents had wanted him to enter the church but they both died when Guelfo was quite young, leaving him an orphan. Despite these personal problems young Guelfo decided to attend school so that he could gain a little education but while doing so he also had to earn a living.

At the age of nineteen years Guelfo joined the Italian infantry, serving from 1916 to 1918. He was awarded the Bronze Medal of Military Valour and, as he had been seriously wounded, he also received the War Merit Cross.

His earlier years of study had proved successful and Guelfo Zamboni subsequently received a degree in economics and trade. In 1925 he passed the formal examination to enter the Italian diplomatic service and later became fluent in German.

In 1942 Guelfo Zamboni was appointed the consul general at the Greek town of Thessalonika which was under Nazi control. Thessalonika then held a population of approximately 56,000 Sephardic Jews, many of whom were of Italian descent. The Germans looted all of the town's historic libraries, manuscripts and other such cultural treasures which were sent to the Institute of German Studies at Frankfurt am Main. The 56,000 Jews were arrested, unceremoniously herded into rail wagons and deported to the death camps where most perished.

It was impossible for Guelfo Zamboni to do much to prevent the looting and deportations but he did everything in his power to rescue the Italian Jews and to offer some succour to hundreds of Greek Jews. He would issue 'provisional' Italian citizenship to the Greek Jews which stated that they were now provisional Italian nationals. In total he was able to save about 350 people from the death camps.

Zamboni was recalled to Rome in June 1943 when his humanitarian work was continued by Italian diplomat and First World War hero Giuseppe Castruccio who was able to organise 'rescue trains' to transport Jews who owned Italian passports to Athens, then under Italian control.

Guelfo Zamboni was awarded the title 'Righteous Among the Nations' in 1992, although he had never sought any kind of recognition for his work in saving the Jews. He died in 1994.[23]

Monsignor Hugh O'Flaherty

Meanwhile, in Rome an Irish priest, Monsignor Hugh O'Flaherty, known as the Scarlet Pimpernel of the Vatican, was responsible for saving a great many Jews from the gas chambers. O'Flaherty had once been a Vatican diplomat and therefore was able to call upon a variety of contacts 'in high places' to aid him with his humanitarian endeavours. He was joined by a network which included the well known Irish singer Delia Murphy, the wife of the Irish ambassador, Dr Thomas J. Kiernan.[24]

Monsignor Hugh O'Flaherty

–Photograph courtesy Molière, Wikimedia Commons.

O'Flaherty had been born at County Cork in February 1898. At the age of twenty years he enrolled at Mungret College in County Limerick to study for the priesthood. He was transferred to Rome in 1922 where he completed his studies and remained working for the Holy See. He served as a Vatican diplomat to Egypt, Haiti, Santo Domingo and Czechoslovakia and was appointed monsignor in 1934. During the Second World War Monsignor O'Flaherty visited many prisoner-of-war camps in Italy attempting to locate soldiers who had been reported as missing in action. When he occasionally found them still alive and well in captivity he would contact the families through Radio Vatican.

When Italian fascism crumbled in 1943 thousands of Allied prisoners were released. However, following the German occupation these former prisoners had to go on the run from the Nazis. With the assistance of a group of other people, including priests, Free French secret agents, communists, Irish balladeer Delia Murphy and even a Swiss count, O' Flaherty managed to evade the Nazi authorities and to hide a large number of former prisoners and Jewish refugees. The Nazis attempted to arrest him and even to assassinate him on a number of occasions but O'Flaherty was under the protection of the Vatican. This resulted in the head of the Gestapo in Rome, Lieutenant-Colonel Herbert Kappler, ordering the painting of the now infamous white line on the pavement at the opening of St. Peter's Square, signifying the official line between the Vatican and the remainder of Rome. Kappler stated that if O'Flaherty were to cross the line he would be killed. These events were later portrayed in a television film, *The Scarlet and the Black*, released in 1983 and starring Gregory Peck as Hugh O' Flaherty.

Exact numbers are not known but it has been recorded that Monsignor O'Flaherty and his associates were able to conceal many thousands of Allied former prisoners and Jewish refugees from the Nazi authorities. These were housed in flats, farms, convents and private houses of ordinary Italian people. Large numbers of refugees and former prisoners were also able to flee to safer countries with O' Flaherty's assistance.

After the war Hugh O' Flaherty was recognised with several distinguished awards including Commander of the Order of the British Empire (C.B.E.). He suffered a stroke during Mass in 1960 and died at the home of his sister in Cahersiveen on 30 October, 1963.[25]

Germany

Alfred Delp

There were, of course, many German Gentiles who resisted the deportation of Jewish people including a Jesuit priest named Father Alfred Delp. While serving as a rector of St. Georg Church in Munich, Father Delp was responsible for assisting Jews to escape into Switzerland. His was to be a life of intellectual thought, religious devotion and humanitarian endeavour.

Alfred Delp was born at Mannheim on 15 September, 1907, the son of a Catholic mother and Protestant father. He was baptised a Catholic but later attended a Protestant school and was confirmed in a Lutheran church.

Delp joined the Society of Jesus in 1926 and after completing philosophy studies he went to work as a prefect and sports teacher at the *Stella Matutina Kolleg* in Feldkirch, Austria. However, in 1933 he was forced by the Nazis to return to Germany and went to the Black Forest where the Jesuits had opened the *Kolleg St. Blasien* for those students who had been evicted from Austria. Delp later completed his studies in theology at Valkenburg, Holland, and Frankfurt.

In 1937, the same year he completed his studies, Delp was ordained a Catholic priest at Munich. It had been his intention to undertake a Ph.D. at the University of Munich but for political reasons he was rejected for admission. From 1939 he worked on the staff of the Jesuit publication *Stimmen der Zei (Voices of the Times)* but in April 1941 the Nazis suppressed the publication. It was then that Father Delp was assigned as rector to St. Georg Church and where he would fulfil his work to save many of the persecuted Jews, assisting them to escape to Switzerland.

The Jesuit, Augustin Rösch, was Father Delp's immediate superior in Munich and it was Rösch who introduced Delp to the underground organisation known as the Kreisau Circle. From that time Delp met regularly with its members and became more deeply involved with the operations of the group.

Alfred Delp

–Photograph courtesy Graf Foto, Wikimedia Commons.

However, when the 20th July bomb plot against Hitler failed, the Gestapo immediately arrested and tortured anyone who might have any kind of connection to the German resistance. Eight days after the assassination attempt Delp was arrested in Munich, although he had never been directly involved in the plot to kill Hitler.

Alfred Delp was transferred to the infamous Tegal prison in Berlin where he continued to say Mass and write reflections on religious and spiritual matters. On 11 January, 1945, Alfred Delp and several of his associates, Helmuth James Graf von Moltke, Franz Sperr and Eugen Gerstenmaier were brought before one of the highly prejudicial and infamous Nazi 'People's Courts' *(Volksgerichtshof)* presided over by the 'blood justice' judge Roland Freisler (who had been one of the attendees at the infamous Wannsee conference in January 1942). The People's Court almost always sided with the prosecution, no matter what the case, and it was generally thought that being brought before the court was tantamount to a death sentence. Freisler acted as judge, jury and prosecution. Approximately ninety per cent of all cases tried before Freisler ended with the death sentence or life imprisonment, the sentences frequently having been determined even before the trial had begun.

The much hated Nazi judge, Roland Freisler.

—Photograph courtesy German Federal Archives, (http://www.bundesarchiv.de), Wikimedia Commons.

After a farcical trial Alfred Delp, Helmuth von Moltke and Franz Sperr were found guilty of high treason and sentenced to death by hanging. They were then returned to prison to await the execution of their sentences.

While in prison Alfred Delp was offered his freedom if he would agree to leave the Jesuits. However, he refused the offer.

Alfred Delp was executed at the Plötzensee prison in Berlin on 2 February, 1945, only three months before the death of Hitler and the German capitulation. While walking in handcuffs to his death, Delp is reported to have said humorously to the Reverend Peter Buchholz, the prison chaplain who was accompanying him, 'In half an hour I'll know more than you do.'[26]

In typical Nazi fashion, Heinrich Himmler had ordered that all those who were executed as a result of the July 20th plot against Hitler should be cremated and their ashes spread over sewage fields. Accordingly Alfred Delp's ashes were disposed of somewhere near Berlin.

The day after Alfred Delp's execution, Roland Freisler, the Nazi judge who had condemned Delp and his friends to death, was himself killed during an Allied bombing mission over Berlin.[27]

Father Bernhard Lichtenberg

Similarly, Father Bernhard Lichtenberg was a German Catholic priest in Berlin who openly prayed for Jews during the evening prayer service.

Bernhard Lichtenberg was born at Ohlau (now Olawa) in Prussian Silesia, on 3 December, 1875, the first of five children. His was to be a life of devotion to the church. He studied theology at Innsbruk and was ordained in 1899. The following year he was appointed as the pastor of Charlottenburg in Berlin where he also served for a period as a member of the Centre Party's local parliament.

In 1931 he became canon of the cathedral chapter of St. Hedwig and was appointed provost of the cathedral in 1938, right at the heart of the Jewish pogrom in Berlin. Bernhard Lichtenberg felt very strongly about the actions the Nazis were taking against the Jews and protested them vigorously. Following the tragic events of *Kristallnacht*, Lichtenberg prayed openly for the salvation of the Jews, despite the powerful anti-Semitic propaganda and attitudes that were sweeping Germany and Austria. He also protested against the arrests and murder of the infirm and the mentally ill.

To begin with, the Nazi authorities simply dismissed his actions as inconsequential, but Bernhard Lichtenberg went on to even stronger forms of dissent, organising protest rallies, sometimes right outside the gates of the concentration camps.

Finally the Germans struck. Bernhard Lichtenberg was arrested and placed on a transport to the Dachau concentration camp. However, by now he was no longer a young man, the years of work and of ardent protest had wearied him and Lichtenberg collapsed and died while being transported to the camp.

In 1996 Pope John Paul II beatified Bernhard Lichtenberg, the Mass was held in the same stadium that Hitler had constructed for the 1936 Olympic Games.[28]

Albert Göring

One of the more astonishing cases of Germans assisting with saving the Jewish populations under Nazi control is that of Albert Göring, brother to *Reichsmarschall* Hermann Göring, one of the founders of National Socialism, commander of the *Luftwaffe*, president of the Reichstag, interior minister, prime minister of Prussia and a close friend and associate of Adolf Hitler. It hardly seems conceivable that two brothers could exist at such distant ends of the ideological spectrum.

Albert was the fifth child of Heinrich Ernst Göring and his wife, Franziska 'Fanny' (née Tiefenbrunn). Heinrich was a former

Reichskommissar to German South-West Africa and German consul to Haiti.

Even as a young man Albert Göring's attitudes to National Socialism and Nazism were well known. Working as a filmmaker and doubtless enjoying the protection afforded him by the position of his brother, Albert made no secret of the fact that he abhorred Nazi policies, especially in relation to the persecution of the Jews. On one occasion he is reported to have joined a group of Jewish women who had been forced to scrub the streets on hands and knees. When the SS officer in charge of the scene discovered that Albert was Hermann Göring's brother he immediately ordered that the activity was to stop and the women were allowed to go on their way. Albert is also reported to have intervened when his former employer Oskar Pilzer was arrested. Albert was able to use his influence to have Pilzer freed and later assisted Pilzer and his family to escape from Germany. Apparently this was not an isolated case and Albert is reported to have helped many other Jewish people to escape the clutches of the Nazis.

After he had been shipped off to Czechoslovakia as the export director of the Skoda works, Albert encouraged the workers to carry out minor acts of sabotage. He also made contact with the Czech resistance movement. He was able to forge his brother's signature and is reputed to have created documents which allowed dissidents to escape. When he was subsequently arrested Albert was, once more, able to use his brother's name and influence to obtain his release. Albert sometimes sent trucks to the Nazi concentration camps demanding that they be filled with labourers. When these vehicles returned carrying their loads of Jewish workers the vehicles were stopped in isolated areas and the camp inmates allowed to escape.

At the end of the war Albert Göring was interrogated by the Nuremberg Tribunal but after many grateful people testified on his behalf no charges were laid. He was subsequently arrested by the Czechs but released after others had testified to the good work he had carried out on behalf of the Jewish people during the war.

Albert Göring returned to Germany where he worked as a writer and translator. He was generally shunned because of his family name. Living finally on a small pension, he later married his housekeeper so that the pension could be transferred to her upon his death. Albert Göring died about a week later on 20 December, 1966.[29]

Poland

Zegota

There were, of course, many organisations and people in Poland who did not adhere to the anti-Semitic influences of the Nazis. Among the leading organisations was the *Zegota*, the Council to Aid Jews, which operated under the auspices of the Polish government in exile. *Zegota* operated about one hundred cells, mainly in Warsaw and distributed relief funds to thousands of Jews. It was especially important in saving the lives of Jewish children.

Since the establishment of the Yad Vashem in Israel more than six thousand non-Jewish Polish men and women (more than any other country in the world), have been recognised as being 'Righteous Among the Nations', for their assistance to Jewish people at the time of the Holocaust. During the war, Poland would be split virtually in two, half under Soviet domination with the Nazis controlling western and central Poland. About seven hundred of the people who would be honoured by Yad Vashem actually lost their lives while trying to hide and otherwise protect Jewish people. It was a highly dangerous undertaking with the death penalty always looming.

Dr Eugeniusz Lazowski

Another Pole, one of many who would assist Polish Jews to survive, was Eugeniusz 'Eugene' Lazowski, a medical doctor. He would become known as the Polish Schindler. Dr Lazowski saved about eight thousand Jews from deportation to the death camps by faking an epidemic of typhus.[30]

Eugeniusz 'Eugene' Slawomir Lazowski was born at Czestochowa, north of Kraków, Poland, in 1913. Prior to the outbreak of the Second World War Lazowski studied medicine, obtaining his degree from the Jozef Pilsudski University in Warsaw. He served in the Polish military at the time of the German invasion, was captured and spent some time as a prisoner-of-war before escaping. He then returned to live with his wife and daughter at Rozwadow, a historic town with a significant Jewish population situated about forty miles north of Lublin. There he began practising medicine in association with a university friend named Dr Stanislaw Matulewicz. It was Matulewicz who discovered that if a person were to be injected with killed typhus bacteria then that person would subsequently test positive to typhus without experiencing any of the symptoms. The original test had been made on one of Dr Matulewicz's friends who was on leave from a work-camp in Germany. This friend knew that if he was forced to return to the work-camp he would probably not survive. Realising the risks involved, he volunteered to be a guinea pig in an attempt to prevent his return to Germany. The 'vaccine' was injected and a blood sample sent to a laboratory in Germany. The results of the test were sent by telegram a few days later stating that the 'patient' was suffering from 'Epidemic Typhus' and that he should not be returned to Germany. The ruse had been completely successful.

At that time the Germans were moving into gear to conscript the Polish population into forced labour and also to deport all its Jews to concentration and extermination camps. Lazowski lived next to one of the ghettos and came up with a plan to assist in saving many of the residents of several villages in the Rozwadów and Zbydniów areas from forced labour battalions and deportation. Secrecy was vital and those people who were in need of immediate assistance would hang a white piece of cloth on their back fence as a signal that they wanted to see the doctor and obtain his collusion in avoiding deportation. By injecting 'patients' with the fake vaccine Lazowski was able to convince the Germans, who were almost paranoid about hygiene and disease, that there was a raging typhus epidemic in the area.

The Germans went in great fear of typhus as it is highly contagious and deadly. They placed all the 'patients' into quarantine and did not themselves go into the quarantined areas for fear of contracting the disease.

Utilising this unique method of saving the Poles and Polish Jews, both Dr Lazowski and Dr Matulewicz were able to save around eight thousand Jews in twelve ghettos from transportation or summary execution. The Germans took typhus very seriously and their stand on the issue was to kill all Jews who had contracted the disease but to isolate non-Jews. Therefore it was necessary for the doctors to inoculate non-Jewish 'patients' in the areas surrounding the ghettos forcing the Germans to abandon those areas and thus saving the Jews in the ghettos. This was an extremely dangerous mission. Because of the very nature of their operations, involving a large number of people, the doctors were always open to betrayal by collaborators. Had they been caught they would certainly have been killed.

In 1958 Dr Lazowski emigrated to the United States, having obtained a scholarship from the Rockefeller Foundation. In 1976 he was appointed professor of paediatrics at the State

University of Illinois. He wrote more than one hundred scientific dissertations and also his memoirs, published successfully under the title of *My Private War*, which was reprinted several times. The book was later made into a television documentary.

Dr Lazowski retired from his medical practice in the late 1980s. He died at Eugene, Oregon, in 2006, where he had been living with his daughter.[31]

Maximilian Kolbe

One of the more well known Polish church leaders and humanitarians was Maximilian Kolbe, who was later to be canonised for his actions.

Maximilian Kolbe was born Raymond Kolbe in Zdunska Wola, Poland, then part of the Russian Empire, on 8 January, 1894. He came from a relatively poor and struggling family. His father was Julius Kolbe, an ethnic German and his mother Maria, née Dabrowska, was a Pole. The family subsequently moved to Pabianice where both parents worked at basket-weaving. Maria also worked as a midwife and operated a small shop from the house they were renting. However, the family was soon to experience separation and heartache. In 1914 Julius Kolbe joined the Polish Legions and was captured by the Russians who quickly hanged him for fighting for the independence of partitioned Poland.

Yet Raymond Kolbe's entire life was to be influenced by a vision he received of the Virgin Mary. Kolbe later wrote that Mary appeared to him holding two crowns, one white, the other red, and asking Kolbe to choose one of them, saying that the white crown would mean that Kolbe would persevere in purity while the red meant that he would become a martyr. Kolbe later wrote, 'I said that I would accept them both.'[32]

In 1907 both Raymond Kolbe and his brother, Francis, decided to join the Conventual Franciscans and illegally crossed the border between Russia and Austria-Hungary to enrol in the Conventual Franciscan seminary at Lwów. Raymond entered the novitiate in 1910, was given the religious name of Maximilian and took his final vows in Rome in 1914.

Maximilian Kolbe earned a doctorate in philosophy in 1915 and a doctorate of theology in 1919. That same year he returned to Poland and founded the monastery of Niepokalanów, situated near Warsaw. In addition to establishing a seminary, a radio station and a number of publications, Kolbe also created a monthly periodical the *Rycerz Niepokalanej*.

Kolbe left for Japan in 1930 where he would spend the following six years. There he built a monastery on one side of a mountain on the outskirts of Nagasaki. According to Shinto beliefs the monastery was not in harmony with nature. When the Americans dropped the atomic bomb on Nagasaki in 1945 the monastery remained unharmed but the other side of the mountain was devastated by the blast.[33]

Upon returning to Poland and during the years of Nazi persecution, Kolbe was able to provide shelter to two thousand Jewish refugees at his friary at Niepokalanów.

Fr. Maxmilian Kolbe

—Photograph courtesy http://www.v-like-vintage.net, Wikimedia Commons.

However his humanitarian efforts eventually came to the notice of the Gestapo and Kolbe was arrested on 17 February, 1941. In May he was transferred to Auschwitz. From that time onwards his life expectancy could be measured in months, rather than years.

About two months later, at the end of July, 1941, three prisoners managed to escape from Auschwitz. In retaliation, the deputy camp commander, *SS Hauptsturmführer* Karl Fritzsch, chose ten men at random and ordered that they were to be starved to death. One of the selected men, Franciszek Gajowniczek, called for mercy, shouting, 'My wife, my children', and Maximilian Kolbe immediately offered to take his place.

Thrown into a bleak underground cell, the men were left without food and water. Over the following days the guards would often see Maximilian Kolbe celebrating Mass, singing hymns and encouraging the other condemned men that they would, 'soon be with Mary in Heaven'.

After two whole weeks only Kolbe remained alive. The camp guards needed to vacate the cell for other unfortunate prisoners so they simply gave Maximilian Kolbe a lethal injection of carbolic acid. It has been reported that when he saw the syringe Kolbe simply held up his arm and calmly waited for the injection. Coincidentally, his body was pushed into the camp crematoria on 15 August—the feast day of the Assumption of Mary.

Maximilian Kolbe was beatified by Pope Paul VI in 1971 and canonised by Pope John Paul II on 10 October, 1982.

Karl Fritzsch, the much loathed former Dachau camp guard who had ordered the death by starvation of Kolbe and his fellow prisoners, was never punished for this or his many other war crimes. It was Fritzsch who, reportedly, had first experimented with the use of the pesticide Zyklon B (prussic acid) as a method of mass murder, Zyklon B had been stored at Auschwitz for use in exterminating vermin from the camp and Fritzsch decided to try it on a group of six hundred Soviet prisoners-of-war and two hundred and fifty sick prisoners.

Karl Fritzsch is reported to have died during the defence of Berlin in May 1945, although this theory has since been disputed and his actual fate is unknown.[34]

Irena Sendler

As mentioned earlier in this publication, one woman who did a great deal to assist with saving Jewish children from the Holocaust in Poland was Irena Sendler.

Irena Sendler was born Irena Krzyzanowska on 15 February, 1910, the daughter of Dr Stanislaw Krzyzanowska and his wife, Janina. In 1917 Irena's father died of typhus which he contracted while treating patients whom other doctors had refused to tend.

As a young adult Irena attended Warsaw University where she studied Polish literature. She became a member of the Socialist Party and opposed the 'ghetto-bench' system at the university, defacing her grade card in public protest. She was then suspended from the university for three years. Irena's first husband was Mieczyslaw Sendler.

When Germany occupied a large part of Poland in 1939, Irena, who was then working for the Warsaw Social Welfare Department, was determined to do what she could for the persecuted Jews. Living in Warsaw she and numerous helpers forged more than three thousand documents for Jewish families. The task was fraught with danger as people assisting and hiding Jewish refugees were liable to be shot or sent to the concentration camps where they would almost certainly be gassed along with the Jews they had been trying to help.

Irena Sendler, 1942.

–Wikimedia Commons

In August 1943 Irena, then known under her *nom de guerre* of 'Jolanta', was nominated to head up the Jewish children's section of *Zegota* (q.v.)—the underground Council to Aid Jews. As an employee of the Warsaw Social Welfare Department Irena possessed a special permit allowing her to visit the Warsaw Ghetto to check its residents for signs of typhus. With the aid of other employees of the department, Irena, in association with the Central Welfare Council (RGO), was able to smuggle babies and children out of the ghetto in ambulances and trams. She even had babies wrapped as packages. These children were then placed into hiding with Polish families or with the Warsaw orphanage of the Sisters of the Family of Mary or Catholic convents.

Among those who assisted Irena with this hugely dangerous undertaking were Zofia Kossak-Szczucka, a writer and resistance fighter, and Matylda Getter, the mother provincial of the Franciscan Sisters of the Family of Mary. In total, Irena and her friends were able to save around 2500 children from the ghetto.

Irena Sendler risked her own life every day and the Gestapo eventually caught up with her. She was arrested, severely tortured and subsequently sentenced to death. Astonishingly, Irena was able to save her own life by bribing the guards when she was taking the final walk to her execution. Her name actually appeared on a bulletin announcing that she had been executed.

For the rest of the war Irena was forced to remain in hiding but she continued to support efforts to save the Jewish children.

Her marriage to Mieczyslaw Sendler ended in divorce in 1945 and two years later Irena married a Jewish friend, Stefan Zgrzembski, whom she had met at university. The couple would have three children. However Irena divorced Zgrzembski in 1959 and remarried her first husband Mieczyslaw Sendler. Sadly, that match also failed once again and Irena lived in Warsaw for the remainder of her life. She died on 12 May, 2008, having been recognised by Yad Vashem in 1965 as 'Righteous Among the Nations'. The tree of Irena Sendler, planted at Yad Vashem, now stands at the entrance to the Avenue of the Righteous. In October 2003 Irena received Poland's highest honour, the Order of the White Eagle.[35]

Henryk Slawik

Another Polish hero of the Holocaust was Henryk Slawik, journalist, editor, soldier, who, in the face of considerable danger to himself, worked diligently to save the lives of thousands of Polish Jews.

Henryk Slawik had been born to an impoverished Polish Silesian family on 16 July, 1894 and was educated at an academic secondary school. In 1922 he was elected president of the Workers' Youth Association and was among those who helped to set up the 'Workers' Universities'. In 1929 he married Jadwiga Purzycka and between the years 1934 to 1939 served as president of the Polish Journalists' Association for Upper and Lower Silesia.

When the Germans invaded Poland in September 1939 Slawik joined the mobilised police battalion which was then attached to the Krakow Army. On 17 September, after the Soviet Union had joined in the war against Poland, Slawik crossed the Hungarian border and was interned at a prisoner-of-war camp.

Some time later József Antall (Snr), a member of the Hungarian Ministry of Internal Affairs, who was then responsible for civilian refugees, saw Slawik at one of the camps and recruited his aid. Slawik spoke fluent German and because of this he was taken to Budapest where he established the Citizens' Committee for Help for Polish Refugees. In association with József Antall, Slawik worked to assist the plight of many prisoners-of-war and displaced persons and also worked clandestinely to assist exiled Poles leave the internment camps and to travel to France or the Middle East to join the Polish Army. Slawik was also a delegate of the Polish Army in exile.

His work in these endeavours was the perfect training ground for what was to follow. When the Hungarian government issued racial decrees, separating the Polish refugees of Jewish descent from all others, Slawik began to issue the Jews with false documents which described them as Catholics. He was also responsible for assisting several hundred Jews to join the Yugoslav partisans.

Yet one of Slawik's most important elements of humanitarian work was the establishment of an orphanage for Jewish children, which went under the guise of the 'School for Children of Polish Officers'. In order to assist with the deception the school would regularly receive visits from Catholic Church authorities.

In 1944 Henryk Slawik was forced to go underground. He assisted with the escape of many Jewish refugees, including those at the orphanage. Unfortunately, Slawik was arrested in March 1944 and tortured savagely to try to make him name his Hungarian colleagues. This he steadfastly refused to do. Slawik was then transported to the Mauthausen concentration camp where he was subsequently shot. His wife was also arrested and sent to the Ravensbruck concentration camp. Miraculously she survived the ordeal and after the war was able to trace their daughter in Hungary who had been hidden from the Nazis by the Antall family.

It has been estimated that Henryk Slawik assisted about thirty thousand Polish refugees in Hungary, about five thousand of whom were Jews. He was recognised by Yad Vashem as 'Righteous Among the Nations' on 26 January, 1977.[36]

Archbishop Andrey Sheptytsky

Archbishop Andrey Sheptytsky, the archbishop in charge of the Ukrainian Greek Catholic Church was responsible for hiding hundreds of Jewish people in his home and in various Greek Catholic monasteries in Poland during the German occupation.

Andrey Sheptytsky was born Roman Aleksander Maria Sheptytsky in a town called Prylbychi, about forty kilometres north-west of Lviv, then part of the Austrian Empire, on 29 July, 1865. He came from a distinguished line and his maternal grandfather was Aleksander Fredro, (1793-1876) the well known Polish poet, playwright and author.

Andrey Sheptytsky was educated initially at home and later attended school in Kraków. As a young man he joined the Austro-Hungarian Army but his term of service was to be cut short through illness. He returned to Kraków where he studied law, receiving a doctorate in 1888. It was during this time that he visited Italy and was granted an audience with Pope Leo XIII. He also travelled to Kiev and Moscow. During his student years he learnt to speak Hebrew in order to be able to relate on a broader level with the Jewish community.

Archbishop Andrey Sheptytsky

—Photograph courtesy infoukes.com, Wikimedia Commons.

Andrey Sheptytsky entered the Basilian monastery at Dobromyl and took the religious name of 'Andrew' after Saint Andrew. He was ordained in 1892 and studied at the Jesuit seminary at Krakow where he received a doctorate in theology in 1894. He was made rector of the monastery of St. Onuphrius at Lviv in 1896. Three years later, in 1899, he was nominated by Emperor Franz Joseph to fill the vacancy of the Ukrainian Greek Catholic Bishop of Stanyslaviv. The pope concurred and Andrey Sheptytsky was consecrated as bishop at Lviv in September that year and appointed Archbishop of Lviv in January 1901.

Following the outbreak of the First World War Archbishop Andrey Sheptytsky was arrested by the Russians and imprisoned. He spent the remainder of the war incarcerated and was not released until 1918 when he returned from Russia to Lviv.

During the Second World War Andrey Sheptytsky worked diligently to save the lives of hundreds of Jewish refugees by harbouring them in Greek Catholic monasteries. He also issued the now well known pastoral letter, 'Thou Shalt Not Kill'. He died in 1944 and was interred at St. George's Cathedral in Lviv.[37]

China and Japan

Shanghai was a considerably important transit point for European Jews who wished to emigrate to other destinations such as the U.S. and many found their way there with the assistance of the International Committee for European Immigrants in China (known as the I.C.). The committee worked out of an office in the Cathay Hotel in Shanghai.

Members of the International Committee for European Immigrants in their office at the Cathay Hotel, Shanghai.

–United States Holocaust Memorial Museum, courtesy of Valerie S. Komor.

Jewish refugees Fritz Huber and his bride, Lauri, from Berlin, photographed in Shanghai.

—United States Holocaust Memorial Museum, courtesy of Fred Deutsch.

It had been formed under the aegis of Sir Victor Sassoon, a rich Iraqi Jew with British citizenship who owned the Cathay Hotel. The committee was organised by Paul Komor, a Hungarian businessman with the aid of Eduard Kann, Aladair Kelen and Michael Speelman. Speelman would later form the Committee for the Assistance of European Refugees in Shanghai (known as the Speelman Committee), after which the I.C. concentrated its efforts on providing I.D. cards to those refugees whose papers and passports had been confiscated by the Nazis.[38]

In fact China was one of the most generous nations for refugees, even under Japanese domination. Between 1933 and 1941 when the flow of refugees was virtually stopped by the Nazis who were then sending them almost directly into the gas chambers, more than thirty thousand Jewish refugees entered the port of Shanghai, a greater number than those taken in by Canada, New Zealand, South Africa and British India combined.

Feng Shan Ho

Among the most humanitarian would be a man named Feng Shan Ho, the Chinese consul general at Vienna who would later freely hand out visas to Jewish refugees.[39]

Feng Shan Ho had been born at Yiyang, Hunan, on 10 September, 1901. His father died when Ho was just seven years of age. Ho was a dedicated and clever school student; he studied at the Yali School in Changsha and subsequently entered Yale-in-China University. He later attended Munich University in 1926 and was awarded his Ph.D in political economics in 1932. Three years later Ho joined the Chinese Foreign Ministry and was posted to Turkey. He then became the first secretary at China's legation in Vienna, taking up the post in 1937. The following year Austria was annexed by Germany, the legation was transformed into a consulate and Ho suddenly found himself the new consul general.

When it became obvious to Ho that the Jews of Austria were doomed, he was determined to do something to offer whatever aid he could. The Évian conference had failed spectacularly, almost all the countries of the world were now refusing entry to any significant numbers of Jewish people, so Ho began issuing visas for China. He did this expressly against the orders of his superior, the Chinese ambassador in Berlin, Chen Jie. Within the first three months of being appointed consul general Feng Shan Ho issued 1200 visas to Jewish refugees.

Despite pressure from his superior Ho continued with his humanitarian efforts until ordered to return to China. It is not known exactly how many visas he eventually issued but the number is certainly in the thousands. Ho received a 'black mark' in his personal file but was allowed to continue with his career. He later served as China's ambassador to Egypt, Mexico, Bolivia and Colombia.

Feng-Shan Ho settled finally in San Francisco where he wrote his memoirs, *40 Years of My Diplomatic Life*, which was published in 1990. He died at San Francisco, aged ninety-six years, on 28 September, 1997. His humanitarian work remained unknown during his life but in 2001 Feng-Shan Ho was posthumously recognised by Yad Vashem with the award of 'Righteous Among the Nations'.[40]

***

During the war the Japanese government, rather surprisingly, in light of its atrocities in China and Manchuria, agreed to ensure the safety of the Jews in China, Japan and Manchuria.

General Seishiro Itagaki, a Japanese Army officer is credited with proposing to the Five Ministers' Council (the highest Japanese decision-making council) that a policy be adopted prohibiting the expulsion of Jews in Japan, Manchuria and China as standard Japanese national policy. The Japanese prime minister, Prince Fumimaro Konoe, is remembered for adopting the policy. However, after the war Seishiro Itagaki was hanged as a war criminal for allowing inhumane treatment of prisoners-of-war.[41]

Kiichiro Higuchi

One high ranking Japanese officer who is remembered for his humanitarian efforts in helping to find refuge for the Jews in China was Kiichiro Higuchi who was the major general of the Harbin Special Branch in 1938 and allowed Jewish refugees to enter Manchuria from across the Soviet border. Some of his men looked after the refugees, fed them, and settled them at Harbin or Shanghai or arranged exit visas for them.[42]

Despite German protest General Hideki Tojo (later executed by the Allies for war crimes) accepted Jewish refugees although after 1941 the Japanese placed all the Jews in Shanghai into what became known as the Shanghai Ghetto. After the war and due to the Chinese Civil War of 1946-50 many of the Jewish residents at Shanghai would emigrate to the U.S. and Israel.[43]

***

Among the refugees to find asylum at Shanghai would be Oskar and Berta Fiedler, who were married at Vienna in 1938. (See passport). It must have been an extremely worrying period for them, to be married in a city at a time when Vienna was at the centre of anti-Jewish fervour. They were able to flee from Austria in November 1938, several months after the failure at Évian and just days after the *Kristallnacht* pogrom. They arrived at Shanghai aboard the Italian liner *Conte Bianco Mano* in mid-December that year and found temporary accommodation at the Embankment building which was also owned by Sir Victor Sassoon.

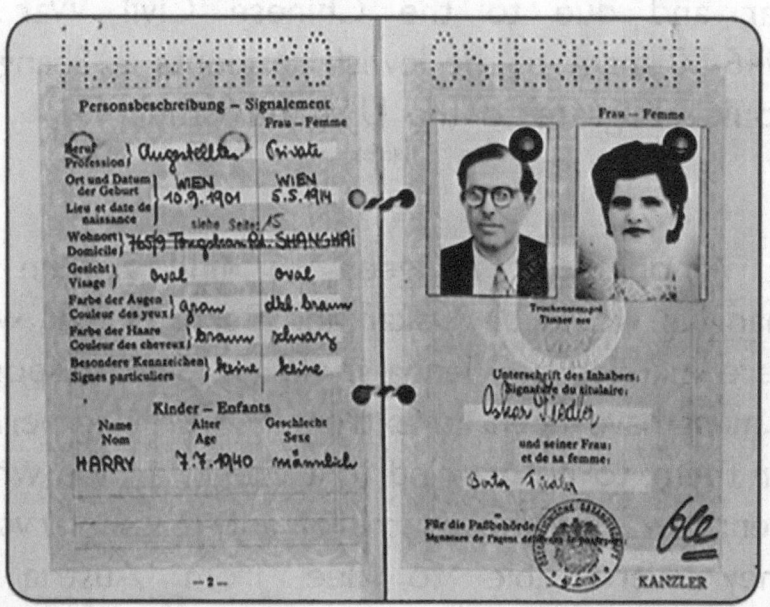

The passport issued by the Austrian Embassy in Shanghai to Oskar and Berta Fiedler.

—United States Holocaust Memorial Museum, courtesy of Harry Fiedler.

This shelter was administered by the International Committee for European Immigrants (I.C.). The couple's son, Harry Fiedler, would be born in Shanghai on 7 July, 1940. The family later moved to the Hongkew Ghetto, remaining there until 1945. In October 1949, just one week before the communist takeover of Shanghai, the family would be able to emigrate to Canada.[44]

Sweden

Count Folke Bernadotte

The activities of Count Folke Bernadotte during the war would later become well known. Bernadotte would be responsible for negotiating the release of about 31,000 people, mainly Jews, to Sweden.

Folke Bernadotte, the Count of Wisborg, was born at Stockholm on 2 January, 1895, the son of Count Oscar Bernadotte (formerly Prince Oscar of Sweden) and his wife, Ebba Munck af Fulkila. His grandfather had been King Oscar II of Sweden.

Bernadotte trained to be a cavalry officer and was commissioned a lieutenant in 1918, later being promoted to the rank of major. He served as Swedish commissioner-general at New York's World Fair in 1939-40. In 1943 he was appointed vice-chairman of the Swedish Red Cross.

During the final months of the war and on the initiative of the Norwegian diplomat Niels Christian Ditleff, Bernadotte acted as the chief negotiator with the task of rescuing a large number of inmates from Nazi concentration camps.

The mission to rescue these prisoners, which had been negotiated through Heinrich Himmler, became famous for its 'white buses', painted entirely white with the distinctive red cross on their sides. The mission would take about two months to complete and the buses with their Red Cross staff would encounter many extreme hazards while operating in German-controlled areas which were often being saturated by Allied bombing. The staff consisted of about 308 people which included medics and volunteer soldiers.

Count Folke Bernadotte

–Photograph courtesy U.S. Holocaust Memorial Museum. Photograph Number 80532, courtesy U.S. National Archives, Wikimedia Commons.

The convoy was made up of thirty-six hospital buses, nineteen trucks, seven cars, seven motorbikes, a tow truck, field kitchen and a massive amount of stores and food including all the petrol the convoy would require for the entire rescue mission. A total of 21,000 people were initially rescued and after Germany's surrender the white buses mission continued bringing another 10,000 people from the camps to Sweden. It was one of the largest humanitarian rescue missions in history.

In May 1948, three years after the end of the war in Europe, Count Bernadotte was appointed the United Nations mediator in Palestine. However, on 17 September, 1948, Bernadotte was assassinated by members of *Lehi*, a Jewish terrorist group, (also known as the Stern Gang), who believed that the count was nothing more than a British stooge and a threat to the emerging state of Israel.[45]

Per Anger and Raoul Wallenberg

Meanwhile, Per Anger, the Swedish diplomat to Budapest, with the assistance of Raoul

Wallenberg were able to save many Hungarian Jews by issuing them with provisional passports to protect them from arrest and deportation to the concentration camps.

Per Johan Valentin Anger had been born at Göteborg, Sweden, on 7 December, 1913. He studied law at the University of Stockholm and the University of Uppsala, graduating in 1939. After being drafted into the army he was subsequently offered a trainee position with the Ministry of Foreign Affairs at the Swedish legation in Berlin. Working initially with its trade department, he soon became involved in relaying intelligence to Stockholm about Germany's impending attacks on Norway and Denmark. In 1942, after a brief sojourn in Stockholm, he was transferred to the Swedish legation at Budapest. In 1944 Per Anger became deeply involved in attempting to assist the Hungarian Jews. He began to issue provisional Swedish passports and special certificates to the Jews, protecting them from internment and deportation to the death camps. About seven hundred of these documents were initially issued and although the legality of the documents remained in question, the Hungarian government agreed to recognise them as legitimate and to consider their bearers as Swedish citizens.

In these endeavours Per Anger worked with the now well known humanitarian Raoul Wallenberg who had been sent in with the support of the United States War Refugee Board, the World Jewish Congress and the Swedish government. When Wallenberg arrived at Budapest he quickly seized upon and expanded Per Anger's initiative, issuing protective passes and providing safe houses in the city. After that time Anger and Wallenberg worked closely together in their endeavours to save the Jews of Hungary from deportation.

When the Soviets took control in 1945 both Anger and Wallenberg were arrested. Three months later Anger was released but Wallenberg simply disappeared into the complex maw of the Soviet prison system. He was never heard of again and it was presumed that he had been killed by the Soviets.

After the war Per Anger served in a variety of Swedish diplomatic posts and continued to search for clues as to Wallenberg's fate. During the 1980s he met personally with Soviet president Mikhail Gorbachev but still nothing concrete was established. During the meeting Gorbachev showed little interest and implied that he had no influence over the K.G.B. In 1957 the Soviet authorities had released a document which appeared to demonstrate that Wallenberg had died of a heart attack while in Lubyanka prison. However, there have been numerous other rumours about the circumstances of his death including the claims that he had been killed with C-2 poison as part of a test at the poison laboratory of the Soviet secret services or that he had been executed at Lubyanka in 1947.

These findings have since been widely disputed and the circumstances surrounding the disappearance and presumed death of Wallenberg remain unclear. In 2013 Raoul Wallenberg became the first person to receive honorary Australian citizenship.[46]

Britain

Despite the disappointing results of Évian, it has to be said that Britain was doing what it thought was right and between December 1938 and the beginning of the war in September 1939 almost 10,000 unaccompanied refugee children from Central Europe would be allowed into the country. These children would arrive in a series of ships which became known generally as the *kindertransports*. The first would arrive at Harwich on 2 December, 1938, with children from Berlin and Hamburg. The second would arrive on 12 December from Vienna. Three days later on 15 December another 370 children would arrive from Hamburg and other areas of northern Germany. Around seventy per cent of the children on these transports would be Jewish who had been chosen by Jewish organisations in Germany, Austria and Czechoslovakia. More transports with thousands of children would soon follow.[47]

Sir Nicholas Winton, Beatrice Wellington, Doreen Warriner and Trevor Chadwick.

Leading the way in the provision of some of the *kindertransports* would be British stockbroker Sir Nicholas Winton in association with several other people including Beatrice Wellington, Doreen Warriner and Trevor Chadwick. Following *Kristallnacht* Sir Nicholas and his associates would organise *kindertransports* from Czechoslovakia and Austria bringing children, mainly Jewish children, to England and neutral Sweden.[48]

Nicholas Winton had been born at Hampstead in London. His parents were of German/Jewish origin and had moved to London in 1907. The original family name had been Wertheim but this had subsequently been anglicised and the family had converted to Christianity.

Nicholas Winton attended Stowe School and later studied at a night school while doing volunteer work at the Midland Bank. His experience at Midland led him to obtaining a position with Behrens Bank in Hamburg and subsequently at the Wasserman Bank in Berlin. He would remain in Berlin until 1931 when he moved to France and commenced work at the *Banque de Credit* in Paris. Returning finally to London, he worked as a stockbroker at the London Stock Exchange.

In 1938, with the cloud of Nazi domination looming over Europe, Nicholas Winton was about to leave England to travel to Switzerland for a holiday when he suddenly changed his mind (and his life) and decided instead to go to Prague, Czechoslovakia, to help a friend who was then involved in refugee operations to assist the persecuted Jewish people.

In Prague Winton established an organisation that would offer aid to those children of Jewish families who were most at risk. The 'office' of the organisation was a dining room table at Winton's hotel in Wenceslas Square.[49]

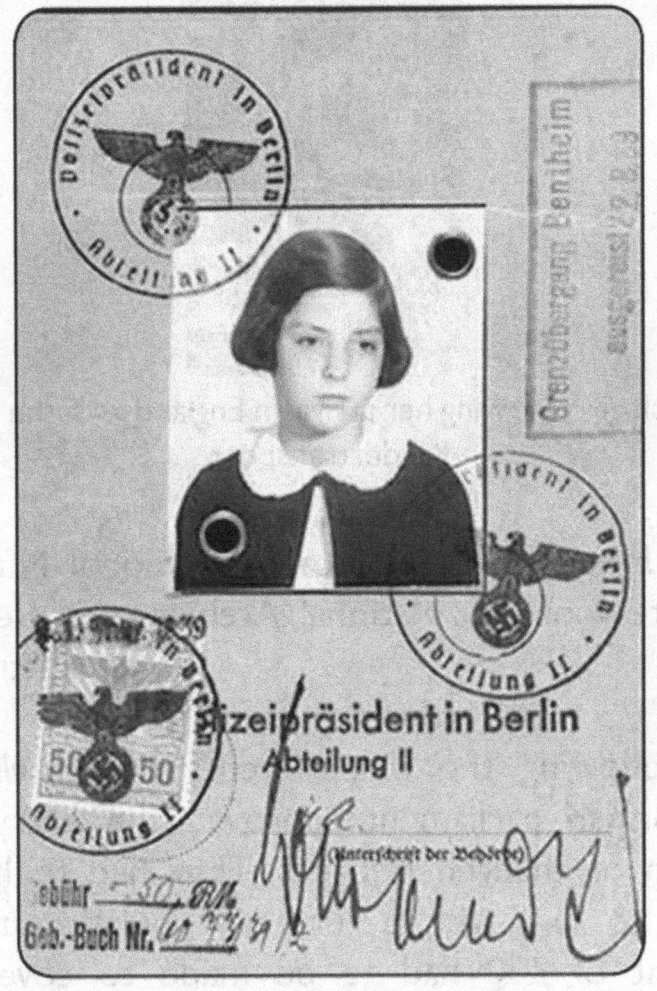

The passport issued to eleven-year-old Gertrud Levy before her departure from Germany on a Kindertransport.

—United States Holocaust Memorial Museum, courtesy of Gerda Levy Lowenstein.

A Jewish girl following her arrival in England with the second Kindertransport.

—United States Holocaust Memorial Museum, courtesy of U.S. National Archives and Records Administration.

Following the tragic events of *Kristallnacht*, the British parliament approved the entry into Britain of children refugees. They had to have a place to live with a further stipulation that a deposit of £50 had to be made to cover the cost of the child's return to the country of origin following the end of the war.[50]

One of the principal obstacles in Winton's plans was to be the border crossing into the Netherlands. The children destined to find refuge in England would be required to take the ferry from the Hook of Holland. However, after *Kristallnacht* the Dutch authorities, like so many others, had closed its borders to Jewish refugees.

The border guards were ruthless in hunting down refugees attempting to cross the Dutch border and when caught, the refugees were immediately returned to Germany and the terrible fate that awaited them in the gas chambers of the Nazi death camps.

However, Winton persevered and was able to get many of his charges across the borders, due largely to guarantees he had obtained from the British. Additionally Winton was able to assist with the migration of Jewish refugees through the Hook of Holland from Vienna and Berlin. He was assisted in his endeavours by numerous people, whom he later publicly acknowledged, including the Dutch national Gertruida Wijsmuller-Meier (known as Tante Truus [Aunt Truus] [See separate entry]), Beatrice Wellington, Doreen Warriner and Trevor Chadwick. Winton later wrote: 'Chadwick did the more difficult and dangerous work after the Nazis invaded; he deserves all the praise.'

Doreen Warriner was an academic from University College, London, and she played a huge role in helping to save political refugees from Europe. In doing so she assisted with the evacuation of many Jewish families. It was Warriner who set up an office on Vorsilska Street from which many of the other rescuers worked, including Winton. She remained in

Prague until April of 1939 after which it became far too dangerous for her as she had been involved in smuggling anti-Nazis illegally across the border into Poland. She knew that the Gestapo was about to arrest her. One of her more memorable achievements was the rescue of two groups of women and children who were taken from the railway station at Prague to safe places in hotels, hostels and private accommodation. This was achieved on the day after the Nazis had entered the city and the streets were literally crawling with Germans. Her replacement was the 'indomitable' Canadian Beatrice Wellington.

Trevor Chadwick, a teacher by profession from Swanage, Dorset, had originally arrived at Prague in order to bring out two refugee boys and take them to his school. He also collected another child and returned with them to England. He then went back to Prague to assist with the rescue of many other refugees.

In total Winton and his associates found homes in Britain for 669 children, many of them orphans, their parents having been sent to the gas chambers at Auschwitz.

After the war (during which he served in the R.A.F.), Winton, like so many other heroes of the Holocaust, would never speak of his work in saving Jewish refugees. In 1988 his wife, Greta, found an old scrapbook in their attic; the book contained lists of names of the children Winton had saved, plus the names of their parents, and the names and addresses of the British families who had taken in the children.

In 1983, several years before his work on the Czech *kindertransports* became known publicly, Winton was awarded an O.B.E. in the Queen's Birthday Honour's List for his work in establishing the Abbeyfield homes for the elderly. In the 2002 New Year's Honours List, in recognition of his work on the *kindertransports*, Winton was knighted. The following year he received the Pride of Britain Award for Lifetime Achievement.

Although Nicholas Winton had been baptised as a Christian, his parents had been entirely Jewish until their conversion to Christianity, therefore Winton was not eligible for the Yad Vashem award of 'Righteous Among the Nations' which is reserved for those of non-Jewish backgrounds. However, in 2010 the British government named Winton a 'British Hero of the Holocaust'.

Upon his 100th birthday Judy Leden, the daughter of one of the boys Winton had saved, flew him over White Waltham airfield. The *Jewish Chronicle* also published a profile of his life and achievements.[51]

Nicholas Winton died at the Wexham Park Hospital at Slough, England, on 1 July, 2015, aged 106 years.

Frank Foley

Interestingly, the British secret service agent in Berlin, Frank Foley, who, before the war was working as a spy with the cover of a passport officer, would save around ten thousand Jewish refugees by issuing them with forged passports to Britain and Palestine. Sometimes Foley would go into the internment camps, despite the fact that he was not acting with diplomatic immunity, to get people out, hiding them at his own home while obtaining passports for them. He subsequently became known as the 'British Schindler' and was recognised by Yad Vashem as 'Righteous Among the Nations'. He died in May 1958. In 2010 Foley was posthumously named a 'British Hero of the Holocaust'.[52]

Turkey

Namik Kemal Yolga

One of the Turkish heroes of the Holocaust was Namik Kemal Yolga, another career diplomat. Yolga had been born in 1914 and in 1940 was posted as the Turkish vice-consul to Paris, this being his first overseas diplomatic appointment. Following the German invasion of France and the roundup of its Jewish citizens and those Jewish refugees who had sought sanctuary there, the victims of the arrests were sent initially to the Drancy deportation camp from where they were to be railed east to some of the major death camps.

When Turkish Jews were arrested the Turkish Embassy in Paris sent a strongly-worded demand to the German Embassy stating that under the Turkish constitution the citizens of Turkey were not discriminated against because of their race or religion. They pointed out that as nationals of Turkey the Turkish Jews should not be subject to arrest by the Germans. This ploy seemed to work as Yolga would then drive to the deportation camp and individually collect those Turkish Jews who had been interned there, taking them back to Paris and arranging safe houses for them to stay.

Yolga later served as the Turkish ambassador to Rome, Paris, Caracas, Teheran (Tehran) and Moscow.[53]

Hungary

Sára Salkaházi

Sára Salkaházi was a Hungarian Catholic who gave her life in an attempt to save the lives of hundreds of Jews during the Holocaust.

Sára Salkaházi was born Sára Schalkház (also reported as Salkaház) at Kassa, Hungary, (now Kosice, Slovakia) on 11 May, 1899, her parents, Leopold and Klotild Schalkház being middle class people of German origin who owned the Hotel Schalkház (or Salkahaz) at Kassa.

As a child Sára was considered to have been something of a 'tomboy' who liked to joke a lot but had a deep 'social sensitivity'. When a teenager she began to write plays and would shut herself up in her room, deep in thought and prayer.

As a young woman Sára was not particularly attracted to a life in the church. She studied at Kassa and earned an elementary teacher's degree, but for political reasons she only worked as a teacher for about a year. Thereafter she worked at a variety of jobs including that of a reporter and bookbinder. As a young writer she participated in the activities of the literary society of the Hungarian minority of Slovakia and edited the official paper of the National Christian

Socialist Party of Czechoslovakia, being a member of the governing body of that party. She wrote many short stories with themes focused on the challenges facing the poor, and on moral issues and injustices.

Before finally taking her religious vows Sára had been engaged to be married but she later broke off the engagement. In 1930 Sára Salkaházi took her religious vows with the Sisters of Social Services at Budapest. She wanted to train for missionary work and to be sent to Brazil. However, this dream never eventuated. Sara was reputed to have possessed a rather 'difficult' character perhaps a little too individualistic and rebellious for the sisterhood, and because of this and probably because of the outbreak of war she was never to set foot in Brazil.

By 1944 Sára Salkaházi was helping to shelter hundreds of Jewish refugees at a building in Budapest owned by the Sisters of Social Service. She knew well the dangers she and her wards faced should they be arrested and was under no illusion that should they be rounded up then summary execution would almost certainly follow. She made a formal pledge to God, in the presence of her superior, that she was prepared to sacrifice herself providing the other sisters were not harmed.

Operating in Budapest during this period was the much hated pro-Nazi group known as the Arrow Cross Party, under the leadership of Ferenc Szálasi, an entity which became the scourge of the Jews and any others who resisted in any way the functions and actions of the Nazi Party.

Sadly, a woman who had been employed by the Sisters of Social Service to work at the 'safehouse' betrayed the house to members of the Arrow Cross Party and two days after Christmas, on 27 December, 1944, they surrounded the house and arrested everyone there. At that time Sára Salkaházi had not been in the house, and could have escaped, but once she heard of the arrests she gave herself up, not wanting to abandon her charges, and admitted that it was she who was in charge of the house.

The Arrow Cross Party members took immediate action. Sára Salkaházi, her Jewish charges, plus a Christian co-worker were taken to the banks of the Danube, stripped naked and shot to death. Like thousands of other victims of Arrow Cross who had been shot and dumped into the Danube, Sára's body was never recovered and her final days were largely unknown until 1967 when several members of the Arrow Cross were being tried for war crimes.

Sára Salkaházi was beatified by Pope Benedict XVI in September 2006, the beatification ceremony taking place outside St. Stephen's Basilica in Budapest. This was the first beatification to take place in Hungary since that of St. Stephen in 1083.[54]

After the war no fewer than 6200 indictments for murder were served against Arrow Cross Party members and some Arrow Cross officials were executed for their countless war crimes including the leader of the party, Ferenc Szálasi. In 2006 a former high ranking member of Arrow Cross, Lajos Polgár, was found in hiding in Melbourne, Australia. The case against him was later dropped and he died of natural causes in July that year.[55]

Romania

Traian Popovici

We have seen earlier in this text how, both before and during the war, Romania was another particularly anti-Semitic state and anti-Semitism became exponentially worse following the German occupation in 1941.

In 1939 Romania had a population of around 750,000 Jewish people. By the end of the war around 400,000 had disappeared. In relation to the 'Final Solution', Romania proved to be one of Hitler's more enthusiastic allies.

During the war the Romanian government passed many legislative measures aimed at persecuting the Jews and stealing their property. The *Centrul National de Romanizare,* (the National Centre for Romanization) was established whose task it was to confiscate all Jewish property and hand it over to non-Jewish Romanians.

Among those who assisted Jewish residents in Romania was Traian Popovici, a lawyer and the mayor of Cernauti, who is reputed to have saved around twenty thousand Jews from deportation.

Traian Popovici

—Archives familiales, author Inconnu, Wikimedia Commons.

Traian Popovici had been born at Rusii Manastioarei, close to the town of Suceava, Austria, on 17 October, 1892, the eldest of four children. Both his father, Ioan Popovici, and grandfather, Andrei Popovici, were deeply patriotic priests.

Traian Popovici was educated at the Orthodox High School, Suceava, from 1903 to 1911 and later attended the Faculty of Law at the University of Cernauti. He graduated in law and subsequently completed his Ph.D.

From 1778 to 1918 Cernauti had been a part of the Austro-Hungarian Empire and known as Czernowitz. However, following the fall of the Austro-Hungarian monarchy in 1918 the city came under Romanian rule and was known as Cernauti.

In 1941 Romania's military dictator, Marshal Ion Antonescu, (executed for war crimes in 1946) requested Popovici to become the mayor of Cernauti. However, he refused as he did not wish to serve a fascist government. Popovici's friends insisted that he could do some good by becoming the mayor and finally he accepted the position.

Cernauti was occupied by the Germans in June 1941, only days after they had launched their attack on the Soviet Union. The Germans immediately ordered that all Jews be registered. A certain number of young Jewish men, totalling somewhere between three and five thousand, were ordered to appear at designated areas every Monday, known as 'Black Mondays', and of these, ten percent were shot. The remainder were held until after the nine p.m. curfew and then allowed to return home. However, the curfew meant that they were 'fair game' for the Romanian Army soldiers patrolling the streets and many more were shot on sight.

In his role as mayor of Cernauti, Traian Popovici came into direct confrontation with Corneliu Calotescu, the governor of Bucovina—the district in which Cernauti was located—over Calotescu's anti-Semitic policies. It was Calotescu who established the *Cabinetu Militar*, the aim of which was to 'destroy' the Jews of Bucovina.

In October 1941 Romanian prime minister and dictator Ion Antonescu instructed Popovici to create a ghetto for the Jews at Cernauti. Popovici strongly opposed the setting up of a ghetto but there was little he could do to prevent it. Failure to move to the ghetto was punishable by death. By the following month the Cernauti Ghetto was in place and thousands of Romanian Jews were living in squalid, overcrowded conditions unfit for human habitation. The ghetto consisted of four city blocks surrounded by guards and barbed wire. Hundreds of people were crammed into small houses. In one bedroom alone 112 people were forced to live together. People lived on the stairs, in attics, in back yards, in hallways, courtyards, cupboards and every inch of possible space.

During this time approximately twenty-eight thousand Romanian Jews were deported in freight cars to a concentration camp in neighbouring Transnistra where many died from starvation, lack of medical care and other forms of brutal ill-treatment.

Fighting to save as many Jews as possible, Traian Popovici convinced the governor and Ion Antonescu that the Jews of Cernauti were vital to the region's economic viability and he was allowed to compile a modest list of people who would be excluded from the deportation order. Popovici began to issue permits for exemptions and the numbers grew far in excess of what had been allotted. In total Popovici was able to save, initially at least, around twenty thousand Jews from deportation.

In the spring of 1942, when it had become clear that Popovici had exceeded his authority in saving too many Jews, he was himself sent to Bucharest. Following his departure from Cernauti another five thousand Jews were arrested and deported to Transnistra where many of them died.

Cernauti once had a population of more than fifty thousand Jews. Less than a third of those actually survived the war. After the war Cernauti became a key node in the *Berihah* (Hebrew, literally 'escape') organisation which assisted in the emigration of Jews to Palestine. After the collapse of the Soviet Union in 1991 almost all the Jewish population of the city emigrated to Israel or the United States.

Popovici died in 1946. Today he is honoured by Yad Vashem as 'Righteous Among the Nations'. In June 2000 a street in Bucharest was named 'Dr Traian Popovici Street.[56]

Chapter 13

Escape and Rescue

Within the scope of this publication, focussed as it is on the events surrounding the Évian conference, it would be impossible, both from a physical and a contextual point of view, to include most or all of the many endeavours made to rescue the stranded Jews of Europe once they had been abandoned to their fate at Évian. However, there were many humanitarian efforts made and the following examples, few though they are, simply demonstrate that despite the events at Évian, despite the dangers of confronting and challenging the horrors of Nazi persecution, there were people and organisations who were prepared to play their role in attempting to rescue as many refugees as possible. In some cases their attempts proved disastrous for the unfortunate refugees, while in others the efforts of these people and organisations proved to be particularly effective. The following stories have been selected simply to provide an example of these wonderful humanitarian endeavours.

The Kladovo Transport

In the autumn of 1939, after it had become perfectly clear from the failure of Évian that European Jews were entirely on their own and would have to take whatever measures necessary to save themselves, the *Hehalutz*[1] Zionist youth movement in Vienna organised what was known as Ehud's transport, the transport being named after Zionist leader Ehud Ueberall (later known as Ehud Avriel), the secretary-general of the *Hehalutz* organisation and a *Mossad* envoy at Vienna who had secured funding for the rescue mission. Ehud Ueberall had actually obtained permission from Adolf Eichmann to take one thousand Jews from Vienna to Bratislava.[1]

The operations of the transport were carefully planned by Moshe Agami, and conducted by Aryeh Dorfman, Emil Schaechter and Josef Schaechter who were to accompany the refugees on their perilous journey. The group, consisting of more than one thousand central European Jewish refugees, would attempt to escape to Palestine via the Black Sea.

---

1   Hehalutz: was an association of Jewish youth whose aim was to train men and women to settle on the land in Israel.

Ehud's transport, which later became known as the Kladovo transport, was an illegal operation that would be strongly resisted by the British authorities controlling immigration into Palestine.

As the pogrom gathered pace, momentum and ferocity, *Hehalutz* leaders in both Berlin and Vienna drew up lists of possible candidates for inclusion in the planned transport. While most of those selected were affiliated in some way with *Hehalutz,* several other Zionist organisations were also represented plus more than three hundred Viennese Jews who were not affiliated with any Zionist organisations. The selection process took into consideration the degree of danger each individual was in and also whether or not they could contribute financially to the rescue mission. Moshe Agami's plan was to gather all the refugees together in the capital city of Bratislava, just across the Austrian border with German-controlled Czechoslovakia, (Slovakia) and then to transport them by riverboat down the Danube through Czechoslovakia, Hungary, Yugoslavia and Romania to the mouth of the Danube at the Romanian port of Sulina. Ehud Ueberall had actually paved the way at Bratislava. Slovakia was then a pro-Nazi state and Ueberall had travelled to Bratislava in order to bribe the police chief to allow the *Uranus* to depart from the river port.[2]

Once at Bratislava the refugees would be transferred to a larger vessel which would take them to Palestine via the Black Sea. It would be the responsibility of the *Mossad le Aliyah Bet* (the Palestinian Jewish group organising illegal immigration) to find the larger vessel and to get it to Sulina to meet the refugees. However, shortly before the date set for the departure of the group there was considerable doubt that *Mossad* would be able to have a ship waiting for them at the mouth of the Danube. Despite this, it was decided that the group should depart anyway, with the hope that by the time they reached Romania a suitable vessel would be waiting for them.

In mid November, 1939, all the members of the group were summoned from Germany and Poland to Vienna and then instructed to leave in smaller groups for Bratislava. By the time all had gathered at Bratislava the group numbered about 1200 people. The refugees boarded the excursion boat *Uranus*, which was owned by the Danube Steam Boat Navigation Company (known as the DDSG.) (which was decorated with a swastika flag). During the first week of December, 1939, the vessel set out for Romania. At the Hungarian border the *Uranus* was stopped and ordered to return to its point of departure. However, on 13 December the vessel once again set out on its long journey to the Black Sea. Yet further problems soon arose. The DDSG company ordered the *Uranus* to return, the owners believing that there would be no ship waiting for the refugees at Sulina. Moshe Agami was able finally to persuade the company to allow the riverboat to continue as far as the Hungarian/Yugoslavian border. There the twelve hundred passengers were transferred mid-river to three smaller Yugoslav excursion boats: the *Kraljica Marija; Czar Dusan* and *Czar Nichola II* which would take the refugees through to Sulina. (These boats have also been recorded as the *Tzar Dusha,* the *Tzar Nickolai* and the *Tzarina Marina*).

However, the Romanian authorities subsequently stopped the vessels from proceeding as it was clear that the Danube was in the process of freezing over and weather conditions would make the journey impossible during the winter months. They directed the three boats to the small winter harbour at the Yugoslav town of Kladovo.

The refugees were now trapped at Kladovo, described as being a, 'small Gypsie village' (now part of Serbia) from which the name of the transport was later changed. Kladovo was an isolated town, about fifty-four kilometres from the nearest railway station and, during winter, almost completely cut off from the outside world.

The refugees believed that once the river had thawed the following year they would be allowed to continue their journey down to the Black Sea. They could not go back and were prevented from going forward. Yet somehow they had to survive. Conditions on the now frozen river were appalling; the men, women and children were crammed onto the three small river boats without any real sanitation. Hot food was a rare luxury and the boats were exposed to severe snow and winds.

The Federation of Jewish Communities in Yugoslavia, whose leader was Sime Spitzer, (also reported as Max Spitzer) moved as quickly as possible to bring some relief to the stranded refugees. In an effort to alleviate the terrible overcrowding aboard the three riverboats, in January 1940 they rented a barge, the *Penelope*, and some of the refugees were transferred to that vessel. Over the following months the men, women and children on these vessels struggled to survive under terrible conditions. Additionally, the owners of the three boats began urging the refugees to vacate the vessels. In May that year 650 members of the group were able to move into a variety of accommodation ashore including the homes of local farmers or Gypsies. Some were moved into tents and barracks. Malnutrition and insect infestations brought outbreaks of scabies and furunculosis (boils). Additionally there were some cases of polio and typhus.

The refugees, however, battled on. They realised by now that their stay in Yugoslavia would be long and so began to set up organisations within themselves to help alleviate their problems. In July 1940 they opened a small school at Kladovo and adult education classes were arranged for those still on board the boats. In September 1940, the group was moved upriver to a Serbian refugee camp at Sabac on the Sava River, where their accommodation consisted of an old flour mill and grain storage sheds. There the refugees set about making life as tolerable as possible; they set up two theatres, a school, and held a variety of cultural events.

In March 1941, about two hundred young members of the group, plus a small number of older people who had relatives in Palestine who had vouched for them, were allowed to obtain legal immigration papers and transportation for Palestine. They would be allowed to leave in groups of fifty. Three of these groups were able to leave just prior to the German occupation of Yugoslavia.

The coming of the Germans to Yugoslavia meant, of course, an end to the group's plans.

Funding for the transport was completely cut and the refugees found themselves dependent for food and supplies on the Croatian Jewish community of Ruma. Men and women in the transports were later conscripted for forced labour and in July 1941 the group was moved again, this time to the city's sinister fortress which had been specifically transformed into a concentration camp to be known as Sava.

In October 1941 Serbian partisans killed twenty-one German soldiers. The Germans were quick to retaliate, taking reprisals against the civilian population. General Franz Böhme ordered that for every German soldier killed, one hundred people would be summarily executed.

On 11 October, 1941, all the Jewish males at the Sava concentration camp were taken to Zasavica. There, along with a group of 160 Gypsies, all were placed into death-pits and shot.

In January 1942 all the women and children in the transport were taken to the concentration camp at Sajmiste, near Belgrade, where Jewish women and children from all over Serbia were already interned. The camp was situated on a former fairground and the prisoners, more than seven thousand of them, lived under appalling conditions. Many of them froze or starved to death during the harsh winter months and the 'survivors' were subsequently herded into the back of enclosed transport lorries and gassed. Their bodies were later discarded in a field. Only one member of the Sava group is known to have survived the war. (After the war General Franz Böhme was arrested in Norway and charged with war crimes. He committed suicide on 29 May, 1947, by jumping from a prison window at Nuremberg).

One of the young men who had been fortunate enough to be selected from the group and transferred legally to Palestine was Erich Nachhaeuser (later known as Ehud Nahir) (pictured).

Erich, the son of Max and Regina Nachhaeuser, had been born at Vienna on 27 June, 1918, the third child in the family.

Group portrait of members of the Hashomer Hatzair Zionist youth aboard one of the riverboats (Kraljica Marija).

Top row from left to right: Zeev Kulka; Josef Cohen; Dov Eshel; Erich Nachhaeuser; Max Stricker; Yehezkel Tanenbaum; Arieh Erez and Avi Marienberg.

Front row: Margalit Figer; Yael Pagi; Batya Horovitz; Ruth Galilee; Shoshana Dukes; Hannah Rosenwasser and Miriam Pick.

—United States Holocaust Memorial Museum, courtesy of Ehud Nahir.

Members of the Hashomer Hatzair from the Kladovo transport at the Sabac refugee camp. Erich Nachhaeuser standing third from left.

—United States Holocaust Memorial Museum, courtesy of Ehud Nahir.

Soon after his birth Erich's mother had died from the Spanish influenza epidemic which was raging around the world following the end of the Great War. Max Nachhaeuser died when Erich was just four years of age. From then until he was aged fourteen Erich lived at a Jewish orphanage in Vienna, later securing an apprenticeship to a tailor. He subsequently became involved in the *Hashomer Hatzair* Zionist youth movement. In 1938 he went to live at an agricultural farm near Vienna, planning at that time to emigrate to Palestine. Following the tragic events of *Kristallnacht,* Erich became even more anxious to leave Austria as quickly as possible and it was then that he was selected to join what later became known as the Kladovo transport.

After the group had been granted the immigration visas for Palestine, Erich joined the first batch to leave, having been selected as a group leader. The youths travelled through Greece, Turkey, Syria and Lebanon eventually arriving in Palestine three weeks later. Sadly, the last batch of youths who had received certificates allowing them to enter Palestine had not left Yugoslavia before the German invasion and these too were killed in the camps with all the other desperate refugees. Erich's older brother, Otto, also survived the war but his sister, Stella, was killed.[3]

A memorial to the victims of the Kladovo transport was dedicated at the small Serbian river port in 2005.

Varian Fry and the Emergency Rescue Committee

During the war, when it had become abundantly clear that the Jews of Europe were doomed, there were, of course, numerous efforts made to save those who were still alive. One of these functioned under the auspices of the Emergency Rescue Committee (ERC), the forerunner of the International Rescue Committee.

Following the defeat of France in 1940 and the establishment of the new French government under Marshal Philippe Petain, it quickly became clear that the Jewish population of France was in dire peril. Under Article 19 of the 22 June, 1940 French armistice, Hitler had instituted the infamous 'surrender on demand' of all German refugees.

The 'surrender on demand' clause of the armistice raised considerable consternation in America. Clearly, time was running out for the Jewish émigrés, many of whom were very high on Hitler's death list. Formed in June 1940, initially it was the objective of the ERC to assist with the rescue of hundreds of anti-Nazi refugee intellectuals and artists who had managed to flee from the various Reich territories and were then held within the borders of Vichy France. Under the terms of the French agreement with Hitler, these and thousands more would soon be deported back to one of the many concentration camps within the Reich areas.

Frank Kingdon was appointed chairman of the new ERC and the work commenced immediately to locate and rescue about two hundred of the endangered intellectuals and artists. It was planned to bring them all back to America and the operation should have taken about three weeks.

To begin their operations in Vichy France the committee would need an emissary. They chose a man named Varian Fry, a journalist and editor for the Foreign Policy Association who enjoyed a strong relationship with the Y.M.C.A. Because of these connections Fry was able to be issued a visa for Vichy France at a time when they were extremely difficult to obtain.

Varian Fry had been educated at Hotchkiss and Taft School and Harvard University. In 1927 he and a friend named Lincoln Kirstein founded the influential literary journal *Hound and Horn*. Fry later married Kirstein's sister, Eileen. It was while working as a foreign correspondent for the U.S. journal *The Living Age* that Fry had first visited Berlin. The date was 1935 and he personally witnessed some of the Nazi atrocities against German Jews. The sight of such atrocities shocked him and he returned to America with a burning desire to help.

Following his ERC appointment Fry arrived at the port of Marseilles via Lisbon on 4 August, 1940, (just a few days before the commencement of the Battle of Britain). He immediately set to work hiring a small staff and opening a legal French relief organisation known as the *Centre Americain de Secours* (American Relief Centre) which would serve as a cover for their real and illegal activities.

The narrow objectives of the ERC in attempting to rescue just the intellectuals and artists were quickly thrown into disarray, however, when it was learnt by refugees that an American national had arrived at Marseilles and was organising rescue measures. Fry was quickly swamped with requests for assistance and immediately realised that he could not restrict himself to the original target group and that the time necessary for this rescue work would be far in excess of three weeks.

Over the following thirteen months Fry and his modest organisation did everything they could for the desperate refugees. They were able to dispense some modest funding, for those most in need, accommodation was found for many of the homeless, and Fry also aided the refugees in obtaining false documents. He sought the release of many who were still held in French internment camps and investigated escape routes out of France.

Fry and some of his staff including Albert Hirschman, who had been serving as a volunteer in the French Army, rented a modest villa on the outskirts of Marseilles, the *Villa Air-Bel*, where they were joined by two important refugees: Andre Breton, the well known surrealist author, and Victor Serge, a former Russian revolutionary. Fry was able to hide refugees at the villa until they could be smuggled out of the country, travelling across the border into Spain and then onto Portugal from where they could make their way to America. Fry assisted others to escape on ships leaving Marseilles for the French colony of Martinique in the West Indies.

Of particular help to Fry was an American vice-consul at Marseilles named Hiram Bingham IV, who battled against State Department anti-Semitism and on his own responsibility issued thousands of visas, both legal and illegal, to Jewish refugees.

By now, however, Fry's 'cloak and dagger' activities had come to the attention of the French police. In December 1940 the villa was raided and Fry and his colleagues were arrested. They were held on board a ship in the harbour for a few days while Marshal Petain was visiting the port.

Fry was also beginning to feel the pressure from U.S. authorities. The U.S. Department of State wished to maintain good relations with the Vichy French. In January 1941 Fry's passport was confiscated. Despite this setback Fry decided to continue with his rescue mission receiving a great deal of opposition from both the U.S. and Vichy French authorities.

Varian Fry

—Author's collection

Fry was arrested in August 1941, given just one hour to pack and then taken to the Spanish border. Upon arriving back in the U.S. Fry was furious that his operations had been closed down. He subsequently wrote that after his office at Marseilles had been closed, '...One of the most horrible manhunts in all history...' had begun. Jewish men, women and children had been rounded up and placed into cattle-cars for deportation to the concentration camps for extermination. Following Fry's return to the U.S. a colleague in Marseilles, Jay Allen, attempted to continue with the rescue operations but with only limited success. Allen was actually arrested by the Nazis and held for months on charges of illegal border crossing.

Fry was among the first to warn of the Holocaust. In the December 1942 issue of *The New Republic* he wrote a scathing article titled *The Massacre of the Jews—the Most Appalling Mass Murder in Human History*. He called upon the U.S. government to allow unrestricted immigration to those refugees who were being persecuted by the Nazi regime.

Yet his work in France had been hugely successful. About 2000 refugees had been rescued from Vichy France and about 2500 more had received solid support from Fry and his organisation.

Among the lucky ones to escape were artists Marc Chagall, Max Ernst, Andre Masson and Jacques Lipchitz; writers Heinrich Mann, Lion Feuchtwanger and Franz Werfel; scientists Otto Meyerhof and Jacques Hadamard and the political scientist Hannah Arendt.

Upon his return to the U.S., Varian Fry's efforts to bring attention to the plight of the European Jews went largely unnoticed, despite his press articles. The ERC dismissed him; the U.S. Army refused to allow him to enlist and his wife divorced him. He found great difficulty in finding work and despite a book he wrote about his experiences in France he finally slipped quietly into obscurity. In 1967 he died unexpectedly of a heart attack in Connecticut where he had been employed teaching Latin and Greek to high school students.

Shortly before his death the French government awarded Varian Fry the *Croix de Chevalier de le Legion d' Honneur*. This was to be the only award Fry would receive during his lifetime. In 1991 the United States Holocaust Memorial Council awarded him the Eisenhower Liberation Medal and in 1994 Varian Fry was recognised by Yad Vashem Holocaust Memorial as one of the 'Righteous Among the Nations'. This was an honour never before given to any American and one which Fry shares with Oskar Schindler and Raoul Wallenberg.

During the announcement of the award, Secretary of State Warren Christopher stated:

> Regretfully during his lifetime, his heroic actions never received the support they deserved from our government. Even today Varian Fry's tale of courage and compassion is too little known in the United States.... We owe Varian Fry our deepest gratitude, but we also owe him a promise—a promise never to forget the horrors that he struggled against so heroically, a promise to do whatever is necessary to ensure that such horrors never happen again.[4]

In 1997 Irish film director David Kerr made a documentary titled *Varian Fry, the American Schindler* and the following year Varian Fry was awarded Commemorative Citizenship of the State of Israel.

In October 2000 the square in front of the U.S. Consulate in Marseilles was renamed Place Varian Fry and the city of Berlin has also named a major street in Fry's honour.[5]

The following year, 2001, a feature film, *VarianS War*, coproduced by Barbara Streisand with William Hurt as the lead actor, was made for television broadcast. Varian Fry's own memoir, originally published in 1945 under the title of *Surrender on Demand*, was republished in 1997. In 2005 a street in Fry's hometown of Ridgewood, New Jersey, was renamed in his honour.[6]

***

Bill Freier (Willi Spira) at an unidentified French internment camp.

–United States Holocaust Memorial Museum, courtesy of Donald Carroll.

One of the émigrés who assisted Fry with his endeavours was Wilhelm Spira (later known as Bill Freier), (pictured) a political cartoonist and caricaturist from Vienna.

Political cartoonists in a Nazi dominated environment could expect only a short life expectancy and following the Anschluss in March 1938 Spira was arrested. Yet he was subsequently released and quickly fled to Paris. There he adopted the name of Bill Freier (meaning 'more free')

Spira's safety in France was, however, transient, and following the German occupation Spira was certain that he would quickly be arrested because of a political cartoon he had published in the British publication, *London Opinion*.

Following the French armistice Spira was interned at the Vichy internment camp of Le Vernet. However, he subsequently escaped and fled to the port of Marseilles. It was while he was working at painting portraits on the Vieux Port that Spira first met Varian Fry.

Fry was always on the lookout for people who may have been able to assist him in his endeavors to rescue the Jewish refugees in the city. Spira was ideal because, as an artist, he could make a perfect forgery of the Vichy identity card. The blank cards were actually quite easy to obtain but it was necessary to have the special *Commissaire de Police* stamp on the card and the official signature. These Spira was able to reproduce to perfection. Spira became one of Fry's most valuable assets and he was able to assist many refugees to find sanctuary using the false ID cards.

Unfortunately Spira was caught in the act of forging documents and arrested by the Vichy police. He was released shortly afterwards but soon re-arrested. Spira's wife, Mina, who was then pregnant, went to Fry asking for his assistance in obtaining Spira's release, but there was nothing more that Fry could do. Spira was later deported to Poland where he was incarcerated at a sub-camp of Auschwitz. It seemed that little could be done to save him. He was subsequently transferred to several other concentration camps, including Buchenwald and Theresienstadt, surviving all of them.

A tragic and poignant scene at the Buchenwald (German for 'Beech Forest') concentration camp following its liberation by the US 9th Armored Infantry Battalion on 11 April, 1945.

This photograph was taken on the 18 April by Ardean R. Miller, a member of the US Signals Corps, a week after the camp's liberation.

—National Archives, Washington.

Following the liberation of the camps Spira returned as quickly as possible to France in order to find his wife and child, a son, now four years of age named Francois. However, shortly after the family had been reunited, Mina suffered a breakdown which left her mentally incapacitated. She was admitted to an asylum where she died in 1953. Spira remained in Paris for the rest of his life, working as a caricaturist and photographer. He died in 2000.[7]

The Jewish Overseas Emigration Association

In September 1940, the Jewish Overseas Emigration Association (H.I.C.E.M.) began to make plans to bring Jewish children to the United States on special State Department visas. The program was specifically designed to rescue children under the ages of thirteen, although children as old as sixteen were also admitted to the program if they were accompanying their younger siblings.

It was planned that relatives then living in the U.S. would subsidise the cost of the trip while the Joint Distribution Committee (J.D.C.) would facilitate and finance the cost of children who did not have relatives in the U.S. H.I.C.E.M. would make all the necessary arrangements including the provision of French exit visas, Spanish and Portuguese transit visas and reservations on the ships at Lisbon.

On 5 March, 1941, the *Oeuvre de Secours aux Enfants* (OSE) in France sent H.I.C.E.M. a list of five hundred children who had been identified as candidates for the rescue mission. OSE was the French/Jewish organisation which saved hundreds of refugee children during the war and ran many orphanages. The listed children were released from various French internment camps and transported to OSE children's homes while awaiting emigration. As we have seen in earlier chapters of this publication, which demonstrate the American and Vichy French governments' attitude to Jewish refugees, both those governments were slow in processing the necessary visas and in some instances the children were forced to wait a full year before the required papers were processed.

Finally, at the end of May 1941 the first convoy of 111 children left the train station at Marseilles. The children were accompanied by OSE members Isaac and Masha Chomski who were working in cooperation with Morris Troper of the J.D.C. and the American Friends Service Committee.

The train carrying the children was able to stop at Oloron, close to the Gurs concentration camp so that many of the children could bid a fond farewell to the parents who were incarcerated at the camp. The children had saved their morning food ration so that they could give it to their parents. It was later reported that the meeting between parents and children was so traumatic for all concerned that it was decided in future transports to discontinue the practice.

A group of Jewish refugee children waiting to board the SS Mouzinho at Lisbon, 10 June, 1941.

–United States Holocaust Memorial Museum, courtesy of Milton Koch.

The children travelled from France through Spain and Portugal to Lisbon where they boarded the SS *Mouzinho*. The ship sailed on 10 June, 1941. Two more convoys of children were similarly rescued. The second convoy arrived at Lisbon in late summer 1941. In all the three transports were able to rescue 311 Jewish children.[8]

The Orphelinat Israelite de Bruxelles Children's Home

There were, of course, innumerable instances of the rescue of Jewish people who were suffering under the heel of Nazi oppression—far too many for all to be mentioned within the scope of this limited publication. However, some persons and organisations also deserve special mention. Among these was the *Orphelinat Israelite de Bruxelles* Children's Home in Belgium run by young Jewish refugees Jonas Tiefenbrunner and his wife Ruth.

Jonas Tiefenbrunner had been born at Wiesbaden, Germany, on 18 June, 1914, his parents having moved there from Poland two years previously. His was a deeply religious family and Jonas had eight siblings. Jonas was active in the Orthodox Zionist Ezra youth movement. He also belonged to an agricultural collective in Frankfurt where he met his future bride, Ruth Feldheim.

In November 1939, when his parents had been forcibly returned to Poland, Jonas was able to escape to Belgium where he joined a brother, Phillip, who was then living at Antwerp. At a town named Heide, just north of Antwerp, Jonas founded a youth home and yeshiva for religious boys aged between fifteen and seventeen who had been sent to Belgium on one of the *kindertransports*.

Here the young students were able to work on nearby farms while also continuing with their schooling and religious studies.

Meanwhile Ruth Feldheim had also managed to flee to Belgium and had found work as a cook at another children's home. She and Jonas again met and the couple married on 9 May, 1940—the day before the German invasion of the Low Countries.

Following the arrival of the Germans in Belgium both Jonas and Ruth were arrested as enemy aliens. However, they were soon released. Yet the children in the home had by now been dispersed and Jonas set out on a bicycle in an effort to find them. He subsequently re-established his children's centre in a former aged person's home on the *General Drubbelstraat*. Under German occupation it was a considerable struggle just to survive. Food and other urgent necessities were in extremely short supply but Jonas was aided by the sudden and quite unexpected donation of a large sum of money from a person who simply rang the doorbell and handed over the funds. These funds enabled Jonas to carry on his work for some time until he began to receive the support of the *Association des Juifs en Belgique* (AJB) which assumed the responsibility for the centre in late 1941.

The home, known unofficially as *Chez Tiefenbrunner*, was subsequently moved to the *Rue des Patriotes* in Brussels. The Germans did not interfere with the running of the facility or deport the children because they needed to maintain the pretense that only able-bodied adults were being deported to the camps as workers. All the children at the centre were under the age of seventeen, most being refugees from Germany and Austria.

Jewish refugee children at the Orphelinat Israelite de Bruxelles children's home, at Rue des Patriotes.

—United States Holocaust Memorial Museum, courtesy of Judith and Joseph Schreiber.

Despite his own relatively young age, Jonas was the patriarch of the centre which he ran as a large religious household. Each child was blessed individually every Sabbath and there were daily religious services. All Jewish holidays were observed and the children were taught both secular and Jewish subjects.

On several occasions the much feared Gestapo raided the centre looking for those over the age of seventeen or adults who may have been in hiding there. Jonas was also arrested but released soon afterwards and no harm came to the children under his care.

However, in August 1944, as Allied troops began to move into German held territory following the D-day landings, an SS officer named Lieutenant Burge attempted to deport all the Jewish children to Germany. Yet Jonas had been able to obtain intelligence about the coming arrests and he moved everyone into a convent which was being run by a friend and associate, Father R.P. Robinet.

Jonas, Ruth and all the children survived the war. Jonas later opened a new home at Mariaburg for children who had been interned in concentration camps and orphans who had spent the war in hiding. He subsequently moved the facility to Antwerp. He continued to be the director of the home until 1960. He died of heart failure, two years later, aged just forty-eight years.[9]

The Teheran Children

Following the German invasion of Poland on 1 September, 1939, and the beginning of the Second World War, hundreds of thousands of Jews—already brutally aware of the powerful anti-Semitism sweeping across Europe—hastily packed a few meagre possessions and fled across the eastern Polish border into the Soviet Union. This was a time of mass confusion made even more impossible following the Soviet Union's invasion of Poland on 17 September that year. During all this war, confusion, despair, bombing and bloodshed many of the Polish children became separated from their parents or were orphaned.

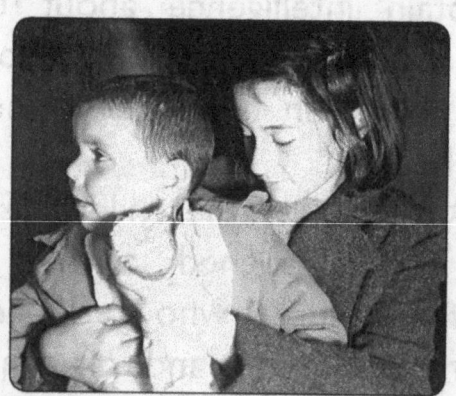

Two of the 'Teheran children' at Athlit, Israel.

—United States Holocaust Memorial Museum, courtesy of David Laor.

At the beginning of 1940 the Polish Jews then in the Soviet Union or in territories controlled by the Soviets became the object of mass expulsions to Siberia. They spent weeks travelling in crowded conditions aboard cattle-cars, enduring freezing conditions, hunger, thirst and disease, finally arriving in Siberia where they were forced to live under appalling conditions. The only positive aspect of these deportations was the fact that the deportations took the refugees away from the rolling horror of the Nazi extermination machine.

On 22 June, 1941, Hitler launched Operation Barbarossa, the German invasion of the Soviet Union. As a result of the invasion the Soviets declared an amnesty for the Polish refugees and released them. They also released tens of thousands of Polish prisoners-of-war and allowed the creation on Soviet soil of a Polish army, known as Anders' Army' after its commander, General Wladyslaw Anders, who had been released from a Soviet prison in Moscow.

Following the German attack on Soviet territory the British and Soviet troops occupied Iran, forcing the abdication of its shah, Reza Shah Pahlavi, who had steadfastly retained Iranian neutrality up until that time. However, Reza Shah Pahlavi's successor, his son, Mohammed Reza Pahlavi, made it possible for British and U.S. supplies to be transported through Iran into the Soviet Union. The supply route became known as the 'Persian Corridor'.

In 1942 the Soviets allowed the resettlement into Iran of about 24,000 Polish civilians and Anders' Army recruits. These people were allowed to transfer to Iran as from the spring of 1942 and the flow of people continued until late summer that year. Among these refugees were about one thousand Jewish children, many of whom were orphans. These children were brought to Teheran (Tehran) from all over the Soviet Union, travelling by train and ship. This mass transport was made possible largely due to the efforts of the Jewish Agency for Palestine whose representatives had negotiated with both the Polish government-in-exile and the Soviets. When the children were brought to Iran they were met by representatives of the Jewish Agency for Palestine. About 720 children arrived during the period April to August 1942 and were housed in tents at Dustan Tappeh, a former Iranian airforce base on the outskirts of Teheran which became known as the 'Teheran Home for Jewish Children'. Many of the children were malnourished and suffering from a variety of illnesses including tuberculosis. More children were soon to follow. Other organisations which assisted in this huge project included the local Jewish community in Iran, the Women's Zionist Organisation in the United States, the American Joint Jewish Distribution Committee and the Youth Immigration department of the Jewish Agency.

Following intensive negotiations between the British administration in Palestine and the Jewish Agency all the children finally received certificates allowing immigration into Palestine.

In early January 1943, 716 children, plus a number of adults, many of whom were also refugees, were taken by trucks to Bandar Shahpour, on the shores of the Persian Gulf, to board the steamer *Dundera*, bound for Karachi. From there the refugees were taken aboard the ship *Noralea* which sailed through the Red Sea to Suez where they disembarked to board a train for the Atlit refugee camp in northern Palestine. Another transport containing 110 children arrived overland via Iran on 28 August, 1943. In total 870 'Teheran Children' arrived in Palestine during the course of this epic project. Thirty-five of these children would later die, either as civilians or as serving soldiers, during Israel's War of Independence in 1948-49.[10]

The Fort Ontario Project

Another rescue mission found its base at the historic site of Fort Ontario near the city of Oswego in Oswego County, New York State.

Located on the east side of the Oswego River, on rising ground overlooking Lake Ontario, Fort Ontario is a place of great historical significance, having been constructed by the British in 1755 during the French and Indian War. It has since been destroyed and rebuilt on numerous occasions and prior to the U.S. involvement in the Second World War had housed the 2nd Brigade of the 1st U.S. Infantry until the brigade had been deactivated on 1 June, 1940.[11]

Known officially as the Fort Ontario Emergency Refugee Shelter, Fort Ontario was perceived as being the perfect facility to house a large number of European refugees. Its use as a refugee centre had initially been proposed by the World Jewish Congress and also by the forceful and highly persuasive Hillel Kook [Peter Bergson] (q.v.) of the Committee for a Jewish Army and later the Emergency Committee to Save the Jewish People of Europe, based in Washington. It was not until February 1944 that the U.S. War Refugee Board's director, John Pehle, endorsed the Fort Ontario proposal formally and presented it to the U.S. administration. The plan had, apparently, come into effect following a unilateral decision of the U.S. and British governments to open camps to house many of the surviving Jews of Europe. Britain would open four such camps in the Middle East; two would be opened in North Africa and one in the U.S.

In June 1944 the U.S. Allied Control Commission published the following notice:

Displaced Persons Sub-Commission
Allied Control Commission
Notice and Application
June 20, 1944

The President of the United States has announced that approximately one thousand non-Italian refugees will be brought to the United States from Italy. The refugees will be maintained in a refugee shelter to be established at Fort Ontario near Oswego in the State of New York, where, under appropriate conditions, they will remain for the duration of the war. The refugees will be brought to the United States outside the regular immigration procedure. The shelter will be equipped to take good care of the refugees and it is contemplated that they will be returned to their homes at the end of the war.

It is planned to select and move applicants for this refugee shelter as soon as possible. Preferences will be given to those refugees for whom no other haven or refuge is immediately available. Therefore, if you desire to make application, please fill out the form below. Please use only one form for yourself and all members of your immediate family. Notification of acceptance for movement will be given as quickly as possible after your application has been received.[12]

A total of 982 refugees were selected for the Fort Ontario project. Approximately seventy-five per cent of these were sourced from transit camps in Southern Italy including Bari, Ferramonti, Santa Marie de Bagni and Compagna. The remaining twenty-five per cent would come from Rome which had capitulated to the Allies earlier that month (4 June, 1944). These people, many of whom had fled from their countries of origin in Europe, had largely remained in hiding during the German occupation of Italy. About 165 of these refugees were children under the age of seventeen.

The age-old problem of religious discrimination was an important issue for the U.S. administration and in an effort to prevent local complaints it was decided that the contingent of refugees should have a percentage of non-Jewish people. Of the 982 selected for the project 874 were Jews, most of whom had fled originally from Yugoslavia and Austria.

The group was assembled at the port of Aversa and boarded the U.S. Army transport ship, *Henry Gibbons*. In addition to the refugees the ship also carried a number of wounded American soldiers. As part of a convoy of sixteen other ships and thirteen warships the *Henry Gibbons* sailed on 8 July, 1944, about a month after the D-day landings in Normandy. It was a perilous journey, particularly when still in the Mediterranean, and the convoy was under constant threat of attack from the air or by submarine.

The *Henry Gibbons* docked at Pier 84, New York, on 3 August that year. None of the refugees was allowed to land and all were kept on board for the night. The following day they were taken to a hut on the wharf where they were ordered to remove all their clothes and then disinfected with DDT. The clothes were also disinfected. All the refugees had signed declarations agreeing to return to their countries of origin after the war. They were not issued with any documentation but instead were given tags to wear around their necks. These tags were labelled: 'U.S. ARMY Casual Baggage', with just an identification number.

The refugees were then placed on two harbour ferries which took them across the Hudson to Hoboken at New Jersey and the terminal dock of the rail line. About one hundred U.S. military police acted as guards.

The refugees were then entrained for Fort Ontario. When they arrived at the camp the refugees were shocked. The facility was surrounded by a chain-link fence on top of which were three rolls of barbed wire. It looked suspiciously like a concentration camp.

Fort Ontario refugees with their classmates on the steps of the public high school in Oswego, New York.

Back row left to right: Eddie Levitch; Kostia Zabotin; Bruno Kaiser; Paul Bokroshh; Ralf

Kutznitcki; Zachy Romano; Joseph Hirt; Jenny Bear;

Gordana Milinovitch and Anita Baruch, with Alfons Finci standing behind. Third row: Ernst Spitzer; Nelly Bokrosh.

Second row: Koki Levy; Leon Levitch; Alice Mandler; Rosa Moschev; Thea Weiss; Paul Arnstein.

Front row: Ivo Lederer; Steffi Steinberg; Lea Hanf; Edith Weiss; Grete Spitzer and Ivo Svecenski.

–United States Holocaust Memorial Museum, courtesy of Hans Thalheimer.

Conditions at the fort were fairly basic and the refugees would remain incarcerated at the camp for the following eighteen months. The inmates were placed under strict quarantine for four weeks, after which children were allowed to leave the camp to attend schools and adults were given permission to take day jobs but had to return to the camp each evening. Many of the refugees had relatives or friends living within the U.S. but they were not allowed to visit them.

The refugees settled in as best they could. They provided themselves with cultural activities but their restricted living conditions were fraught with divisiveness. It became a difficult and somewhat hostile situation.

Following the German surrender in May 1945, the U.S. administration came under considerable pressure from various Jewish groups, relief agencies, congressmen and even members of President Truman's cabinet, to do something to release the incarcerated refugees. Finally, in December 1945, Truman issued a directive which permitted the immigration of displaced persons from American zones of occupation and also removed the restrictions placed upon those refugees who were already in the U.S.

Recently arrived refugees wait in line to complete their registration at the Fort Ontario Emergency Refugee Shelter.

—United States Holocaust Memorial Museum, courtesy of U.S. National Archives and Records Administration.

In January 1946 the inmates of the camp were taken by bus to Niagara Falls, Canada, issued with an American visa and then allowed to cross the Rainbow Bridge into the U.S. so that they could apply officially for citizenship. Today the Fort Ontario complex houses what is known as the Safe Haven Museum and Education Centre.[13]

Among the Fort Ontario refugees was teenager David Hendel (later Hendell-pictured below), the son of Eisig and Hana Hendel. David had been born at Zagreb, Croatia, on 11 September, 1928. His father was a textile merchant. David had one sibling, a sister named Ruth who had been born on 26 April, 1935. Following the German invasion of Yugoslavia the Hendel family fled to the Italian zone; Hana and Ruth were the first to leave followed by David and his father, Eisig, who managed to get to the Italian zone after several unsuccessful attempts.

The family stayed at lin Susak for several weeks before moving to Ljublijana, in Slovenia, where they remained for a few months. David's grandmother, Yetta Weissman and Hana's sister, Bertha Kremer, with her two sons, Wilko and Herman Kremer, soon joined the family at Ljublijana. They had fled from Zagreb following the killing of Bertha's husband, Aron Kremer, and David's grandfather, Mordechai Weissman, both of whom had been murdered by the *Ustashi*, the state secret police.

Refugees at the Fort Ontario Emergency Refugee Shelter.

Left side: Edith Broner; Silvio Levy; Ernest Spitzer; Lili Broner; Bruno Kaiser and Ivo Svecenski.

Right side: Herman Kremer; David Hendel; Thea Weiss and Neli Bokros. Table on right: Lea Hanf.

—United States Holocaust Memorial Museum, courtesy of Dr David Hendell.

From Ljublijana the family eventually found their way to Italy, living at Rovigo until September 1943 when the Germans invaded. The group then moved to Rome where they lived under false papers. David and his cousin, Herman

Kremer, attended a Catholic Vatican school, the *Coleggio San Leone Magno.*

Jewish youth at the Fort Ontario Emergency Refugee Shelter.

Included in this photograph are: Elfi Strauber; Liesel Bader; Ruth Hendel;

Walter Arnstein; Ernest Spitzer; Leo Levic; Wilko Kremer; David Hendel;

Henny Notowitz; Adam Munz; Fortunee Levic; Paul Bokros; Ivo Lederer;

Paul Arnstein; Neli Bokros and Herman Kremer.

The pen and ink drawing on the wall by Adam Munz.

–United States Holocaust Memorial Museum, courtesy of Dr David Hendell.

Following the liberation of Italy several of the Hendel family volunteered to become part of the Fort Ontario Project. They shipped aboard the *Henry Gibbons* with almost one thousand other refugees and were taken to New York State. Following the presidential directive allowing them to immigrate to the U.S., David and his family moved to New York City. David later served for two years in the U.S. military and subsequently qualified as a dentist at the Columbia University School of Dental and Oral Surgery.[14]

The Mefkure Disaster

The motor schooner *Mefkure* was a wooden-hulled vessel which, in 1944, had been chartered along with two other ships to take Jewish refugees from Romania to Istanbul. The other ships were the *Bulbul* and *Morina*, both carrying approximately three hundred Jewish refugees. Once in Turkey the refugees aboard the ships would attempt to enter Palestine by whatever means possible. All three ships would sail under the protection of neutral Turkish and Red Cross flags but not carry any navigation lights. The ships left the Romanian port of Constanta just before dawn on the morning of 5 August, 1944. It is not known how many refugees were aboard the *Mefkure* at the time of its sailing and estimates have varied from 289 to 394. The Romanian Navy provided an escort from the harbour which was mined at the time.

It was after midnight and the *Mefkure* was in the Black Sea, about twenty-five miles north-east of Igneada, Turkey, when the ship was suddenly illuminated by flares fired from an unseen vessel. The captain of the *Mefkure* failed to respond and held his course. However, the vessel firing the flares was a Soviet Shchuka-class submarine the Shch-215. When it failed to attract any kind of response from the *Mefkure* the submarine's skipper launched a torpedo attack. In addition to this attack the crew of the Shch-215 fired a large number of rounds from the submarine's 45mm gun and 650 rounds from its 7.62mm machine guns. The resultant destruction aboard the *Mefkure* was devastating. The ship caught fire and rapidly sank, the survivors being machine-gunned in the water. The *Mefkure's* commanding officer, Captain Kazim Turan, along with six of his crew, were able to save themselves by escaping in a lifeboat. However, of the hundreds of men, women and children passengers only five of the refugees were able to survive the attack.

Both the *Bulbul* and the *Morina* survived the passage to Turkey.[15]

The Kasztner Train

A train transport from Budapest to Switzerland via the Bergen-Belsen concentration camp in Northern Germany was, despite great fears, effective in saving more than 1600 people in 1944. Yet since the war the organisation and selection process surrounding this transport, plus the content and context of negotiations carried out with the SS, have been steeped in controversy, and one of the principal people involved in this enormous humanitarian effort, Rudolph Kasztner, has been vilified, condemned and finally assassinated by right-wing Israeli terrorists.

During the 1940s an organisation known as the Budapest Aid and Rescue Committee was formed with the aim of assisting the escape of Jewish refugees, particularly Hungarian refugees and those from Slovakia and Poland who had fled to Hungary. There were several principal leaders in this committee: Rudolph Kasztner, a highly intelligent and articulate Zionist from Cluj; Joel Brand with his wife, Hansi; Samuel Springmann, Ottó Komoly, an engineer who lived in Budapest, Erno Szilagyi and several others.

Rudolph Kasztner had been born at Kolozsvár, Austria-Hungary, in 1906. Kolozsvár became known as Cluj, Romania, in 1918 but was returned to Hungary in 1940. Kasztner studied law but subsequently worked as a journalist and political commentator, his principal interest being politics. He was the political and parliamentary correspondent for the publication, *Uj Kelet (The New Middle East)* and in this role was able to develop acquaintances with some of the more influential members of the political establishment. Fluent in five languages, he was an assistant to Dr József Fischer, a member of the Romanian parliament. In 1934 Rudolph Kasztner married Fischer's daughter, Erzsébet (Elizabeth, who was known as Bogyó).

Rudolph Kasztner broadcasting at Kol Yisrael, Israeli State Radio Station, where he was the host of a Hungarian program.

—Photograph courtesy Wikimedia Commons.

When Transylvania was annexed by Hungary in 1940 Rudolph Kasztner left Cluj and moved to Budapest. An ardent Zionist, he joined the *Ihud* Party

However, following the Nazi takeover of Hungary in March 1944 all Hungarian Jews and those Jews who had escaped to Hungary from Nazi controlled Europe were slated for deportation. The situation for the Nazis was now critical. They had already seen what the Jews were capable of when pressed into a corner, the uprising in the Warsaw Ghetto had proved that the Jews, both men and women, were capable of putting up a powerful struggle to survive. The deportations from Warsaw to the concentration camps had been extensive and only a relatively small number of Jews had been left in the ghetto just before the revolt. However, here in Hungary there were 250,000 Jews in Budapest alone with a further 650,000 spread throughout the country. If they fought for their survival as had the Warsaw Jews then it would have been difficult, if not impossible, for the Germans to put down such a revolt. The Russians were drawing close to the Hungarian border and Adolf Eichmann was presented with a major manpower shortage. Hitler wanted all the Jews in Hungary to be pushed into the gas chambers but the logistics of doing so were enormous. These statistical and military difficulties created the platform upon which negotiations to save at least some of the Jews could be founded. They also created the accusations that Kasztner did a deal with Eichmann to assist with placating the majority of the Jewish population, allaying their fears so that they would board the deportation trains willingly, without a fight, in exchange for a small number of them being allowed to escape to Palestine.

When the Jewish Rescue Committee learned that it might be possible to 'buy' Jewish lives from the SS, as odious as this appeared, the committee believed that the ransom method of saving Jews might well be exploited. They were left with little choice.

The first meeting between the SS and the committee took place on 5 April, 1944. Dieter Wisliceny, the SS officer in charge (hanged in 1948) offered to place a hold on the deportations to the concentration camps in exchange for the sum of US$2 million. It was an expensive proposal but the committee immediately saw it as a way to save a significant number of Jewish people.

In April 1944 the first instalment of about $92,000 was delivered by Rudolph Kasztner to associates of Adolf Eichmann, the SS officer in charge of the deportations. Time was of the essence as around 12,000 Jews were being deported to the concentration camps every day. Shortly afterwards the balance of the first instalment was delivered. On April 25th Eichmann offered to 'sell' one million Jews in exchange for a large quantity of military vehicles and other goods. These items were to include military trucks, 200 tons of tea, 800 tons of coffee, two million cases of soap (the story, widely circulated since the war, that the Germans were making soap out of Jewish corpses has since been proven a myth)[16] and a large but unspecified quantity of tungsten. There was, of course, no chance that the U.S. authorities would agree to an exchange of military equipment. Joel Brand was sent by Adolf Eichmann to Istanbul in order to negotiate the ransom.

In July 1944 Heinrich Himmler's representative, SS Colonel Kurt Becher, took over the negotiations with Rudolph Kasztner and Kasztner was able to rescue a 'token' transport of 1684 Jews plus an agreement to send twenty thousand Jews to a 'safe work camp' in Austria for the remainder of the war.

It was arranged that a train of cattle-cars would take those who were to be saved from Budapest to Switzerland. Kasztner later stated that he thought of the rescue train as a kind of 'Noah's Ark' because it contained a wide cross-section of the Jewish community. The passengers were chosen by the committee and included 199 Zionists from Transylvania and 230 from Budapest; 126 Orthodox and Ultra-Orthodox Jews, including forty rabbis. There were many professions represented including scholars, artists, journalists, bankers, housewives, farmers, peasants, teachers and nurses. About

388 people from Rudolph Kasztner's home town of Cluj were also aboard the train, including a number of Kasztner's family. His mother, Helen Kasztner, his brother, Erno, Rudolph Kasztner's pregnant wife, Bogyo with her father, Jozsef Fischer, along with a number of Bogyo's relatives were also aboard. The inclusion of so many from Rudolph Kasztner's hometown and family members later gave rise to severe criticism about the selection process of those who were to be saved but logically it could hardly be expected that Kasztner would not include members of his own family on the rescue train.

Of course, there was no honour among the Nazis. Himmler and Eichmann had given their word that the refugees would be sent to Switzerland but there was absolutely nothing to prevent them from reneging on the deal and sending the hapless victims straight to the gas chambers. And that is exactly what appeared to be their plan.

When the train reached the Hungarian-Austrian border it should have been allowed to proceed west towards Switzerland. Instead it turned towards Germany and there was considerable consternation on board as many of the passengers believed they were being sent to one of the, by now, notorious extermination camps. At Linz, in Austria, the passengers were disembarked and sent to a military delousing station. There they were given rough medical inspections and herded into showers. For many of these refugees, who now knew of the Nazi ruse of using fake shower-rooms as gas chambers, this was the height of terror. Stripped naked and standing in line for hours, many were convinced that their last moments would soon arrive.

However, finally, the passengers were returned to their train but still their fears were not allayed, especially when the train continued to travel deep into Germany, arriving eventually at the notorious Bergen-Belsen concentration camp in the north of the country. It now appeared certain that the refugees were doomed.

However, upon arriving at the camp the passengers were segregated into a separate section, the *Ungarlager* (Hungarian camp), and provided with 'reasonable' if plain food, (reasonable compared to other concentration camp inmates who were generally starved and worked to death).

Behind the scenes Kasztner was negotiating desperately to have the Hungarian Jews released so they could continue their journey. He and Colonel Kurt Becher travelled to the Swiss border to meet with representatives of the Joint Distribution Committee. A letter of credit was produced which allowed for the release of some of the Hungarian Jews.

Finally, in August, about 318 refugees were crammed on board a train and transported to Switzerland. The remainder were kept captive while further negotiations took place. It was to be an expensive operation. Kasztner agreed to Becher that US$1000 would be paid for every Hungarian Jew. The funds, comprising of gold and platinum bars, gold coins, jewellery and currency was raised from the Budapest Jewish underground and valued, at that time, about US$1.86 million.

In December almost all the remainder followed, although about seventeen continued to be detained at Belsen. A total of about 1670 people had been saved by the Kasztner transport, a significant effort but only a very small percentage of the Jews of Hungary, and the negotiations to save a total of one million Jews in exchange for trucks and stores would never come to fruition.

After the war Rudolph Kasztner was severely criticized for the way in which the selection process for the rescue train had been carried out and he was accused of collaboration and informing. Kasztner emigrated to Israel in 1947 where he became a manager in the intelligence section of the Prime Minister's Department and was also appointed spokesperson for the minister for trade and energy. However, his wartime actions and the selection process for the rescue train became a major controversy in Israel. Malchiel Gruenwald was an elderly former Hungarian Jew who published a newsletter periodical called *Letters to Friends in the Mizrahi*. In August 1952 he published issue number 51 which included a damning article vilifying Kasztner for his actions during the war and calling into question the selection process of Jews to be saved from the gas chambers. He claimed that the ransom method had only led to further Nazi deportations and accused Rudolph Kasztner of theft, collaboration with the enemy, the betrayal of the Allies, and giving positive character references to Colonel Kurt Becher and other SS officers which allowed Becher to escape prosecution for war crimes. Becher would later go on to be a well known multimillionaire businessman whose basis for success was believed to have been the wealth he stole or ransomed from the Jews during the war.

Kasztner was then a member of the ruling *Mapai* (Labor Party) and was informed by the attorney general that he would have to clear his name by taking legal action against Gruenwald. Otherwise Kasztner would have to resign.

In 1 January, 1954, Kasztner took action for libel against Gruenwald. However, the trial was hardly impartial. Gruenwald was represented by Shmuel M. Tamir, a member of the *Herut* (Revisionist) Party and an opponent of the *Mapai*. Presiding over the trial was Benjamin Halevi, who had his own personal battle with *Herut*.

After pouring over three thousand pages of trial transcripts for nine months, Halevi delivered his verdict on 22 June, 1955. He found for the defendant, Gruenwald, and stated that Rudolph Kasztner had failed to warn the Jews who were to be deported that they were heading for death in the gas chambers, and that he had saved a few at the sacrifice of many. The judge added that Kasztner had, 'sold his soul to the devil'. This verdict actually triggered the fall of the Israeli Cabinet.

Rudolph Kasztner resigned his position with the government and became a recluse. He would speak to no one of his rescue mission, telling reporters that he was 'living a loneliness blacker than night and darker than hell'. His wife suffered from acute depression and their daughter was vilified at school.

Rudolph Kasztner appealed the decision and in 1958 the Supreme Court rejected all the major decisions made during the trial and was strongly critical of the whole proceedings.

Sadly, by then it was too late for Rudolph Kasztner.

Just after midnight on 4 March, 1957, three men seated in a jeep waited in the dark outside Kasztner's home in Tel Aviv. The men were Yosef Menkes, Ze'ev Eckstein and Dan Shemer. As Rudolph Kasztner drove up to his home and parked his car, Eckstein got out of the Jeep and walked towards Kasztner. He asked if he was Rudolph Kasztner and when Kasztner confirmed it Eckstein pulled out a pistol and fired at point blank range. The first bullet was 'spent' or misfired but Eckstein quickly fired two more shots. One hit the car door and the third struck Rudolph Kasztner in the chest.

Rudolph Kasztner was rushed to hospital where he was able to describe his attackers to officers of Shin Bet, Israel's internal security service. He died of his injuries twelve days later. After a lengthy investigation Shin Bet was able to identify the three assassins. Dan Shemer confessed and implicated Eckstein as the shooter. Eckstein also confessed and implicated Yosef Menkes. The police tracked down the Jeep and found the murder weapon and fingerprints. Twenty members of their organisation, the right-wing group *Lehi*, were subsequently arrested.

The three main conspirators all received life sentences which, however, were pardoned after seven years.

Rudolph Kasztner's granddaughter, Merav Michaeli, was voted to the Israeli parliament in 2013.[17]

Rescue Children Inc.

The war was over and tens of thousands of orphans were left in Europe like the detritus of a broken generation—starved, homeless, emaciated, hollow-eyed, almost wild, they somehow had survived the horrific years of Nazi oppression and a concerted effort to murder them *en masse*. The children were found in a grim variety of situations: crawling from the sewers where they had lived for years; materialising from the forests where they had worked with partisans; from the ruins of the ghettoes; from beneath the rubble of destroyed cities; in remote corners of now abandoned concentration camps, they emerged like wraiths to tell their terrible stories of struggle, death and survival.

Prior to the war, according to lists subsequently compiled by a variety of Jewish agencies, there had been approximately one million Jewish children under the age of fourteen living in Poland. At the end of the war just five thousand had been left. When the concentration camp at Majdanek had been liberated by Soviet forces in 1944, a total of nineteen starving children had been found, just those few whom the Nazi executioners had not had time to kill before they had fled the camp.

But what was to be done with these thousands of homeless orphans? One of the many organisations which came into existence in an attempt to deal with the problem and give succour to the orphans was the *Vaad Hatzala*, an emergency relief organisation which was brought into effect by the Union of Orthodox Rabbis of the United States and Canada. The *Vaad Hatzala* had originally been formed on 13 November, 1939, and during the war had been responsible for the rescue of more than two thousand children, finding homes for the orphans throughout Europe.

However, after the war, in June 1946, as the rising tide of orphans demanded immediate action, the *Vaad Hatzala* formed Rescue Children Inc. as a separate identity which would work to raise funds, find homes and locate relatives of the lost children. Rescue Children Inc. established centres in France, Belgium, Sweden and Germany; its *modus operandi* was to raise the necessary funding through an 'adopt a child' program whereby donors would 'adopt' a child or children and give one dollar per day for the child's food, welfare and education, totalling $365 each year.

There were nine centres in France under the direction of Sam Levy; one of its buildings, known as the *Maison Du Diable* (Devil's House) was actually rented from an agent of the British royal family. Additionally, several bomb-damaged estates surrounding Paris were handed over to Rescue Children Inc. by Pierre de Gaulle, president of the Municipal Council of Paris and the brother of General Charles de Gaulle. One centre alone at Aix-les-Bains was home to about 360 children, part of a group of 500 who, with the financial aid of the J.D.C., had been brought out of Poland by the chief rabbi of Palestine, Rabbi Isaac Herzog. At Villejuif and Barbizon the rescue homes were under the supervision of *le Comite des Oeuvres Sociales de la Resistance*, (COSOR) This was an agency of the French government which had been established to care for the families of deportees, prisoners-of-war and people who had been executed by the Germans.

All the children in the rescue homes were interviewed to establish the names and possible locations of any surviving family members. When children gave the names of relatives who might have survived, advertisements were taken out in newspapers in an attempt to locate the missing relatives so they might have an opportunity to be reunited with the child.

Sponsors who 'adopted' a child were encouraged not only to fulfil their financial obligations but also to interact with the 'adopted' child by writing to 'their' child and sending birthday gifts etc in order to establish a personal relationship with the child and to assist with the child's sense of 'belonging' once more. It was an important part of the child's rehabilitation back into a more normal society.

Rescue Children Inc. and the J.D.C. worked closely together and had children registered with the Chief Rabbi's Council in France. Together they were able to arrange for groups of children to be transferred to homes in Israel.

During the years 1945 and 1946 alone the Rescue Children Inc. supported 2200 orphans of the Holocaust.[18]

Appendix A

Myron C Taylor's report to (President Roosevelt)

The following text is Myron C. Taylor's highly confidential report to President Roosevelt, written at the end of the Évian conference. The text of this report may be found in U.S. Department of State file, 840.48, Refugees, 585. USNA film 1284, reel 20.

On June 23, 1938, Messrs. Pell and Brandt reported for duty with me at Paris. Previously I had read all available material bearing upon the problem of political refugees [or involuntary emigrants as they have come to be called], and I received at my home in Florence the representatives of numerous private organizations. I therefore had a clear picture of the situation when I received my letter of guidance.

In accordance with this letter I immediately went south to establish contact with the representatives of the French, the British, the Argentine and Brazilian governments.

Ambassador Bullitt very kindly arranged to take me on June 24, 1938, to call on M. Bonnet, the French Minister for Foreign Affairs, through whom I made an appointment to meet Senator Henri Berenger, the Chairman of the French Delegation.

On June 27, 1938, accompanied by Mr Pell, I called upon Senator Berenger at the Luxembourg Palace and outlined our ideas with regard to the Évian Meeting. Moreover, I gave the Senator a copy of my proposed opening speech and invited his comments. M. Berenger was extremely cordial and pledged his delegation to cooperation with us at Évian. Specifically, after some friendly discussion, he agreed to open the meeting as Chairman and appeared to be willing to accept the permanent chairmanship.

On June 28, 1938, I received an informal note from Senator Berenger saying that his Government was in complete agreement with the points contained in my opening statement and repeating his desire to be of real assistance.

In the meantime, I had made rather strenuous efforts through our Embassy at London to establish contact with the British Government. I made it clear that I should be willing to review the situation with Lord Winterton or Sir Michael Palairet at Paris, or would go to London, if it was more convenient for them. After some delay I received word that they, the British, were extremely fearful of publicity and if it could be assured that Sir Michael Palairet would see me privately in Paris, without any word to the press, he could arrange to come. I sent back word that I was as anxious as they to avoid publicity, and pointed out that no word of my presence in Paris had, up to that time, appeared in the press and, in fact, no word did appear until July 4, when the French Foreign Office inspired a brief notice which appeared in local Paris newspapers including the *New York Herald Tribune*. Accordingly, it was agreed that Sir Michael Palairet would come to Paris on June 31st.

Meanwhile, I had word that the French and British had been discussing the situation. I therefore sent Mr Pell to see Sir Ronald Campbell, Minister at the British Embassy, for the purpose of reassuring him as to our desire to avoid any mention of our meeting in the press. Mr Pell learned, during his conversation with Sir Ronald, that the French had given the British Embassy a rough translation of the text of my proposed speech. Mr Pell, in consequence, handed Sir Ronald a copy of the original English text and said that I hoped it might be transmitted immediately to Lord Winterton.

Sir Michael Palairet came to my private apartment at the Ritz on the afternoon of Thursday, June 31, prepared to discuss with me on the basis of this speech. He expressed the hope that we might make certain changes which I reported to you in the Paris Embassy's telegram No 1041, of July 1, 5p.m. He, moreover, made it clear that the aim of the British was to subordinate any machinery which might be set up at Évian to the existing League machinery, and was emphatic in urging the necessity of limiting the scope of the new activity to refugees and potential refugees from Germany including Austria. I took this occasion to give him a copy of our draft resolution which he said would be studied by the services in London, in order that we might open negotiations immediately upon arrival of the British Delegation at Évian.

That same day I communicated a copy of the Resolution to Senator Berenger.

Previously, I had made an informal call on Ambassador Le Breton, of the Argentine Republic, at his Embassy. I outlined in full to him our plans for the Évian Meeting and it was agreed that we should have further technical discussions during the ensuing week. Unfortunately the very next day Mme. Le Breton died after a plane trip to London, and as a consequence our conversations with the Ambassador were interrupted.

We also communicated with M. Lobo, the Brazilian Delegate, who was at Geneva at the time. He came to Paris, and we reviewed this situation in detail.

Subsequently, he kept in touch with Mr. Pell, who furnished him with such information as he required. We also received calls from most of the other Latin American delegates. Almost without exception they told us that they had received no instruction whatsoever from their governments, that they had merely been told that they were to go to a refugee meeting at Évian and discover its purposes. I gave each one of the visiting Ministers a copy of the agenda and such other information as he requested. Several called later on Mr Pell who furnished them with documents and other useful material.

I should add that during this period in Paris, I received representatives of innumerable private organizations and sent none away without a personal interview. Perhaps the most notable of my private callers was Dr. [Otto] Hirsch, the representative of the Jewish community in Germany. Shortly after my arrival in Paris, I had a letter from Consul Geist, at Berlin, saying that Dr. Hirsch would like to discuss the situation with me and that the German authorities had no objection to his coming to Paris. I telegraphed the Embassy at Berlin indicating that if it was deemed advisable for me to see Dr. Hirsch I should be very glad to do so. Dr Hirsch came and was most helpful in giving concrete details as to the situation in Germany and as to the extent of the problem.

On July 5, our Delegation took up quarters at Évian. That evening Lord Winterton and Sir Michael Palairet arrived by plane from London and dined with me. In the course of the conversation they took a very strong stand on behalf of the League Commission and said that they could not agree to any machinery which would diminish in any respect the standing of Sir Neill Malcolm, or his organization. They said that they envisaged real difficulty in this respect and hoped that we would agree that the intergovernmental committee should have the statutes of the advisory committee of governments to the League Commission which was called for in the recommendation made by the Council of the League of Nations on May 14, 1938. I said that while our Government was anxious that the organization which we proposed to set up and the League Commission should collaborate and be complementary, we would not be able to agree to participate in an advisory body to the League Commission such as the British Delegates described.

I might observe at this point that we had already been made aware of the fact that the League Secretariat was hostile in the extreme to the Évian meeting and was most anxious to have it fail. I do not believe that this was the attitude of the Secretary General, M. Avenol; in fact I was assured by Governor [John Gilbert] Winant, who very kindly came to see me on the afternoon of July 5, that the Secretary General saw definite advantage in the Évian meeting; it was, however, distinctly the attitude of the League bureaucracy as a whole, notably of Major Abrams, who has in charge refugee activities of the League. I learned from various sources that he was extremely active in stirring up hostility to the meeting, particularly among the Latin American Delegates over whom the League Secretariat has great influence.

In any event, the British Delegates decided with us that it would be advisable to appoint an informal drafting committee to consider the resolution and when it had reached an agreement on a text to report to the chiefs of the delegations. This drafting committee should consist of Mr Makins, for the British Delegation; M. Bressy, for the French Delegation, and Mr Pell for the American Delegation.

The following morning, July 6, at our suggestion, the British, the French and ourselves met in Senator Berenger's office. The question immediately arose as to who would be chairman of the meeting. I reminded M. Berenger that it was understood in Paris that he would accept this responsibility. He immediately countered by saying that since the meeting had been called on the initiative of President Roosevelt, and was American in its inspiration and direction, it was imperative for me to accept the chairmanship. The British were inclined to support Senator Berenger's stand. I made it clear that I was extremely disappointed and said I could not accept before consulting my Government. [See my No 1, July 6, 4p.m.].

After considering the situation, I reluctantly came to the conclusion that a compromise was inevitable and that a graceful solution might be for Senator Berenger to remain as Honorary Chairman, while I accepted the active chairmanship. When I suggested this solution to Senator Berenger the following morning, he was delighted and agreed to open the meeting while I took charge during the period of active negotiations in open and executive sessions.

The opening session of the meeting took place on the afternoon of July 6, with M. Berenger in the Chair. I reported briefly the substance of this meeting in my No 2, July 6, 8p.m., and a full stenographic account is included in the Minutes of the meeting which I enclose.

Beginning the evening of July 6, and for several days thereafter, Pell, Makins and Bressy labored to find the text of a resolution upon which they could agree.

Makins was inclined at first to take a very rigid stand against our text. Bressy supported him throughout and in addition made it clear that the French Government would not agree to the presence of the intergovernmental committee in Paris, on the grounds that it would attract undesirable elements and would prove an embarrassment in French relations with Germany.

On the evening of July 7, Lord Winterton invited me to dine with him. Pell and Brandt, for us, and Palairet and Makins, for the British, were also present. The evident object of this dinner was to persuade us into an acceptance of their concept of the intergovernmental committee as an advisory body to the League Commission.

They told us at length of the great work that Sir Neill Malcolm had done; what a remarkable character he was; how useful it would be if we could throw our weight behind him and the League. At this point I read the statement contained in my No.4, July 7, 2p.m., with the changes suggested by you, and said frankly that there was no object in our deceiving one another; that we could not accept a subordinate position for the intergovernmental body; that it seemed to me that the two organizations could very usefully be complementary and that there was plenty of room for the activity of both. I then outlined in detail our plan for a Committee with a British Chairman, four Vice-Chairmen, and an American Director, and made a strong plea to Lord Winterton for an understanding of our aim. Lord Winterton seemed to be tremendously impressed, his whole attitude changed immediately. Later he informed me that he had been so struck by our presentation of the case that he had communicated with the Prime Minister who had authorized him to modify the views of the British Delegation. He then also accepted the suggestion of a British Chairman and mentioned Lord Plymouth, but later said the government had suggested that he accept the chairmanship himself, which pleased him greatly as it [as late as Sunday, July 17, when I saw him in Paris] still does.

This explains why, when on the morning of this day, the British, supported by the French, presented a counterproposal to our Resolution—the full text of which I sent you in my telegram No 8. July 8,

7p.m.—that same evening there was a noticeable change in their attitude, as indicated in the modifications which they were prepared to make in their own text which I reported in my telegram No 10. July 8, 10p.m.

In the conversations with Pell and Bressy over the weekend, Makins was decidedly more cooperative, so that by noon of July 11, he, Pell and Bressy had reached an agreement on a text [see my no 14, July 11, 12 noon], which was then referred for consideration to Senator Berenger, Lord Winterton and myself. It was then that by a display of very great seriousness and firmness we eliminated the clause which made the League services [Commission and Nansen Office] members of our Committee. In view of the pushing character of Sir Neill Malcolm and Dr. Hansson, we were convinced that they would be too active and might make much trouble. We modified a few passages and then Winterton and Berenger said that since the meeting was called on American initiative and I was Chairman, I should do the negotiating with the other Delegations in order that there might not be any differentiation between them.

During the next twenty-four hours I saw the representatives of every Delegation, first singly then in groups, such as the small European power group, and the Argentines, Brazilians, Chileans and Peruvians. Subsequently, Pell had technical conversations with each Delegation and made such minor modifications in the text as were necessary to meet their views. After considerable shifting of words and redrafting of phrases, we were able to draw up a text which appeared to be acceptable to all Delegations. I then held an off-the-record meeting of Chiefs of Delegations in my office, at which we discussed the Resolution paragraph by paragraph, and made further minor changes in phraseology. We seemed to be in agreement when a group of Latin American representatives, notably the Central American Delegates and the Delegates of Colombia, Venezuela, Uruguay and Chile came to me with the tale that they were not able to approve the Resolution, explaining that they were under heavy pressure from Germany on account of the barter agreements, and that in this situation they thought it preferable to make a complete reservation of their position. I attempted to persuade them to change their minds, explaining what an unfortunate effect an apparent difference of views would have and assuring them that there was nothing in the Resolution as drafted which could possibly offend Germany. This led us to have a second and larger meeting in my office the following [Wednesday] morning. We again read the Resolution, paragraph by paragraph, and again the difficulty arose with the groups above named. I had already stated many times that the Resolution as phrased was a recommendation. The objections continued, however, until, finally, on the suggestion of Mr Lobo, who was invaluable in seconding my efforts, I agreed to make a statement to the effect that each country could decide in its sovereign right how far it would take action on the basis of the Resolution. This seemed to meet their objections, and on this basis I obtained an assurance from each objecting Delegation that it would not reserve its position. The only exception was the Colombian Delegation which said that it was obligated by its instructions to make a complete reservation.

Since all the Delegations were in agreement, I decided that it was unwise to wait until the next day for the formal presentation of the Resolution to the Meeting. I therefore called an executive session that afternoon and the Resolution was approved without dissenting voice. [See my No 21, July 14, 5p.m. for the text]. It was, moreover, agreed that I should continue to serve as Chairman until a permanent Chairman was elected at London and that in the interim I should receive communications from participating governments in order to emphasize the continuity of our work.

On the following morning, July 15, we held the closing session, when I made the statement which I telegraphed to you in my No 24, July 15, 12 noon, and Lord Winterton, then Senator Berenger, spoke. Other speakers were Judge Hansson, the Chairman of the Technical Committee and M. [A.] Costa du Rels, of Bolivia, who made strong proLeague statements which led to a request by Lord Winterton that the conclusions of the Intergovernmental Meeting be communicated to the Secretary General of the League of Nations.

After the speeches were concluded, I proposed that Senator Berenger, as Honorary Chairman, should take the Chair and dismiss the Meeting. He was evidently delighted to do so and delivered a charming and highly laudatory address. The Meeting closed with the fullest evidence of goodwill all around and a desire to achieve a concrete result. I believe that the friendly atmosphere was in part influenced by the fact that I, as Chairman, made a point of entertaining at one time or another all the principal delegates and their staffs. This created a more favorable atmosphere and enabled me to make several speeches off the record in which I made the humanitarian and emotional appeal which it was difficult for me to do in the public sessions. I was very much impressed with the increasing seriousness with which the work was conducted as the meeting progressed, and I am happy to say that it concluded on a very high note.

I should add that two subcommittees were set up by the intergovernmental committee: the first was the Subcommittee set up to hear the representatives of private organizations and to receive their memoranda. The Chairman of this Subcommittee was Lieutenant-Colonel White, of Australia; Mr McDonald represented us.

This Subcommittee heard a representative of every private organization which had registered with the Secretary General. They then delegated to the Secretary General, M. Paul-Boncour, who was assisted by Mr. [Alfred] Stirling, of Australia, [External Affairs Office, London] the task of drawing up a synopsis of the views of the private bodies. At the last minute this synopsis which had been shown to us was mysteriously suppressed. Later, I learned that the paper No 5[1]—which is enclosed—was substituted for it and that Mr Erim, Sir Neill Malcolm's assistant, made off with the accompanying material for the files of the High Commissioner's office. We are seeking to recover this material which, however, we had taken the pains to duplicate in our private files.

The second Subcommittee was the technical group, which had as Chairman Judge Hansson, and had the duty of hearing a statement of the laws and practices of each country with regard to political refugees, and statements of the number and type of immigrants which each country was prepared to receive. Mr Brandt represented us on this Subcommittee and, in fact, he together with Mr Cooper of the British Delegation, did the greater part of the work and prepared the final report and the Resolution based on it.

At the Meeting on July 8, Brandt presented to the Technical Subcommittee the statement of our immigration policy which was previously approved by the Department. [See my No 12, July 10 4p.m.]. In this connection, I should observe that after Brandt had made his statement, he was roundly attacked by Sir Neill Malcolm, the League High Commissioner, who implied that we should not have called this Meeting unless we were prepared to modify our immigration laws. I think it is only frank to state that Sir Neill Malcolm's attitude during the whole proceedings was one of open hostility. Sir Neill, as you may know, is a semi-invalid, who does the work of the League Commission in time which he can spare from his duties as head of the North Borneo Company. In actual fact, the work is done by his Turkish Assistant, Mr Erim, who is a member of the League Secretariat, and by Lord Duncannon, a young boy of some ability who has just left college and is preparing to run for Parliament. As far as I can make out, Sir Neill's chief virtue is that he obeys the orders of the British Foreign Office and of the League Secretariat without question, and does not even attempt to act independently. The consensus among the private organizations is that Sir Neill is pleasant but of very little real value and that it would be a tragedy were he to be chosen as the permanent High Commissioner of the League, as apparently he and the British Government wish.

I have the impression that Judge Hansson is another candidate for the permanent High Commissionership. He is an agreeable, pleasant spoken man, but proved to be completely ineffective as Chairman of the Technical Subcommittee. Very evidently he is not in the good favor of the British.

As I look over the situation, I am satisfied that we accomplished the purpose for which the Intergovernmental Meeting at Évian—which we consistently regarded as an initial session—was called. We have obtained approval of machinery which should prove effective, if skilfully used, to alleviate the condition of political refugees; we have established the continuity of governmental effort through the agreement of the British to hold a further meeting at London on August 3. We have laid the groundwork for the Director who will find that the way is paved for him to engage in negotiation with Germany immediately upon his arrival. We have done what is equally important: we have won the British, the French and others to the idea of doing something immediately to deal with the situation which, if allowed to develop in major proportions might prove disastrous. I have every confidence that Lord Winterton and Senator Berenger are now fired with real enthusiasm for this work and are prepared to continue an active and constructive interest.

I find many of our Latin American colleagues extremely troublesome. They have nothing constructive to offer and enter objection after objection, in many cases for purposes of self-advertisement. Notable exceptions are M. Lobo, of Brazil, and Ambassador Le Breton, of the Argentine, who are both men of experience and wisdom. Undoubtedly there will be a tendency on the part of some Latin American governments to separate themselves from this work in its continued form at London, and I think it should be weighed whether their value as countries of settlement is sufficiently great to warrant our urging them to come, if it is to be merely for the purpose of blocking progress.

In any event, I believe that you could help us at Washington by explaining to them the importance of making a show of inter-American unity and of assisting in this great humanitarian enterprise.

With regard to the projected negotiations with Germany, some evidence has reached me that there is at least a disposition in certain German quarters to cooperate in an orderly solution of this problem. Of course, the approach to the German Government will have to be very carefully prepared. I shall give serious thought to the manner of approach between now and the arrival of the Director and am sure that you will consider this aspect of the question very carefully. It is clear from the evidence which we have at hand that disaster lies ahead unless the Germans can be persuaded in an orderly manner. At the present time there is very little possibility of large-scale settlement of political refugees. The process of infiltration may be accelerated somewhat, but not to an extent which will permit the absorption of hundreds of thousands of involuntary emigrants from Germany, and after them from other points in Central Europe. It is absolutely essential therefore that the

German Government should collaborate, if it wishes in fact to solve its problem and not reduce the undesirables in its population, that is undesirable from its point of view, to the status of little better than serfs.

As you perhaps realize, we had very serious difficulties over the question of the scope of the Governmental Committee. The British, supported by the French and many others, were adamant in insisting that the scope should be strictly limited to involuntary emigrants from Germany including Austria. They explained to us at great length and on numerous occasions that it would be fatal to give the slightest encouragement to the Poles, the Romanians and others in Central Europe, since they would immediately begin to put such pressure on their minorities that we would have an incalculable problem on our hands. Incidentally, Makins told Pell in strict confidence that prior to the Évian Meeting Signor Mussolini had indicated to the British Ambassador at Rome that he would resent any suggestion of extending the scope to include Italian refugees and would regard it as a personal affront. In reply, we did everything in our power to persuade the

British and others that the problem of refugees from other points than Germany, including Austria, was with us in any event, and that there could be no harm in making the scope more general. The only compromise we were able to obtain on this point was the inclusion of the word 'develop' in the terms of reference of the intergovernmental committee in its continued form. The British and French have agreed privately to interpret this word 'develop' as meaning that if it becomes necessary the scope of the Committee can be extended. I am afraid that there is little possibility of obtaining further assurances at the present time.

As I have reported to you, we have succeeded in arousing a keen interest on the part of the British, the French and others, in the continuing intergovernmental committee. Lord Winterton evidently finds the prospect of assuming the chairmanship much to his liking, and I understand that he has discussed this and other aspects of the plan with Lord Halifax and other members of the British Cabinet. Senator Berenger has informed me that his Government has agreed that he may serve as one of the Vice-Chairmen, and all seemed very much pleased that I should continue at least for a time as another Chairman. The British are most anxious that a third Vice-Chairman should be a representative of Denmark and all are in agreement that a fourth Vice-Chairman should be a Latin American. I have some reason to believe that the French would like to place M. [A.] Costa du Rels, of Bolivia, who works very closely with them, in this position, I should much prefer to have M. Lobo, of Brazil, who was extraordinarily cooperative at Évian and, without of course taking an initiative, I shall do what I can to support him if his name is put forward by the Latin American group.

Interest focuses naturally on the Director, and all are hopeful that he will be able to make a successful approach to the German Government. Great importance is attached to the fact that he is an American, since all are agreed that because of political involvement in one sense or another, the national of another country could not succeed.

In conclusion, I am convinced that it is of the highest importance to maintain the continuity of this work and not to let it drop for a single instant.

It has got off to a good start; it must be carried on in the spirit of the Évian meeting and with the same energy and determination.

Appendix B

List of delegates at Évian

List of delegates of Évian. Source: U.S. Department of State file Refugees 568, USNA film 1284, reel 20.

Australia

Lieutenant-colonel the Hon. T.W. White, DFC, VD, MP. minister for trade and customs.

Alfred Stirling, external affairs officer, London.

A.W. Stuart-Smith, Australia House, London.

Argentine Republic

Dr Tomas A. Le Breton, ambassador to France.

Carlos A. Pardo, general secretary of the permanent delegation to the League of Nations.

Belgium

R. de Foy, general director administrator of the *Surete Publique*.

J. Schneider, director of the Foreign Office.

Bolivia

Simón Iturri Patino, minister in France.

M.A. Costa du Rels, ambassador, permanent delegate to the League of Nations.

United Kingdom

The Right Hon. the Earl Winterton, MP, Chancellor of the Duchy of Lancaster.

Sir Charles Michael Palairet, KCMG, minister plenipotentiary.

Sir John Schuckburgh, KCMG, CB, Colonial Office, deputy undersecretary of state.

J.G. Hibbert, MC, principal, Colonial Office.

E.N. Cooper, OBE, principal, Home Office.

R.M. Makins, assistant adviser on League of Nations Affairs, Foreign Office, (secretary to the delegation.)

Private secretaries to Lord Winterton:

Captain Victor Cazalet, MP.

T.B. Williamson, Home Office.

Brazil

Helio Lobo, minister first class.

Jorge Olinto de Oliveira, first secretary to the Brazilian Legation.

Canada

Humphrey Hume Wrong, permanent delegate to the League of Nations.

W.R. Little, commissioner for European emigration in London.

Chile

Fernando Garcia Oldini, minister to Switzerland and representative accredited to the International Labour Organisation, with the rank of envoy extraordinary and minister plenipotentiary.

Colombia

Luis Cano, permanent delegate to the League of Nations, with rank of envoy extraordinary and minister plenipotentiary.

Professor J.M. Yepes, legal counsellor to the permanent delegation accredited to the League of Nations.

Abelardo Forero-Benavides, secretary of the permanent delegation to the League of Nations, (secretary).

Costa Rica

Professor Luis Dobles Segreda, *chargé d'affaires* at Paris.

Juan Antiga Escobar, envoy, minister to Switzerland. Permanent delegate accredited to the League of Nations.

Cuba

Juan Antiga Escobar, envoy extraordinary and minister plenipotentiary in Switzerland, permanent delegate to the League of Nations.

Denmark

Gustav Rasmussen, Ministry of Foreign Affairs.

Trosls Hoff, Ministry of Justice.

Dominican Republic

Virgilio Trujillo Molina, envoy, Minister to France and Belgium.

Dr Salvador E. Paradas, *chargé d'affaires* representing the permanent delegation to the League of Nations.

Ecuador

Alejandro Gastelu Concha, with rank of *chargé d'affaires*.

United States of America

The Honourable Myron C. Taylor, ambassador on special mission.

James G. McDonald, adviser, chairman of President Roosevelt's Advisory Committee on Political Refugees.

Robert T. Pell, technical adviser, Division of European Affairs, Department of State.

George L. Brandt, technical adviser, formerly chief of the Visa Division, Department of State.

Hayward C. Hill, secretary of the delegation, American consul, Geneva.

George L. Warren, assistant to McDonald, executive secretary, President Roosevelt's Committee on Political Refugees.

France

Henri Berenger, ambassador.

M. Bressy, assistant director of the International Bureaux Section at the Ministry of Foreign Affairs.

M. Combes, director at the Ministry of the Interior.

M. Georges Coulon.

M. Fourcade, head of bureau at the Ministry of the Interior.

François Seydoux, of the sub-department for Europe at the Ministry of Foreign Affairs.

Baron Brincard, sub-department for the League of Nations at the Ministry of Foreign Affairs.

Guatemala

Jose Gregorio Diaz, envoy extraordinary, minister to France.

Haiti

Leon Robert Thébaud, commercial *attache* at Paris, with the rank of minister.

Honduras

Mauricio Rosal, consul at Paris, with rank of envoy extraordinary and minister plenipotentiary.

Ireland

Francis Thomas Cremins, permanent delegate to the League of Nations.

John Duff, assistant secretary of the Department of Justice.

William Maguire, deputy assistant secretary of the Department of Industry and Commerce.

Mexico

Primo Villa Michel, envoy extraordinary and minister plenipotentiary to the Netherlands.

Manuel Tello, *chargé d'affaires* to the League of Nations.

Nicaragua

Constantino Herdocia, minister to Great Britain and France with the rank of envoy extraordinary and minister plenipotentiary.

Norway

Michael Hansson, president of the Nansen International Office for Refugees and former president of the Egyptian Court of Mixed Appeals.

C.N.S. Platou, general director of the Ministry of Justice.

Finn Moe, journalist, representative of private organisations of refugees in Norway.

R. Konstad, director of the Central Office of Norwegian Passports.

New Zealand

C.B. Burdekin.

Panama

Dr Ernesto Hoffman, consul general at Geneva and delegate accredited to the League of Nations.

Paraguay

Gustavo A. Wiengreen, envoy extraordinary and minister plenipotentiary of Paraguay.

Netherlands

W.C. Beucker-Andreae, head of the Legal Section at the Ministry of Foreign Affairs.

R.A. Verwey, *directeur du service de l'Etat des assurances contre le chomage et des bourses du travail, ministere des affaires sociales.*

I.P. Hooykaas, adviser to the Ministry of Justice.

Peru

M. Francisco Garcia Calderon, minister to France, with rank of envoy extraordinary and minister plenipotentiary.

Sweden

G. Engzell, head of the legal department of the Ministry for Foreign Affairs.

C.A.M. de Hallenborg, chief of bureau at the Ministry for Foreign Affairs.

Eric Drougge, secretary at the Administration of Labour and Social Affairs.

Switzerland

Dr Heinrich Rothmund, director of the police division at the Federal Department of Justice and Police.

Henri Werner, legal adviser to the police division at the Federal Department of Justice and Police.

Uruguay

Dr Alfredo Carbonell-Debali, delegate plenipotentiary of Uruguay.

Venezuela

Carlos Aristimuno-Coll, envoy extraordinary and minister plenipotentiary in France of the United States of Venezuela.

Appendix C

Text of resolution adopted at Évian

Text of resolution adopted on 14 July, 1938, by the intergovernmental committee on political refugees at Évian, France. Source, U.S. Department of State press release, number 335, 15 July, 1938. Film 840.48 Refugees/529.

1. Considering that the question of involuntary emigration has assumed major proportions and that the fate of the unfortunate people affected has become a problem for intergovernmental deliberation;

2. Aware that the involuntary emigration of large numbers of people of different creeds, economic conditions, professions and trades, from the country or countries where they have been established is disturbing to the general economy, since these persons are obliged to seek refuge, either temporarily or permanently, in other countries at a time when there is serious unemployment; that in consequence countries of refuge and settlement are faced with problems not only of an economic and social nature but also of public order, and that there is a severe

strain on the administrative facilities and absorptive capacities of the receiving countries;

3. Aware, moreover, that the involuntary emigration of peoples in large numbers has become so great that it renders racial and religious problems more acute; increases international unrest; and may hinder seriously the processes of appeasement in international relations;

4. Believing that it is essential that a long range program should be envisaged, whereby assistance to involuntary emigrants, actual and potential, may be coordinated within the framework of existing migration laws and practices of governments;

5. Considering that if countries of refuge or settlement are to cooperate in finding an orderly solution of the problem before the committee they should have the collaboration of the country of origin and are therefore persuaded that it will make its contribution by enabling involuntary emigrants to take with them their property and possessions and emigrate in an orderly manner;

6. Welcoming heartily the initiative taken by the President of the United States of America in calling the intergovernmental meeting at Évian for the primary purpose of facilitating involuntary emigration from Germany including Austria, and expressing profound appreciation to the French

Government for its courtesy in receiving the intergovernmental meeting at Évian;

7. Bearing in mind the resolution adopted by the Council of the League of Nations on May 14, 1938 concerning international assistance to refugees:

Recommends:

8. [a] That the persons coming within the scope of the activity of the intergovernmental committee shall be [1] persons who have not already left their country of origin [Germany including Austria], but who must emigrate on account of their political opinions, religious beliefs, or racial origin and [2] persons as defined in [1] who have already left their country of origin and who have not yet established themselves permanently elsewhere;

[b] That the governments participating in the intergovernmental committee shall continue to furnish the committee, for its strictly confidential information, with [1] details regarding such immigrants which each government is prepared to receive under its existing laws and practices and [2] details of these laws and practices;

[c] That in view of the fact that the countries of refuge and settlement are entitled to take into account the economic and social

adaptability of immigrants, these should in many cases be required to accept at least for a time changed conditions of living in the countries of settlement;

[d] That the governments of the countries of refuge and settlement should not assume any obligations for the financing of involuntary emigration;

[e] That, with regard to the documents required by the countries of refuge and settlement, the governments represented on the intergovernmental committee should consider the adoption of the following provisions:

> In these individual immigration cases in which the usually required documents emanating from foreign official sources are found not to be available, there should be accepted such other documents serving the purpose of the requirements of law, as may be available to the immigrant.
>
> And that, as regards the document which may be issued to an involuntary emigrant by the country of his foreign residence to serve the purpose of a passport, note be taken of the several international agreements providing for the issue of a travel document serving the purpose of a passport, and of the advantage of their wide application;

[f] That there should meet at London an intergovernmental committee consisting of such representatives as the governments participating in the Évian meeting may desire to designate.

This committee shall continue and develop the work of the intergovernmental meeting at Évian and shall be constituted and shall function in the following manner:

There shall be a chairman of this committee and four vice-chairmen.

There shall be a director of authority, appointed by the intergovernmental committee, who shall be guided by it in his actions. He shall undertake negotiations to improve the present conditions of orderly emigration. He shall approach the governments of the countries of refuge with a view to developing opportunities for permanent settlement.

The intergovernmental committee, recognizing the value of the work of the existing refugee services of the League of Nations and of the studies of migration made by the International Labor Office, shall cooperate fully with these services, and the intergovernmental committee at London shall consider the means by which the cooperation of the committee and the director with these services shall be established.

The intergovernmental committee at its forthcoming meeting at London will consider the scale on which its expenses shall be apportioned among the participating governments;

[g] That the intergovernmental committee in its continued form shall hold a first meeting at London on August 3, 1938.

Notes and Sources

Principal sources used in this history are located in the United States National Archives, from Record Group 59, file 840.48.

Abbreviations used in notes:
USNA: United States National Archives.
USSD: United States State Department.

Acronyms

AFSC—American Friends Service Committee.
AJB—*Association des Juifs en Belgique.*
CAEJR—*Comite d'Assistance aux Enfants Juifs Refugies.*
COSOR—*le Comite des Oeuvres Sociales de la Resistance.*
DDSG—Danube Steam Boat Navigation Company.
DORSA—Dominican Republic Settlement Association.
ERC—Emergency Rescue Committee.
H. I.C.E.M.—Jewish Overseas Emigration Association.
IC—International Committee for European Immigrants.
IZL—.*Irgun Zvai Leumi* (the military arm of the Revisionist Zionist movement).
J.D.C.—Joint Distribution Committee.
OSE—*Oeuvre de Secours aux Enfants.*

R.S.H.A.—Reich Security Head Office.
RGO—Central Welfare Council.
ZOW—*Zwiazek Organizacji Wojskowej* (the Union of Military Organisation).

Introduction

[1]　USSD file 840.48, Refugees 552 USNA film 1284, reel 20.
[2]　*Maryborough Chronicle*, Monday 2 October, 1933, p 5.

Chapter One: The Need for Évian

[1]　Seyss-Inquart was made *Reichsstatthalter*, governor of Austria, after the *Anschluss*. In May the following year he was transferred to the Netherlands as Reichs commissioner, a post he ruled with quite remarkable brutality. He was hanged at Nuremberg in 1946.
[2]　Refugees 214, USNA film 1284, reel 19.
[3]　Memorandum on the International Conference on Jewish Migration, Akzin, Benjamin, p 1, USSD file 840.48, Refugees 203, USNA film 1284, reel 19.
[4]　Akzin, p 2.
[5]　Akzin, p 3.
[6]　Ibid.

[7]   Refugees, 368 1/2, USNA film 1284, reel 19.
[8]   Ibid.
[9]   *The Star*, Johannesburg, Friday 29 April, 1938.
[10] Ibid.
[11] Ibid.
[12] USSD file 840.48, Refugees, 57, USNA film 1284, reel 19.
[13] Ibid.
[14] Ibid.
[15] Refugees 586, general statements, p 1, USNA film 1284, reel 20.
[16] Refugees 586, general statements, USNA film 1284, reel 20.
[17] Ibid.
[18] Refugees 277, USNA film 1284, reel 19.
[19] Nansen International Office for Refugees, Report on the Liquidation of the Office, Geneva, 14 June, 1937; http://enwikipedia.org/wiki/Nansen_International_Office_for_Refugees.
[20] Refugees 57, USNA film 1284, reel 19.
[21] Ibid.
[22] Refugees 277, USNA film 1284, reel 19.
[23] Refugees 309 1/2 USNA film 1284, reel 19.

[24] Ibid.
[25] Ibid.
[26] *Maryborough Chronicle*, Monday 30 October, 1933, p 8.
[27] Ibid.
[28] Ibid.
[29] *Maryborough Chronicle,* 9 July, 1938.
[30] Refugees 309 1/2 USNA film 1284, reel 19.
[31] Refugees 57 USNA film 1284, reel 19.
[32] Refugees 59, USNA film 1284, reel 19.
[33] Ibid.
[34] Survey of present conditions and outlooks for Jewish emigration in the most important immigration countries. Refugees 365 1/2, USNA film 1284, reel 19.
[35] Ibid.
[36] Ibid.
[37] Ibid, pp 3-4.
[38] USSD file 840.48 Refugees 66, USNA film 1284, reel 19.
[39] Ibid.
[40] Ibid.
[41] USSD file 840.48, Refugees A. USNA film 1284, reel 19.
[42] Ibid.
[43] USSD 840.48 Refugees/1. USNA film 1284, reel 19.

[44] USSD, file 840.48, Refugees/2, USNA film 1284, reel 19.
[45] USSD, file 840.48, Refugees 5, USNA film 1284, reel 19.
[46] Refugees 173, USNA film 1284, reel 19.
[47] Ibid.
[48] *Maryborough Chronicle*, 3 August, 1938.
[49] Refugees 729, USNA film 1284, reel 21.
[50] *Maryborough Chronicle*, 3 September, 1938.
[51] USSD file 840.48, Refugees 7, USNA film 1284, reel 19.
[52] Refugees 365 1/2 USNA film 1284, reel 19.
[53] Ibid
[54] Refugees 1501, USNA film 1284, reel 24.
[55] http://wikipedia.org/wiki/Dudley_Aman,_1st_Baron_Marley; Biography of Lord Marley, http://web.onetel.com/~pelhamwest/westfamily/west6-lord-marley.htm.
[56] Refugees 1518, USNA film 1284, reel 24.
[57] Ibid.

Chapter Two: Responses and Reactions

[1]   Refugees 61, USNA film 1284, reel 19.
[2]   USSD file 840.48, Refugees 15. USNA film 1284, reel 19.
[3]   Ibid.
[4]   USSD file 840.48, Refugees, 20, USNA film 1284, reel 19.
[5]   Ibid.
[6]   USSD file 840.48, Refugees 26, USNA film 1284, reel 19.
[7]   USSD file 840.48, USNA film 1284, reel 19.
[9]   Refugees 365.5, USNA film 1284, reel 19.
[10] USSD file 840.48, Refugees 27, USNA film 1284, reel 19.
[11] USSD file 840.48, Refugees 29, USNA film 1284, reel 19.
[12] USSD file 840.48, Refugees 35, USNA film 1284, reel 19.
[13] Ibid.
[14] Refugees 987 USNA film 1284, reel 22.
[15] Refugees 1014, USNA film 1284, reel 22, and *Trinidad Guardian*, 20 November, 1938.

[16] Refugees 1263 GDG, USNA film 1284, reel 23.
[17] Refugees 1342 USNA film 1284, reel 24.
[18] USSD file 840.48, Refugees 38, USNA film 1284, reel 19.
[19] Refugees 39, reel 19.
[20] Refugees 365.5, USNA film 1284, reel 19.
[21] Ibid.
[22] Refugees 365.5, USNA film 1284, reel 19.
[23] Refugees 586, general statements, p 22, USNA film 1284, reel 20.
[24] Refugees 586, general statements, p 23, USNA film 1284, reel 20.
[25] USSD file 840.48, Refugees 52, USNA film 1284, reel 19.
[26] Ibid.
[27] Refugees 52 USSD 1284, reel 19.
[28] USSD file 840.48, Refugees 52, USNA film 1284, reel 19.
[29] USSD file 840.48, Refugees 55, USNA film 1284, reel 19.
[30] USSD file 840.48, Refugees 56, USNA film 1284, reel 19.
[31] Refugees 67, USNA film 1284, reel 19.
[32] Refugees 365.5, USNA film 1284, reel 19.

[33]   Refugees 586, general statements, p 24, USNA film 1284, reel 20.
[34]   Refugees 68, USNA film 1284, reel 19.
[35]   Refugees 69, USNA film 1284, reel 19.
[36]   Refugees 72, USNA film 1284, reel 19.
[37]   Ibid.
[38]   Refugees 365.5, USNA film 1284, reel 19.
[39]   Ibid.
[40]   Ibid.
[41]   Refugees 64, USNA film 1284, reel 19.
[42]   Refugees 365.5, USNA film 1284, reel 19.
[43]   Refugees 365.5, USNA film 1284, reel 19.
[44]   Ibid.
[45]   Refugees 586, general statements, p 19, USNA film 1284, reel 20.
[46]   Refugees 75, USNA film 1284, reel 19.
[47]   Refugees 272, USNA film 1284, reel 19.
[48]   Refugees 78, USNA film 1284, reel 19.
[49]   Refugees 81, USNA film 1284, reel 19.
[50]   Refugees 84, USNA film 1284, reel 19.
[51]   Ibid.
[52]   Ibid.
[53]   Refugees 88, USNA film 1284, reel 19.
[54]   Refugees 103, USNA film 1284, reel 19.

[55] Refugees 104, USNA film 1284, reel 19.
[56] Refugees 105, USNA film 1284, reel 19.
[57] Ibid.
[58] Refugees 107, USNA film 1284, reel 19.
[59] *The Broom*, 21 March, 1938, p 1.
[60] Refugees 107, USNA film 1284, reel 19.
[61] Refugees 114, USNA film 1284, reel 19.
[62] *Maryborough Chronicle*, 14 July, 1938.
[63] Refugees 117, USNA film 1284, reel 19.
[64] Ibid.
[65] According to U.S. documents, the Allies were so outraged over the massive Swiss supplies of munitions to Germany that they were considering an economic boycott of Switzerland. In a letter from Admiral William Leahy to Cordell Hull, Leahy had claimed that the Swiss munitions to Germany were so great that they were: '...materially decreasing the military effectiveness of our air attacks on the Axis'. For further details see

	Toowoomba Chronicle, 11 January, 1997, p 7.
[66]	Refugees 117 3/7. USNA film 1284, reel 19.
[67]	Refugees 117 5/7, USNA film 1284, reel 19.
[68]	Refugees 117 6/7, USNA film 1284, reel 19.
[69]	Refugees 122, USNA film 1284, reel 19.
[70]	Ibid.
[71]	Refugees 131, USNA film 1284, reel 19.
[72]	Refugees 145, USNA film 1284, reel 19.
[73]	*Neue Freie Presse*, 29 March, 1938.
[74]	Refugees 154, USNA film 1284, reel 19.
[75]	Refugees 165, USNA film 1284, reel 19.
[76]	Ibid.
[77]	Refugees 249, USNA film 1284, reel 19.
[78]	*Kansas City Journal Post*, 10 April, 1938, p 6A.
[79]	Ibid.
[80]	*Kansas City Journal Post*, 10 April, 1938, p 6A, and Refugees 164, USNA film 1284, reel 19.

[81] Refugees 164, USNA film 1284, reel 19.
[82] Refugees 173A, USNA film 1284, reel 19.
[83] Refugees 173/3/10 USNA film 1284, reel 19.
[84] Refugees 182, USNA film 1284, reel 19.
[85] *Maryborough Chronicle* 7 January, 1953 p 1.
[86] Refugees 173/6/10, USNA film 1284, reel 19.
[87] Refugees 173 C, USNA film 1284, reel 19.
[88] Refugees 173/8/10, USNA film 1284, reel 19.
[89] *New York Times*, 7 May, 1959; enwikipedia.org/wiki/Myron_Charles_Taylor.
[90] Refugees 275, USNA film 1284, reel 19.

Chapter Three: Pressures Increase

[1] Refugees 188, USNA film 1284, reel 19.
[2] Refugees 190, USNA film 1284, reel 19.
[3] Refugees 194, USNA film 1284, reel 19.
[4] Report of Wadsworth, George, *Palestine Reaction to American Proposal for*

	International Refugee Committee, p 1. Refugees 195, USNA film 1284, reel 19.
[5]	Wadsworth, p 2.
[6]	Wadsworth, p 5.
[7]	Ibid.
[8]	Wadsworth pp 2-4.
[9]	Refugees 211, USNA film 1284, reel 19.
[10]	*Maryborough Chronicle*, Friday 23 June, 1939, p 7.
[11]	Refugees 218, USNA film 1284, reel 19.
[12]	Refugees 365 1/2, USNA film 1284, reel 19.
[13]	Refugees 219 GHC, USNA film 1284, reel 19.
[14]	Untitled report, Hecker, W p 4, Refugees 225, USNA film 1284, reel 19.
[15]	Hecker, pp 4-6.
[16]	Refugees 225, USNA film 1284, reel 19.
[17]	Refugees 253, USNA film 1284, reel 19.
[18]	*Hansard*, House of Commons, 3 May, 1938, cols 698-699.
[19]	Refugees 227, USNA film 1284, reel 19.
[20]	Refugees 228A, USNA film 1284, reel 19.

[21] Ibid.
[22] Refugees 247 GDG, USNA film 1284, reel 19.
[23] Refugees 247 GML, USNA film 1284, reel 19.
[24] Refugees 228, USNA film 1284, reel 19.
[25] Refugees 430, USNA film 1284, reel 20.
[26] Ibid.
[27] Refugees 289A, USNA film 1284, reel 19.
[28] Ibid.
[29] Refugees 329, USNA film 1284, reel 19.
[30] Refugees 340, USNA film 1284, reel 19.
[31] Ibid.
[32] Refugees 298A, USNA film 1284, reel 19.
[33] Refugees 326, USNA 1284, reel 19.
[34] Refugees 326 GDG, USNA film 1284, reel 19.
[35] Refugees 332, USNA film 1284, reel 19.
[36] Ibid.
[37] Refugees 355, USNA film 1284, reel 19.

[38] Refugees 355 G/HC, USNA film 1284, reel 19.
[39] Refugees 348, USNA film 1284, reel 19.
[40] Refugees 299A, USNA film 1284, reel 19.
[41] Refugees 300, USNA film 1284, reel 19.
[42] Refugees 306, USNA film 1284, reel 19.
[43] Refugees 330 USNA film 1284, reel 19.
[44] Refugees 310, USNA film 1284, reel 19.
[45] Ibid.
[46] *Voelkischer Beobachter*, 13 May, 1938, p 8.
[47] Refugees 367, USNA film 1284, reel 19.
[48] Refugees 586, 'Declaration of Norwegian Delegation on the Immigration Laws and their Application to Norway', pp 1-3, USNA film 1284, reel 20.
[49] Refugees 365 1/2, USNA film 1284, reel 19.
[50] Ibid.
[51] Refugees 1321 GDG, USNA film 1284, Reel 24.

[52] http://enwikipedia.org/wiki/List_of_individuals_and_groups_assisting_Jews.

[53] For more on this see Ephraim, Frank, *Escape to Manila*, University of Illinois Press, 2003. See also: www.jewishgen.org/databases/Holocaust/0105_philippines.html.

[54] Refugees 374A, USNA film 1284, reel 19.

[55] Refugees 382, USNA film 1284, reel 19.

[56] Refugees 586, declaration by Chilean delegate, p 1, USNA film 1284, reel 20.

[57] For details of this ambitious project see: Tokayer, Marvin and Swartz, Mary, *The Fugu Plan*, Paddington Press Ltd, New York, 1979.

Chapter Four: The Problems of South America

[1] *The Jewish Refugee and the Argentine Immigration Problem*, Hunter, Winifred A. p 4, Refugees 186, GDG, USNA film 1284, reel 19.

[2] Hunter, p 5.

[3] Ibid, p 9.

[4] Ibid, pp 10-14.

[5]	Ibid, pp 15-16.
[6]	Ibid, p 8.
[7]	Ibid, p 21.
[8]	Ibid, pp 24-28.
[9]	Ibid, pp 24-28.
[10]	Ibid, pp 30-31.
[11]	Ibid, p 24.
[12]	Ibid, p 29.
[13]	Refugees 243, USNA film 1284, reel 19.
[14]	Ibid.
[15]	Refugees 308, USNA film 1284, reel 19.
[16]	Refugees 318, USNA film 1284, reel 19.
[17]	USSD, file 840.48, Refugees 11, USNA film 1284, reel 19.
[18]	Refugees, 365 1/2, USNA film 1284, reel 19.
[19]	Ibid.
[20]	Ibid.
[21]	Ibid.
[22]	Ibid.
[23]	Refugees 365, USNA film 1284, reel 19.
[24]	Ibid.
[25]	Refugees 365 1/2, USNA film 1284, reel 19.

[26] Refugees, 586, general statements, pp 15-16, USNA film 1284, reel 20.
[27] *The Daily Courier*, Connellsville, Pa.; en ://wikipedia.org/wiki/Sim%C3%B3n_Iturri_Pati%C3%B1o.
[28] Refugees 365.5, USNA film 1284, reel 19.
[29] Ibid.
[30] Ibid.
[31] Ibid.
[32] Ibid.
[33] Ibid.
[34] Refugees 219 GHC, USNA film 1284, reel 19.
[35] Refugees 272, USNA film 1284, reel 19.

Chapter Five: A Progression of Disappointments

[1] Refugees 523, USNA film 1284, reel 20.
[2] Ibid.
[3] Refugees 398 GMB, USNA film 1284, reel 20.
[5] Refugees 401 GML, USNA film 1284, reel 20.
[6] Refugees 409 DG, USNA film 1284, reel 20.

[7] Refugees 409 G/HC, USNA film 1284, reel 20.
[8] Ibid.
[9] Refugees 1123 GMB, USNA film 1284, reel 23.
[10] Refugees 411, USNA film 1284, reel 20.
[11] Ibid.
[12] Refugees 425 GML, USNA film 1284, reel 19.
[13] Refugees 185, USNA film 1284, reel 19.
[14] Refugees 185 GDG, USNA film 1284, reel 19.
[15] Refugees 215, G/HC, USNA film 1284, reel 19.
[16] Refugees 341, USNA film 1284, reel 19
[17] Refugees 707, USNA film 1284, reel 21.
[18] Ibid.
[19] Refugees 1356, USNA film 1284, reel 24 and Refugees 1434 USNA film 1284, reel 24.
[20] Refugees 712, USNA film 1284, reel 21.
[21] Refugees 1310 A, USNA film 1284, reel 24.

[22] Refugees 1402, USNA film 1284, reel 24.
[23] Refugees 430, USNA film 1284, reel 20.
[24] *New York Times*, Sunday 26 June, 1938, and file, Refugees 437, USNA film 1284, reel 20.
[25] *Oxford Dictionary of National Biography*, Oxford University Press, 2004, online edition; en.wikipedia.org/wiki/Michael_Palairet.
[26] Refugees 442 SEC 4, USNA film 1284, reel 20.
[27] Refugees 445, USNA film 1284, reel 20.
[28] Refugees 442, USNA film 1284, reel 20.
[29] Refugees 447, USNA film 1284, reel 20.
[30] Ibid.
[31] Refugees 450, USNA film 1284, reel 20.
[32] Refugees 446, USNA film 1284, reel 19.
[33] Refugees 458, USNA film 1284, reel 20.
[34] Refugees 484, USNA film 1284, reel 20.

Chapter Six: The Conference and World Disillusion

[1] Refugees 586, USNA film 1284, reel 20.
[2] Refugees 586, *Statement of Details Regarding the Number and the Type of Immigrants Which the Government of the United States is Prepared to Receive Under its Existing Laws and Practices*, pp 1-4, USNA film 1284, reel 20.
[3] en.wikipedia.org.wiki/Nahum_Goldmann; *Who Shall Live and Who Shall Die*, (quoting Nahum Goldmann), director Laurence A. Jarvik, 1982.
[4] Refugees 586, USNA film 1284, reel 20.
[5] *Maryborough Chronicle*, 8 August, 1938.
[6] Refugees 586, USNA film 1284, reel 20.
[7] Ibid.
[8] Taylor, A.J.P., *The Oxford History of England, English History, 1914-1945*, p 419.
[9] *Maryborough Chronicle*, 6 August, 1938.
[10] Ibid.
[11] *Maryborough Chronicle* Saturday 7 March, 1936, p 13.
[12] *Maryborough Chronicle* Saturday 10 October, 1936, p 11.
[13] Ibid.

[14]   Reproduced in the *Maryborough Chronicle*, 15 November, 1938.
[15]   *Maryborough Chronicle*, 17 December, 1938.
[16]   Refugees 586, verbatim report, 15 July, 1938, Lord Winterton's speech, p 3, USNA film 1284, reel 20.
[17]   Refugees 1327, USNA film 1284, reel 24.
[18]   *Maryborough Chronicle*, 23 November, 1938.
[19]   Refugees 1400A, USNA film 1284, reel 24.
[20]   *Washington Post*, 16 April, 1978.
[21]   *Hansard*, 11 July, 1938, cols 891-892.
[22]   *Hansard*, 14 July, 1938, cols 1507-1509.
[23]   Refugees 586, USNA film 1284, reel 20.
[24]   Ibid.
[25]   Refugees 586, French statement to technical subcommittee, p 1, USNA film 1284, reel 20.
[26]   Refugees 586, USNA film 1284, reel 20.
[27]   Refugees, 586, technical subcommittee confidential statement by Brazil, p 1, USNA film 1284, reel 20.
[28]   Refugees 586, USNA film 1284, reel 20.

[29] *Washington Post*, 16 April, 1978.
[30] Koifman, Fabio, *Quixote nas Trevas*, Rio de Janeiro/San Paulo, 2002; http://enwikipedia.org/wiki/List_of_individuals_and_groups_assisting_Jews.
[31] Refugees 586, USNA film 1284, reel 20.
[32] Refugees 586, USNA film 1284, reel 20.
[33] Refugees 289D Supplement, USNA film 1284, reel 19.
[34] *Maryborough Chronicle* Thursday 15 March, 1934, p 2, and *Commonwealth Parliamentary Handbook and Record of Elections for the Commonwealth of Australia, Eleventh Edition*, 1945 to 1953, p 287.
[35] Refugees 365 1/2, USNA film 1284, reel 19.
[36] Ibid.
[37] Refugees 586, USNA film 1284, reel 20.
[38] Ibid.
[39] Ibid.
[40] Refugees 586, Memorandum of Australian Immigration Laws, pp 1-2, USNA film 1284, reel 20.
[41] *Maryborough Chronicle*, 20 July, 1938.

[42] *Maryborough* Chronicle, 6 October, 1938.
[43] *Maryborough Chronicle*, 23 June, 1938.
[44] Ibid.
[45] *Maryborough Chronicle*, 1 August, 1938.
[46] *Maryborough Chronicle*, 11 April, 1938.
[47] *Maryborough Chronicle* Saturday 3 December, 1938, p 11.
[48] *Maryborough Chronicle*, 8 August, 1939.
[49] *Maryborough Chronicle*, Wednesday 18 January, 1939, p10.
[50] Refugees 365.5, USNA film 1284, reel 19.
[51] Ibid.
[52] Refugees 586, USNA film 1284, reel 20.
[53] Refugees 586, general statements, session three, p 2, USNA 1284, reel 20.
[54] H.H. Wrong biography www.thecanadianencyclopedia; http://enwikipedia.org/wiki/H._H._Wrong.
[55] Refugees 586, USNA film 1284, reel 20.
[56] Refugees 365.5, USNA film 1284, reel 19
[57] Ibid.
[58] Ibid.

[59] Refugees 586, USNA film 1284, reel 20.
[60] *Weekend Australian*, 21 November, 1998, p 17.
[61] Refugees 586 USNA film 1284, reel 20.
[62] Letter to the author from Gosta Engzell dated 17 March, 1994, and telephone conversation between Gosta Engzell and author, 26 March, 1994.
[63] Refugees 586, USNA film 1284, reel 20.
[64] Refugees 1498, USNA film 1284, reel 24.
[65] Refugees 722, USNA film 1284, reel 21.
[66] Ibid.
[67] http://enwikipedia.org/wiki/List_of_individuals_and_groups_assisting_Jews.
[68] Refugees 586, general statements, pp 4-9, USNA film 1284, reel 20.
[69] Refugees 586, general statements, p 10, USNA film 1284, reel 20.
[70] Refugees, 586, Colombian statement to technical subcommittee, pp 1-6, USNA film 1284, reel 20.
[71] Refugees, 601, USNA film 1284 reel 21.

[72] Refugees 964 G/GC, USNA film 1284, reel 22.
[73] Refugees 586, general statements, pp 29-30, USNA film 1284, reel 20.
[74] Refugees 689, USNA film 1284, reel 21.
[75] Refugees 889, USNA film 1284, reel 22.
[76] Refugees 1060.5 PS/FMF, USNA film 1284, reel 23.
[77] Refugees 1308, USNA film 1284, reel 24.
[78] Refugees 1524, USNA film 1284, reel 24.
[79] http://enwikipedia.org/wiki/List_of_individuals_and_groups_assisting_Jews;en.wikipedia.org.wiki/Sosua.
[80] Refugees 586, general statements, Nicaragua, Costa Rica, Honduras and Panama, 11 July, 1938, meeting, pp 1-2 USNA film 1284, reel 20.
[81] Refugees 586, USNA film 1284, reel 20.
[82] Ibid.
[83] Refugees 586, Cuban statement to technical subcommittee, pp 1-3, USNA film 1284, reel 20.

[84] Text description for photo number 59915, U.S. Holocaust Memorial Museum.
[85] Text description for photo number 31815, U.S. Holocaust Memorial Museum.
[86] Text description for photo number 31794, U.S. Holocaust Memorial Museum.
[87] Refugees, 586, Venezuelan statement to technical subcommittee, USNA film 1284, reel 20.
[88] Refugees 586, USNA film 1284.
[89] Refugees, 586, statement to technical subcommittee, pp 1-2, USNA film 1284, reel 20.
[90] Refugees 586, USNA film 1284, reel 20.
[91] http://enwikipedia.org/wiki/List_of_individuals_and_groups_assisting_Jews; wikipedia.org/wiki/Paul_Gruninger.
[92] *Washington Post*, 16 April, 1978.
[93] Refugees 725, USNA film 1284, reel 21.
[94] http://zachor.michlala.edu/english/manhigim/manhigim_t.asp?num=5&chug=manhigim.
[95] *Toowoomba Chronicle*, 15 March, 1997, p 8.

[96] Jewish arrivals in Switzerland, 1938-1945, (database) JewishGen.org.

[97] Embassy of the United States, Lima, letter number 515, file 800, film 840.48, Refugees/536.

[98] Enclosure number 1 to dispatch number 515, dated 11 July, 1938, from Lima Embassy. Refugees 536, USNA film 1284, reel 20.

[99] Refugees 586, general statements, p 27, USNA film 1284, reel 20.

[100] Refugees 586, general statements, pp 12-14, USNA film 1284, reel 20.

[101] Letter to U.S. Department of State, 13 July, 1938, number 147. U.S. Archives film 1284, reel 20, file 840.48 Refugees/537.

[102] *El Diaro Ilustrado* Santiago, Chile, 13 July, 1938.

[103] *El Imparcial* Santiago, Chile, 12 July, 1938.

[104] Meijer, Daphne, L. *Unknown Children, the Last Train from Westerbork* (Internet paper).

[105] Refugees 586, general statements, p 26, USNA film 1284, reel 20.

[106] Refugees 586, statement to technical subcommittee, pp 1-3, USNA film 1284, reel 20.

[107] www.yadvashem.org/yv/en/righteous/stories/duckwitz.asp; http://enwikipedia.org/wiki/Rescue_of_the_Danish_Jews.
[108] http://enwikipedia.org/wiki/List_of_individuals_and_groups_assisting_Jews.
[109] *Washington Post,* 16 April, 1978.

Chapter Seven: Press Reports in South America

[1] Refugees 553, USNA film 1284, reel 20.
[2] Ibid.
[3] Ibid.
[4] Ibid.
[5] Refugees 562, USNA film 1284, reel 20.
[6] Ibid.
[7] Ibid.
[8] http://enwikipedia.org/wiki/List_of_individuals_and_groups_assisting_Jews.

Chapter Eight: Faltering Progress

[1] Refugees 484, USNA film 1284, reel 20.
[2] State Department file 840.48 Refugees 577 GDG, USNA film 1284, reel 20.
[3] Refugees 583A and 584, USNA film 1284, reel 20.

[4] Refugees 586, technical subcommittee report, p 2, USNA film 1284, reel 20.
[5] Ibid.
[6] Refugees, 586, report of technical subcommittee, USNA film 1284, reel 20.
[7] *Maryborough Chronicle*, 20 June, 1938.
[8] Reproduced in the *Maryborough Chronicle* 6 July, 1938.
[9] *Maryborough Chronicle*, 7 July, 1938.
[10] *Maryborough Chronicle*, 17 November, 1938.
[11] Refugees 489, USNA film 1284, reel 20.
[12] Letter from John C. Wiley, file no 840.1. Refugees, 569, USNA film 1284, reel 20.
[13] Refugees 494A GML, USNA film 1284, reel 20.
[14] Refugees 495, USNA film 1284, reel 20.
[15] Refugees 510B, USNA film 1284, reel 20.
[16] Refugees 513, USNA film 1284, reel 20.
[17] Quoted in memorandum to U.S. secretary of state from U.S. Embassy Montevideo, number 347, USNA film 1284, reel 21.

[18]	Refugees 1176 GDG, USNA film 1284, reel 23.
[19]	Diplomatic serial number 2965, Department of State Washington, File 840.48, Refugees, 550A, USNA film 1284, reel 20.
[20]	Refugees 586, verbatim report of sixth public meeting, closing session, pp 2-3. USNA film 1284, reel 20.
[21]	Refugees 516A, USNA film 1284, reel 20.
[22]	Refugees 524, USNA film 1284, reel 20.
[23]	Refugees 524 and 525B, USNA film 1284, reel 20.
[24]	Refugees 572, USNA film 1284, reel 20.
[25]	Grabman, Richard, *Bosques' War*, 2007; wikipedia.org/wiki/Gilberto_Bosques_Saldivar
[26]	*La Razon*, 11 July, 1938.
[27]	Quoted in U.S. Department of State file, 840.48, Refugees, 552, USNA film 1284, reel 20.
[28]	Refugees 527, USNA film 1284, reel 20.

Chapter Nine: The Palestinian Question

[1] U.S. Department of State file 840.48, Refugees, 581. USNA film 1284, reel 20.
[2] Ibid.
[3] Ibid.
[4] Refugees 561, USNA film 1284, reel 20.
[5] Ibid.
[6] Ibid.
[7] *Palestine and Trans-Jordan*, 9 July, 1938. Enclosure to State Department dispatch 656 of 11 July, 1938, from the U.S. consul general in Jerusalem, USSD file 840.48, Refugees, 561, USNA film 1284, reel 20.
[8] Refugees 586, verbatim reports, 15 July, 1938, Lord Winterton's speech, pp 1-2, USNA film 1284, reel 20.
[9] USSD file, 840.48, Refugees 586, USNA film 1284, reel 20.

Chapter Ten: The Aftermath of Évian

[1] Quoted in Refugees 593, USNA film 1284, reel 21.
[2] *Manchester Guardian*, 16 July, 1938.

[3]   Quoted in Refugees 640, USNA 1284, reel 21.
[4]   Refugees 676, USNA film 1284, reel 21.
[5]   Refugees 589A, USNA film 1284, reel 21.
[6]   Refugees 596, USNA film 1284, reel 21.
[7]   Refugees 651, USNA film 1284, reel 21.
[8]   Refugees 975, USNA film 1284, reel 22.
[9]   Refugees 1395, USNA film 1284, reel 24.
[10] Refugees 1516, USNA film 1284, reel 24.
[11] Refugees 1467E, USNA film 1284, reel 24.
[12] Refugees 1469, USNA film 1284, reel 24.
[13] Refugees 591, USNA film 1284, reel 21.
[14] Refugees 657, USNA film 1284, reel 21.
[15] Refugees 662, USNA film 1284, reel 21.
[16] Ibid.
[17] Refugees 571 SEC 3-4 GMB, USNA film 1284, reel 20.
[18] Refugees 592, USNA film 1284, reel 21.
[19] Ibid.

[20] Refugees 664, USNA film 1284, reel 21.
[21] Refugees 710, USNA film 1284, reel 21.
[22] Refugees 674, USNA film 1284, reel 21.
[23] Refugees 685, USNA film 1284, reel 21.
[24] Caption accompanying photograph number 60708A. United States Holocaust Memorial Museum.
[25] Refugees 686, USNA film 1284, reel 21.
[26] *Jewish Telegraphic Agency News*, Tuesday 30 August, 1938, p 2.
[27] Refugees 737, USNA film 1284, reel 21.
[28] Refugees 824 G/HC, USNA film, 1284, reel 22.
[29] Refugees 1357, USNA film 1284, reel 24.30
[30] Refugees 1335, USNA film 1284, reel 24.
[31] Refugees 706A, USNA film 1284, reel 21.
[32] Refugees 717, USNA film 1284, reel 21.
[33] Refugees 713, USNA film 1284, reel 21.

[34] Ibid.
[35] Refugees 720, USNA film 1284, reel 21.
[36] Refugees 733, USNA film 1284, reel 21.
[37] Refugees 772, USNA film 1284, reel 21.
[38] Ibid.
[39] Refugees 777, USNA film 1284, reel 21.
[40] Ibid.
[41] Refugees 777 GDG, USNA film 1284, reel 21.
[42] Refugees 796 USNA film 1284, reel 21.
[43] Refugees 796 GMB, USNA film 1284, reel 21.
[44] Refugees 807 G/HC, USNA film 1284, reel 22.
[45] Ibid.
[46] Refugees 820, USNA film 1284, reel 22.
[47] Refugees 832 GDG, USNA film 1284, reel 22.
[48] Refugees 856, USNA film 1284, reel 22.
[49] Refugees 875 GE, USNA film 1284, reel 22.

[50] Refugees 1109, USNA film 1284, reel 23.
[51] Refugees 859, USNA film 1284, reel 22.
[52] Refugees 877, USNA film 1284, reel 22.
[53] Refugees 878, USNA film 1284, reel 22.
[54] Refugees 1196, USNA film 1284, reel 23.
[55] http://en.wikipedia.org/wiki/History_of_Albania.
[56] http://enwikipedia.org/wiki/List_of_individuals_and_groups_assisting_Jews.
[57] Caption for photograph number 34949, United States Holocaust Memorial Museum, courtesy of Johanna Neumann.
[58] Refugees 1320 GDG, USNA film 1284, reel 24.
[59] Refugees 1320 GDG, USNA film 1284, reel 24.
[60] Refugees 861, USNA film 1284, reel 22.
[61] *Aftenposten,* Monday 19 December, 1938.
[62] Ibid.
[63] Refugees 862, USNA film 1284, reel 22.

[64]   Refugees 1331, USNA film 1284, reel 24.
[65]   Refugees 876, USNA film 1284, reel 22.
[66]   Refugees 882A, USNA film 1284, reel 22.
[67]   Refugees 890, USNA film 1284, reel 22.
[68]   Refugees 884 GE, USNA film 1284, reel 22.
[69]   *Maryborough Chronicle*, 25 February, 1983, p 15.
[70]   Refugees 1016, USNA film 1284, reel 22.
[71]   Refugees 1337, USNA film 1284, reel 24.
[72]   *Vancouver Sun*, 11 November, 1938.
[73]   *Victoria Daily Times*, 16 November, 1938.
[74]   Refugees 1337, USNA film 1284, reel 24.
[75]   Ibid.
[76]   Refugees 1383, USNA film 1284, reel 24.
[77]   *Action Catholique*, 21 November, 1938.
[78]   *Le Canada*, 21 January, 1939.
[79]   *Maryborough Chronicle* Monday 14 November, 1938, p 1.

[80] Julius Streicher, the profoundly anti-Semitic editor of *Der Sturmer*, the anti-Jewish publication that loudly supported the expulsion of all Jews from Germany. Streicher was tried at Nuremberg and hanged in 1946.
[81] Reproduced in the *Maryborough Chronicle* Thursday 10 November, 1938, p 1.
[82] Reproduced in the *Maryborough Chronicle*, 15 November, 1938.
[83] Ibid.
[84] Ibid.
[85] Reproduced in the *Maryborough Chronicle*, 17 November, 1938.
[86] Ibid.
[87] Ibid.
[88] *Washington Post*, 16 April, 1978.
[89] Refugees, 1201, USNA film 1284, reel 23.
[90] Refugees 1477, USNA film 1284, reel 24.
[91] *Maryborough Chronicle*, 19 November, 1938.
[92] Refugees 1051, USNA film 1284, reel 23.
[93] Refugees 1087 GE, USNA film 1284, reel 23.

[94] *Truth* 16 October, 1938, and Refugees 1057, USNA film 1284, reel 23.
[95] Refugees 1338, USNA film 1284, reel 24.
[96] Refugees 896 GE, USNA film 1284, reel 22.
[97] Ibid.
[98] Ibid.
[99] Ibid.
[100] Refugees 900, USNA film 1284, reel 22.
[101] Refugees 933 GDG, USNA film 1284, reel 22.
[102] Refugees 939 GE, USNA film 1284, reel 22.
[103] Refugees 939 G/HC, USNA film 1284, reel 22.
[104] *Maryborough Chronicle*, 18 November, 1938.
[105] Refugees 1072 FP, USNA film 1284, reel 23.
[106] Memorandum to the undersecretary of state from President F.D. Roosevelt, 10 December, 1938, Refugees 1072, USNA film 1284, reel 23.
[107] Refugees 1077 GDC, USNA film 1284, reel 23.

[108]	*The Great Weekend*, 20 June, 1987. http://enwikipedia.org/wiki/Lidice For an excellent television documentary on the assassination of Heydrich see: *Nazi Hunters*, 'Reinhard Heydrich', N.M. Productions and I.M.G. Entertainment, 2009.
[109]	Refugees 1081 GE, USNA film 1284, reel 23.
[110]	Confidential telegram from J.V.A MacMurray, U.S. Embassy at Istanbul, to U.S. Department of State, number 899 dated 13 December, 1938, USNA film 1284, reel 23.
[111]	http://enwikipedia.org/wiki/List_of_individuals_and_groups_assisting_Jews.
[112]	Schacht was instrumental in generating the funds needed for German rearmament, although an ardent Hitler supporter, he was imprisoned after the 20 July bomb plot. He was found not guilty of war crimes and acquitted at the Nuremberg trials in 1946.
[113]	Refugees 1108, USNA film 1284, reel 23.
[114]	Refugees 1119, USNA film 1284, reel 23 and Refugees 1238, USNA film 1284, reel 23.

[115]	Refugees 1119, USNA film 1284, reel 23.
[116]	Refugees 1142, USNA film 1284, reel 23.
[117]	Refugees 1177, USNA film 1284, reel 23.
[118]	Refugees 1205, USNA film 1284, reel 23.
[119]	Refugees 1258 GDG, USNA film 1284, reel 23.
[120]	Refugees 1284, USNA film 1248, reel 23.
[121]	Refugees 1297 GMB, USNA film 1284, reel 23.
[122]	Refugees 1187 USNA film 1284, reel 23.
[123]	Refugees 1197, USNA film 1284, reel 23.
[124]	Refugees 1182, USNA film 1284, reel 23.
[125]	Refugees 1303, USNA film 1284, Reel 24.
[126]	Refugees 1314, USNA film 1284, reel 24.
[127]	Refugees 1306 GDG, USNA film 1284, reel 24.
[128]	Letter from William Phillips to President Roosevelt, dated 5 January, 1939, USNA film 1284, reel 24.

[129] Refugees 1319, USNA film 1284, reel 24.

[130] Refugees 1328, USNA film 1284, reel 24.

[131] Refugees 1386, USNA film 1284, reel 24.

[132] Refugees 1408, USNA film 1284, reel 24.

[133] Refugees 1411, USNA film 1284, reel 24.

[134] Refugees 1433 GB, USNA film 1284, reel 24.

[135] Refugees 1411, USNA film 1284, reel 24.

[136] Refugees 1476, USNA film 1284, reel 24.

[137] Refugees 1488, USNA film 1284, reel 24.

[138] Refugees 1510, USNA film 1284, reel 24.

[139] *New York Times*, 7 May, 1959; enwikipedia.org/wiki/Myron_Charles_Taylor.

Chapter Eleven: The Ongoing Struggle

[1] *Maryborough Chronicle* Tuesday 16 January, 1940, p 1

[2] Ibid.
[3] *Washington Post,* 16 April, 1978.
[5] Reproduced in the *Maryborough Chronicle,* 18 November, 1938.
[6] http://enwikipedia.org/wiki/List_of_individuals_and_groups_assisting_Jews.
[7] http://enwikipedia.org/wiki/Rescue_of_Jews_by_Poles_during_the_Holocaust.
[8] wikipedia.org/wiki/Witold_Pilecki.
[9] wikipedia.org/ wiki/Eduard_Schulte; wikipedia.org/ wiki/File:Riegner_Telegram.jpg.
[10] *Who Shall Live and Who Shall Die,* (quoting Gerhart Riegner) director Laurence A. Jarvik, 1982.
[11] wikipedia.org/wiki/File:Riegner_Telegram.jpg.
[12] *Washington Post,* 25 November, 1942, p 6; *Who Shall Live and Who Shall Die,* director Laurence A. Jarvik, 1982
[13] *Who Shall Live and Who Shall Die,* director Laurence A. Jarvik, 1982.
[14] *Weekend Australian,* 27 November, 1993.
[15] *New York Times,* 7 May, 1943.
[16] *Executive Order Creating War Refugee Board,* www.jewishvirtuallibrary.org; http.en.wikipedia.org/wiki/War_Refugee_Board; *Who Shall Live and Who Shall Die,* (quoting John Pehle) director

Laurence A. Jarvik, 1982; http://enwiki pedia.org/wiki/Henry_Morgenthau,_Jr.
[17] www.jta.org/1944/02/23/archive/ira-a-hi rschmann-appointed-war-refugee-board.
[18] Shoah Resource Centre, the International School for Holocaust Studies; www.nytimes.com/1989/10/10. obituaries/ira-hirschmann-is-dead-at-88.
[19] *Who Shall Live and Who Shall Die*, (quoting Nahum Goldmann and Peter Bergson) director Laurence A. Jarvik, 1982.
[20] http.en/wikipedia.org/wiki/Ben_Hecht.
[21] www.ushmm.org/wlc/es/articles.php?Mo duleId=10007041; http://wymaninststitu te.org/special/rabbimarch/pg03.php; htt p://en.wikipedia.org/wiki/Hillel_Kook; *Who Shall Live and Who Shall Die*, (quoting Peter Bergson [Hillel Kook]) director Laurence A. Jarvik, 1982.
[22] http://en.wikipedia.org/wiki/Ben_Hecht.
[23] *Weekend Australian*, 24 October, 1998, p 33.

Chapter Twelve: The Courageous

[1] Kranzler, David, *The Man who Stopped the Trains to Auschwitz*, Syracuse University Press, Syracuse, 2000; wikipe

dia.org/wiki/Jose_Castellanos_Contreras; http://enwikipedia.org/wiki/List_of_individuals_and_groups_assisting_Jews.

[2] www.nytimes.com2010/01/12; *Los Angeles Times*, 12 January, 2010.

[3] http://enwikipedia.org/wiki/List_of_individuals_and_groups_assisting_Jews.

[4] Meijer, Daphne L. *Unknown Children, the Last Train from Westerbork*, http://demos3.apple.com.

[5] www.ajr.org.uk/index.cfm/section.joirnal/issue.Sep01/article=573; www.thejc.com/news/world-news/59442/kindertransport-memorial-unveiled; http://enwikipedia.org/wiki/Gertruida_Wijsmuller-Meier; Meijer, Daphne L. *Unknown Children, the Last Train from Westerbork* Internet paper; http://en.wikipedia.org/wiki/History_of_the_Netherlands.

[6] http://enwikipedia.org/wiki/List_of_individuals_and_groups_assisting_Jews.

[7] http://enwikipedia.org/wiki/List_of_individuals_and_groups_assisting_Jews.

[8] wikipedia.org/wiki/Archbishop_Damaskinos.

[9] http://enwikipedia.org/wiki/List_of_individuals_and_groups_assisting_Jews; wikipedia.org/wiki/Omelyan_Kovch;okinternation

alfoundation.org/About%20Omelian%20Kovch.html.
[10] www.raoulwallenberg.net/saviors/others/le-chambon-sur-lignon.
[11] wikipedia.org/wiki/Eduardo_Propper_de_Callejon.
[12] Ibid.
[13] http://enwikipedia.org/wiki/Aristides_de_sousa_mendes.
[14] http://enwikipedia.org/wiki/List_of_individuals_and_groups_assisting_Jews; http://enwikipedia.org/wiki/Aristides_de_Sousa_Mendes.
[15] http://enwikipedia.org/wiki/List_of_individuals_and_groups_assisting_Jews.
[16] *The Iranian Schindler who Saved Jews from the Nazis*, www.bbc.co.uk/news/magazine-16190541, BBC 21 December, 2011; wikipedia.org/wiki/Abdol-Hossein_Sardari.
[17] Blum, Johannes, *Restance-Pere Bruno Reynders*, monograph, published by *Les Carrefours la Cite*, 1993; http://enwikipedia.org/wiki/Henri_Reynders
[18] Dimitar Pechev biography, http://www.raoulwallenberg.net; Assa, A and Cohen, A., *Saving the Jews in Bulgaria*, State Publishing House, Sofia, 1977; http://en.wikipedia.org/wiki/List_of_individ

uals_and_groups_assisting_Jews>; en://wikipedia.org/wiki/Dimitar_Peshev.

[19] Ramati, Alexander, *The Assisi Underground*, Stein and Day, New York, 1978; wikipedia.org./wiki/Rufino_Niccacci.

[20] http://enwikipedia.org/wiki/Giovanni_Palatucci.

[21] www.giorgioperlasca.it/; http://en.wikipedia.org/wiki/Giorgio_Perlasca; www.answers.com/topic/giorgio-perlasca; wikipedia.org/wiki/History_of_Hungary.

[22] http://enwikipedia.org/wiki/List_of_individuals_and_groups_assisting_Jews; www.oocities.org/remember_wwII/sered.html; en.wikipedia.org/wiki/Jasenovac_concentration_camp

[23] wikipedia.org/wiki/Guelfo_zamboni.

[24] http://enwikipedia.org/wiki/List_of_individuals_and_groups_assisting_Jews; Ohara, Aiden, *I'll Live Till I Die*, Drumlin Publications, Leitrim 1997; wikipedia.org/wiki/Delia_Murphy.

[25] http://en.wikipedia.org/wiki/Hugh_0%27Flaherty; Fleming, Brian, *The Vatican Pimpernel: the Wartime Exploits of Monsignor Hugh O'Flaherty*, Collins Press, 2008.

[26]   Delp, Alfred, *The Prison Writings*, Orbis, 2004.

[27]   Delp, Alfred *Advent of the Heart*, Ignatius Press, 2006, wikimedia.org/wiki/Alfred_Delp;wikipedia.org/wiki/Roland_Freisler.

[28]   Spicer, Kevin P., *Resisting the Third Reich*, Northern Illinois University Press, 2004; wikipedia.org/wiki/Bernhard_Lichtenberg.

[29]   http://en.wikipedia.org/wiki/Albert_G%C%B6ring.

[30]   http://enwikipedia.org/wiki/Rescue_or_Jews_by_Poles_during_the_Holocaust.

[31]   http://enwikipedia.org/wiki/Eugene_Lazowski; *Fake Epidemic Saves a Village from Nazis*, http://web.archive.org; www.holocaustforgotten.com/eugene.htm.

[32]   Darch, John H. *Saints on Earth*, Church House Publishing, 2004.

[33]   www.guardian.co.uk/commentisfree/belief/2012/oct/10/maximilian-kolbe-sainthood-meaningful.

[34]   www.guardian.co.uk/commentisfree/belief/2012/oct/10/maximilian-kolbe-sainthood-meaningful; wikipedia.org/wiki/Maximilian_Kolbe; wikipedia.org.wiki/Karl_Fritzsch; www.deathcamps.org/occupation/auschwitzmen.html.

[35] Paldiel, Mordecai, *The Path of the Righteous*, Ktav Publishing House, 1993; wikipedia.org/wiki/Irena_Sendler.

[36] www.holocaustforgotten.com/Slawik.htm; wikipedia.org/Wiki/Henryk_Slawik.

[37] Pelikan, Jaroslav, *Confessor Between East and West*, William B. Eerdmans Publishing Company, 1990; *Thou Shalt Not Kill*, pastoral letter, www.ji.lviv.ua/n28texts/ne-ubyj.htm; wikipedia.org/wiki/Andrey_Sheptysky.

[38] Text description for photo 94738, U.S. Holocaust Memorial Museum.

[39] http://enwikipedia.org/wiki/List_of_individuals_and_groups_assisting_Jews.

[40] www.yadvashem.org/yv/en/righteous/stories/ho.asp.

[41] Maga, Timothy P., *Judgement at Tokyo*, University Press of Kentucky, 2001; wikipedia.org/wiki/Seishiro_Itagaki.

[42] Toyaker, Raabi Marvin, *The Fugu Plan*, Gefen Publishing House, 2004; wikipedia.org/wiki/Kiichiro_Higuchi.

[43] http://enwikipedia.org/wiki/List_of_individuals_and_groups_assisting_Jews.

[44] Caption accompanying photograph number 08846, United States Holocaust Memorial Museum.

[45] Macintyre, Donald, *Israel's Forgotten Hero*, www.independent.co.uk/news/world/middle-east/israels-forgotten-hero-the-assassination-of-count-bernadotte-and-the-death-of-peace-934094.html; wikipedia.org/wiki/Count_Folke_bernadotte.

[46] *New York Times*, 29 August, 2002; wikipedia.org/wiki/Raoul_Wallenberg; http://enwikipedia.org/wiki/List_of_individuals_and_groups_assisting_Jews; wikipedia.org/wiki/Per_Anger.

[47] Text description for photo 69285, U.S. Holocaust Memorial Museum.

[48] http://enwikipedia.org/wiki/List_of_individuals_and_groups_assisting_Jews.

[49] www.auschwitz.dk/Winton.htm.

[50] *Nicholas Winton, British Saviour*, www.raoulwallenberg.net.

[51] Porter, Monica, *Sir Nicholas Winton: a Reluctant Holocaust Hero*, www.thejc.com/lifestyle-features/sir-nicholas-winton-a-reluctant-holocaust-hero. See also wikipedia.org/wiki/Sir_Nicholas_Winton

[52] http://enwikipedia.org/wiki/List_of_individuals_and_groups_assisting_Jews; http://en.wikipedia.org/wiki/Frank_Foley.

[53] Stanjford, J. Shaw, *Turkey and the Holocaust*, New York University Press; wikipedia.org/wiki/Namik_Kemal_Yolga.

[54] www.raoulwallenberg.net/?en/saviors/women/2997/sara-salkahazi-slovakia.3421.htm; http://frpost.com/servlet/Satellite?cid=1154526001018&pagename=JPost/JPArticle/ShowFull; wikipedia.org/wiki/S%C3%A1ra_Salkah%A1zi; www.salkahazisara.com/bio_en.html.

[55] wikipedia.org/wiki/Arrow_Cross_Party.

[56] http://enwikipedia.org/wiki/Traian_Popovici; http://czernowitz.ehpes.com/popovici/popovicibio.html; www.jewishvirtuallibrary.org/jsource/biography/Popovici.html; en.wikipedia.org/wiki/Chernivtsi; JTA Global News service, 21 June, 19+-44, http://www.jta.org/1944/06/21/archive; www romaniantimes.at/news/Panorama/2011-01-14/1262/Hoffman.

Chapter Thirteen: Escape and Rescue

[1] Photographic details for image number 32969, United States Holocaust Memorial Museum; *The Darien Story*, http://www.dariendilemma.com.

[2] *The Darien Story*, http://www.dariendilemma.com.

[3] Photographic details for image number 32969, United States Holocaust Memorial

Museum; *The Darien Story*, http://www.dariendilemma.com; www.aufrichtigs.com

[4] www.varianfry.dk/aftermath.htm; www.rescue.org/varian-fry.

[5] www.varianfry.dk/aftermath.htm

[6] http://en.wikipedia.org/wiki/Varian_Fry; caption for photograph number 34485, United Stated Holocaust Memorial Museum.

[7] Caption for photograph number 34485, United Stated Holocaust Memorial Museum.

[8] Caption for photograph number 59625, United States Holocaust Memorial Museum.

[9] Caption for photograph number 60079, United States Holocaust Memorial Museum.

[10] Photographic caption for United States Holocaust Memorial Museum number 05746; www.ushmm.org/wlc/en/article.php?ModuleId=10007498; www.jewishgen.org/databases/holocaust/0102_Tehran-children.html; Messenger, Charles, *World War Two Chronological Atlas*, Bloomsbury Publishing, London 1989.

[11] www.recognitionscience.com/cgv/oswego.htm.

[12] Ibid.

[13]	Caption for photograph number 38546, United States Holocaust Memorial Museum; www.recognitionscience.com/cgv/oswego.htm.
[14]	Caption for photograph number 38546, United States Holocaust Memorial Museum.
[15]	Ofer, Dalia, *Escaping the Holocaust, Illegal Immigration to the Land of Israel*; Oxford University Press, 1990; en.wikipedia.org.wiki/MV_Melft%C3%BCre.
[16]	www.ihr.org/leaflets/soap.shtml
[17]	For further details see: Shoshana, Barri, *The Question of Kastner's Testimonies on behalf of Nazi War Criminals*. Journal of Israeli History, issue 2-3, pp 139-165; Gabor, Kadar and Zoltan, Vagi, *Self-financing Genocide: the Gold Train, the Becher Case and the Wealth of Hungarian Jews*, Central European University Press, 2004; Kranzler, David, *The Man Who Stopped the Train to Auschwitz*, Syracuse University Press, 2000; en.wikipedia.org/wiki.Rudolf_Kastner; www.kasztnermemorial.com; www.jewishgen.org; en.wikipedia.org/wiki/Kastner_train; Alford, Kenneth D and Savas, Theodore, P., *Nazi Millionaires,*

Greenhill Books, London, 2002, pp 39-54.

[18] http://libfindaide.yu.edu:8082.

Bibliography

Primary sources

This book has been based almost exclusively on information derived from many thousands of U.S. Department of State documents that have now been released to the public and are available from the National Archives in Washington DC. These documents may all be located on microfilm reels, 'Refugees', with the prefix 1284.

Secondary sources

The following publications have also been of assistance in providing some background material. Abella, Irving, and Troper, Harold, *None Is Too Many*, Random House, New York, 1982.

Aarons, Mark and Loftus, John, *The Secret War Against the Jews*, Reed Books, Australia, 1997

Blum, Johannes, *Restance-Pere Bruno Reynders*, monograph, published by *Les Carrefours la Cite*, 1993.

Clare, George, *Last Waltz in Vienna*, MacMillan, London, 1981.

Cross, Colin, *Adolf Hitler*, Hodder and Stoughton, London, 1973.

Darch, John H., *Saints on Earth*, Church House Publishing, 2004.

Delp, Alfred, *The Prison Writings*, Orbis, 2004.

Delp, Alfred *Advent of the Heart*, Ignatius Press, 2006.

Fleming, Gerald, *Hitler and the Final Solution*. Hamish Hamilton, London, 1985.

Gabor, Kadar and Zoltan, Vagi, *Self-financing Genocide: the Gold Train, the Becher Case and the Wealth of Hungarian Jews*, Central European University Press, 2004.

Garcia-Granados, Jorge, *The Birth of Israel*, Alfred A Knopf, New York, 1949.

Grunberger, Richard, *Hitler's SS*, Weidenfeld and Nicholson, London, 1970.

Hart, Kitty, *Return to Auschwitz*, Sidgwick and Jackson, London, 1981.

Hassan, Crown Prince Hassan bin, *Palestinian Self Determination*, Quartet Books, New York, 1981.

Kranzler, David, *The Man Who Stopped the Trains to Auschwitz*, Syracuse University Press, Syracuse, 2000.

Landau, Elaine, *We Survived the Holocaust*, Franklin Watts, New York, 1991.

Langer, Walter, *The Mind of Adolf Hitler*, Secker and Warburg, London, 1972.

Lee, Asher, *Goering, Air Leader*, Duckworth, London, 1972.

Longmate, Norman, *How We Lived Then*, Hutchinson, London, 1971.

Maga, Timothy P., *Judgement at Tokyo*, University Press of Kentucky, 2001.

Manvel, Roger and Fraenkel Heinrich, *Heinrich Himmler*, Heinemann, London, 1965.

Neave, Airey, *Nuremberg*, Hodder and Stoughton, London, 1978.

Ofer, Dalia, *Escaping the Holocaust, Illegal Immigration to the Land of Israel;* Oxford University Press, 1990.

Paldiel, Mordecai, *The Path of the Righteous*, Ktav Publishing House, 1993.

Patterson, Charles, *Anti-Semitism, the Road to the Holocaust and Beyond*, Walker Publishing Company, New York, 1982.

Pelikan, Jaroslav, *Confessor Between East and West*, William B. Eerdmans Publishing Company, 1990.

Ramati, Alexander, *The Assisi Underground*, Stein and Day, New York, 1978.

Shirer, William L., *The Rise and Fall of the Third Reich*, Pan, London, 1960.

Spicer, Kevin P., *Resisting the Third Reich*, Northern Illinois University Press, 2004.

Taylor, Fred, *The Goebbels Diaries*, Hamish Hamilton, London, 1982.

Tokayer, Marvin and Swartz, Mary, *The Fugu Plan*, Paddington Press, New York, 1979.

Whiteman, Dorit Bader, *The Uprooted*, Plenum Press, New York, 1993.

Newspapers, Magazines and Periodicals

The following publications have been sourced during the research stages of this history:
Action Catholique, (Canada).
Aftenposten, (Norway).
Chattanooga News, (U.S.).
Danzinger Vorposten, (Nazi Germany).
Das Schwarze Korps, (Nazi Germany).
Debrest's Weekly News Service, (U.S.).
El Debate, (Uruguay).
El Diaro Illustrado, (Chile).
El Emparcial, (Chile).
Frankfurter Zeitung, (Austria).
Helsingin Sanomat, (Finland).
Kansas City Journal Post, (U.S.).
La Canada, (Canada).
La Cronica, (Peru).
La Fronda, (Brazil).
La Manana, (Uruguay).
La Mercurio, (Chile).
La Nación, (Chile).
La Razon, (Brazil).
La Tribuna Popular, (Uruguay).

Maakansa, (Finland).
Maryborough Chronicle, (Australia).
National Zeitung, (Nazi Germany).
Neue Freie Presse, (Austria)
New York Sun, (U.S.).
New York Evening Post, (U.S.).
New York Times, (U.S.).
Palestine and Trans-Jordan, (Jerusalem).
Palestine Post, (Jerusalem).
The *Broom* (U.S.).
The *Times*, (U.K.).
The *Sunday Times*, (U.K.).
The *Manchester Guardian*, (U.K.).
The *Daily Telegraph*, (U.K.).
The *Truth*, (Australia).
The *Star*, (South Africa).
Toowoomba Chronicle, (Australia).
Toronto Globe, (Canada).
Trinidad Guardian (Trinidad).
Vancouver Sun, (Canada).
Vancouver News-Herald, (Canada).
Victoria Daily Times, (Canada).
Voelkischer Beobachter, (Austria).
Washington Post, (U.S.).
Weekend Australian (Australia).

About the Author

Tony Matthewes

Author & Historian

Tony Matthews is a Queensland author who has dedicated almost his entire adult life to writing and researching Australian history. He also writes extensively on military and espionage history with a specific emphasis on both world wars. He is the author of more than thirty books including several historical novels.

He worked in the television industry for many years, writing, producing and directing, and during that time wrote a number of highly acclaimed historical documentaries which were broadcast on the Seven Network and ABC Television. He has also written and narrated more than five hundred historical programmes for ABC Radio. Dr Matthews' books and articles have been published in Australia, England, the United States and Europe and his television documentaries have been widely distributed to schools, universities, colleges and libraries across Australia.

Please visit the author's website for more details of his published and broadcast works.

Author's website: https://drtonymatthews.weebly.com

Back Cover Material

In July 1938 the United States, Great Britain and thirty other countries participated in a vital conference at Évian-les-Bains, France, to discuss the persecution and possible emigration of the European Jews, specifically those caught under the anvil of Nazi atrocities. However, most of those nations rejected the pleas then being made by the Jewish communities, thus condemning them to the Holocaust.

There is no doubt that the Évian conference was a critical turning point in world history, The disastrous outcome of the conference set the stage for the murder of six million people. Today we live in a world defined by turmoil with a disturbing rise of authoritarian governments and ultra right-wing nationalism. The plight of refugees is once more powerfully affecting public attitudes towards those most in need. Now, on the 75th anniversary of the liberation of Auschwitz and the end of the Second World War, it's time to reflect on the past to ensure we never again make the same mistakes.

Tragedy at Évian also Shines a spotlight on some of the astonishing and courageous stories of heroic efforts of individuals and private organisations who, despite the decisions made it

Évian, worked under extremely dangerous conditions, frequently giving their own lives to assist in the rescue of the Jewish people.

Index

A
Aberbach Adolf (Aron), 424
Anna, 424
Action Catholique (Roman Catholic publication), 578
Administration of Labour and Social Affairs, 385
AFSC (American Friends Service Committee), 533
Aftenposten (newspaper), 570
Aliens Act of 1937, 46
Allied Maritime Transport Council, 474
American Chamber of Commerce, 235
American Civil Liberties Union, 76
American Committee for Christian German Refugees, 117
American Friends Service Committee (AFSC), 533
American Jewish Committee, 76, 102
American Red Cross, 117
Angrieff (publication), 62, 65
Anschluss (the union of Germany and Austria), 367, 424, 432, 487, 558
Arab Women's Committee, 513
Aranha Oswaldo, 341
Argentine Embassy (Poland), 235
Ariadne (steamer), 391
Aristimuno-Coll Carlos, 82, 427
Armstrong Hamilton Fish, 136, 161, 298
Aryan C. Leon de, 106, 109

Association for the Protection of Jewish Immigrants, (see: Sociedad Protectors de Immigrantes Israelitas), *230*
Auschwitz, *284, 421, 536*
Australian Jewish Welfare Society, *353, 365*
Austrian Jewish Community (Kultusgemeinde), *487*

B

Baerwald Paul, *79, 96, 117, 136, 161*
Baker George F., *143*
Baldwin Roger N., *79*
Balfour Declaration, *293*
Bernard, *136, 161*
Bases for the Establishment of a Jewish Colony in Los Andes (document), *238*
Belgian, *82*
Belgian Foreign Office, *185*
Belzec, *284*

Benton J. Webb, *558*
Bentwich Professor Norman, *10, 484*
Berat camp, *562*
Berenger Henri, *305, 308, 337, 339, 471, 530*
Bergmann Ministerialdirektor, *572*
Bernadotte Count Folke, *455*
Bernstein Enrigue, *460*
Beucker-Andreae W.C., *383*
Biddle, Jnr. A.J. Drexel, *274, 277, 279, 282*
Blair Frederick Charles, *379, 576*
Bocker John, *530*
Boetge-Pilku, Lizalotte, *562*
Brandt George L., *171, 177, 182, 185*
Bridgard Fernardo Navas de, *397*
Brinkmann Reich State Secretary, *572*
British Embassy (Bucharest), *129*

British Foreign Office, 522
British Imperial Fascist League, 321
Brown Lieutenant-Colonel Pearson B., 171
Buchenwald camp, 418, 583
Bullitt William C., 298
Burdekin C.B., 347, 370

C

CAEJR (Comite d'Assistance aux Enfants), 533
Calderon Francisco Garcia, 441
Calvert Reverend Samuel McCrae, 112, 136, 147, 161
Calvert Publicity Company (Baltimore), 62
Camacho Manuel Avila, 502
Canadian Corps Association, 578
Canadian Jewish Congress, 410
Cano Luis, 397
Cap Arcona (steamer), 496
Cape Argus (newspaper), 46
Carbonell-Debali Dr Alfredo, 73
Cardenas President Lazaro, 87, 502, 570
Caroline Medical Institute Stockholm, 391
Carr Wilbur J., 196
Casa Rosada palace, 383
Chamberlain Neville, 607
Professor Joseph P., 112, 136, 161
Chateau de La Hille, 533
Chattanooga News (newspaper), 547
Churchill Winston, 136
Ciano Count Galeazzo, 38
Cohen Benjamin, 460
Rudolf (later Dr Rudolph Jacobson), 416
Columbia University, 112, 136
Comitato Assistenza Ebrei Profughi, 43

Comite d'Assistance aux Enfants Juifs Refugies (CAEJR), *533*
Commercial Economy Board, *474*
Committee of Asuncion, *59*
Committee of Protection of Lima, *247*
Committee on Care of Transient and Homeless, *93*
Committee on Immigration and Naturalization, *102*
Committee on Political Refugees, *136, 288*
Committee to Facilitate Emigration From Austria and Germany Of Political Refugees, *499*
Concha Alejandro Gastelu, *251*
Congress of Jewish Youth, *244*
Conte Verde (Italian vessel), *541*
Cornell University, *143*
Cotti Flavio, *439*
Council for Foreign Relations, *136*
Council for German Jewry, *370, 484*
Council of Citizens, *324*
Council of National Defence, *474*
Covington, Burling and Rublee (law firm), *474*
Cremins Francis Thomas, *427, 430*

D

Dachau (concentration camp), *286, 416, 418, 435, 487, 583*
Daniels Josephus, *87, 499*
Dawson William, *464*
Department of Colonization, *377*
Department of Immigration and Colonization Ottawa, *373*
Department of Mines and Resources (Canada), *379*
Department of the Cuban Treasury, *161*

Despatcher (publication), *19*
DesPortes Fay Allen, *238, 241*
Devisen Central (Austria), *484*
Diaz Jose Gregorio, *271*
Dickstein Samual, *102*
Dieckhoff Hans (German ambassor to Washington), *601*
Dies Senator Martin, *57, 59*
Distinguished Flying Cross (awarded to Thomas Walter White), *350*
Division of Current Information (Department of Defense), *158*
Division of European Affairs (State Department), *134*
Dominican Republic Settlement Association (DORSA), *407*
Dow Edward A., *244*
Drancy transit camp, *421*
Drougge Eric, *385*
Dubois Elinor, *533*
 Maurice, *533, 536*
Duckwitz Georg Ferdinand, *450, 452*
Duke of Windsor, *487*
Duncannon Lord, *435*
Dunne John Borough, *117*

E

Egyptian Court of Mixed Appeals, *200*
Einstein Albert, *57, 550*
Eisenhower Dwight, *136*
El Mercurio (newspaper), *460, 462*
Emerald (warship), *21*
Engzell Gosta, *385*
Epstein Werner, *536*
Errazuriz Maximiliano, *441, 460, 462*
Escobar Juan Antiga, *413*
Évian conference, *10, 19, 32, 39, 54, 68, 71, 73, 82, 87, 112, 120, 164, 171, 188, 191, 192, 200, 201, 211, 247, 251, 257, 260, 269, 271, 288, 293, 302, 337, 341, 345, 356, 360, 370, 379, 403, 410, 441, 445,*

458, 462, 474, 487, 496, 503, 509, 511, 513, 516, 520, 547, 583, 593, 595, 598
Évian-les-Bains, *164, 288, 302*
extermination camps, *284, 609*

F
Federal Council of Churches of Christ, *112, 136*
Federal Department of Justice and Police, *432*
Federal Trade Commission, *474*
First National Bank (Boston), *226*
First World War (Great War), *3, 143, 216, 337, 347, 370, 388, 432, 445, 586, 604*
Fleming Frances, *321*
Flerman Mendel, *530*
Foreign Affairs (publication), *73*
Foreign Language Information Service, *102*
Forster Peter, *567*

Fosdick Raymond B., *112, 117*
Foy R. de, *185, 188, 345*
Frank Alexander, *533*
   Elka, *533*
Frankfurter Zeitung (newspaper), *536*
Friediger Dr Max, *450*
Funk Dr Walter, *529, 574*

G
Gayda Signore Virginio, *46*
Gerechter Alice, *559, 562, 564*
   Johanna, *559, 562, 564*
   Siegbert, *559, 564*
Gerechter family, *559, 562, 564*
German-American Settlement League, *112*
German Foreign Office, *554, 601*
German Jewish Relief Fund, *353*
German Reich, *337, 544, 558*
German secret police, *539, 554*

Gestapo, *174, 479, 484, 487, 489, 502, 544, 556, 567*
Gildemeester Van Gheel, *174, 177, 196, 197, 482, 484, 489*
Goebbels Josef, *62*
Goldman Rabbi Solomon, *166*
Goldmann Nahum, *316, 318*
Goldschmidt-Brodsky Madame, *533*
Goodmann H.A., *487*
    Hermann, *572, 574, 581*
Great Council of Red Men, *158*
Great Depression, *3, 79, 357, 373, 441*
Greenwood Arthur, *324*
Grüninger Paul, *432*
Grynszpan Herschel, *581*
Guillermo Kraft & Cia Ltd., *232*

H

Habe Hans, *339*
Hadassah (Women's Zionist Organisation), *153*

Hallenborg C.A.M. de, *385*
Hansson Michael, *3, 200, 201, 476*
Harris Basil, *117, 136, 161*
    Sir Percy, *362*
Harvard University, *474*
Havas Agency, *235*
Hay General (..), *87*
Hebrew Immigrant Aid Society, *556*
Hebrew Sheltering and Immigration Society, *102*
Hecker W, *164, 166*
Hecker and Yellen (civil engineers), *164*
Hedtoft Hans, *450*
Heijplaat (also reported as Heijplatte) (Rotterdam region), *418*
Henriques C.B., *450*
Herald (newspaper), *324*
Hermanns Grete, *418, 421*
Hilde, *418, 421*
    Julius, *418*
HIAS-JCA, *43, 373*
H.I.C.E.M. (Jewish Overseas Emigration Association), *43*

Hilfsverein Deutschsprechender Juden, *225, 226, 230*
Himmler Heinrich, *574*
Hirsch Adolfo, *226, 232*
Hitler,
  Adolf, *15, 27, 46, 48, 51, 54, 65, 68, 79, 99, 109, 230, 247, 257, 265, 328, 337, 388, 416, 445, 450, 458, 489, 574, 583, 609*
Hoare Sir Samuel, *328*
Hoffman Jnr. Conrad, *604*
Holocaust, *213, 416, 418, 421, 424, 452, 536, 541, 562, 567, 572, 581, 590*
Holzbock Werner, *241, 244*
Hotel Royale, Évian, *188, 191*
House of Commons, *169, 321, 324, 328, 337, 362*
House of Lords, *46*
Hull Cordell, *24, 30, 32, 51, 54, 57, 62, 73, 79, 93, 99, 102, 127, 131, 134, 149, 166, 177, 185, 188, 241, 244, 267, 269, 288, 290, 298, 489, 490, 499, 506, 522, 547, 595*
Hunter Winifred A., *216, 219, 221, 225, 226, 232, 238*

I

Immigrants Selection Board, *46*
Immigration Act of 1 July, 1924, *24*
Immigration Department, *161*
Intergovernmental Meeting on Political Refugees, *496*
International Bureau for the Rights and Aid to Political Refugees, *567*
International Refugee Conference, *279*
Italian-Greek War of 1940-41, *562*

J

Joachim, *424*
Julian, *424*
Jacobsohn Erich, *416, 418*
  Margarete, *416*
  Rudy, *416*
Jacobson Dr Rudolph, *416*

James McCutcheon and Company, *136*
Jewish Agency for Palestine, *277, 290, 293*
Jewish Colonisation Association, *225, 226*
Jewish Joint Distribution Committee, *96, 117*
Jewish Labour Federation, *21*
Jewish National Council, *21*
Jewish People's Committee for United Action Against Fascism and AntiSemitism, *102*
Jewish Philanthropic Society, *370*
Jewish Telegraphic Agency, *536, 544*
Joint Distribution Committee (J.D.C.), *76, 96*
Junior Order of United American Mechanics, *120*

K
Kenedy Louis, *136, 161*
Kennedy Joseph P, *120, 547, 554, 607*
    President John F., *120*
Kenyan Legislative Council, *328*
King MacKenzie, *574, 578*
King Christian X, *447*
Krakow ghetto, *435*
Kristallnacht, *416, 468, 583, 588, 590, 595, 601*
Kuffler Arthur, *174, 484, 489*
Kultusgemeinde (Jewish community, of Vienna), *484, 487*

L
La Nacion (newspaper), *460, 462*
Lange Dr (..), *539*
Latcham Richardo, *460*
La Tribuna Popular (publication), *464, 590*
League Commission, *524*
League Council, *6*
League of Nations, *3, 6, 10, 288, 300, 397, 427, 490*
Le Breton Tomas A., *379, 383*

Lee Charles H., *73*
  Senator Josh, *93*
Le Vernet (internment camp), *533*
Liebman Charles W., *136*
Llamadas (landing permits), *68*
Lobo Helio, *339, 341*
Lodz Ghetto, *435*
London Naval Conference (1930), *474*
Long Boaz, *247, 251*
Louw Eric, *48*
Lowenherz Dr Joseph, *484, 487*
Lyons Joseph, *360*

M
Mainz Frank L., *265*
Majdanek (concentration camp), *536*
Manchester Guardian (newspaper), *517*
Manhattan (steamer), *182*
  Thomas, *550*
Marley, Lord (Dudley Leigh Aman, D.S.C.), *46*
McBride Harry, *547*

McDonald James Grover, *10, 112, 147, 161*
McEwen John, *360, 362*
Meir Golda, *316*
Melchior Dr Marcus, *450*
Messersmith George, *57, 76, 93, 96, 99, 117, 171, 180, 271, 274, 550, 574*
Metal Julio, *526*
Mexican Foreign Office, *87*
Meyer Eugene, *136*
Michelsen Alfredo, *403*
Milton George, *547*
Ministry of Labour (Peru), *247*
Moffat Pierrepont, *134*
Molina Virgilio Trujillo, *403, 406*
Morella (steamer), *158*
Morgan J.P., *143*
Morgenthau Jnr Henry, *136*
Morrison Herbert, *324*
Mussolini Benito, *38, 39, 46*
Mutual Farmers Pty. Ltd., *365*

Myron C. Taylor (freighter), 147
  Naef Roesli, 533, 536

N
Nansen Dr Fridtjof, 3
Nansen International Office for Refugees, 3, 6, 200, 247, 300
Nansen passport, 211
Nansen Relief Organisation, 3
National Council of Catholic Men, 136
National Council of Jewish Women and others, 102
National Council of Palestine Jews (Vaad Leumi), 509
National Defence Party, 511
National League for American Citizenship, 73
National Negro Congress, 588
Nations of Asylum, 379, 458, 588, 590, 598, 601
Nazi Party, 536

Neue Freie Presse (newspaper), 120
Neumann Professor Heinrich, 487
New York Evening Post (newspaper), 588
New York State Assembly, 143
New York Sun (newspaper), 588
New York Times (newspaper), 112, 136, 288
Nieww Holland (steamship), 360
Nobel Peace Prize, 3, 131
Normandie (steamer), 604
Norweb R. Henry, 406, 407
Nuremberg war crimes trials, 529

O
Office International Nansen pour les Refugies, 3
Oldini Fernando Garcia, 441
Oronsay (steamer), 367

Osterdman Fanny, *418*

P

Palairet Sir Charles Michael, *288, 296*

Palestine and Trans-Jordan (newspaper), *511*

Palestine Illustrated News (newspaper), *156*

Palestine Post (newspaper), *156*

Parliamentary Advisory Committee (for the aid of Jews in eastern Siberia), *46*

Patino Simon Iturri, *257*

Patterson Charles, *416*
    Jefferson, *197, 200*

Pell Robert Thompson, *171, 177, 180, 182, 185, 192, 471, 476, 529*

Personal Report to the President,
    See: Report to the Secretary on the Acquiescence of this Government to the Murder of the Jews,

Philips Frederick Jacques 'Frits', *455*

Phillips William (U.S. ambassador to Rome), *38, 43*

Pilku Laun, *562*
    Lizalotte, *562, 564*
    Njazi, *562, 564*

Polish Embassy (Tokyo), *213*

Polish Jewish Relief Fund, *353*

Potter, M.D. Ellen C., *93*

President Harding (steamer), *177*

President's Advisory Committee on Political Refugees, *136, 147, 288*

Protestant War Veterans of New York City, *171*

Q

Queen Mary (liner), *522*

Quezon President Manuel (Philippines), *205*

R

Rasmussen Gustav, *445, 447*

Rath Ernst von, *581, 583*
Razovsky Cecilia, *96*
Red Cross, *117, 455*
  Belgium, *533*
  Swiss, *533, 536*
Refugee Economic Corporation, *136, 226, 232*
Reich government, *62*
Reichstag, *48*
Revisionist Zionists, *277*
Ribbentrop Joachim von (German foreign minister), *601, 609*
Riga Ghetto, *421*
Righteous Among the Nations, *213, 536, 567*
Ritz Hotel, *564*
  (Paris), *185*
Rivas Florencio, *468*
Roberts Mrs H., *321*
Rockefeller Foundation, *112, 117*
Romanian Foreign Office, *129*
  President Franklin D., *10, 12, 32, 35, 51, 73, 96, 103, 106, 109, 112, 115, 117, 123, 127, 131, 136, 143, 153, 161, 177, 192, 247, 265, 274, 293, 296, 316, 318, 373, 406, 464, 471, 503, 509, 511, 544, 576, 588, 601, 604, 609*
Rothmund Dr Heinrich, *432, 435*
Rothschild Lord, *536*
Rothschild-Palais, *536*
Rublee George, *177, 298, 471, 474, 476, 499, 522, 529, 541, 547, 550, 554, 572, 574, 590, 595, 598, 601, 604, 609*
Rummel Reverend Joseph F., *136, 161*
Ruppin Dr Arthur, *509*
Russo-Japanese War of 1904-1905, *211*
Roman Aleksander Maria,
  See Sheptytsky: Archbishop, Andrey,
Shin Bet,

S

Sachsenhausen concentration camp, *583*
Saint Cyprien internment camp at, *421*
Saldivar Gilberto Bosques, *502, 503*

Santo Tomas University, *207*
Schattmann Erwin, *73, 76*
Schechtman Dr Joseph, *274, 277, 279*
Schneider J., *185*
Schwartz Dr Zolly C. von, *129*
Second World War, *318, 350, 576*
Secours Suiss aux Enfants (Swiss Children's Aid), *533*
Seiden Juliette, *134*
  Rudolph, *131, 134*
Shipley Ruth, *24*
Siegel Gerd, *421*
Simmons John Farr, *296*
Sobibor, *284*
Socialist Party conference, *321*
Sociedad Protectors de Immigrantes Israelitas (the Association for the Protection of Jewish Immigrants), *226*
Soden sanitarium, *586*
South African Broadcasting Corporation, *46*
Souza Dantas Luis Martins de, *345*
Spanish Civil War, *6, 221*
Speers James M., *117, 136, 161*
Spickler Elsie, *416*
SS Quanza (vessel), *572*
State Council of Pennsylvania's Order of Independent Americans, *103, 106*
Stein Else, *421*
  Kurt, *421*
Steincke K. K. (Danish minister for justice), *593*
Sternbuch Mrs Recha, *435*
Stimson Henry Lewis, *136*
St. Louis (steamship), *416, 418, 421, 424*
Stolper Professor, *182*
Storfer Berthold, *487*
Strabolgi Lord, *46*
Streicher Julius, *583*
Sudetenland transfer, *567*

Sugihara Consul Senpo (also given as Chiune), *213*
Summers Lord, *357*
Sunday Times (newspaper), *517*
Swedish Foreign Office, *38*
Sweetser Arthur, *6*

T
Taylor A.J.P, *318*
Taylor Myron Charles, *139, 142, 143, 147, 158, 169, 171, 174, 177, 180, 182, 185, 188, 192, 201, 265, 267, 279, 288, 290, 293, 296, 298, 300, 302, 305, 308, 313, 318, 471, 490, 496, 506, 516, 520, 522, 524, 526, 529, 547, 574, 604*
Taylor William Delling, *143*
  William Underhill, *143*
Taylor (née Mack) Anabele (also reported as Anabel), *169*
Taylor (née Underhill) Mary, *143*

Telegraph (newspaper), *482*
The American Jewish Joint Committee, *79*
Thébaud Leon Robert, *413*
The Broom (newspaper), *106*
The Times (newspaper), *517*
Thompson Dorothy, *24, 73, 76, 112*
Toronto Globe and Mail (newspaper), *62, 576*
Treaty of Versailles, *3*
Treblinka (concentration camp), *284*
Tricase Porto displaced persons' camp, *564*
Trinidad Guardian (newspaper), *65*
Trujillo President Rafael Leonidas, *407, 410*
Truman Harry S., *143*
Truth (Brisbane newspaper), *593*
Turnour Edward (Lord Winterton), *318*

U

Ubico President [Jorge], *241*
United Australia Party, *360*
United Palestine Appeal, *166*
United States Lines Company, *136*
University of Uppsala, *391*
U.S. advisory committee, *180*
U.S. Committee for the Care of European Children, *533*
U.S. Department of Defense, *158*
U.S. Department of State (also U.S. State Department), *6, 24, 30, 32, 38, 43, 46, 51, 54, 57, 59, 65, 68, 71, 73, 76, 82, 86, 91, 93, 103, 112, 115, 117, 120, 127, 129, 134, 147, 149, 153, 164, 166, 169, 171, 174, 177, 180, 182, 185, 188, 192, 196, 197, 205, 207, 216, 225, 232, 238, 244, 247, 251, 253, 260, 265, 267, 271, 274, 277, 279, 286, 288, 300, 318, 341, 353, 373, 379, 406, 407, 427, 462, 471, 476, 482, 496, 506, 511, 524, 526, 529, 539, 544, 547, 554, 556, 574, 576, 578, 593, 598, 601, 604, 607, 609*
(Brussels), *185*
(Buenos Aires), *503*
(France), *544*
(London), *32, 117, 496*
(Mexico), *87, 474*
(Milan), *43*
(Montevideo), *68*
(Paris), *191*
(Prague), *196*
(San Domingo), *38*
(Santiago), *441, 462*
(Vienna), *30*
(Warsaw), *274*
U.S. Legation (Prague), *192*
U.S. Steel, *143, 147*

V

Vaad Leumi (National Council of Palestine Jews), *509*

Vancouver News-Herald (newspaper), *578*
Vancouver Sun (newspaper), *576*
Vichy, *345, 536*
Victoria Daily Times (newspaper), *576*
Villa Michel Primo, *87, 91, 502*
Voelkischer Beobachter (newspaper), *196*

W

Waay Gaspard de, *533* Lucienne de, *533*
Wadsworth George, *153, 511, 544*
Waller George Platt, *269*
Wannsee conference (January 1942),
Warsaw Ghetto, *435*
Washington Post (newspaper), *136*
Wasthitz Dr (..), *21*
Weddell Alexander W, *503*
Weiner William, *102*
Weiss Henrietta, *530*

Weizmann Dr Chaim, *277, 290, 293*
Welles Sumner, *93, 99, 112, 129, 136, 158, 182, 185, 277, 347*
Westerbork camp, *421*
White Lieutenant-Colonel Thomas Walter, *347, 350, 356, 365*
White Australia Policy, *595*
White House, *106, 109, 112, 115, 117, 164*
Wiengreen Gustavo A., *413*
Wiley John Cooper, *174, 177, 286, 482, 484, 487*
Wilson Hugh, *536, 572, 601, 604*
   President Woodrow, *153, 474*
Winterton Lord (Edward Turnour), *308, 318, 328, 356, 471, 513*
Wise Rabbi Stephen, *102, 136, 161, 293*
Woodhead Sir John, *509*

World Jewish Congress, *305, 316*
World Zionist Organisation, *277, 293*
Wrong Harold Verschoyle, *370*
    Humphrey Hume, *370, 377*

Y

Yad Vashem Holocaust Memorial, *213, 536, 567*
Yeats-Brown, Captain (..), *350*
Yepes Professor Jesus Maria, *397, 400, 403, 490*
Y.M.C.A., *604*

Z

Zabotynski (Zionist Revisionist leader), *274, 277*
Zionist Organisation, *153, 277, 293*
Zionist Revisionist Movement (Poland), *274*
Zionist Revisionists, *274*
Zog King (of Albania), *564*

www.ingramcontent.com/pod-product-compliance
Lightning Source LLC
Chambersburg PA
CBHW010300010526
44108CB00044B/2702